ENERGY
AND THE
EARTH MACHINE

Also by Donald E. Carr

DEATH OF THE SWEET WATERS
THE BREATH OF LIFE
THE ETERNAL RETURN
THE SEXES
THE DEADLY FEAST OF LIFE
THE FORGOTTEN SENSES

ENERGY
AND THE
EARTH MACHINE
DONALD E. CARR

W·W·NORTON & COMPANY·INC·NEW YORK

Library of Congress Cataloging in Publication Data
Carr, Donald Eaton, 1903–
Energy and the earth machine.
Bibliography: p.
Includes index.

1. Power resources. 2. Human ecology. 3. Energy
policy. 4. Energy conservation. I. Title.
TJ163.2.C37 1976   333.7   75–44431
ISBN 0–393–06407–7

Published simultaneously in Canada
by George J. McLeod Limited, Toronto

Printed in the United States of America

1 2 3 4 5 6 7 8 9

To Monica and Christina

CONTENTS

Dost thou know, my son, with how little
wisdom the world is governed?
—OXENSTIERNE

INTRODUCTION

We have been having energy crises in the world since man started to burn things to keep warm and to melt ore. Yet sudden economic swings of monstrous character are phenomena of recent times. For the hunting cultures the scarcity of food animals precipitated a gradual sort of paleolithic energy crisis and inspired the development of neolithic agriculture. Thousands of years later the Roman Empire fell apart primarily because of a shortage of firewood in the Mediterranean area. This lack forced the smelters to move northward to the German forests, and by the end of the Empire the Romans were in the ignominious position in which the British now find themselves—importing metals from people who had once been their colonials, people to whom they had taught the metallurgical art.

Northern wood, water power, and to some extent wind power got the Western World—by now an emaciated skeleton—through the Dark Ages; but in the sixteenth century another shortage of firewood laid the foundation for the Industrial Revolution. When things were picking up in the Renaissance decades, an incredible amount of wood was burned. There was a much greater demand for firewood than for timber. For example, the evaporation of brine to produce 1,700 wagonloads of salt required 6,000 wagonloads of wood. The reduction of a ton of iron ore took 12 loads of charcoal equivalent to about 8 big beech trees. It is noteworthy that from the end of the sixteenth to the middle of the seventeenth century there was an inflation that all Europeans complained bitterly about. Prices in general tripled, but firewood went up eightfold. It is, in fact, quite likely that the inflation—comparable in magnitude to that in the early 1970s—was triggered by the inordinate price of fuel.

The European people had a lot of coal, but they did not like it and they had to learn to use it industrially in agonized stages. Coal was substituted sooner for heating homes than for making bricks and glass, for baking, for malt drying, and for smelting lead, tin, copper, and iron. Steam power was developed primarily to pump water out of British coal mines. From the reign of Elizabeth I through that of Charles I, 1 in every 7 patents issued had to do with the pumping of water.

Even when the West was deep into the Industrial Revolution, an extraordinary amount of wood continued to be burned, in America, mostly for homes; and sometimes we tend to forget how recently King Petroleum took over from King Coal, and that before the Civil War, people in Boston were writing essays on the coming firewood scarcity. Even in the 1970s, we in the United States get as much energy from firewood as we do from nuclear generating plants, and it is only since the 1950s that horsepower from farm tractors has exceeded horsepower from horses.

In the history of energy transactions there are small cyclic shortages within greater cycles. For example, from the colonization period until the Civil War the major source of artificial lighting in the Americas and Europe was whale or sperm oil. In fact, the world's supply of artificial light depended almost exclusively on the whaling industry. When the price of sperm oil went out of sight, coal oil became competitive, then kerosene from petroleum. However, the great shocks in the economics of energy, such as the enormous increases in the price of seventeenth-century firewood and in petroleum in 1973, can hardly be ascribed to grim conspiracies. The older I get the less I believe in the conspiratorial interpretation of history and the more I believe in the Cleopatra's nose theory—that happenings like the world energy crisis take place because men are careless and time slips by them. All of a sudden they notice that the universal spot price for crude oil is over $10.00 a barrel. This is a happening of raw terror; one can only appreciate its impact if one has been long in the business. It is like a sudden realization when afflicted with a chest pain that one is certainly going to die, if not now, then a few chest pains later.

The feeling of desperation, when luxuriating Americans and Europeans momentarily fail to get enough motor fuel to generate their normal quota of smog, is the desperation of a people spoiled rotten and made petulant by an overabundant planet. It is only since we have compared the blue and lush beauty of our world, through the eyes of astronauts, with the stifling dungeons of Venus and Mercury and the barren, metallic typhoons of Mars that we have come to fall in love with our planet over again and to realize what a precious sphere it is—how quickly we can poison its lovely surface—but how wondrously it responds to the educated caress of conservation.

This book is concerned with energy in many forms, but it is also concerned with man's mind and man's fate and the moods and resources of the planet Earth.

ENERGY
AND THE
EARTH MACHINE

1 The Clock of Stupidity

In public affairs, stupidity is more dangerous than knavery.
—WOODROW WILSON

Stupidity and pride grow on one bush.
—F. E. HULME.

THE WASTED PROPHECIES

One of the peculiarities of the human animal is his lack of group providence. He is easily scared and even killed by personal voodoo, but as a social creature he will not accept any warning that interferes with daily business. Commission after commission, expert after expert can sound the alarm, but the human creature as a company, or even as a category (consumers), will grunt and glide through extrapolations and predictions, like sea cows through a tangle of water hyacinths. Then when the tide goes out and the creatures are stranded they will yell, "Why didn't somebody tell us?"

Who is "somebody?" Who foretells the economic tides? It is not the president of the United States, because he is commonly one of the last to be convinced of any chance or mischance. He is the one who sets up panels and commissions and task forces and ignores their conclusions. He is the pal of all the rich dealers; he takes their advice, but in the end he founders because the rich dealers fall out among themselves.

In the United States, economic prophecy has a bad track record, not because the predictions did not come true, but because they came true in unexpected ways. For instance, if in 1928 a gypsy fortuneteller, after glancing at your palm, had hissed, "You will be financially ruined," you would not have expected that she was in fact foreseeing the Great Depression, in which virtually everybody was ruined. When the Paley Commission in 1952 foresaw that the American petroleum reserves would start on their curve of exhaustion about 1965 and that the United States might face an energy crisis in the 1970s, they did not include in their visions the titanic reserves of the Middle East; they could not expect that from the time of their report, the world would suffer, not from the pinching out of oil supplies, but from a continuous, dispiriting, world-wide glut of oil. This glut had taken in the minds of international oil-company executives such a sinister aspect that it overwhelmed all their thinking for decades. They were simply in no condition to imagine an *overpriced* glut. They could not forsee a state of affairs in which the United States would suffer because it could not afford to bring into North America the practically limitless reserves of Middle East petroleum at a quadrupled price. Had the law of supply and demand suddenly been repealed? The economic world of the autumn of 1973 was an Alice's Wonderland where the disembodied spirits of John Maynard Keynes and Adam Smith and even John D. Rockefeller moaned in disarray.

BEFORE THE PROPHECIES

It is useful to go back a few generations.

The original John D. Rockefeller was a man with two immensely sharpened specialties: He knew how to get along with the banks and he knew how to stroke the railroads. At the turn of the century the railroads had more clout than the banks (a situation very hard to imagine in our day), which can be illustrated by a true story about California. In those days before the turn of the century most of the important legislation was considered in Sacramento on the last day of the session when everybody was drunk. The Southern Pacific Railroad, which had the members of the legislature on its unofficial payroll, had devised a foolproof technique for conducting this final day's session to its pleasure. Two clerks read the bills to be voted upon, one with a blue tie and the other with a red tie. If "red tie" made known the bill, the legislators were to vote aye; if "blue tie" read the bill, they were to holler nay. This was a simple, rugged system and it worked very well until teetotalers, such as Hiram Johnson, came along to slay the railroad dragon.

At about the same time, the oil monster came under attack, but not before John D. Rockefeller had established a petroleum system that still prevails in this country (although it had to be modified for international operations). John D. would have no truck with exploration for oil or even production of it. That was for the damn fools who wanted to gamble. The Rockefeller money was made by refining and distributing the products, which is why the American oil industry today is still divided among independents, who find and produce about 80 percent of the domestic oil, and the majors, who are integrated (to produce, refine, and distribute), but very few of whom produce as much oil as they refine.

As long as petroleum was essentially a one-product commodity (kerosene), John D. was riding a lovely monopoly. While sloppy competition dumped by-product gasoline in the river at Cleveland (Cleveland's river was even then a source of fire rather than water), John D.'s foreman burned it thriftly under furnaces to distill the kerosene and lube oil. In five-gallon cans, the kerosene turned up in places like China. Rockefeller's only competition for this world-wide business, Shell (who got kerosene from the great Russian wells at Baku), made a fearful merchandising mistake. Sending the kerosene to China by bulk in the first Russian-invented oil tankers, Shell discovered to its dismay that the five-gallon container was half the attraction: One could make chairs and even houses of these cans. John D. had realized this, because he had been fascinated as a boy with the cans that carried whale oil. The manufacture of the cans was more important to Rockefeller than the distillation of the kerosene.* A possibly apocryphal story of the "thirty-nine drops" says that John D., in wandering around his can-welding factory, came to counting the number of drops of solder that the welders used to make a can. It was always forty. He suggested that they try thirty-eight. This gave a defective can—a leaker. Try thirty-nine, he suggested. Thirty-nine worked, so thirty-nine it was and probably is to this day.

By the time John D.'s Standard Oil trust was broken up in 1911, the age of gasoline had arrived and the petroleum industry began to wonder whether it could ever keep up with the hungry myriads of tin lizzies (Model-T Fords) that began to swarm on the roads. The drama of Spindletop (the greatest gusher in Texas history) had come and gone. Although it was not immediately apparent, something else had come and gone, too: The oil industry in America was no longer an independent enterprise. Oil had become the servant of the automobile. Oil millionaires took off their hats and bowed and scraped when they met Detroit millionaires.

The United States, however, was regarded as bereft of really big oil pools. In 1901, Russia was producing more oil at the tall rigs at Baku than the entire United States. But the mode of exploitation, or the tone of gathering Russian oil, was as different from the American style as the ballet is different from a hoedown. Henri Deterding, the eccentric Dutchman, who founded Royal Dutch and later amalgamated it with Shell of England (named thus because Marcus Samuel, its gentle owner, had run a bric-a-brac shop in London that specialized in satisfying the Victorian collection craze for sea shells), borrowed Rothschild money and made Batum and Baku the Black Sea equivalents of modern day Miami Beach and Las Vegas. Stately ladies of lenient virtue were summoned from all of Russia and the conversation was mainly in French. Deterding with his incredible energy buzzed like a bumblebee from flower to flower. Even Chekhov and Turgenev visited the Black Sea sources of oil.

Although "Colonel" Edwin L. Drake,† with his mud-bespattered top hat, was credited with discovering oil, it was Russian engineers, civil servants of the czar, who had shown how to produce it in gentlemanly fashion. The expensive parties and the ostentatious consumption of caviar and champagne are believed by some Marxian historians to have been responsible later for the special, bitter fervor of Georgian communists, such as Stalin.

It is not that America was failing to find oil. Pools were opened up in

---

*It is ironic that the perfect process to make a smoke-free kerosene was discovered only after the automobile had made gasoline the ranking commodity. This was the Rumanian Edeleanu process in which the crude kerosene stock was extracted under pressure with liquid sulphur dioxide.
†Drake was not a colonel but an ex-streetcar conductor and his understanding of oil production was confined to primitive water-type pumps. The poor fellow died, most likely of a cirrhotic liver, in a worse state of poverty than that he had emerged from.

California and Oklahoma and sometimes, as in Seminole, Oklahoma City, and Long Beach, the strikes were dramatic and foolish (but they were not as ponderous and long-lived as those at Baku). For example, at Signal Hill (behind Long Beach) in 1920, the discovery of oil led to possibly the most preposterously crowded drilling orgy in the history of the business. Two competing rigs would drill at each end of one grave in a violated cemetery. Meanwhile, below the hill, makeshift service stations sold gasoline, freshly cooked from the high-gravity crude oil, at 9 cents per gallon. But that was in the morning. In the afternoon the sign would be turned upside down and the gasoline would be sold at 6 cents per gallon. So much natural gas was wasted, without even taking the trouble to flare it, that at one point the sky over Signal Hill caught fire and burned all day in a series of explosions that sounded curiously like the oomphs of some gigantic camel belching.

The really great discovery in pre-Depression North America was the Golden Lane in Mexico. The wells there were individual giants, but Deterding got as much oil from them as did American plungers such as Edward L. Doheny, Harry F. Sinclair, and Frank Phillips. Besides, it was not long before Mexico nationalized the whole industry. This impressed American businessmen very unfavorably, indeed, and created a reversed incentive for digging in one's own back yard, even if it had to be on government-owned land, such as Teapot Dome in Wyoming.

The Teapot Dome reserve technically belonged to the Navy but the Navy allowed itself to be snookered by some fast end plays into giving up its responsibility over this reserve to the Department of the Interior, then headed by Albert Fall. For the ridiculous sum of $130,000, Fall allowed access to Teapot Dome by Sinclair and Doheny. So rough were the business morals of the 1920s that this scandal had very little staying power. Surrounded on every hand by Great Gatsbys and Al Capones, making tens of millions of dollars per year on the hideous fraud of Prohibition, the go-getters of this age could not work up much sour saliva at the fact that Albert Fall had sold out his country for less than the average yearly salary of the vice-president of a third-rate oil company. Warren Harding's personal story attracted more attention as the tragedy of a wife deceived; one could hear more statements to the effect, "I don't blame her for poisoning him" than "Kick all the crooks out of Washington."

OIL HITS BOTTOM

The United States had its own inappropriately timed Bakulike discovery when "Dad" Joiner in 1930 working on the Widow Daisy Bradford's farm in Rusk County, Texas, brought in the first gusher of the tremendous East Texas field. As could be expected, "Dad" Joiner did not make much money, but was outslickered by a poker-playing genius, Harold Lafayette Hunt, who went on accumulating money until he had the unofficial billionaire championship of the United States and in 1960 lavished money on Southern Baptist ministers to compose pieces for radio on "Why the election of a Catholic president would destroy religious freedom in the United States."

The rush to exploit East Texas ruined the oil business in this country—almost for good. It was the depth of the Great Depression, and nobody knew what to do with the oil. The price shuddered down to 5 cents per barrel at one time, and in order to enforce prorationing and the edicts of the Texas Railroad Commission, National Guard troops were sent down to police the mess.

When one stops to think that some "good ole boys" in the petroleum industry (including myself) have seen oil vary in price from a nickel a barrel to $20 a barrel (in 1973 spot auctions of Iran crude), is there any reason to wonder that some of us look at it all as a kind of charade in a madhouse? The cost of energy now not only dictates the price of food but, as Bella Abzug so astutely pointed out in the House of Representatives, even the price of pantyhose.

HOW TO LOSE FRIENDS

In the thirties the American hold on Venezuelan and Middle Eastern oil production became powerful through a series of frenzied political acts that we shall review in the next chapter. Meanwhile, we need to emphasize that simultaneously with the emergence of Exxon (formerly Esso or Jersey), Texaco, Standard Oil of California, Mobil, and Gulf as fierce international oil producers, they lost their Americanism and somehow along with this, some of their stability and sense. During the early part of World War II, for instance, they went out of their way to gyp the U.S. Navy on bunker fuel prices, but actually sold to the Japanese at a discount.

Along with internationalism and the exciting wheeling and dealing that went along with building up an immense postwar European market, the managers completely forgot that they were, after all, American citizens. In a 1973 CBS documentary concerned with the Phillips Petroleum Company, the top executive was painted into a corner where, lacking the wit to keep his mouth shut, he was tricked into admitting that if it came to a showdown between the good of his company and of his country, he would choose his company. Such sensational muddleheadedness is always remembered when nothing else is. I have talked to dozens of people who know nothing about the oil business but who saw this documentary; all they remembered was that the chairman chose his company above his country.

This is far from being an isolated asinine public relations booboo. The oil companies commit them almost daily and have been doing so ever since they had money enough to hold API (American Petroleum Institute) conventions and to take out full-page advertisements in the *Wall Street Journal.*

A convention of the API was layered into the technical men, who go to hear talks on geological, chemical, and engineering subjects and the executives, some of whom go to get drunk for four days and to play high-stake dominoes. Although some patina of class and quietude has covered the brashness of the 1930s and 1940s, when rich Texans in San Francisco (for example) began their evening meals by stuffing $20 bills down the bosoms of waitresses and in Tulsa naked call girls shrieked on hotel fire escapes, as they were sprayed from inside and above by seltzer water, the API convention is still more of a wild party than a meeting of minds. It has much the same effect on respectable observers as the high-class swinery of Victorian-age Baku had on nascent communist leaders.

Although the spectacular antics of the API orgies of forty years ago has given way to a totally boring exchange of complaints against the government, and one sees even white wine consumed rather than Scotch whiskey, one can perceive little improvement in the art of communication. In fact, the foul-mouthed lustiness of the "good ole boys" has yielded to a kind of sissified nonsense—the illiteracy of the language of "public relations."

It may be that this lack of common literacy emerges from the massive mental lethargy of the industry's moguls. There is no challenge to be met any longer by being a fanatic, like a Rockefeller or a Deterding. The world has been made safe from, not for, fanatics. Probably the last truly energetic managers were the late "Mr. Mac" (Leonard F. McCollum of Continental) and Fred Hartley—as a young man—of Union Oil of California (I intentionally omit such exotics as Armand Hammer and Enrico Mattei). When the company no longer seems to hang together and everybody prefers golf to work, the $300,000 chairmen or chief executive officers have no solution. What they do is hire a glossy consulting firm which specializes in company reorganizations. There is no room for literacy or energy.

The lack of what I have called literacy is not really so much an unfamiliarity with cultured pursuits as a lack of appreciation of how ordinary people think. At a time when an energy crisis has inflamed the layman to suspect the big oil companies of conspiracy and when the layman is assured in return by them in expensive TV commercials and full-page newspaper ads that all the new profits will go straight into finding non-Arabian petroleum, what kind of gesture is it for one giant oil company (Gulf) to announce that it is planning to buy a circus? Even worse, why should an even larger company (Mobil) pay $800 million to buy up Montgomery Ward? Montgomery Ward has no sources of energy. It is a vast consumer of energy. What impels a Mobil top executive to accumulate a private cache of home heating oil of thousands of gallons, thus infringing not only the antihoarding regulations but the rules of the municipal fire department?*

The inadequacy of democratic common sense in the oil industry is further demonstrated by its immensely expensive propaganda counterattack in the fall of 1973 and the winter of 1974. On TV and in the newspapers, they described returns on equity, the high cost of exploration, and other subjects which the consuming public doesn't understand and doesn't want to understand. The public can comprehend simple, brutal things, such as the Arabian embargo and waiting in line to buy gasoline, but no number of Philadelphia lawyers and casuists can give the oil industry an honest name, when the waiting in line is juxtaposed with record high profits.

---

*So full of nervous tics are the managers of Mobil that Vice-President Herman Schmidt told a news conference that if the amendments removing the tax credits on foreign oil production became law, his company, after being a pillar of American society for over 100 years, would have to move out of the country.

It is extremely easy to sell the people on the fable that we have a fake energy shortage and that it was caused by the oil companies holding out for higher gasoline prices and driving independent marketers out of business. For Frank Ikard of the American Petroleum Institute—a former congressman—it is desperately hard to unsell it. One reason is that, because of an animal fear of the mighty moguls of Detroit, the oil industry cannot summon the courage to talk realistically about the costs of the automobile culture. Because of the ruinous practice (introduced by Alfred Sloan, the patron saint of General Motors) of changing models every year, the American auto industry has made depreciation such an overwhelming percentage of the price of personal transportation that any changes in the costs of fuel or lubrication are by comparison almost imperceptible. (This is why European governments can tax "petrol" with relative impunity. The European car owner is enough of an amateur accountant to realize that the stability in market value of his automobile is more than enough to pay for the ridiculous price of his fuel.) Since a car is normally the second most expensive possession that an American acquires, and he is quite hip to car-pricing tactics, the astonishing thing is that he remains such an uncomplaining sucker in the gigantic fraud of the yearly model changes and its effect on multiplying the rate of depreciation of his car.

Oil companies go out of their way to set up defenses for the car makers in regard to air pollution, but I have never heard of an automobile manufacturer doing anything for the oil business. My first superior in petroleum research, when I was fresh out of Cal (known by everybody but Californians as "Berkeley") was a brash and brilliant Georgian (who has since made himself many times over a millionaire) and I can recall that he advised me never to forget that the petroleum business with all its pomps was a mere suburban appendage of Detroit. With any heart and will, this need not be the case, since the oil industry, instead of being a slave to one form of internal combustion engine and the people who make it, could graduate into the general energy business; and it could spend its money on things other than circuses and mail-order houses; it could spend money, for example, on nonpolluting transportation.

One trouble is that there does not seem to be any skill or magic involved in being a top oil executive. What does he do for his half-million dollars a year? Can he not learn at least not to appear as a fool on television* and not to give huge company handouts illegally to presidential candidates?

If there is some sort of social revolution or even (which would amount to the same thing in the oilmen's minds) a partial nationalization—as in France and Great Britain—of certain companies, the first thing to be examined should be the process of picking managers and chief executives. As it is now, the man who can mysteriously gain some smell of money (as an accountant or salesman) and is over six feet tall and keeps his fingernails clean and is either an ex-athlete or has been a coach of a Little League baseball team, finds himself tapped by the board of

---

*A vice-president, not in an engineering role where it might be excusable, had to admit before a senate subcommittee that he did not know even approximately the public value of his company's stock.

directors for some exercise in increased responsibility—or at least increased visibility—perhaps assistant to the president. If he doesn't fumble the ball on the first snap, it is then simply a matter of waiting for people to retire or die.

One of the reasons that American oil companies are stupidly managed is not only that the chief executive officers are likely to be incompetent but they compound their puerility by surrounding themselves with committees. Aside from the enormous and expensive overhead involved in having executive committees, operating committees, planning departments, and other Pentagonlike groupings, this trend to complicate everything results in the well-known phenomenon, long ago expressed in American business folklore, that "a camel is a horse designed by a committee."

European and Japanese businesses often run circles around American firms, not because they have a better or a cheaper product but because they have a simple mechanism for making decisions. Pick a good top manager and a good sales manager. The rest is kitty litter.

THE ALMOST FATAL BOO-BOO

The clock of stupidity does not chronicle only the unwisdom of petroleum tycoons. We shall see in Chapter 3 that the oil industry has been politically pampered as no other in regard to tax benefits and sweetheart arrangements (for example, the Texas Railroad Commission). However, since the breakup of the Standard Oil Trust, oil companies trade these benefits, which are too complicated for most people to understand, for a built-in and generalized distrust. Occasionally the distrust erupts in governmental or judicial actions, having very grave, almost fatal results in an economy which is as energy-oriented as that of the United States.

When the metallurgical art progressed to the point that thin-walled pipe of sufficient strength could be successfully welded to yield long pipelines capable of pumping gas at high pressures (about 1935), the age of natural gas was born. Natural gas is the superpremium of all premium fuels, in industry, for home use, and for burning under the boilers of electrical utilities. Indeed, natural gas networks have much the feel of public utilities, such as the telephone system and the rural electrification grids; and it was not surprising that natural gas pipelines, as they came on the scene, were put immediately under the scrutiny of the Federal Power Commission (FPC).

This commission of five men, satisfied to control the prices and availability of pipeline transfers, balked at the increasing demands on the part of certain powerful politicians that their control should extend to the wellhead price of natural gas going into interstate pipelines. (The National Gas Act of 1938 stated that provisions of the Act should not apply to producers or gatherers.) The gas producers held their breath as the matter was taken to the Supreme Court and the decision was made in the so-called Phillips Case in 1954. This was, of course, the Warren court and its decision, roughly, was that the FPC should control interstate natural gas prices and at the lowest level of their existing intrastate prices.

Although I have maintained some sentimental attachment to the Warren court, on account of other decisions that I admire, the Phillips Case decision was abominably shortsighted and the work of men who obviously had no feeling for energy and economic realities, who indeed had no business poking their noses into the prices of anything. Because of the decision, one can argue with justice that the future of the fossil-fuel business (petroleum and coal both) in the United States was put in serious jeopardy for 20 years.

One can easily see the disastrous foolishness of the decision. If you put a strict contract ceiling price on such an attractive and sexy fuel as natural gas, everybody will grab at it. All customers will be spoiled. Rightfully they will object to paying 2 or 3 times per therm (or the equivalent amount of energy) in the form of liquid fuel or coal. Thus, either the price of heating oil and coal must go down or the price of natural gas must go up. Since, in the name of widows and orphans, the price of interstate natural gas was kept down and frozen in long-term contracts, the natural gas and petroleum industry (in most cases, the same) got into the habit of saying to hell with it. The number of explorations declined with the price of domestic crude oil. Coal prices went down to the point where the coal industry became a sort of shabby poor relation. And we began to run out of gas.

At the time of the 1954 Phillips decision, about 60 percent of each barrel of domestic crude went into gasoline and distillates, while 40 percent went to No. 6 heavy residual fuel, commonly used by electric utilities and industry as boiler fuel. The artificially cheap natural gas made available by wand-waving on the part of the Warren court undercut the No. 6 fuel, and for years it was sold at a minus profit. It was worth less than garbage. Technology tried to solve this problem by new cracking and coking processes that produced gasoline and distillates from the heavy fuel and still more gasoline by cracking the distillates.

As a result of this trend, in the early 1960s we had an enormous oversupply of gasoline. The refining companies with their own dealerships moved as much gasoline as possible by bribing customers with steak knives, plastic tumblers, trading stamps, and gambling games. The rest was sold to independent marketers who promptly started price wars. Refining companies averaged about 2 percent on investment during these sorry times, which was not enough to pay the interest on investments for the construction of more refineries. Thus the catastrophic Phillips Case decision had a further effect: While it discouraged exploration and production in the United States after 1954, in the 1960s it was the refining end of the business that said to hell with it. During the sixties, therefore, the major oil companies emphasized the building of refineries in foreign countries where distillate and heavy fuel markets had not been destroyed by the availability of cheap natural gas.

Within the giant perimeter of this slow cyclone of senseless action, we can perceive little dust devils of sheer insanity. For example, in the midst of a looming shortage of natural gas, we see residences, especially in the Middle West, being converted from oil to gas heating. This comes about because the industrial gas consumers are being cut off in favor of higher priced residential users. At the top of the crazy list, probably is the construction of plants to produce SNG (synthetic or substitute natural gas) by cracking naphtha, propane, and even the whole crude oil into gas (methane). As of May 1, 1973, there were 26 plants of this kind in various stages of development in this country with a theoretical capacity equal to the domestic refining through put of Gulf and Mobil combined.

It would take quite a lot of rhetoric to justify this nonsensical operation. One can imagine trying to explain it to an angel from outer space—a sort of Bob Newhart angel. He says, "Let me see if I get this straight now. On this planet you produce large amounts of gas and liquids in one place, where you burn the gas; is it to light the desert at night? Well, anyway, you save the liquids and flare the gas. Then in another part of this planet you take the liquids and make them into gas, with a large loss of energy because you have to heat the liquids to high temperatures to decompose them into gas. It is the gas that you use, right? Then if the gas is so precious, why do you charge so little for it and burn so much of it in the desert?"

Incredible as it may seem, the British Labor party is set up to repeat the same folly with gas from the North Sea. A government instrument, the British Gas Corporation, is a monopoly buyer of North Sea natural gas and has already retarded development of this luscious but fragile and dangerous field by holding prices down below the liquid equivalent in energy.

MISCELLANEOUS MANIA

There has been plenty of stupidity to go around. As Will Rogers said, "If stupidity got us into this mess, why can't it get us out of it?" It wasn't the same men, but perhaps stupidity is all we have. Consider in recent years the administrations, the bureaucracy; and consider Congress.

Kennedy gave energy little thought and Johnson believed in such sacred Texas doctrines as the depreciation allowance and the containment of gasoline wars. From Truman through Johnson we can sum up the administration viewpoint on energy as "benign neglect," but with Nixon we enter a period approaching dementia.

The story is odd. In the middle 1960s, for example, a New York independent oil entrepreneur, John M. Shaheen, started to build refineries in Newfoundland and Nova Scotia. His 3 Canadian refineries have a total planned capacity of 600,000 barrels per day. This is more refinery capacity than has been built in the United States for 5 years and it represented a good deal of wheeling and dealing both politically and legally with Canadian politicians. Who was Shaheen's lawyer in all this shadow play? It was Richard M. Nixon of the firm of Nixon, Mudge, Rose, Guthrie, Alexander and Mitchell.

In 1968 a gigantic refinery (300,000 barrels per day) was planned at Machiasport, Maine, by the Occidental Petroleum Corporation, to operate mainly on Libyan crude, or whatever this large independent could pick up. Armand Hammer, head of this company, was willing to put up the money and take his chances. Major oil company opposition to this refinery was so explosively bitter that Exxon and the API finally took their case to President Nixon. The Machiasport refinery was never built.

In 1969, when a task force headed by the then labor secretary, George Shultz, began a study of import controls, the Canadian government delivered a note to Washington which could have built an enduring system of energy management of the North American continent. The note stressed the importance of Canadian oil remaining (as it had) free of import restrictions and expressed a desire for the intelligent sharing of Canadian resources with its southern neighbor, emphasizing the natural partnership in continental defense and the like. It asked an end to border restrictions on the delivery of Canadian oil and natural gas to the United States and acceptance by Washington of the view that Canada's oil and gas reserves are as much a part of U.S. strategic resources as those of Texas and Louisiana. In spite of, or perhaps because of, his former machinations for Mr. Shaheen, Nixon's answer to this tentative note from Canada was, on March 10, 1971, to slap absurd restrictions on petroleum imports from that country. Canada did not forget this insulting treatment, and in 1973 and 1974 (when import quotas had been abolished) they placed rigorous controls on oil exports into the United States and refused to respond to advances on the part of Nixon and Henry Kissinger.

The final abolition of the import quotas in 1973 was, in any case, like pulling teeth. The task force of 1969 unanimously had recommended this move and even most of the majors were by then in favor of it, since Middle East oil had started modestly upward in world price. For some odd and opaque reason Exxon alone insisted on retention of the quota and Nixon went along. As late as September 1972, when the country was on the eve of a serious winter fuel shortage,* Nixon was assuring Congress he did not foresee any difficulties whatever. Nixon's spokesman, General George A. Lincoln, of the now-defunct Office of Emergency Preparedness, acted as official Pollyanna.

He dismissed the task force and appointed another one, with George Shultz conspicuously excluded. Two months later, Nixon did just what John Ehrlichman said he had no intention of doing: He abolished the oil import quotas.

Such shifty open-field running is hard to predict, unless one assumes that Nixon was ready to do whatever a consensus of major oil executives favored. The shiftiness in 1972 and 1973 apparently reflected the fact that for a few months there was no consensus. Texaco and Mobil, for example, argued against Exxon. A close look at Exxon would have shown that their production capabilities both

---

*Through the miracle of the moods of the jet stream, we have had recent successive winters of unprecedented mildness. A severe winter in 1972–73 or 1973–74 would have been the slap in the face to wake us up.

in the U.S. and abroad were so large that it didn't really matter so much to them which way the ball bounced.

One of the important questions that came up with the discovery of the Alaska North Slope field (the biggest single American discovery since East Texas) was whether the pipeline should run from Prudhoe Bay to Valdez or down the Mackenzie Valley, picking up Canadian oil and ending in the Midwest rather than in the already better served California market. The choice for *oil* transportation was the Alyeska (Valdez terminal) route, but there was still a good argument for a Canadian *gas* line rather than one paralleling the Alyeska oil pipeline, since the extra amount of Canadian gas that could be picked up was very considerable.

The word had gotten out that Canada would insist upon a 51 percent ownership of any such line, and to disavow this rumor the Canadian government delivered an official denial to the U.S. embassy in Ottawa. For some undetermined reason this document was never made known to Congress. Nixon was more interested in a proposal by the El Paso Natural Gas Company to build a gas line on the right of way of the oil pipeline to Valdez, where the gas would be liquefied and shipped by special tankers to California (or Japan).

Now, El Paso is one of those raunchy, hungry firms. It has been in and out of federal courts for two or three decades, facing up to accusations of violating antitrust laws, of engaging in monopoly practices, and of overcharging consumers. During these court adventures it has had the good sense to pay at least $1 million in fees for the services of the law firm of Nixon, Mudge, Rose, Guthrie, Alexander and Mitchell.

I suppose one could make a lot more of these Nixonian linkages with past clients.

The men he surrounded himself with, possibly excepting Schultz and later, William Simon, were inexpert in the energy field. Governor John A. Love's chief claim to a historical asterisk was that he had come east from Colorado in 1968 to warn against the Machiasport refinery project, on the grounds that it would delay shale oil development projects in his home state. At that particular time this was a shortsighted notion. John E. Ehrlichman, who held the position of "energy czar" for a few months, probably had the brains to understand it all, but he was too busy with political pots and pans.

In Congress there were brilliant and assiduous men and women, but they were poorly understood, unappreciated by the press, and too subtle to attract supporters. Consider Adlai Stevenson, III. Of all the members of the House of Representatives, he has been the only one (with the exception of Patricia Schroeder of Colorado) to insist, time after time, upon the essential two-tier or dichotomous nature of the U.S. oil business. From the drastic proposals he directed toward the major oil companies, he invariably excluded the independents—either in petroleum or natural gas. This applies to the depletion allowance and to many other things, including the pricing of new crude and stripper crude (produced at less than 10 barrels per day per well). He and Ms. Schroeder have appreciated that the small wildcatter is a strange and valuable creature; in the end he discovers in this country most of the new oil and gas, hidden beyond the patience of the big boys in stratigraphic traps in the mountains and in the unlikely and endless plains. Special treatment, they believe and propose, is necessary to prevent the independents from becoming extinct, as the grizzly bear is going to be extinct.

What, for example, is the independent's role in exploration and production on the continental shelf? Here the government auctions off leases at prices that even the big companies can meet only by combining into bidding teams. Would it be desirable, for example, to allow only small companies, in return, to bid for production of oil from government reserves such as Elk Hills and "Pet Four" in Alaska? The Navy's Elk Hills reserve near Bakersfield, California, already has been possibly nibbled to death by Standard Oil of California which has pumped millions of barrels from wells located within 2,500 feet of the reserve boundaries. In January 1974 the Navy politely asked Stancal to lay off. Stancal refused. (This company is noted for its extreme aggressiveness. It has some shadowy legal document implying that if any company can exploit Elk Hills, it is Stancal, although Shell Oil also has some legal pretensions. At any rate it would be a miracle if the Navy ever burns any Elk Hills fuel oil under its boilers.)

Naval Petroleum Reserve No. 4 ("Pet Four") on Alaska's northwest shore, adjacent in a general sense to the North Slope or Prudhoe Bay discovery, may just possibly be one of the largest oil resources in the world, possibly 100 billion barrels, compared to 10 billion barrels for the North Slope and perhaps 600 billion barrels of proven reserves for the whole world. Pet Four looks too big to be nibbled away, but Adlai Stevenson has reason to believe that federal officials are fudging on Pet Four boundaries to allow major oil companies to drill in the reserve's 2-million-acre buffer zone and thus tap the Navy oil pool. Alaskan senators favor throwing this mysterious and magnificent property open to private development. This is a place to watch—it may have enough oil to generate a thousand Teapot Dome scandals.

In reviewing the exceptional—the intelligent—minds in Congress one should not overlook the unhonored prophet, Senator Jennings Randolph of West Virginia, who in 1959 saw enough trouble ahead to call for the congressional formulation of a national energy policy. He suggested that in Congress the policy be discussed by a permanent joint committee; but his resolution to this effect was referred to the Senate Committee on Rules and Administration, where it died and was not even vouchsafed the grace of an autopsy. The corpse was disinterred for the purpose of partisan "I-told-you-so's" during the madhouse scenes of December 1973.

It was in this wild month, when the country actually had more heating oil and gasoline in storage than the year before, but had officially acquired an energy crisis, that Congress showed its capacity for hysteria. It is during such periods when a deadline for action is set (and invariably missed) that one could develop nostalgia for the California legislature of 1898, with everybody unashamedly drunk and the blue- and red-necktied clerks in systematic action.

Some of the congressmen admitted that they had no notion of what they were voting on. Amendments pyramided and anybody without an amendment was as *manqué* as a diplomat without his pants. Senator Ernest Hollings pointed out that the old saying aboard ship in World War II now applied: "When in danger, when in doubt, run in circles, scream and shout."

In the midst of extremely unscholarly debates on solar energy, the dangers of nuclear devices, the villainy of the ecologists, the villainy of the oil companies, Charles W. Sandman of New Jersey incredibly brought up the ancient story that goes, "Years ago there were auto engines that could get 30 to 35 miles per gallon. But in order to boost gasoline sales, the major oil companies bought all the patents for these engines and removed them from the market." Representative James A. Burke of Massachusetts, an inflamed Irish-American, said that he wouldn't ever have his picture taken next to an oil drum. Amid the jabber about geothermal power, a revival of windmills, hydrogen fusion, fuel cells, et cetera, Mr. Teno Roncello, a plain-spoken gentleman from Wyoming, shouted that the chamber should get back to business and forget about all these "erotic" forms of energy. Presumably he meant exotic, but so great was the general brouhaha and so late the hour and the date that apparently nobody except Morris Udall of Arizona noted this remarkable slip of the tongue.

One of the far from humorous results of the congressional orgy was that they failed to act on matters of international and internal urgency. Coming back after Christmas, still red-eyed and mad, they put an end to the International Development Association, the poor countries' window at the World Bank that was supporting the defense against starvation and river blindness in West Africa. But they failed to act against one of the worst disgraces and causes of winter suffering in this country—the propane swindle.

Propane, the major constituent of liquefied petroleum gas (LPG), has always been a nostalgic word for me because when I first went to work as a chemical engineer I was given the job of developing a very neat process, which consisted of dissolving lubricating oil in liquid propane to remove the asphalt and wax in petroleum residuum. In a mixing bomb, the asphalt comes out of the bottom in long puffy turds, but the smell is the cool, clean one of propane.

Since those days, propane has become in effect the poor man's natural gas. Since it can be stored in simple pressure packages, people who can not afford a house piped up to natural gas utility systems use propane for cooking and heating. Three years ago the price was 8 cents a gallon. It has shot up to 34 cents per gallon and more. An old Oklahoma woman writes, "It's the only fuel I can get where I live. My husband is blind and ill in a nursing home . . . so all these rises I can't stand, for my husband and I together we draw $100.78 per month from Social Security." A 78-year-old Arkansas widow reports that her total income is $81.50 per month from Social Security. Propane, which she uses only for heat, cost her $36.00 per 100 gallons in January 1974, compared to $8.17 for a colder January 1973 (Forty-five percent of her 1974 total winter income went to propane!)

What conceivable excuse is there for multiplying the price of a simple by-product of natural gas production, so that on a thermal equivalent basis it costs the poor people 5 times as much as natural gas itself? One excuse is, "It's that Cost of Living Council again." It seems that in 1973 under Cost of Living Council rules, only the 23 top oil companies were subject to commodity price control. This meant open market for propane suppliers from whom the 23 top companies normally buy to round out their sales line. With the majors hog-tied, the brokers and independents were free to bid the propane price up, and they did.

Much of the propane produced in Oklahoma, for instance, was stored out of state for many months and sold 2 or 3 times before being distributed. There was no shortage. There was in fact a surplus. Some concerns that offered to sell propane at fancy prices couldn't be found in telephone directories and 3 of them were located in a Texas town of just 300 population. The Internal Revenue Service is trying, also, to find the propane broker who gave a Los Angeles hotel as his business address. As for the wholesaler who bought from and sold to brokers, such transactions would have helped his profit margins more than sales to normal customers, because they eliminated the need for trucking and other distribution costs.

It is in situations like this, where a severe outbreak of unquarantined greed threatens the lives of the poor and helpless, that one begins to tire of the superior smiles of the William Buckleys, or even of the strong, impeccable logic of editorals in the *Wall Street Journal*. It is all very well to state that high, uncontrolled prices will "clear the market" (a pet expression), because of the law of supply and demand, but somebody who can't afford a gas-supplied home and certainly can't afford firewood (now the most expensive combustible of all) is likely to die of pneumonia before the market clears. Besides, where there is so little elasticity, as there is in the price of fuels, the market may never clear to the extent that the 78-year-old-widow can survive a rugged winter.

The clock of stupidity is attached to a bell, and it tolls for your descendants. Millions of Americans, have disassociated themselves from all thoughts of the energy crisis (which they now regard as a forgotten false alarm). I quote from the *New Yorker*, March 18, 1974, "Our prophets are without honor. Now, when a problem is ordained a crisis, it becomes all the rage. Congressmen hold hearings and Presidents announce programs. There are conferences and commissions and TV specials. We write books about it . . . and then suddenly we become bored with it."

Yet, there must be exceptions to the epidemic state of instant boredom. I would rather hope that it is only the few who have no grandchildren, who become bored with it; those who live for the present and believe the universe will disappear after their death. But they need not fear; they will continue to have their quota of costly fuel to produce their quota of smog for years to come. What we are concerned about is what happens after that.

2 Frogs and Scorpions

*Man is a rational animal who always loses his temper when he is
called upon to act in accordance with the dictates of reason.*

—OSCAR WILDE

Ray Vicker of the *Wall Street Journal* has made known a modern parable told
by a sophisticated Lebanese trader:

> A frog was about to swim across the Nile River when he was accosted by a
> scorpion, who begged to be carried along. "Oh, no!" objected the frog. "You'll sting
> me and I'll die."
>
> The scorpion said, "Why would I be so foolish? If I stung you, I'd drown."
> After thinking this over, the frog agreed to ferry the scorpion across, but in the
> middle of the river the scorpion stung the frog.
>
> "Look what you've done, you damn fool," mourned the dying frog. "Now we'll
> both perish."
>
> The scorpion replied, "I know, I know. But don't forget, this is the Middle
> East!"

One could, with equal justice, apply this parable to the international oil
business itself. It is full of frogs and scorpions.

Foreign oil operation is very different from North American operation and
it has not been easy for born Texans to get used to carving up the enormous pie
of Middle East petroleum resources while standing about in an English grouse
moor with tall, tweeded Englishmen smoking pipes and being urbane. There was
a time in the early 1920s when it looked as if the British had a lock on everything
from the Mediterranean to Indonesia. In the Western Hemisphere Royal Dutch/
Shell had most of the Mexican and Venezuelan production and, through its
subsidiary Shell Oil Company, an important slice of the production and sales in
the United States. *Sperling's Journal,* an English magazine much trusted by
Winston Churchill and Lloyd George, said in September 1919, "America is
running through her stores of domestic oil and is obliged to look abroad. The
British position is impregnable. All the known oilfields, all the likely or probable

oilfields outside the U.S. are in British hands, under British control or financed by British capital." It took just two decades for American impudence and bumptiousness to reverse this lockmanship.

In the last chapter we noted that the Standard Oil patrimony was not slanted toward the brute task of finding and producing oil, since John D. regarded oil as a sort of gift of nature, oozing from convenient rocks where collecting it was a pumper's chore and all the skill and money lay in the transporting and refining of it. Before the demand grew enormous with the advancement of the automobile, Standard had been legally carved up and some of the muscular morsels remaining had the job of rounding up oil by finding it themselves or by buying it from independent producers, a class of people peculiar to this country and indeed somewhat abhorrent to Europeans. Oil operations, as carried out by Europeans, Asiatics, South Americans, Africans, or Russians have little place for the independent, the wildcatter who is gambling the shirt on his back, his wife's uncle's savings, and some money from the richest friends in town—usually his dentist. Although it is this kind of person who still make up the backbone of the American petroleum industry (they discover 80 percent of all domestic oil), they are as rare abroad as professional cowboys. Exploration and production by the British, French, and others, are under the guidance of great cartels and of government bureaus—even of foreign ministers.*

One may say that the only true European independent was Calouste Gulbenkian ("Mr. Five Percent"), who eventually became a billionaire, not because he knew anything about oil (he probably had never seen a drop of it) but because he had an instinct for cartel politics and the march of money. As Gulbenkian said, "Petroleum companies are like cats—it's hard to tell when they're fighting or making love." But Gulbenkian learned not only how to tell the difference, but how to promote the love matches and referee the fights.

THE OIL OF RUSSIA, HOLY AND UNHOLY

Before considering those passionate struggles of the years after World War I, it is worthwhile emphasizing once again that at the turn of the century, Russia was producing more oil than America. Also of great interest is that, at the start at least, Baku with its great gushing wells was exploited much as the Middle East came to be exploited 40 or 50 years later—by foreigners. In the case of Baku, the foreigners were three Swedish brothers, Ludwig, Robert, and Alfred Nobel. Among various accomplishments in this family was the invention of the torpedo by their father, Emmanuel. Ludwig and Robert built the magnificent and difficult St. Petersburg dockyard, and Alfred invented dynamite and attained philanthropic immortality through his Nobel prizes.

The Nobel brothers' master stroke in Baku was to establish by tactics typical

*This is not to say that the U.S. government has little influence on native American operations or on the logistics of international oil concerns bossed from the United States. In general, since World War II, at least, operations have been so linked with cold war matters that, as we shall see, at least one critical coup connected with oil was handled by the CIA.

of John D. Rockefeller a virtual monopoly over the transportation of oil from the Caucasus to the rest of Russia and the world. There was no railroad to the Black Sea. The Nobel brothers had to take the oil up the Volga River and thence by rail to the Baltic Sea. The Nobel stranglehold on Baku loosened when other operators borrowed enough Rothschild money to build railways to Batum. Eventually the construction of the Suez Canal, concurrently with the development of oil tankers (which almost invariably exploded at some stage in their life, and still do), made the lucrative Far Eastern market available to such Black Sea entrepreneurs as Henri Deterding of Royal Dutch.

After the Bolshevik Revolution of 1917, oil production, along with everything else in Russia, went into the doldrums; but there was still a good deal of petroleum left in the Caucasus. All the foreign holdings were expropriated, but with the tears that the USSR exhibits in such matters, the door was left open about one-sixteenth of an inch for reimbursement of some nature. Indeed, the Royal Dutch/Shell people, deep in the labyrinth of their London headquarters have a spider-spotted topographic map showing the location of their once mighty wells in the "lost province" of Baku, which they still dream of as one dreams of the lost land of Thule; they perceive a mathematical chance of getting the wells back in the form of access to other Russian properties.

Judging by the behavior of the Russian dictators during and after World War II, this mathematical chance is so near zero that pragmatists may assume that it is zero. The USSR in fact developed such a xenophobic attitude with respect to petroleum that several expert observers (including Christopher Tugendhat) attribute Hitler's invasion of Russia to the refusal of Stalin to allow joint Russian-German exploitation of the Russian oil reserves. Germany at war needed large amounts of fuel to keep the Panzers rolling and the *Luftwaffe* in the air, and it is noteworthy that the main thrust of the German armies into Russia was toward the Caucasus.

After the fall of the Third Reich, the USSR staged a formidable comeback in petroleum, stumbling, for example, on the immensely rich Tuymazy and Oktyabrak fields in the Ural-Volga basin (often called the Second Baku), 700 miles due east of Moscow. Russia regained its traditional position as the second largest oil producer, after the United States, but Stalin and, after him, Nikita Khrushchev, made sure that the Second Baku was not open to the foreign industrial princes. Russia from then on not only kept the foreigners out, she refused to import a single drop of oil from outside the Iron Curtain. (Natural gas was a different story, and one of the heroic deals that the Shah Pahlevi of Iran is continually setting up involved the exchange of Iranian gas for Russian rubles and technical assistance.)

A third Baku was found near the town of Tyrumen in Western Siberia, and Russia now apparently had more than enough oil, for the time being, to satisfy her own economy. She became an oil-exporting country, but she exported in return for things she needed, including steel pipe and political outposts. The steel pipe she got from Italy, for example. The sugar she got from Cuba went directly to countries that Russia had trade with, since Russia had plenty of sugar of her own.*

The doctrine that Russia had enough oil was based on Khrushchev's eccentric notion that his country would never have private automobiles; that, instead, it would rely on state-owned rental fleets. Khrushchev was trying to suppress, whether he knew it or not, one of the most powerful desires of modern man, and it was doubtless one of the reasons for his downfall. The private car is not only a precious thing for Europeans, it is a symbol of comfort and prestige to all Western mankind, a symbol more radiant than drink, fine food, and splendid women. It is a credit to Leonid Brezhnev's insight that he recognized this social fact immediately and began to set up deals with Fiat of Italy and Renault of France to create mass facilities for the manufacture of Russian cars. He has a long way to go, however, because for one thing, there are fewer paved roads in all of Russia than in just the state of Michigan.

Perhaps the riskiest oil policy that the Russians use is to treat the Eastern European countries like barely tolerable poor cousins. In the 1960s East Germany, Hungary, Czechoslovakia, Poland, and Bulgaria were paying from 17 to 20 rubles per ton for the same Russian oil that Japan, Italy, and West Germany were getting for 7 rubles. The Russian excuse is that the East European countries overcharge the Soviet Union for the machinery they provide in exchange for the oil. They complain also of the poor quality of that machinery. (On the face of it this appears a dubious charge, since some of the East European countries, especially Czechoslovakia and East Germany, are noted for their master machinists.)

If the hunger for private automobiles is satisfied, Russian oil is not enough to satisfy the Eastern European appetite also, thus the Eastern Europeans have taken to a rather gentle wheeling and dealing on their own. Rumania signed a $100 million barter arrangement with Iran in which Rumania would send tractors and ploughs in return for oil. Bulgaria also joined the queue for Iranian oil and East Germany signed with Algeria. Deals too numerous to detail and too vague to trust continue to be negotiated.

The rather cautious differentiation which Russia makes in regard to petroleum and natural gas policies shows up in her immensely ambitious plans and accomplishments in gas technology. In the 1960s the vast Friendship Pipeline was built to link the Communist bloc countries with central Russia's source of natural gas supply over 2,500 miles away from most of them. The Soviet plans for exporting natural gas are even bolder. They want to build the largest natural gas line in the universe, from the Ukraine to Trieste to supply Italy with up to 12 billion cubic meters a year. The line would pass through Austria and then be extended across Northern Italy to France, thus tying the Soviet fields into the intricate West European distribution system which has hitherto been based on the gas supply in Algeria and Libya, Holland (the great Gröningen field), and the Lacq reserves in France. If this scheme comes off, it will after a fashion, make

*This was temporarily not the case during the sugar crisis of 1974.

the Soviets a sort of silent partner in the European Common Market.

I have noted previously that I did not believe in the reality of conspiracy as a serious factor in the mess that United States energy is in—or indeed in history. I must reverse this attitude when I speak of strong socialistic nations. In their case it is safer to assume that conspiracy is always involved. The very nature of the socialist charter assures that conspiracy is the way things are done. It is true that many of their conspiracies are foolish failures, but a conspiratorial society—being composed of mere human creatures—is not guaranteed to act less stupidly than a free society.

WORLD WAR I

We must try to put ourselves back into what seems an almost unfathomable past —the days of the first great assembly-line production of the Model-T Ford, unequaled until the years of the Volkswagen Beetle two generations later; the growth of rivals for the residues of the Standard Trust, notably Gulf and Texaco; the explosion and dying off of Spindletop; and in Europe, the merging of Henri Deterding's Royal Dutch and gentle Marcus Samuel's Shell. And the "guns of August."

Shell was run in an unbelievably amateurish fashion. In Marcus Samuel's mind it did not merit any more management than the collection and dispensing of sea shells, his first love. The way in which he tried to sell the use of petroleum fuel to the British Navy was typical. The Royal Navy in the early 1900s was full of the usual harrumphing old-style alcoholic admirals, who had to be shown with plainness and vigor that petroleum bunker fuel was equal to or better than coal for heating the boilers of their mighty ships. The test was a disaster. Samuel's engineers could have done better trying to burn sea shells. They used the wrong kind of vaporizer burners, with the result that the test ship and everybody in the vicinity (including royalty) was enveloped in a dense cloud of choking soot and smoke. In the eyes (and noses) of the admiralty this new-fangled stuff was a most improper fuel, and thus Samuel's dream of capturing the largest single market in the world disappeared.

Samuel had some Indonesian oil production in the Kutei field of Borneo. He built a refinery there with Russian equipment that seems to represent a really historical monster of amateur engineering. It could only be made to work after a fashion by, so to speak, running it backward. Nevertheless, some years later this Borneo crude, because it contained a highly unusual concentration of toluene, proved important during the war for making TNT.

In 1907 Samuel's troubles came to a head. He had invested heavily in Texas oil, but Spindletop dribbled out. Tankers had to be converted into cattle ships. He begged the British government for help in getting into Burma and to give him another chance to show the Admiralty that petroleum would burn; but the British government had decided that Shell, with its reserves in the Dutch East Indies, was not "British" enough to receive any more favors. Samuel's only refuge was to fall into the protective arms of Henri Deterding of Royal Dutch. Although the deal was a 60/40 split in Royal Dutch's favor, the persistence of the Shell name and symbol and the location of the headquarters in London have given the world the impression that the Shell group is British.

Deterding was everything that Marcus Samuel was not: dynamic, supercompetitive, a fierce gambler. He developed new fields in Rumania, he bought up the Rothschild interests in the Caucasus and, just before the war, he brought in a great gusher in Mexico. For a million pounds he obtained the unexercised exploration rights in Venezuela of a small American company—perhaps the best property investment ever made. (For 300,000 pounds he bought from Cartier's an emerald parure in order to attain exploration rights over the incomparable person of a Madame Lydia Pavlovna, but he found he could not meet the bill until the arrival of his director's fees a few months later. We know little more of Lydia. She may just as well have been the Lydia of Groucho Marx's hoarse ditty.)

As prologue to World War I, one other crucial chapter in oil was written; this time in the Middle East. German geologists, as early as 1871, had visited the vilayets of Baghdad and Mosul in Mesopotamia (now Iraq) and reported that the land positively stank of petroleum. Persia also smelled interesting, although it constituted a much more ambitious stretch of geography, and in 1872 Baron Julius de Reuter, founder of the news agency, took out a mineral concession there —and did nothing with it.* For decades the Hohenzollerns had a rather mystical dream of a Berlin to Baghdad railroad and in 1888 the Ottoman Railway Company, controlled by the Deutsche Bank got right-of-way concessions in Anatolia and Mesopotamia, including mineral rights which, if they had been exercised promptly by Turkey, would have made that nation independent of Germany in the impending world war.

Turkey was advised by a very young man, a King's College graduate and mining expert, Calouste Gulbenkian. Gulbenkian's great mistake in his early years of advisership was turning down a concession to all of Persia, which was instead grabbed up by an Englishman, William Knox D'Arcy, displacing Julius de Reuter. As D'Arcy's explorations failed, the British government came to the rescue, with its usual unexplainable sense of cruciality, and encouraged an appeal to the Burmah Oil Company. The funds that Burmah put up were in turn running out, but at the last moment, at 4:30 in the morning of May 26, 1905, a vast gusher blew in and the oil industry of the Middle East found itself born along with a new company, Anglo-Persian (in 1935 changed to Anglo-Iranian, and in 1957 to British Petroleum). Burmah took the preferred stock (which is why this venerable old nervous wreck of a company still survives), while Field Marshal Lord Kitchener was among the milling mob competing for common shares. A pipeline had to be laid to the coast and a refinery built and by 1913 not a drop of oil had been sold.

Fortunately the young upstart, Winston Churchill, was first lord of the

---

*Apparently because they have preferred to conquer rather than explore, the Germans have a strangely dim record in the oil business. They have in recent years tried to make up for past history by offering outrageously generous government loans which the lender has to repay only if oil is found.

Admiralty and in 1911 had again brought up the matter of petroleum as a preferred naval fuel. Recent tests indicated that petroleum would not only burn under marine boilers but, by substituting oil for coal, one could add an extra gun turret or, alternatively, increase sustained speed by several knots. With visions of a superfleet that would sail circles around the Germans in a shoot-out, Churchill wanted to guarantee the availability of petroleum fuel for his navy and he conceived the notion that the best guarantee was part ownership of an oil company. His proposal to buy 51 percent of the new Anglo-Persian Oil Company was approved by Parliament and took effect as the first but not the last example of mutual government-private management in this business— a development, incidentally, which profoundly shocked the Texans and filled them with dreams of horror, especially since Senator James Phelan of California was about to suggest a federal company to help explore the world for oil.

By the end of the war, the British Army alone had 79,000 automobiles and trucks and 34,000 motorbikes, compared with 827 cars and 15 motorbikes at the start. The shortage of fuel also affected the German Army, forcing it to rely on horses to do the work of trucks and motorcycles. Although the Allies failed to take advantage of their superior mobility and the war ended up in a dispiriting stalemate, the behind-the-lines comparison was startling. London buses were never taken off the road and, in the United States, private motoring was never interrupted.

In the Middle East the postwar question was, Who should get what loot? It was quite obvious that the United States, although it was feeling very oil-poor (we are back to where we were when we quoted the smug English statement from *Sperling's Journal*) did not have enough muscle to displace the British and French, although, upon Woodrow Wilson's death and Warren Harding's election, the stage was set for some American hell-raising, had the country not turned so isolationist. But politics change with the emptying of the tanks.

What probably prevented an unpleasant three-cornered round of fisticuffs was the discovery of the immense Lake Maracaibo field of Venezuela. Suddenly there, with oily hands and oily smile, stood the oilman's perfect South American ruler, General Juan Vincente Gomez, welcoming them from the salting up fields of Mexico: nominal royalties and taxes, no restrictions, nothing but a few million a year here and there for General Gomez's private pot. Production went from 2 million barrels in 1922 (all from Shell) to 106 million barrels in 1928, when Venezuela replaced Russia as the world's second largest producer. And in the "new Venezuela," Standard of Indiana, Gulf, and especially Standard of New Jersey (Creole Oil Company) pulled abreast of and eventually ahead of Shell.

In California, Wyoming, Oklahoma, Texas, and elsewhere new reserves were found and, in fact, 1921 turned out to have been the last year of the American shortage. From 1922 until about 1969 the United States produced more oil than its refineries could handle. In a sense this was a fatefully tragic circumstance, since it engendered in the average American citizen a xenophobia up to that time equaled only by China. We had everything. Why bother at all about the rest of the world? The oil companies, of course, were not all controlled by xenophobia; there was a good deal of old-fashioned, nonisolationist greed left.

THE CARCASS OF THE TURKISH EMPIRE

Meanwhile back in the Middle East, Gulbenkian was earning his 5 percent playing the French against the British. He suggested, for instance, that France should ask the British for the Deutsche Bank's quarter-share in the Turkish Petroleum Company, a lootable acquisition of wartime. This had the effect of stirring up a whole zoo of rapacious animals; but eventually a reasonably placid temporary agreement was reached at the San Remo conference in 1920, when Britain and France divided the Arab territories between them as League of Nations mandates. (Since that bitter old man, Henry Cabot Lodge, had caused America to cut off its nose to spite its face, this country, not a member of the League, was unable to avail itself of the elegant ruse of mandates.)

Mesopotamia, which shortly became Iraq, fell to British tutelage and Syria went to the French. The French were given 25 percent of the Turkish Petroleum Company and Gulbenkian again got his 5 percent. Deterding was curiously lost in the shuffle, but mainly because he had relied on French interests and when Raymond Poincaré came to power, the mind of the ex-generalissimo was filled with the notion that France should also have a national oil company. Indeed, this dream (as all dreams of the victors in those days of German inflation and hopelessness) came immediately to realization in the form of the Compagnie Française des Pétroles. The government had, however, only 40 percent voting rights, and technically the company was not the national tool of France in the sense that British Petroleum (then Anglo-Persian) continued to be the tool of British nationalism.

It seems to be a law of nations that when a great country is in no need of a particular commodity everybody hastens to thrust the commodity upon it. As hemispherically the Americans were so well fixed, now they were cordially invited to participate in another carving-up party for the whole of the Middle East, and the Americans accepted, with Walter Teague of Standard of New Jersey as leader of the American group.

The carving consisted of what is known historically as the Red Line Agreement. This looks very peculiar on a map—as if a child with a crayon had been playing with an atlas, and in fact that was virtually what happened. The red line was drawn by the French delegation to include the nearly imaginary southward perimeter of the defunct Turkish Empire. (So ghostly was this concept that the line could well have been drawn to include all of Afghanistan, and all of Africa for that matter.) The whimsical red line included the Arabian peninsula, with the exception of Kuwait, but did not include Iran. Within the included area the various companies agreed mutually to "arrange for" rather than compete for concessions, and nobody was supposed to slicker a friendly company without due notice and the consent of the mass cartel.

The negotiations surrounding these matters (most of the countries represented being fond of and expert in haggling) dragged on interminably and the visiting Americans grew so restless that by 1930 all had gone home, except Standard of New Jersey and Socony Vacuum, who had important markets in Europe and the Far East.

In the meantime, at Baba Gurgen near Kirkuk in Iraq, very close to the "eternal fires of Nebuchadnezzar" where oil seepages had been burning for 3 milennia, an immense gusher was hit on October 27, 1927. For the first time in recorded history the holy fires had to be extinguished to prevent an explosion, as 12,500 tons a day poured out. The field was 60 miles long and richer than the diamond-studded dreams of Moguls. Gulbenkian's 5 percent now elevated him to one of the wealthiest men of all history. The Iraqi government under King Feisal (no relation to the Saudi ruler of later times) received a pittance of 4 shillings in gold for every ton of oil produced.

Iraq looked big enough, but it turned out to be a minnow in an ocean of whales. Snooping around the Persian (or Arabian) Gulf* was an enterprising New Zealander, Major Frank Holmes, with British money in his pockets and desert oil on his mind. The people he contacted were incredibly naïve (a very temporary condition of mind) and they could no more imagine the usefulness of oil than they could imagine the existence of ice. The sheik of Kuwait was advised by his counselors that bringing in a new industry would have the unpleasant effect of raising the wages of the pearl divers. In Bahrein, however, which was suffering from a terrible drought, Holmes was lucky enough to suggest that they dig artesian wells. This worked so well that the grateful Sheik Hamad granted Holmes an exclusive oil option in 1925.

Holmes also had an option in a part of Saudi Arabia, but had no luck in trying to interest the British-oriented companies, such as Shell, Anglo-Persian, and Burmah in either Bahrein or El Hasa in Saudi Arabia. Reluctantly he turned to the Americans. Gulf rather hesitantly took a chance on Bahrein but, being a member of the Red Line syndicate, had to ask permission to drill, and this was promptly refused. Standard Oil of California, not a member of the syndicate and something of a Johnny-come-lately to the international scene (also hungry because it had not participated in blowing the bubbles off the beer of Iraq), was willing to take Bahrein off Gulf's hands. More importantly, Standard of Cal found oil there in 1932. The major companies in Iraq heard the news with utter horror. Who and what was this brigand from California? Gulf Oil Company was infuriated. It knew the brigand from California very well, but in the meantime it had resigned from the Iraq petroleum group and was thus cut off from both of the new, mighty proven fields of the Middle East.

Gulf then sent Holmes, who was now on its payroll, to investigate Kuwait. Negotiations there with the sheik and the British were expedited in London by the fact that the American ambassador to Britain was then Andrew Mellon,

*What you call it depends on which side of the gulf you live.

former president of Gulf. The net result was that Gulf and Anglo-Persian signed a 50/50 deal for the formation of the Kuwait Oil Company, registered in London. Holmes sold out his overriding royalty which, if he had kept it, would now be netting his grandson more than 15 million pounds per year, since Kuwait is virtually floating on oil and contains about one-sixth of the world's proven reserves.

The rivalry for El Hasa in Saudi Arabia (where Holmes's rights had lapsed) was between the Iraq Petroleum group and Standard of California. The Californians had a psychological advantage. King Ibn Saud was a warrior potentate, who had just succeeded in rounding up all the Bedouin factions. As a simple man of battle, he did not understand such things as corporate identities taking the place of individuals or of countries (which after all is a somewhat mystical concept: Would one die, literally, for the General Motors Corporation?). Furthermore he detested lawyers. He preferred deals consummated with hand clasps, one man to another. He had, moreover, conceived a strong dislike of Englishmen, and the Iraq petroleum syndicate seemed to be full of both lawyers and Englishmen.

The deal was decided, however, by a very simple kind of quick thinking. It must be remembered that the Great Depression was now world-wide. Ibn Saud's income depended to a large extent on the Hegira (the annual flow of pilgrims to Mecca and Medina) and depression had cut both the human and coin flow. King Saud asked the oil concession bidders for 50,000 pounds in gold. The Iraq group countered with an offer of 30,000 pounds, but Standard of Cal correctly guessed the king's temper and offered the full 50,000. Suddenly it had itself a large piece of sandy real estate, but it would be many years before the full incredible value of its concession came to be appreciated.

THE WORLD WAR II

The Great Depression, followed by World War II, had a most discouraging effect on large, ethereal galaxies of international accord and the polite cutthroating, of which the British were so fond. The last of the "grouse moor" discussions, perhaps indeed the last chance for Britain to exert its tactics of gentlemanly strangulation, was the Achnacarry Conference of 1928, sometimes termed the Pool Association, sometimes the Grouse Party Agreement. This covered the whole world outside the United States and Soviet Russia. The terms of the agreement were very simple. The gist of the agreement was to avoid duplication of facilities. Obviously this was a wholesome idea, but its relevance became questionable when in 1931 world consumption of petroleum declined for the first time in the twentieth century; it declined still farther in 1932 and fell again in 1933.

The next five years were a time of careful hoarding of petroleum by Hitler's Germany. That they had to pick up turkey necks and squeeze oil cans from obscure places is shown by the following breakdown of principal, non-Communist oil production in 1938:

	Tons per year in millions
United States	161.5
Venezuela	27.7
Iran	10.2
Mexico	5.5
Iraq	4.4

As a matter of fact, Germany was lucky in having a little oil production of its own in the northwest, controlled by German companies. These for obvious reasons came under the supervision of Hermann Göring. A large part of the imported petroleum went into sealed storage. At the time of the invasion of Poland, Germany had about 50 million barrels of total fuel. Twenty-five coal conversion and Fischer-Tropsch plants produced a total additional output by 1941 of 30 million barrels a year of synthetic fuel.

It is not often realized how directly the need for parsimony in fuel usage and the quality of the fuel affected Hitler's campaigns. For example, in the Battle of Britain, the British Spitfires owed much of their superiority to the lavish availability of 100 octane gasoline, up to that time a laboratory curiosity. The whole theory of the *Blitzkrieg* depended upon the scarcity of fuel. One burned up a gust of fuel in furious but carefully planned *Panzer* and *Luftwaffe* attacks, then waited until enough fuel was available for another concerted Blitz. This technique of war making explained both the lull between the Battle of Poland and the Battle of France and the unexpectedly quiet weeks in between the *Luftwaffe*'s attack on London and on other British cities. The *Wehrmacht* and *Luftwaffe* managed to accomplish their unheard of triumphs by using only 12 million barrels of oil products, or about the same as the United States at that time produced every 3 days.

The ripe plum of Rumania's 43 million barrels a year dropped into Hitler's lap before the end of 1940 and proved throughout the war the theorem that it is exceedingly hard to destroy an oil field with explosives.* On the other hand, it is very easy to pulverize synthetic fuel plants. By 1944 more of the Luftwaffe fuel was coming from coal, but by May 1945 Allied air attacks had reduced Germany's output of aviation fuel from 17,000 tons a month to virtually nothing.

The Japanese in the meantime were reduced to making aviation fuel out of pine knots. In July 1941 Japan's oil imports were cut off when the United States, followed by Britain and Holland, imposed a ban on all normal trade with Japan. Some historians believe that it was the ban on oil which triggered the attack on Pearl Harbor. Japan had failed to capture any appreciable amount of petroleum

---

*This is perhaps the single most relevant petroleum lesson we can learn from World War II. Excited Arabs claim that if the American marines tried to take over the Persian Gulf they would find no oil fields left in the region, only smoking holes. In highly classified literature it is shown that unless very large atomic bombs are used, it is impossible to destroy an oil field. Of course, it is not unlikely that nuclear explosives would be used not to fracture the formation, but to permanently contaminate the production.

either in the East Indies or in Borneo, since the Dutch and British, respectively, had thoroughly demolished all surface facilities before fleeing the areas. (The oil could have been produced, but only by spending half a billion dollars on new rigs, tanks, pipelines, and the like.) The Japanese position early in 1945 was so desperate that they offered to give their few remaining battle cruisers to Russia, if the Soviets would supply them with fuel. The answer was, of course, Nyet.

Because of the German submarine campaign and the enormous demand for aviation gasoline, World War II saw the first motor fuel rationing this country had experienced. New England was especially hurt since it relied to a large extent on fuel stocks from Venezuela, and the tankers were being torpedoed, sometimes three a day.

For some inexplicable reason, the World War II rationing is held up by many politicians too young to have observed it firsthand as a horrible example of black market chaos and riotousness, but as we shall point out later, nothing could be further from the truth.

POSTWAR AMENITIES

Just before the start of World War II, Standard of California had decided that its potential reserves in Saudi Arabia and Bahrein were so large that it needed sales outlets it did not possess in a world of economic depression; hence it sold a half-interest in its Saudi Arabian concession to Texaco, which had a sophisticated distribution system in the Eastern Hemisphere. Standard of New Jersey ("Jersey" to everybody in those days), although a member of the Red Line cartel, decided in 1941 that Saudi Arabia looked too good to stay out of and began plotting how to buy in and at the same time avoid the Red Line restrictions. The Red Line had been good to Jersey, since in profits from its share of Iraq Petroleum Company it had multiplied its investment more than 10 times over.

The war gave both Jersey and Socony Vacuum (formerly Standard Oil of New York and now Mobil) an opportunity that could not be fumbled. With the fall of France, the Compagnie Française des Pétroles and Gulbenkian, who went to Vichy, were declared enemy aliens and cut off from their oil, while even the Allies, because of the incredibly successful German submarine depredations, could not move much oil around the world. It was a time for planning the future, rather than for sticking one's neck out. Jersey and Socony advanced the claim that under such confused circumstances the Red Line agreement had automatically dissipated into thin air and to reinstate it, they piously suggested, would be contrary to the American antitrust laws. Without waiting for French or Gulbenkian consent, they began to deal with Standard of California and Texaco; and in 1947 Jersey received a 30 percent share in Aramco for $76.5 million while Socony got 10 percent for $25.5 million. And the real heavy drilling began.

The Aramco presence and, indeed, all American activities in the Middle East had been viewed with a benevolent smile by the Roosevelt administration. Coming home from the 1945 Yalta Conference, Franklin Roosevelt in spite of obvious ill health made a point of stopping to meet King Ibn Saud, much to the annoyance of Winston Churchill, who decided he would have to bestow his presence separately upon this doughty warrior.

The two encounters were so different in nature and conceivably had such important repercussions that it is worth describing them. Arrangements had been made to have the king travel on a U.S. destroyer up the Suez Canal to rendezvous with Roosevelt, who would be waiting on the cruiser *Quincy*. The destroyer *Murray* had been outfitted on the foredeck with a throne upon which Ibn Saud would sit through much of the short voyage. To the dismay of the destroyer's commander, the king showed up not only with a goodly retinue of advisers, sons, and fan-wavers but with his complete harem. Since the destroyer provided room for only about twelve visitors, the captain had to explain that in the ritual of American seamanship it was considered fatally heretical to bring even such beautiful women as belonged to His Majestic Highness upon a ship of war. The women were left behind, but another problem showed up in the shape of a formidable *dhow* that floated up alongside the destroyer, carrying 83 sheep. These were to be loaded aboard so that the king would not have to rely on the desiccated rations of the destroyer but could dine, as he was accustomed, on fresh-slaughtered mutton and lamb. The distracted commander allowed half a dozen animals on board but this was the limit.

Now, Roosevelt had been warned that Ibn Saud was the strictest of Moslem puritans and could be readily insulted even at the sight of alcohol or tobacco. Consequently, during the ceremonious visit on the *Quincy* Franklin indulged neither in his usual martinis nor his cigarettes in the long holder. He presented the king with a brand new DC-3, with the royal insignia on the nacelle. (This 30-year-old gift was still flying in the late King Faisal's stable of private airplanes.)

Churchill's session with the fierce king was by no means so felicitous. First of all, Churchill sent a message in advance, advising the noble king that (1) the religious rules of his own church required that Churchill consume alcohol before, during, after, and between meals; and (2) similar strict religious doctrine necessitated that Churchill puff on a cigar at practically all times in which he was neither eating nor drinking. Doubtless Churchill's wit flowed like wine during the kingly encounter, but Churchillese loses a good deal in the translation and the king saw only what he regarded as a drunken fool waving an enormous piece of tobacco. The Rolls Royce that Churchill gave as a token of the British regard was never taken out of the garage.

THE VENEZUELAN AND IRANIAN REVOLUTIONS

After Roosevelt's death, Harry Truman and Dean Acheson continued the American diplomatic interest in the Middle East, but the wheeling and dealing for oil became obviously tinged with the spookiness of spying, counterspying, insurrection, and counterinsurrection. It became an Eric Ambler sort of half-world, with the smell of Arabian light crude oil and the shadow of nuclear rockets providing background atmosphere.

Not only did Truman's administration provide moral support in the form of CIA agents, but it broke the economic sound barriers in respect to tax alleviation for the American-based international companies. At Truman's insistence, the National Security Council prevailed secretly upon the Internal Revenue Service to allow such companies as Aramco and Gulf to write off royalties paid to oil-producing countries as taxes, dollar for dollar. This became, as we shall see later, an incredible bonanza, but had a rather dismaying effect: The international companies had no incentive to lower crude prices since the taxes were paid as a percentage of an artificial posted price which was not equivalent to but nevertheless controlled the true market price. Up to that time, royalties in oil had been regarded as part of the expense of doing business and were so taxed. The royalties in Venezuela under Gomez, for example, were absurdly low, on the order of 7 to 8 percent. The new system kept nominal royalties but added a kind of superroyalty in the form of taxes which the American IRS allowed to be subtracted, not from the taxable income, but directly from the total tax paid to the United States Treasury. A little figuring will show that this provided a chance for everybody except Uncle Sam and the consumer to get very rich indeed.

Economically, matters had proceeded in a somewhat similar style in Venezuela, and in fact it can be said that Venezuela historically set the example that the others followed. General Gomez died in 1936, having some $200 million in various Swiss banks, and his death was the occasion for riotous rejoicing in the course of which the Foreign Club in Caracas was burned down and other acts of destructive elation were committed at the expense of the Yanqui villains. In 1948 the Lopez Contreras government introduced an income tax law dividing the oil industry's profits equally between the state and the companies. (It cannot be said that this move, amounting eventually to a 50 percent income tax, was received with stunned amazement, since 10 years earlier the Mexican government had taken a more massive and simple tactic—it simply expropriated all foreign oil properties.)

Venezuela's adventure in the new economics of petroleum impressed the producing countries of the Middle East and in a few years the 50/50 profit sharing, or taxing, became a working model for every Middle Eastern nation except Iran. A peculiar man, Dr. Mohammed Mossadegh, had attained power there and threatened from week to week, to bring in the mysterious Tudeh, a large but clumsy Communist party. Shah Pahlevi was not then the powerful and polished kingly dictator he became later; in fact, he lived a most precarious political existence, more or less commuting in and out of exile, depending on how the winds blew and on the price of oil.

Mossadegh represented a kind of character so foreign to people like Truman and Acheson that he might as well have been a Martian. Among his habits was to make long, impassioned speeches and then at an appropriately dramatic moment to faint dead away. In his book *Present at the Creation,* Dean Acheson describes meeting Mossadegh for the first time at the railway station in Washington. The Iranian delegation left their carriage at a funeral pace, like pallbearers, with Mossadegh moving among them, pale and sad—a walking corpse. When Mossadegh caught sight of the welcoming American group, he seemed to be hit with a thunderbolt of joy and delight. He broke loose from his fellows and actually skipped toward the Americans, twittering like a child. If he had had a tail (and Acheson writes as if this were not out of the question), he would have wagged it ecstatically.

In conference with Truman and Acheson at the White House, Mossadegh was trying to describe the needs of his country:

"We have very little, you know," he said pathetically, "only a few sheep, maybe a camel or two . . ."

"Yes, with all that oil," Acheson interrupted, "you remind me of Texas."

Mossadegh burst into delighted laughter. He seemed to be admitting, "Well, I tried to play the part."

What the dangerous little man was really trying to do was to nationalize Iran's oil, and this meant a blow primarily at Britain, since Anglo-Iranian (British Petroleum) was the only important firm involved. Relations between the United States and Europe, including Britain, were at a low ebb because of the Marshall Plan (in international as well as personal relationships the recipient of benefits often resents his benefactor) and Mossadegh wanted, doubtless, to insure that nationalization in Iran would not result in a universal boycott.

This is exactly what happened, however. After nationalization, Anglo-Iranian was not seriously hurt, since it quickly made up for the deficit by drawing more heavily on Kuwait, Qatar, and Iraq, while Iran strangled. No one would buy their oil. During the 2 years of this treatment, the country was moving toward a Mossadegh dictatorship, which had all the earmarks of a prelude to a Communist takeover. The Shah bravely tried to dismiss Mossadegh from office, but within a few days was himself forced to flee to Rome. At this point (although we do not know all the Eric Ambler details) the CIA, in company with British paramilitary forces, evidently moved in to conduct a most unexpected *coup d'état* under General Zahedi, which swept Mossadegh from office; whereupon the Shah returned in triumph.

In his memoirs, the Shah leaves the whole question coyly open, but it was obvious that the CIA had started a new world game, although in fact its Iranian operation was the only one of its adventures which could be termed an unqualified success: At a crucial point in the cold war the Soviet Union had been blocked, not so much from an oil source, as from a clear strategic pathway to the Persian Gulf.

Although Iran's nationalization remained in effect, the Shah agreed to a consortium of 8 top international companies, who produced the oil for a government entity known as the National Iranian Company which then sold it to the individual members of the consortium and shared the profits equally with them. The American members of the top 8 were obliged by their government to sell 5 percent of their share to a number of independents in order to avoid the impression that the consortium was a cartel. The net result was that Iran wound up with the same percentage income arrangement as the other Middle Eastern oil producers, but had lost 2 years of business and its position as leading producer in the region had been taken over by Kuwait.

DISILLUSION IN THE MIDDLE EAST

In historic perspective one can view the Iranian episode as the first disenchantment on the part of the West with the Middle East as the inexhaustible cornucopia of future oil. The exporting countries had begun to act unpredictably. From the viewpoint of the United States, the Suez adventure of 1956, in which the British and French tried to take over the canal, showed that Christians could be just as crazy as Moslems (a point which should have been satisfactorily demonstrated years before by the Mexican appropriation). The Suez incident rudely interrupted oil flow, and people with money wished they were someplace else (free of frogs and scorpions)—someplace like Venezuela of the early 1920s or possibly Australia.

In fact, millions upon millions of dollars were spent in the 1950s and 1960s on a search for an oilman's Shangri-La. The list of major discoveries through the next decade or so is impressive: Gröningen gas reserve, Laduc in Canada, Malaysian and Indonesian off-shore extensions, North Africa, Nigeria, Alaska, the North Sea, northwestern Australia gas reserves, southernmost Mexico. If he is candid with himself, however, none of these discoveries will satisfy the longings of an oilman for the ultime Thule, the Fathomless Reserve upon which one is justified in building a score of refineries, 10,000 service stations, 20,000 TV commercials encouraging a 50,000-miles-per-year motorized way of life. In comparison with the giant of them all (now found to be Saudi Arabia) the newer discoveries were mud puddles. One field (Ghawar) in Saudi Arabia, from which high-gravity crude can be produced for not more than a dime a barrel, is estimated to contain more reserves than all the crude oil that has been used up to this time in history by the United States, and, of course, America has been the greatest of all imaginable energy hogs. (Representing only 6 percent of the world's population, it accounts for 33 percent of the world's energy consumption.)

So one went full circle: Starting out from the Middle East because it threatened to become Mexicanized (with expropriation in the offing), one came back to it because one could not escape its enormous shadow.

The trouble was that there was too much petroleum flowing in the world, but Middle East petroleum was the cheapest to produce. In the late 1950s, as during the 1960s, the price of Arabian light crude was low enough to get all of Europe, India, and Brazil hooked on the Persian Gulf as a source of cheap energy and the Seven Sisters (the major international oil companies) were the pushers of this black narcotic.

In order to prevent the ruination of small independents in the United States,

President Dwight Eisenhower, in 1959, set up the oil import quotas, a step which was also of obvious acceptability to those American companies which had well-established Eastern Hemisphere refining and marketing systems; but it was tough on a new, emergent class of American firms just getting their feet wet in foreign oil production, such as Phillips, Continental, Marathon, Occidental, Union, and the like. They had assumed that the oil they found abroad would come back to the United States where they could handle it, but the quotas slammed the door in their faces. They were forced instead, to sell externally produced crude at low prices to foreigners.

The oil-producing countries were not pleased with the way things were going. Posted prices of crude oil were too low for their liking and, although the integrated international companies could still make money by selling refined products (in fact, the lower the book prices for crude, the higher the refining profit), the producing countries did not have this downstream capability to cash in. In September 1960, mainly at the insistence of Perez Alfonso, the oil minister of Venezuela, a conference of oil-producing nations was held in Baghdad and the Organization of Petroleum Exporting Countries (OPEC) was formed. The stated charter was the stabilization and standardization of world-wide pooled prices of crude oil and, more generally, to avoid being bilked by the international companies.

The galaxy of international petroleum companies had made a full revolution since the Grouse Party Agreement of 1928; and after 1960 the companies never tried on their own to reduce the posted prices.

Even cozier and more incestuous beddings were now in view, mainly because of the seductive behavior of the Italian, Enrico Mattei, who felt he had been insulted and snubbed by the majors in his attempt to make a place in the sun for Ente Nazionali Idrocarburi (ENI), a government-backed corporation which had refineries and petrochemical facilities galore but no oil production to back them up. Mattei was a dynamo: a politician, a newspaper owner *(Il Giorno),* but he had bad luck. He taught the oil exporting countries that they were still sucking the hind teat and he announced, "The people of Islam are weary of being exploited by foreigners. . . . I not only intend to give them a more generous share of the profits but to make them my partners in the business of finding and exploiting petroleum resources."

Mattei signed a very glamorous deal with Iran. (The Shah spent seemingly the main part of his working day signing deals with one party or another, but it must be strongly emphasized that such papers meant little or nothing until the wells were spudded in; and, indeed, the amount of useless and meaningless commercial paper treaties between 1960 and 1974 in the Middle East and Northern Africa adds up to a formidable trash pile.) ENI formed a joint corporation with the National Iranian Company, called Société Irano-Italienne des Pétroles (SIRIP) and each agreed to share both the management decisions and the future profits equally with its partner. On top of this, ENI agreed to pay 50 percent of its profits in taxes. Since the National Iranian Company was a state-owned concern, this meant that altogether the Shah's government would receive 75 percent of SIRIP's total profits.

There was actually more love-making than money in all this, since ENI did not come through with the customary down payment nor did it assume, as was normal, the entire exploration costs. Nevertheless the majors regarded SIRIP with the loathing that one reserves for a king cobra in the bedroom, and indeed the U.S. ambassador in Tehran felt it incumbent upon himself to call upon the Shah and to regret the company His Highness had been keeping. The Shah, always one to reflect the mood of his visitors (a Persian smoothness that doubtless goes back to Darius and Xerxes) stated comfortingly that he did not think ENI had what it takes to find a big new field, but that the arrangement had its merits as a showpiece.

He was right. ENI failed to find a new field in Iran but the Japanese-owned Arabian Oil Company, Standard Oil of Indiana, and (the final shock!) Royal Dutch/Shell concluded agreements on off-shore production with Kuwait, Saudi Arabia, and Iran, incorporating all the financial endearments that Mattei had invented.

THE 1967 TIP-OFF

So fragile are our memories that we forget what actually happened during the Six-Day War of 1967. The impression of a brilliant Israeli *Blitzkrieg* perhaps remains with us, but more important to the oil business was the closing of the Suez Canal and the fact that Libya and the other Arab countries placed an embargo against the United States and Britain. It was not a very efficient embargo and for that very reason, in 1968, the appropriate countries got together to form the Organization of Arab Petroleum Exporting Countries (OAPEC), which was by no means a substitute for OPEC but, so to speak, a club within a club. It excluded Iran, which is predominantly a Shitite Moslem country but one which speaks Farsi instead of Arabic and is of Aryan descent.

It seems incredible that Aramco and the other international oil companies, especially those members of the consortium working in Iran, as well as those in touch with such professional toughs as Colonel Mu'ammar El-Qadafi of Libya, could not foresee the next move. It appears not to have occurred to the board of directors of Aramco, for example, that they were no longer dealing with the equivalent of Australian aborigines, interested in colored beads, but with highly trained young men who had gone to Harvard, Stanford, and UCLA. (So large a proportion of the sons of sheiks, kings, and emirs had degrees from the California universities that one spoke of the California Mafia.) Aramco's fond plan of doubling the Saudi Arabian production to about 20 million barrels a day suddenly confronted a very sophisticated, if brutal, Middle Eastern alternative: the idea that instead of doubling the production one should double the price.

Herbert Stein, who like many American economists, tried overnight in the febrile autumn of 1973 to turn himself into an expert in international petroleum, said that in order to understand the Middle East situation, "All one has to know is that there are 42 gallons in a barrel and that, while Qadafi is the name of a person, Abu Dhabi is the name of a place." It is too bad that Stein did not include the statement, "Shahinshah Pahlevi is the name of a would-be superman," because in retrospect it seems certain that the Shah provided the intellectual drive that changed the course of the world's economic history.

At the Teheran agreement in 1971 the major oil companies agreed to collective bargaining on posted prices rather than unilateral price action. The price of oil was to be tied to an escalation clause, which included inflation.

Unfortunately, this didn't work out too well. The companies tried to get by with only a 2.5 percent increase representing inflation, whereas the Shah and others were pointing to American wheat at $5 or $6 a bushel. The grim saying was revived, "You pay us less for a barrel of oil than we pay for a barrel of water." The devaluation of the dollar did not help matters.

"IF I WERE A RICH MAN . . ."

The same urge that persuaded the American grain farmer that he could get an income of $50,000 to $60,000 a year and leap directly into the upper-middle class by simply being stubborn enough to double and triple the price of grains was latent, like a bomb with a long fuse, in the minds of the members of OPEC. It took only a bold man to light the fuse, and this man was the Shah of Iran.

In the October 9, 1973, meeting in Vienna (this city had then become OPEC's headquarters) the oil companies offered a 15 percent increase in posted prices and adjustments of the inflation factor. OPEC countered with a 100 percent increase in posted price and a mechanism for keeping the posted price at all times 40 percent above the actual selling price. The companies asked for time out. OPEC broke off negotiations and adjourned the meeting sine die.

OPEC then met by itself in Kuwait and announced a new Persian Gulf posted price for Arabian light of $5.119 per barrel up from $3.011, the government share rising from $1.20 to $3.048. This was during the Yom Kippur War, and things were confused by the embargo. The prices were bound to go up further, while the production rate went down (at the separate insistence of OAPEC).

Hell had been popping in the meantime in Libya. Colonel Qadafi had been manhandling the Occidental Oil Company and threatening the majors; unheard of posted prices were being leaked around. In September, Nixon had held a fatuous press conference in which he threatened to isolate Libya the way Iran under Mossadegh had been squeezed in the 1950s. Since there was not the slightest suggestion of a parallel in the two cases, however, the speech succeeded only in increasing Qadafi's susceptible blood pressure and in allowing the Shah of Iran to leapfrog back and forth in his arguments from the Mediterranean to the Persian Gulf.

By December 1973 the Shah had persuaded OPEC (with the very reluctant consent of Saudi Arabia) to set the Persian Gulf posted price at the heart-stopping level of $11.53 per barrel. The justification to the West was the increased price of "commodities" (especially wheat) and the general inflation of things the Middle East had to import. Whatever the justification (and whether the American grain farmer is to blame for it, which possibly in the long run he is) this quadrupling in crude prices represented a paralyzing shock to the world economy, one it may never recover from. It set in motion a further vicious circle in inflation, since more expensive fuel results in still more expensive grain, more expensive pipe, more expensive everything that the OPEC countries import. As the secretary general of OPEC, Dr. Abder Rehanan Khene, a heart specialist in Algeria, suggests, "If the industrialized countries agree to lower the prices of their exports, we will do the same." But the opposite is also implied, and the opposite (the raising of the prices of Western exports) is all too likely; hence the world is faced with a horrifying spiral that seemingly has no mechanism of termination.

Perhaps in the long run a more dangerous question is what the OPEC countries will do with their sudden, overwhelming billions.

IRAN AS A SUPERPOWER

When one is descending from the air upon Teheran, this great city looks remarkably like Los Angeles, scattered pell-mell on a plain with the delectable mountains as a backdrop and the water resorts of the Caspian Sea a three-hour drive to the north. Like L.A., the city is smothered in automotive smog; but if one listens, looks, and smells thoughtfully enough, one will perceive also the fierce effluvia of the will to power. Shahinshah, the king of kings, is willing to trade you gas and oil rights for anything: for refineries, steel plants, petrochemical plants (which the Shah regards as particularly "noble," a word he uses very frequently), but, most readily of all, for arms.

Iran has firmly agreed to buy over 80 Grumman F-14 fighter planes, America's most advanced and expensive weapon systems, making that country the only customer other than the U.S. Navy. Since the withdrawal of British forces east of Suez in the 1960s, Iran has in fact engaged in the most concentrated arming outside of the USSR. The Shah is quite frank about his undeclared war with Iraq and with the terrorist threat to the Persian Gulf oil sheikdoms—especially the "forgotten war" that is still being fought between respectable Arabs and Communist-inspired terrorists in West Oman, a relatively oil-poor sultanate which, however, guards the west shore of the gulf. (Left-wingers now call the Oman rebels and their associates in South Yemen the Popular Front for the Liberation of the Occupied Arabian Gulf—PFLOAG.) PFLOAG is a beloved acronym in Moscow and even in Peking, but decidedly unlovely to Iranian ears.

In an interview with *Time*'s head editorial executives, Cliff Donovan and Murray Gart, Shah Pahlevi admitted that he fears the Iraqis will start some kind of adventure in the Persian Gulf: "The Iraqis have tried to take Kuwait. They aggressed. They stopped—God knows why. They could have crossed the whole country before midday. But their subversive activity is going on everywhere."

In a 1973 junket at the Shah's invitation, Barry Goldwater obtained the same impression: "Iraq is capable of taking over Kuwait in a morning, and knocking out Abadan [the Iranian refining center] before lunch, but by suppertime, Iraq would be dead." According to Goldwater, the Shah is seeking military parity not with any single Arab power such as, say, Egypt, but with Israel and the Arab powers taken all together. He has negotiated a naval base on Mauritius, deep in the Indian Ocean; announced plans to build at Charbabar, the largest land, air, and naval base in that ocean. He has 1,700 tanks. He is getting American "smart bombs." From the new naval gun emplacements on Aber Maser and the Greater Tumb Islands, which he seized over 3 years ago from the United Arab Emirates, he can make spot checks of passing vessels entering the Straits of Hormuz at the mouth of the Persian Gulf to the Gulf of Oman and the Arabian Sea. About 80 percent of the world's shipping tonnage will continue to pass this way, and anybody who controls these waters can, if he has a mind to, cut the jugular vein of the West. The Shah wants superpower status, which with a 35 million population would usually be regarded as impudent, but with an assumed future annual income of $40 to $50 billion, one is never in danger of being called impudent.

There are few problems of what to do with Iran's money. The Shah has gone in for the concept of the capitalist welfare state (although it must be admitted that the poor of Teheran have yet to feel any gracious blessing on their cheeks). Along with his immense military, economic, and power expenditures, including three new nuclear energy plants (coming as the fruits of a trade with France), the Shah has to worry about getting more money. Unlike Saudi Arabia, he wants to increase the oil production to 12 million barrels a day. There is some conflict in reporting here. The Shah was once quoted as sharing Saudi Arabia's concern for preserving the life of the reserves, but it is probably not so much the reporting as the Shah's mind that changes with the seasons and the bottom-hole pressure.

The catchword now is secondary recovery. The Shah is too impatient to wait for the discovery and development of additional fields. As we shall see later on in the first go-round an oil field produces only about 30 percent of the crude it holds. Some of the rest can be recovered by flooding it with water. Alternatively natural gas can be repressured to the formation, in order to increase production efficiency, in which case you have a choice to make between the value of the gas as a fuel or chemical and as a crude oil production agent. The Shah blows hot and cold on this issue, as on so many others.

He is willing to give money to the World Bank and to the International Monetary Fund in order to extend cheap credit to the developing nations who can't afford the incredible hike in petroleum fuel prices, yet at the same time, neither Iran nor the Arabs seemed concerned with the ghastly drought and famine of the sub-Saharan countries, leaving the food drops to Europe and the United States.*

---

*The sudden enrichment of the oil-producing nations has taken them off the list of World Bank clients and put them on the list of world bond buyers. This is also true of a number of other international

Goldwater perceived a sort of native hostility of the Iranians toward the Arabs. There are frequent accounts, probably more hopeful than authentic, of the Shah and Sheik Ahmed Yamani, Saudi Arabia's oil minister, having a "hell of a row." The Shah, unlike Yamani (a silken smoothy), enjoys the kingly prerogative of popping off, sometimes in front of world-wide TV.

When the Shah voiced his displeasure at the undue windfall profits of the international oil companies in the last quarter of 1973, William Simon, secretary of the treasury, indulged himself unwisely in a tantrum in which he referred to the Shah in uncomplimentary terms. Needless to say, such losses of cool can be very expensive in the case of a proud, sensitive monarch, who is not exactly sure who his friends are, but who now has more money in the bank than France or Germany and potentially more money than the United States. Ardeshir Zahedi, Iranian ambassador to the United States, reported that the Shah was deeply injured by Simon's diatribe and added the following remark, which tends to point again to the ultimate trigger of the most important price escalation in the history of the world: "Do you know that while not so long ago we paid the price of half a barrel of oil for 1 bushel of wheat, today we have to sell 3 barrels to buy 1 bushel?" (The arithmetic is quite haywire but the emotional staying power of this cliché is worth noting.)

Even if one hardly expects Simon to keep his temper bottled up, Iran's Shah was more amazed and irritated to hear Henry Kissinger in April 1974 solemnly warn against "trading blocs with oil and other natural resources."

HOW TO SPEND $100 BILLION

To extremely pious Moslems, such as the *nouveaux riches* of Saudi Arabia and Kuwait and Abu Dhabi, the spending of money becomes embarrassing. In the first place one must bear in mind that devout Arabs, such as the late King Faisal, read only the Koran; and that holy book (as did early Christianity) regards monetary interest as impious. Presumably interest against one's own loans is more impious than a return on one's investments, yet even here there is some degree of shyness, as witness the fact that a good many Arabian bank deposits have taken the form of simple savings or even mere checking accounts rather than high-interest-rate certified deposits.

How is it in Kuwait? Kuwait is full of foreigners. In Kuwait the saying is "Which car has the right of way at a traffic circle?" And their answer is "The car driven by a Kuwaiti." Here is a welfare state with a gigantic bureaucracy that does absolutely nothing, except drink innumerable cups of very sweet tea. Nobody can be fired without a special dispensation, and nobody can be made to work, either. Telephone service is free. There are so many big cars that there are Cadillac and Rolls Royce drag races every twilight. The Kuwaiti remind me of the Elois of H. G. Well's *The Time Machine*. They toiled not, neither did they

do-gooder agencies. From now until at least the year 2000 any international beggar or sharpster will have the OPEC members on his sucker list.

spin, while the Morlocks (in this case the Iraqi) watch with evil eyes as the fat, edible children play with their money. At Abu Dhabi the per capita income is headed toward $100,000, but this statistic does not mean, of course, that every Abu Dhabist has that much, only that certain important people have incomes at around $100 million a year.

In order to get an idea of the amount of money Saudi Arabia is programmed to get by 1980, one must resort to parables rather than numbers. We always think, for example, of General Motors and Exxon as giant money-making corporations whose total assets are often larger than the Gross National Product of many countries, even European countries, such as Denmark. But Saudi Arabia by 1980 could afford to buy up General Motors and Exxon combined and hardly feel the expenditure. And they could afford to repeat such expenditures every year thereafter.

Colonel Qadafi, has threatened to "ruin all your industries." If OPEC became malevolent, they could do this easily: They could simply buy up the Western industries and amuse themselves by pulling the wings off. There is no indication that they would want to ruin the West, however, because if the West goes down, they go down with it. As newly alert world businessmen, their instinct is to preserve the market, to prevent a depression, to put a brake on inflation, and thus to see the demand for oil stabilized at a high and profitable level. But they want it used thriftily.

One of the Shah's and now Khene's (the secretary of OPEC) sayings is that we cannot continue to regard petroleum as something to burn. It is too "noble" for that. It must be preserved for petrochemicals. The West, instead, should burn coal, shale oil, uranium, and find ways to capture the direct power of the sun. In the meantime it is only logical that the price of oil should be maintained at a level that represents the price of such substitute energy. This is a subtle and nervy doctrine and indeed has invoked the suggestion "And would you like to help us pay for all this new kind of energy?" And to that (a favorite proposal by David Rockefeller and Chase Manhattan) the answer has been ambiguous, but there have been some interesting rumors. The Province of Quebec has admitted to selling bonds of its public power corporation, now engaged in the construction of the largest hydroelectric project in history near Hudson Bay. Quite coyly the directors will acknowledge only that the bond buyers are "UFO's" (Unidentified Financial Organizations); but when they say this they do everything but take out a prayer rug and make obeisances in the direction of Mecca.

This story has a persuasive ring, because Arab money, although likely to go to energy projects, would still be cautious money and would probably wind up in well-proven and traditional kinds of energy rather than in such gambles as shale oil or solar power plants.

Saudi Arabia has a contract with the Stanford Research Institute for a 5-year economic development plan involving the expenditure of $60 billion within its own borders. The most popular verified investment for Arab money on the outside so far has been real estate. Saudi Arabia is known to own substantial pieces of Mayfair in London and of the Champs Eliseés in Paris. The secrecy is great. As the saying goes, "An Arab won't even tell his brother how much money he has in the bank." Such deals are hard to verify because they usually go through the Swiss who are clever at hiding large transactions, but whose expertise may not be up to the gigantic scale of the Arab monies. In a typical transaction, a Swiss bank will invest funds for the bank's own account and then adjust an Arab nation's deposits accordingly. In this way it is theoretically impossible to tell who is buying what. However, if the Staatsbank of Zurich, with an official funding of $900 million, turns up owning $150 billion worth of Manhattan real estate, some observant Wall Street financier is likely to start sniffing the gold dust trail back to somewhere east of Suez. (This particular imaginary example is unlikely, because it involves a lot of real estate owned by Jews, as is true in many large American cities, and Arab-Jew transactions—even through intermediaries—are at the present time unthinkable.)

Because of the friends made at school in California by Arab money managers, a lot of real estate is bought in that state, also in Texas and Oklahoma, but not necessarily oil property. Small banks in California are being purchased. Libya has established investment banks in Buenos Aires, where Colonel Qadafi finds dangerous people to his liking. Abu Dhabi and Saudi Arabia are considering the construction of a large oil refinery in Puerto Rico. The Saudis also are looking at a project for a refinery and chemical complex in the Philippines. Kuwait bought the Kiawack Isles off Charleston, South Carolina, and plans to spend over $100 million developing them as a residential resort area. Kuwait's agents have also put up cash for property in downtown Atlanta, including the Atlanta Hilton Hotel. All this, however, is peanuts compared with their disposable income.

The Arabs have been going through a cautious spell which must break down at some point. American and European banks have become extremely nervous at accepting large, temporary "call accounts" from the Middle East (from which money may be withdrawn without advance notice), and quickies like treasury bills don't seem to be attractive to the Moslem trader. Arab investors were badly hurt by the collapse of Bernard Cornfeld's I.O.S. Ltd., which sold many mutual funds in the Middle East. Furthermore, Arab businessmen still haven't received full repayment from the bankruptcy of a major Mideast institution, the Intra-Bank, 10 years ago.

One possibility is a kind of economic and even political union of the Arab Mideast with a large, undeveloped but dynamic and oil-poor country. Brazil exactly fits the bill. Brazil has been not only a good customer through Petrobras, its oil-handling agency, but has been regarded as an especially friendly country. There is in fact a large Arab colony in Brazil of over 2 million, mostly of Lebanese descent and important in the business community, especially in São Paulo, that richest and newest of monster cities.

The Brazilians have a lot to offer. However, some American economists think the bulk of the money will come to New York in the form of investments in securities and it may come in time to electrify the stock exchange. Peter B. Kenen of Princeton, a specialist in international finance, points out that "we're the only country in the world in which there's lots of stock available in large enough volumes for these countries to be interested. If Wall Street booms in the next two years, it will be Arab money that pushes it up."

Kenen emphasizes that you can't pick up stocks in European companies. It isn't available. You can't buy European bonds. The issues aren't big enough. So the United States is the capital market to which they must turn. "American industry may start sounding like French industry, bitching about foreign take-over."

There is a hint of wistfulness in this typical Yankee tough talk, but behind the admiration (or at least awe) that the huge Arab treasure house inspires, there is hidden some rather ratlike hostility and even some impudent schemes. The well-known MIT economist, Morris A. Adelman, who missed the boat on predicting the price escalation, has presented an elaborate scenario which shows how to dismantle OPEC: He suggests we limit our imports from OPEC in the form of a single huge quota and put this quota up for sealed competitive bids among OPEC members. This system, he contends, could magnify the tensions that exist among the OPEC countries. (There would be another "hell of a fight" between the Shah and Sheik Yamani). This would shake the cartel (he means OPEC). If it works well in the United States, other countries will try it, and that will be the end of the cartel. This would bring oil prices back down.

Adelman's view that OPEC is in a class with John D. Rockefeller's old Standard Trust and can and should be busted is not shared by many economists. I personally think the idea doesn't even merit discussion. The day has long passed (if it ever existed) when multi-billion-dollar bids can be concealed in envelopes, and any effort we expend on such cloak-and-dagger posturings simply loses us face and friendship.

3 The Peculiar Economics of Petroleum

There are lies, damned lies and statistics.
—BENJAMIN DISRAELI

THE OCCURRENCE OF WITCHES

Although the provenance of petroleum has about it the seemingly random, almost magical quality of a gross fairyland—with oil wells popping up most improperly in the grounds of a state capitol building (Oklahoma City) and even with gay hoods, burnooses, and sound-deadeners in the back yards of Los Angeles residences—there is nevertheless a rationale of sorts about how petroleum was formed and where we ought to look for it. The rationale has many holes and ragged edges, which are especially annoying to biochemists (since petroleum chemistry is a branch of biochemistry, being the chemistry of a special sort of fossils).

There seems little doubt that petroleum originates (I use the present tense, because it is still forming but at a rate too slow for us to perceive) from the dead bodies of small marine organisms of the general nature of algae, diatoms, krill, and so forth. Yet the genesis of petroleum further depends upon geological accidents. Normally these marine organisms, if they are not consumed by fish and countless other aquatic life forms, undergo when dead a process of bacterial decay common to the cessation of all organic life—a process which does not end in gasoline and lube oil but in carbon dioxide and water. The accident that has to happen is that trillions of tiny corpses are buried rather suddenly in sediment and thus protected from being devoured by aerobic bacteria; that is, bacteria which use the oxygen from the air to perform their digestive processes. (Even without bacteria, the mysterious chemical process that we call death would render the fossils susceptible to complete destruction by the oxygen of the air and water.)

Thus fossil fuel, if it is to survive its first stage of metamorphosis, must be protected by a mantle of silt, gravel, or rock; and the easiest way for this to happen is for the dead to be covered by the sediment from a river. Not surprisingly, therefore, many oil fields are believed to represent the deltas of ancient rivers.

Once the sedimentation has occurred, drastic internal chemical conversions take over. These are governed by the pressure (depth) of the deposit and its temperature and, above all, by time. The petrolification of once living things is surely not peculiar to very small organisms of the sea. One can predict a few hundred million years from now the discovery of an oil deposit made out of human bodies. This might come about if some swarming city, such as Shanghai, were hit with a large meteorite (or a gigantic multimegaton bomb) and which resulted in some 5 million of the 15 million bodies in this city being buried under debris perhaps a mile or so deep. In the course of many millions of years the burial ground would be indistinguishable from an oil resource—a modest one, it is true, since even in China the total bulk of human beings is modest compared to the total bulk of small creatures of the seas of the mighty past. But the chemistry of dead human flesh is not sufficiently different from that of the body of a diatom that one could tell human petroleum from diatom petroleum.*

The undreamable organic richness of the past is hinted at, indeed, by the very fact that the preservation of fossil fuel is an accident, and that petroleum represents only a minuscule fraction of the small bodies that lived and died in the sea since life began.

Although the occurrence of oil is a chancy thing, the type of structures that are likely to bear oil can be inferred by geologists and seismography. One is no longer, as in the old wells of California before 1900, clued simply by oozes from cracks in the ground. In a very general way the search for oil should be rationalized on the basis of the most important geological doctrine of modern times— the so-called plate tectonic theory of moving continents. It is surely of interest that the average date of many older oil pool formations coincides roughly with the breaking up of the supercontinent of Pangaea, and that the richest known formations (the Middle East) are not far from the tremendous collision of the subcontinent of India with the continent of Asia.

Seventy-five percent of all the oil so far discovered in the world was found in reservoir structures that were at least partly created by an archlike upward fold in the earth's strata. Translated into the modern concepts of geological history, these could have been ancient river deltas affected by the movements or collisions of continental masses. These folds are known as anticline traps in which a layer of rock has been forced upward roughly like a bulge in a rug. The oil is trapped in the bulge.

*The irritating question is, why does diatom petroleum vary so much? I have seen and experimented with California crudes with a sulfur content higher than their API gravity. They were too heavy to float in water. Yet Pennsylvania crude oil has practically no sulfur and is very light (high in gasoline). The difference seems to be a matter of age: The older the crude oil in geologic time the more gasoline, the less asphalt, and the less sulfur. All petroleum chemists will agree with that generalization, but there are nagging questions. Where, for example, does the sulfur go? Or for that matter, where did it come from? There is not nearly as much sulfur in dead or living tissue as one finds in many crude oils.

Geologically we can deduce the presence of such bulges much as one can deduce the presence of salt domes, but seismographic measurements are a great help in confirming not only the existence and location of the bulge but whether the bulge contains oil, gas, water, or salt. What one does in seismographic exploration is simply to shoot off a stick of dynamite and measure the nature of the echo of the explosion as it is reflected from the depths of the earth to various sonic pickups at the surface.

There is another kind of hiding place for oil that is called a stratigraphic trap. One common sort of stratigraphic trap brings two horizontal layers of rock together to form what looks like a forked stick on its side. The oil is trapped inside the fork. From the fact that three-fourths of the world's oil has been found in anticline traps, we still cannot conclude that stratigraphic traps in the history of oil genesis are only one-fourth as popular a place for oil to be formed as anticlines. The fact is that it is simply much easier to locate and to define anticline structures. Petroleum geology at its present degree of sophistication cannot map stratigraphic traps and most of them are discovered by accident—in this country mainly by independent wildcatters who cannot afford the expense of seismographic crews and who rely on the more or less inspired guesses of young geologists, who are usually partners in the independent venture.

There is a great deal of push behind the development of new methods of listening to the sounds of the earth, not only for reasons of oil exploration but for the prediction of earthquakes. We have come a good way from the time of "Crazy James," the Pennsylvania wizard of the 1880s who discovered oil, much as the water-witch maestros discover water, with a sort of divining rod. It is quite reasonable to expect advances in the technology of finding oil, especially off-shore oil, where it appears that much more accurate seismograms can be obtained.

If the seismography of locating stratigraphic traps makes the exploration for this sort of oil resource much simpler, cheaper, and more accurate than it is today, we might expect a revolution, not only in the technology of exploration but in the over-all economics of the American oil business.* The independent wildcatter then may no longer have even his raw daring to rely on as a selling point for outside investment on the part of rich urologists or rock singers. This would be a pity, since the independent truly represents—like the old corner grocery store —a remnant of self-reliance that one associates with the best of America's past.

SCRUBBING OUT THE OIL THAT'S LEFT

The layman seldom realizes that in the normal production of a given oil field the producer is lucky to recover as much as one-third of the oil actually present. In other words, when the producing rate falls with the gas pressure to a mere dribble, the field has been only one-third exploited. Producers in the new fields of the

---

*Very recent and very significant improvements in seismography, especially the so-called bright-spot technique, have made it almost certain that stratigraphic traps can now be located by precise, although tedious and expensive operations.

Middle East and of Africa have come to appreciate this, and more and more of them are reinjecting the natural gas that comes along with the oil in order to keep the bottom-hole pressure and the flow rate up. This is not so much secondary recovery as a common-sense technique for increasing primary recovery.

Classical secondary recovery involves water flooding; that is, injecting water in such a pattern that it sweeps some of the remaining oil in a converging manner toward a central producing well, after which the oil-water mixture—often an emulsion—is separated. The Osage Indians of Oklahoma are very familiar with the benefits of secondary recovery. The large Burbank field of northeastern Oklahoma was in the middle of Osage property and the royalties on the first go-round made them the richest, Indians on the continent. Then the field pooped out. Years passed and Phillips Petroleum Company decided to carry out an ambitious water flood on the unitized Burbank field. So successful was this secondary recovery operation that royalty checks began to fall again like snowflakes and a second generation of Osages became rich.

In some cases, notably the San Joaquin Valley crude oils of California, the production history is peculiar. For instance, the Midway Sunset field was discovered before 1894 and the Kern River field in 1899 (the discovery well in this case was 60 feet deep and was dug by hand). In spite of nearly 80 years of continuous production, the two ancient fields are now flowing at a rate surpassed only in California by the Wilmington field, a relative youngster in the tidelands of Los Angeles Harbor. The explanation is that Valley crude is very heavy and oozes out of a pump like cold molasses. It responds in lively fashion to steam, and it is the use of hundreds of millions of barrels of water to form injection steam that has rejuvenated the tired old pools and kept them profitable, even though the average producing rate per well is only 18 barrels per day. At this sort of average, which indeed is the over-all national average, a given field may contain a high proportion of strippers, that is, wells producing 10 or less barrels a day.

Under the peculiar regulations enforced by the Federal Energy Administration (FEA), the producer can sell oil from the strippers at free-market price—say, $11 per barrel—while he is restricted to a controlled price of about $5.25 per barrel from those of the wells that pump more than 10 barrels a day. The temptation is the same that was yielded to by Kuwait and Libya—produce at a low rate but get the highest price: The allure of this sort of gamesmanship in California is tempered by the fact that the use of more steam or other secondary recovery techniques may increase the total production from the field to the point where a sizable fraction (that exceeding 1972 production) can qualify as new oil and therefore similarly command the free-market price.*

The reason I dwell on this topic is this: There is little doubt but that secondary or tertiary recovery from established fields is the quickest way to

---

*Since this paragraph was written, the regulations have been relaxed to allow a one-time stripper well to produce more than 10 barrels per day without incurring a price drop. This is known as the "once-a-stripper, always-a-stripper" rule.

increase energy availability in the United States. But this assumes that the major part at least of oil squeezed out by steam or advanced water-washing techniques can be sold at free-market prices of $10 per barrel or thereabouts. After a field like Burbank has been watered out by a conventional flood, there still remains possibly 50 percent of the original crude in the ground. The Bureau of Mines, in conjunction with various companies, is demonstrating tertiary recovery, which usually amounts to a second water flood but carried out in a much more sophis- ticated and efficient manner. It may even involve the addition of hydrocarbon solvents to decrease the viscosity of the crude in place, followed by water flooding.

Technically the reason straight water fails to recover more than about half the oil is the viscosity mismatch between the oil and water. The oil is usually so much more viscous that the water under pressure breaks through in fingers, short-circuiting the oil formation instead of chasing it toward the recovery well. The addition of solvent decreases the viscosity of the oil. However, a fancier way of avoiding this viscosity mismatch is to increase the viscosity of the water by the addition of soluble polymers. The whole operation (for no reason except the desire on the part of chemists to sound scholarly, being called the micellar slug tech- nique) involves, first, the injection of detergents to increase the water miscibility (decrease the surface tension) of the oil; secondly, the injection of a slug of polymer-thickened water; and finally, the injection of ordinary water, as if the oil plus the slug were a single entity to be pushed toward the recovery well.

There is every reason to believe this will work, but at the present price of added chemicals, the tertiary oil might cost $5 a barrel to produce. Until the explosion of world crude prices in December 1973, the price of these goodies would have been prohibitive. The method will be tried out in 1977 in collabora- tion with Cities Service on a large scale in the old El Dorado field of Eastern Kansas that furnished most of the country's military fuel needs in World War I and which is also prized in history for the first use of electrical drilling and pumping, the first use of tubular steel rather than wooden derricks, and indeed it was the first field discovered by the use of a wide-area geological survey.

Other means of producing more oil from a hiding place underground include flooding with carbon dioxide, which is miscible with oil; fire flooding (burning part of the oil in place to heat and crack the formation ahead of a burning zone so that the oil—usually very heavy—is made to generate gas, gasoline, and light fuel oil while still in the ground); and fracturing tight formations.

The opening up of cracks in nearly impermeable rock-oil structures has classically been accompanied by a method dreamed up many years ago by some inventive geniuses of Standard Oil of Indiana. Called hydrofrac, it involves expos- ing such tough structures to high enough water pressures to open up cracks, then to maintain the cracks by particles of gravel contained in the pressurized water. Since it was supposed that the same result, more or less, could be obtained by gigantic explosions within the structure, the Atomic Energy Commission tried to increase natural gas production from tight formations in Colorado by a series of nuclear shots included in an over-all program entitled Project Ploughshare. So far this has proved singularly unsuccessful and, since any nuclear experiment, including the opening of a nuclear power plant, is invariably attended by widespread protest, Ploughshare may be drawing to an end. It would be worthwhile spending some more money on it, if only to find out why it doesn't work.

In areas of the country where there is enough water to play around with, it would seem that greatly stepping up the secondary and tertiary recovery program is the obvious first step in a rational energy-independence policy. Its steel and manpower and capital and time requirements are the least of any conceivable alternative.

UNITED STATES OIL—A GOVERNMENT-FOSTERED INDUSTRY

The *Wall Street Journal,* like many respectable organs of conservative thought, is now written by relatively young men with little if any personal memory of the Great Depression. Indeed, the Great Depression, which still colors the lives of older people, may as well be for these vigorous youngsters a nonevent, a hole in the space-time continuum. Things which happened in it—the doings of the fearful wizard, FDR, for example—might as well have happened in fairyland.

Thus it is refreshing, but at the same time rather pathetic, to see the *Wall Street Journal* sum up the recent energy problem, "To achieve the objectives of Project Independence, the government has to do only one thing, get out of the way."

This makes a good punch line, but could only have been written by a man who was born after 1931, when in the midst of a world that was too poor to buy anything, the titanic East Texas field came roaring in, pouring oil over everything, when what was needed that year was rain water and some shred of confidence. Oil went down to a dime a barrel and still had no takers. The oil business was suddenly all but dead, with hungry men fighting over the moribund body. Feebly it yowled and whined for help. Under the direction of state and federal government sometimes relying on militia, a degree of order was made out of bloody chaos.

In a few years, World War II came about and the question was no longer how to inhibit oil production but how to stimulate it. And by that time the U.S. oil industry had become, to the utter amazement of foreign experts, such as Christopher Tugendhat, a vast creature, petted, powdered, and soothed by government controls and largesse. It didn't want the government to "get out of the way." It wanted the government in its coat pocket, and that was essentially where the government ended up. Each state came up with a commission. The Connally Hot Oil Act of 1935 made it illegal to transport between states oil that had been produced in excess of a quota assigned by the commission of the state of origin.

There would be no more wild outflowings of Texas oil, for the Texas Railroad Commission had the situation strongly under leash and the major oil companies, hand in glove with the commissioners, got only as much oil allowed in production as the companies thought they could sell. The Texas Railroad Commission consists of 3 men drawing comfortable salaries, and still meets under normal circumstances (although what circumstances are normal anymore?) once a month—usually Friday morning in a public room at the Commodore Perry Hotel in Austin. Its sole job is to decide how much oil Texas should produce the following month. Although the commissioners surround themselves with various packets of federal and state statistics, there is only one piece of information that really matters—the total of the estimates submitted by the major companies of the amount of oil they wish to buy. After some correction for the allowance of strippers and special attention to new fields, if any, the commission divides the companies' demand between every well in the state so that in a condition of excess oil, each well can operate for only a certain number of days a month. Since the domestic shortage started in 1972 and became a squawling yahoo in 1973, none of the state commissions, including the Texas Railroad Commission, has put any limitation upon the production of any well except for the pious hope that production flows would not exceed MERs (maximum efficient rates).

TAX BENEFITS LIKE GARLANDS OF POSIES

The lushness of American tax benefits and incentives in the petroleum business have always attracted the attention of envious foreigners, although one would scarcely suspect it from all the clamor that goes on. As we shall see later, there may in the long run be justification for the incentive taxes in the following simple fact of life: Although production is relatively inexpensive, exploration is damnably costly and the likelihood now of finding a new productive well is much less than in winning at roulette.

What is the nature of these tax benefits? In the first place anyone drilling a dry hole can set all his expenses against taxes; the total cost in other words is deductible from the tax base. Apparently the general public has not realized this fact, which represents the real attractiveness of petroleum wildcatting for fat cats looking for tax deductible gambles. But this is not all. Even if the wildcatter finds a well, he can deduct from the tax base all "intangible expenses," such as geological studies, equipment, labor, fuel, and testing, which can usually run up to 60 percent of the total cost. Thus a producer (and the investors behind him), spending $100,000 on drilling a dry hole, deduct $100,000 from the base tax. If he drills a flowing well, spending the same amount of money, he (and they) can deduct $60,000 from the tax base.

In addition, there is the depletion allowance, which is a term as likely to start a fight as the challenge "your sister is a whore." This started out in an inoffensive way in the 1913 income tax bill (a novelty in itself), when Congress thought that all minerals should be written off in the same way that one depreciates the value of, say, a house. At this time, along with platinum, copper, gold, coal, etc. Congress proposed to set off 5 percent of the gross income of the extraction (mineral) industries against the tax base. The idea was merely to compensate the miners for the decline in value of their capital asset that must inevitably take place as production reduced the size of the resource.

By 1926, in the midst of an oil-shortage scare, a staunchly Republican Congress was inspired to increase the depletion allowance in the oil industry to 27 1/2 percent of gross income, an extremely high figure in comparison with other minerals. (Even uranium and platinum receive only a 23 percent depletion allowance.) Moreover, the concept of the allowance had completely changed. After 1926, no longer did it have any parallel with depreciation, because oil companies pay off the original investment in a well by an average factor of 18. (That is, the cost of a well over its producing life is returned in depletion benefits 18 times. On the other hand, obviously we cannot depreciate the total value of any ordinary piece of property, like a house or a refinery, more than once.)

From 1926 to the present, the depletion allowance began to take on a mystical, one might even say a religious flavor, especially in the minds of Texans such as Sam Rayburn and Lyndon Johnson. It was viewed as a kind of heavenly award for asphalt-stained knights who assumed the grave risks of seeking the holy grail of petroleum. Surely after all such travail and gambling with long shots, the finder of the grail should receive more than the ordinary awards of becoming a rich man; he should have his taxes lowered so that he would be encouraged to go on another beautiful and reckless crusade; find more oil; have the tax on producing that reduced, so that in turn he or people modeling themselves in his image would spend a lifetime in searching out the beautiful oil spots in the world (for the depletion allowance for American citizens was not limited to oil found in the United States).

The lyrical nature of this incentive is somewhat reduced if one notes that it is purely an award for producing oil, not looking for it. Indeed, if anything, it has a discouraging effect on exploration, for by spending the same amount of money on extending an already established field, or water flooding it after one has milked it dry the first time around, one is much more certain to get the depletion allowance than by chasing off after ghostly oil that may or may not be found. One of the economic facts of life about which there is absolutely no doubt is that nobody can get a depletion allowance on a dry well. On the other hand, it seems a little silly to receive this tax benefit on every tremendous flowing well in such an all but inexhaustible field as Ghawar in Saudi Arabia.

Although the depletion allowance has begun to fade in importance in comparison with the world-wide acceleration of crude oil prices, there are still ferocious fights about it. There have been some defections, such as those of Arco and Gulf, who believe it is a dead issue and best forgotten. In the case of those major companies who still support it, the motive is, in my opinion, a feeling that the present flush times are transitory—things are too good to last—and one should defend every tax benefit with tooth and claw, because tomorrow the dam may burst and we will be back to $2 a barrel for oil.

However, am I the only writer on this subject to point out that the elimination of the depletion allowance carries with it a devastating bookkeeping discrimination against the independents as producers? Although essentially this discrimination depends on the obvious fact that a major integrated company can chose its profit-taking point (at the wellhead, at the refinery truck-loading overhead lines, at the service station) the raw accounting of simply finding and producing oil shows that, without the depletion allowance, the independent is better off in selling his discovery well immediately to a major company. In other words, without the depletion allowance we have no incentive for independents to produce oil at all. I don't think the legislators, whose hearts ostensibly bleed for small businessmen, realize this fact. I offer in evidence some figures given to me by a brilliant young independent producer whose word I have very profound reasons to trust but who wishes to remain anonymous.

In the detailed arithmetic, which is presented in Appendix A, it is shown what happens when "Poverty Petroleum Company" drills a well which costs $100,000 to complete and $2,000 leasehold costs. The well produces 100,000 barrels in 5 years and goes dry. As shown in the summary of Appendix A, the present-worth value of the profit after taxes to Poverty Pete would be $349,741 when discounted at 10 percent per year if the depletion allowance is retained. If the depletion allowance is eliminated, Poverty Pete would realize only $272,486 present-worth profit if he produced the well until abandonment.

Suppose "Big Giant Oil and Gas Corporation" comes snooping around, looks the property over, and offers to buy it, before any oil had been produced, for $500,000. This would represent $296,497 present-worth profits, after taxes, for Poverty Pete, and he could pull up stakes and retire to Seal Beach, California, or continue looking for another bonanza, but he would not be functioning as a producer, only as a once lucky gambler.

If the depletion allowance is retained, on the other hand, Poverty Pete has the incentive of $53,294 more present-worth profit by producing the well himself rather than by selling it to Big Giant Oil and Gas Corporation.

One may ask, what is the incentive for Big Giant to pay half a million? This is actually the whole point of the exercise. At approximately two-thirds the open market cost of the same crude oil even without depletion allowance, Big Giant is getting an assured source of raw material upon which, after various stages of refining, transporting, and merchandising, he gets his real profit. This is because Big Giant is an integrated company. This is why the president of Arco said, "We don't need the depletion allowance; we can make up for the loss of it by a cent a gallon added to the price of gasoline." Poverty Pete has no such downstream source of profit. Adding 1 cent a gallon to the price of gasoline doesn't help him, because he doesn't sell gasoline. Like every other faceless, consuming statistical unit, he just buys it.

These are the kinds of considerations that intelligent young men in the oil business study very carefully, but apparently they are beyond the imagination of congressmen, newspaper columnists, or professors of economics. In my opinion this example weights heavily in favor of selective retention of the depletion allowance (or some equivalent) in the case of the independent operator; that is, if we want to preserve the independent operator. The present legislation provides depletion protection for only a small percentage of oil produced by independents.

There is also the fact previously referred to that the independent is almost automatically cut out of the next American oil boom—on the outer continental shelf. The government has seen fit to auction off these lease properties in large blocs and the going price is in the hundreds of millions of dollars per bloc. Even the majors usually bid in pairs in order to share these huge gambles. Although a sort of Mutt-and-Jeff bidding system has been proposed by liberal congressmen, in which independents would be allowed a small equity in the bidding by a large integrated major, neither the majors nor the independents seem attracted by this incongruous marriage of giant and dwarf.

The very large companies, such as Exxon, Mobil, Gulf, Standard of California, Texaco, who for the last few years have made most of their money on foreign operations, are in a mood to take off-shore American operations very seriously indeed, for they may be forced to test out Thomas Wolfe's axiom "You Can't Go Home Again." The fun and huge profits have left the foreign operations, as OPEC becomes more and more demanding, as nationalization becomes routine, and the companies see their authority nullified and their share of the loot diminished to that of hired agents.

While the party lasted, the tax incentives were not only attractive, they were downright gross. In addition to the foreign tax credit described in the last chapter there was a special gimmick that depended upon the fact that the OPEC countries taxed at a greater rate than the United States. The rules were then set up so that the international company could treat this difference as a special excess credit and use it for making deals in countries with lower tax rates for things other than oil: oil tankers, for example.

As long as the world price of crude oil stayed near or about $10 per barrel and the foreign tax credit system remained on the books, the big majors could remain reasonably prosperous (although not as prosperous as during 1973 and 1974) and relations between the majors and the American independents would continue to be fairly pacific.* Both the majors and the independents quail in concert in fear that Washington may start a series of rollbacks in prices.

But as noted, much of Congress has insisted on a duality in the oil business and even the noisiest liberal admits an extraordinary tenderness toward the independents, as toward all little people. Hubert Humphrey has asserted that he is "not after the poor little fellow who goes around with a corkscrew digging his little holes." After drying his eyes after imagining this picture of the pathos of littleness (which reminds one somehow of ragged gnomes boring holes in Swiss

---

*This pacifism is under considerable strain because of the steel shortage. Two-year-delivery delays are common on tubular goods, valves, rigs, casing, and so forth. This lack of equipment is so desperate that some independents are plugging up still profitable stripper wells to use the old hardware in new drilling projects; with some justice they accuse the majors of overbuying and hoarding. As an elephant can be kind to field mice by giving them gigantic turds to nibble at, Exxon has gone out of its way to share some surplus hardware with the independents.

cheese), the Minnesotan rages, "No, I am after the *big* guy—the one who has so much money he is trying to buy circuses and chain department stores!"

In spite of the tender loving care that the politicians profess for the small independents and the attempt to drive a wedge between the strata of independents and integrated majors, recent industry meetings of such bodies as the Independent Petroleum Association of America usually wind up with amiable expressions toward the majors. There is a good reason for this. The majors are the best customers for independent oil. The majors have the pipelines and most of the refineries. Without a clear provocation, one does not insult or break political brotherhood with one's best customers.

"BY THE TIME THE FAT MAN IS THIN, THE THIN ONE IS DEAD" (old Slavic proverb)

So far we have used the expression *independent* for a company which explores for oil and produces oil. There is another, nearly extinct kind of independent, who markets oil products. In the last few decades these merchants have scratched out a reasonable living by selling gasoline at a price 2 or 3 cents a gallon lower than that of the well-advertised major brands. In all but the most exceptional instances this cheaper motor fuel is precisely the same as that sold by the majors, which is not surprising since it usually comes out of the same storage tank. One pays the bonus for the imaginary "tiger in the tank" or for the privilege of being served by "the man who wears the star." This kind of independent was a necessary piece of economic gear in the long years of the 1950s and 1960s, when there was an American excess of petroleum, and in fact potentially an enormous world-wide glut. The independent marketer acted as an overflow weir or escape valve for the American integrated companies. In many cases he was even encouraged financially by the majors. As the surplus of motor fuel grew, however, the independents were inclined to start price wars—a most hateful practice and one that necessarily had to be indulged in by the majors, as one builds a counterfire in the mountain brush to save the houses. Everybody lost money except the customer and he is hardly conscious of the saving, because (as mentioned before) the price of motor fuel within limits has little effect on the demand.

The price war becomes a different kind of weapon when the total demand for petroleum equals or exceeds the supply, as it started to do in the late 1960s. There is no need for a weir or overflow valve, and the price-war-prone independent marketer becomes to the majors not a convenience but a damned nuisance. A classic instance of the power of the fat man under such circumstances is the European motor fuel market of 1966 and 1967.

By the beginning of 1968 the independent marketer had captured about 20 percent of the West German market and was gaining ground through Europe. Many of them were taken over by big independents, such as Continental, Signal, Sinclair, and Murphy. Price wars broke out like little brushfires, now in France, now in Denmark, now in Britain, skipping borders, to bring annoyance impartially in and out of the Common Market. Finally the biggest major of them all, Exxon (then Esso) decided to test the soundness of the old Slavic proverb that heads this section. The thousands of glossy Esso service stations in every European country dropped the price of gasoline by as much as 20 percent. By holding to this brutal regime for 2 years, Esso broke the backs of the independents and bent the bones of some of the majors. The total loss to the industry was in Great Britain alone about 30 million pounds per year; but to underline the futility of such ventures, the total sale of motor fuel neither decreased nor increased beyond a rate which could be easily extrapolated from the normal curve. A lot of *thin* people had died, but as far as the motorist was concerned, all this might have taken place in Albania.

The role of the independent marketer is dubious, although in Europe he may have more of a future because of the legal or economic separation of retailer from source; for example, in Great Britain there are strict regulations laying down the number of service stations that any oil refiner may own. But in the United States the independent marketer no longer seems to have any particular role to play. There is no constant surplus, because there is in fact a dearth of refineries. A large independent operator may be forced to buy gasoline from the Caribbean refineries, such as Amerada-Hess, operating on expensive world-market crude oils and will find himself forced to sell at higher prices than the majors' service stations. This means quick oblivion.

Many liberals believe that in a further apocalyptic trust-busting crusade, marketing, refining, production, and exploration should be done by separate corporations. There should be no integrated companies. If this were accomplished, I think we would be in the same sad position that we are in with food. An integrated oil company can decide where to take its profits, if any—at the crude producing end, refining, transportation, or marketing. A company which does nothing but refining, for example, is in the same lamentable dilemma as the cattle feeders. If the price of feed grains goes up and he can get no better price from the slaughterer, he is out of business—and at a time when the grain farmer never had it so good. The American refiner is really in a worse position. (There is plenty of grain but in 1973 and 1975 at least, nobody controlled its price and suddenly wheat was selling at $6 a bushel, with corn not far behind.) If he can find enough old domestic crude oil at $5.25 per barrel he can make money, if he has to rely on new domestic crude at $11 a barrel or on imported crude at $12 to $13 he is not competitive.

This is why practically nobody is building new refineries in this country. Where is the medium-price crude going to come from? A big 300,000-barrel-a-day refinery costs half a billion dollars and has to run full-tilt for 15 or 20 years to pay off. But running full-tilt means a much surer source of supply, a much more comfortable assurance against stricter environmental pollution laws, a much more settled political picture than the oil investor sees ahead of him. So disturbed is the 10-year future that circuses and Montgomery Ward look like good hedges. And the truth of the matter is that, realistically, the oil industry doesn't make enough money to support the future energy requirements of the world.

In spite of all the babying it has gotten in the form of tax relief, its profits have been declining to the point at which, without the 1973 and 1974 boom, many oil companies could have been on the rocks.

HOW DO YOU FIGURE PETROLEUM PROFITS?

The "obscenity" that Senator Henry Jackson and other demagogues have professed to see in recent oil-company profits is based on a kind of optical illusion. They see a whorehouse where there is only a temporarily renovated poorhouse.

For large operations like petroleum, the only sensible way to figure profits is on a percentage return on investment equity; that is, for every dollar invested in the whole enterprise, how much do you get back over a period of time? During the middle 1950s in companies such as Aramco the annual return was very high, above 20 percent. For some other industries (for instance, the pharmaceutical business) it was much higher. The rate of return average for all American manufacturing companies in the 1960s was around 14.5 percent, while for various reasons the average for United-States-based oil companies had slipped to around 11 percent; and many domestic companies with large ratios of refining runs to crude oil ownership were struggling along at 6 to 8 percent, often below the return on certified deposits in savings banks.

In the bad year of 1972, nearly everybody made more money on this basis than the oil companies. Included among good investments were CBS television and radio at 18.0 percent and the New York *Times* at 17.5 percent.

According to some congressmen, such as Les Aspin of Wisconsin, this is a lot of bunk. One cannot deduce true profitability in oil companies from return on equity, because the investment is so complex and so often deferred in the process of exploration and development. Instead, according to Aspin one should calculate an oil company's profits on the basis of the ratio of profit to gross sales. On such a basis, Aspin claims, even in the gloomy year of 1972 the oil industry's profits were 6.5 percent of sales, compared to 4.2 percent for all manufacturers.

But of course Aspin is still asking for the same kind of accounting in another dress, for in computing the profit on sales one still has to include in some way the cost of exploration and development. Moreover, if Aspin's accounting were used by everybody, one would find oneself suddenly fresh out of certain enterprises, such as supermarkets. The profit on sales in a chain of supermarkets is paper-thin, a fraction of 1 percent; so if this were the true criterion of profitability nobody would go into the supermarket business. But the fact is that supermarket chains are extremely profitable. They have a vast turnover per unit of capital investment and the very small investment cost makes the return on equity higher by far than for the petroleum industry.

Another mystifying factor in the petroleum dollar is the way one bookkeeps the inventories, which are so large in international operations that inventory accounting can make the company glow or look busted. Much of the 1973 "obscene" profit depended on the fact that the international oil companies used what is known as the FIFO (first in, first out) inventory system. What this means is that when a barrel of oil is sold from storage it is taken to be the earliest barrel produced or bought by the seller during the fiscal year. On a first in, first out basis, if the company has oil which is bought at $1 and sold at $10, it reports a $9 profit, even though it costs $10 to replace that oil. In the LIFO (last in, first out) method, used by most other businesses, an oil company would be allowed to claim that the barrel it sold from storage was the same barrel it bought from the Arabs yesterday for $10 a barrel. Hence the reported profit would be much lower. (Neither undiluted FIFO or LIFO seems completely honest. One can use FIFO when one wants to impress the stock market and LIFO when one is trying to avoid big taxes.)

THE FEDERAL COMPANY

Mainly because of the feeling of increased frustration on the part of certain congressmen, who were investigating the profits of the American oil companies in 1973 and 1974, a cute idea was proposed by Adlai Stevenson, III, Michael Harrington, and several others, who complained that the smog of secrecy set up around petroleum accounting was so thick that it seemed impossible to find out how the companies carried out their businesses. The companies refused to give their inventories, their estimates of reserves, and this and that and the other thing, claiming that by divulging such information publicly to competitors, they would be mortally wounded.

The notion began to grow (actually it was the same notion that Harold Ickes had suggested in the 1930s) that the United States government should either buy a major part of a big oil company or have its own company—a sort of doll-baby that everybody could play with to see what makes petroleum economics click, hum, or explode. The doll-baby would generate its own data and presumably would parallel the economic behavior of big private companies, as the Tennessee Valley Authority paralleled the workings of private utilities.

Aside from the fact that this Frankenstein creature would start with the advantage of exploiting oil on government-owned land, including the outer continental shelf and possibly Pet Four (the presumably gigantic next-door neighbor of the North Slope field in Alaska),* it would get no special coddling. It would be concerned primarily with production and only with pipelines and refineries as a last resort; that is, if the privately owned majors refused to handle the hateful nationalized crude oil. One could easily imagine such a boycott, since the awful shrieks that majors and independents alike emitted upon hearing of the Stevenson-Harrington plan were enough to pierce both eardrum and heart. "The first step toward complete socialism!" thundered the oil executives and their pet congressmen.

---

*In the latter eventuality the government-owned company would be competing in the same area with another very large government or shared concern, British Petroleum, which latched onto a healthy share of the North Slope oil field.

There is, of course, a good deal of nationalization and seminationalization of fossil fuel resources going on around the world, and this is not confined to the developing countries nor the Iron Curtain countries. Of the noteworthy ventures, British Petroleum has been government-owned to the extent of 51 percent (lately 48 percent) for over 60 years. The Compagnie Française des Pétroles of France is partly owned, and Ente Nazionale Idrocarburi (ENI) of Italy is fully owned.

Perhaps the most instructive parallel, however, is in Canada, where the sole and peculiar virtues of government ownership (the ability and willingness to gamble on a long shot) make themselves apparent. The Canadian government had begged private companies to take a chance on the Arctic islands in the far north, where there was convincing evidence of large gas deposits. Since private capital refused to accept the risks, the Canadian government finally, in the mid 1960s, put up the money to form Panarctic Oils, Ltd. Gas was found and the problem now is only how to get it back from the ice islands. Some consideration is actually being given to flying it part way, to the nearest harbor, in Boeing 747 tanker planes.

In the United States, by far the largest and most successful government-controlled energy operation is, of course, the Tennessee Valley Authority (TVA). Although this started as a flood-control and conservation project, it suddenly seemed to come to life, to have a soul of its own, and to start to act tough. From the hydroelectric power plants that are the inevitable daughters of flood control, TVA went into very large thermal power plants often running on high-sulfur strip-mined coal. TVA is rough as a cob and has outshouldered privately owned utilities, not by reason of special privileges but because of lean, aggressive management. It raised hell when the Environmental Protection Agency insisted on absorption of sulfur oxides from stack gases and it grumped when the land conservation folk pointed in horror at what was left of Kentucky hills that had been subjected to the drag lines of the strip miners. TVA succeeded, in other words, by being more of a capitalist pig than the capitalist pigs. But it made money and produced power for 8 states at bargain prices. It showed the government that owned it a lot about the utility business.

From that standpoint, if one were lucky enough to get the kind of management that TVA got, rather than what Amtrak and the Post Office got, a National Oil and Gas Corporation might be worth considering. But I believe there is a more compelling mission for a national entity of this sort. As most adherents of a national company conceive it, the research activities of the organization would not be limited to petroleum, but would include the development of other fossil fuels, such as the gasification or liquefaction of coal, the recovery of shale oil and sand tar, even the direct utilization of solar energy.

When one considers this aspect of a national company, things begin to take the shape of the future. If we turn the whole concept upside down, regarding the petroleum exploration and production as a base merely to support research and development in the long-shot areas of new sources of energy, we have a powerful and symmetrical megaproject. In fact, on a reduced and domestic scale, it is essentially David Rockefeller's great but unlikely dream of having the multibillionaire governments of the Middle East finance energy projects alternative to oil. The National Oil and Gas Corporation would put all its profits (and with management as sharp as that of TVA, the profits could be large indeed) into research and development that by the twenty-first century could put the mother company out of business. Instead of the measly dribbles now devoted to geothermal prospecting and engineering, solar power, wind power, and other areas that we shall explore later in this book, we would have hundreds of millions of dollars to research these fields, and it would not be money torn from the groaning taxpayer's flesh but collected by producing highly salable energy that the taxpayer would buy, as he would continue to buy it from the private oil companies.

A further merit of this way of financing energy research too expensive or too far out for private funding is that of stability. Congress tires easily and administrations change. It is difficult politics to get hundreds of millions of dollars appropriated every year for projects that few of the congressmen understand. You can sell them on the sun for a year or so but they get tired of the sun, as they got tired of the moon and of visits to Mars and Venus, and so on.

From my personal stance as a retired director of research, I know the high costs of good research. One company that I worked for had the notion that it would make more money on petrochemicals than it would on gasoline and lube oil; that it would become another Du Pont, but it would do this by spending, not the high percentage of sales that chemical companies spend on research, but by having a few dozen bright boys working in a spic-and-span little laboratory. As one would predict, this was not enough to result in a metamorphosis from caterpillar to butterfly. As God intended it to do, this company now makes most of its money producing and selling oil—foreign oil.

Good, sound, intense research in new areas (for example, research on the direct application of solar energy) costs some sizable percentage of what one would estimate the total sales value of such energy. The total annual price of world energy is impossible to predict accurately, but by the end of the century it will probably be in the ball park of $500 billion, of which possibly one-fifth, or $100 billion, might, with intense research and development, come, by A.D. 2000, from expenditure in solar power, either in the form of residential or building heating and cooling devices or in electrical power from solar farms. One percent, a reasonable research fraction, would be $1 billion a year.

One need not be overly optimistic in expecting the profit from a National Oil and Gas Corporation to attain considerably more than $1 billion within a few years of setting it up. A quicker way, naturally, would be simply to divert the return from off-shore lease auctions to research. But this is too much like hocking the family jewels to stay in business, and so would not satisfy the secondary objective of finding out how the oil business is (or should be) run.

HOW LONG IS THERE?

Every time predictions are made that the world is about to run out of oil, some enormous discovery is made. Predictors of calamity have had such a poor track record that they have gone out of business, and their place has been taken by amateurs (such as Ralph Nader) making opposite assertions, namely, that the world has an inexhaustible glut of oil and the price for it is high only because of the infinite gluttony of oil men. However, the energy appetite of the world has proved unpredictable. The U.S. shortages of 1972, 1973, and early 1974 occurred because, as large oil companies feathered their nests in the markets of Europe and Asia, the American demand skyrocketed behind their backs, so to speak. Unanimously they claim that the nation's use of energy simply outsprinted their most generous estimate.

Conservation and a lower birth rate may keep the rate of increase in energy demand below a fever level, but it may take longer to educate Americans to practices of conservation and to a zero increase in birth rate than it will take to develop indefinitely renewable sources of energy, such as the sun's radiation and hydrogen fusion.

I do not have sufficient confidence in the potential reserves of petroleum and in estimates of American off-shore oil even to quote them. They are not even intelligent guesses, they are just guesses, which vary wildly from one authority to another. The U.S. Geological Survey (having during the last two-thirds of a century cried wolf too often) is now in the habit of acting the part of Pollyanna. Critics of their calculations now believe that they have, for example, overestimated the Pacific Coast off-shore reserves by a factor of nearly twenty.

Whatever the amount of petroleum hidden under the sea or desert sands or under the pastures or under the ice, it is not enough. It is not renewable and it is not inexhaustible. As the famous early Nobel-prize-winning chemist Dmitri Mendeleev said, when he had his first look at petroleum (curiously enough in Pennsylvania), "This material is too valuable to burn."

As we have noted in the last chapter, the Shah of Iran has also adopted this motto, and it is a good one for futurists. It is to be hoped that our great-great-grandchildren will see the day when petroleum will be needed only to make chemicals and food. And like the perennial Western cowboy, the oil prospector will be only a character in folklore and on the late, late TV show.

4 King Coal Returns from Exile

We may well call it black diamonds.
—RALPH WALDO EMERSON

God, if you wish for our love, fling us a handful of stars!
—LOUIS UNTERMEYER,
"Caliban, in the Coal Mines"

THE RED-HEADED STEPCHILD

As Carl F. Bagge, president of the National Coal Association, a fiercely sarcastic and bellicose man, has remarked, this country has treated coal over the last 3 decades "like a red-headed stepchild." Although the United States has something in the order of half the world's total coal reserves (counting all kinds from lignite to anthracite) it has in recent years used coal for only 17 percent of its energy requirements. There is somewhat of a Dickensian flavor of nastiness about coal that echoes itself in memorials to the 100,000 killed in American mines since the start of the century and in songs ("Sixteen tons . . . and I owe my soul to the company store . . .") and in folklore (the old miner says, "God made the coal and he hid it, then some fool found it and we've been in trouble ever since").

The previous chapter described the origin of petroleum from small marine organisms in the course of geologic accidents that resulted in protecting the innumerable little corpses from air and oxidizing bacteria. Coal is entirely of plant origin and mostly from the carboniferous epoch some 250 million years ago, when the supercontinent of Pangaea was still intact and millenium after millenium of hot years laid down unimaginably vast compost piles of dead vegetation which was protected from complete oxidation, not so much by geologic accidents as by the thick miasma of carbon dioxide that lay over the swamps. At first most of the vegetation consisted of lycopods (mosslike plants), but later the dominant coal-formers were tree ferns; indeed, even an amateur can sometimes discover the ghostly image of a fern leaf in a piece of cracked coal. The division between the mosses and the ferns is observed as the Desmoinesian-Missourian boundary in this country and the Westphalian-Stephanian in Europe, but both are, so to speak, the same boundary, since Europe and North America were joined as part of the mother continent Pangaea when the mosses and the tree ferns died and became composted into various forms of coal.

Since Pangaea was so big and during most of its intact existence so warm, it is not surprising that coal in one form or another is found in every daughter continent of the planet including Antarctica. In energy units there is several hundred times as much coal as there is petroleum in the world; it is often close to the surface, and it is not surprising therefore that man took to burning it after he had nearly denuded the European scene of his favorite fuel, wood.

Historically the British were far ahead of the rest of Europe in the industrial combustion of coal; even in the fifteenth century (the time of the Tudors) they used the hotter flames from coal to evaporate sea water to yield salt and to burn limestone for lime. The English learned to make coke by dry roasting coal and were far superior to other peoples in substituting coke for charcoal in the smelting of iron and other metals. Because of their expertise with the coal-fired reverberatory furnace in the seventeenth century the English made the best glass, the best earthern pottery, and because of better steel tools, even the best clocks and watches in the world. In the course of improving the operations of the mining of coal, they made the most massive invention since the discovery of the wheel —the steam engine. It was an *ad hoc* development in the continual, nagging search for some way to pump the water out of coal mines. The first and best machine was made by Thomas Newcomen about 1705, not by James Watt.

The extraordinary scientific genius of the British—their glow of inventiveness and engineering courage—made them (a pitifully small island country) the natural leaders of the Industrial Revolution, but at the same time their riven and ossified class system caused most of the cruel absurdities that the age of coal gave birth to: the enormous royalties in coal produced from land owned, surface and subsurface, by the aristocracy; the sinking of the lower classes hired for the degrading and dangerous job of getting the coal out of the ground. Coal was not cheap by the standards of the eighteenth and nineteenth centuries; because the landed gentry took such a bountiful cut, the company owners, to make themselves rich, had to conscript a special class of *miserables* (analogous to the blacks enslaved for the job of picking cotton).

The whole coal system, lacking the landed aristocracy, was transplanted to the colonies. In the United States, where coal was nearly everywhere, mining it became a giant industry, but curiously enough it was a retarded giant. For reasons that are still not completely clear, the average big coal company (for instance, Peabody, the biggest) never made much money, killed more men than a medium-sized war, and was usually taken over by a railroad, by a steel company, by an electric power company, by a mining company (Kennicott, the copper baron, bought out Peabody in a deal that has not yet attained the approval of the courts), by an oil company, or by one of those weird modern octopuses we know as conglomerates.

COAL GEOGRAPHY

Most of the high-grade coal and nearly all of the deep mines are in the area vaguely and often scornfully referred to as Appalachia, a social rather than a topographical entity that includes all of West Virginia, Western Pennsylvania, Western Virginia, Eastern Kentucky, and Tennessee. There is some anthracite (very hard coal) but only in eastern Pennsylvania. A goodly reserve of high-sulfur bituminous coal is found in Illinois, Indiana, Ohio, Western Kentucky, and Kansas; whereas most of the low-sulfur coal in the country is in subbituminous form in the west, including Montana, Wyoming, New Mexico, Arizona, and in the form of lignite (also low-sulfur) in the great Williston basin of North Dakota. Lignite is one stage beyond peat (which also must be considered in the world's energy budget), and one mining engineer has said, "I'm not sure whether the stuff is low-quality coal or just high-quality dirt." Some people have complained that if you throw lignite on a fire, instead of burning, it puts the fire out. Nevertheless, it makes up 25 percent of all American coal reserves (90 percent of it in North Dakota) and when the water is cooked out of it, it makes good enough steam coal to burn in 2 large existing power plants, with dozens more on the drawing board. Lignite is all strip mined, but that is a dirty, powerful word which will be scattered through a large part of this chapter.

The reader will have noted the emphasis on sulfur content. On July 1, 1975, the Clean Air Act was supposed to go into final effect, stipulating either a maximum of 0.7 percent sulphur in coal or a maximum of 10 grams of sulfur dioxide per million British thermal units (Btu)* of heat release when burned in power plants or other industrial furnaces. The bountiful, low-sulfur Western coal does not have a high enough heat content to ship all the way east at present railroad rates, but what tariff the railroads lose the pipelines may gain, for it is practical to pump powdered coal in a slurry with water or, to go one step further, to gasify the coal in the West and ship the substitute natural gas by pipeline. The ultimate step of burning the coal at the mine mouth to generate electric power and transmitting this power by cable always seems such a nice answer, but economically it is murderous because (despite the popular impression) electrical transmission is, next to air freight, the most expensive of all modes of transportation. It is practical only within a radius of a few hundred miles.

THE DEEP, DEADLY MINES

Surface or strip-mining on a large scale is a very recent adventure, but the deep mines have been with us for 150 years. Until quite recently underground mining was quite simple and quite deadly and remarkably inefficient both in terms of tons

---

*A British thermal unit is the amount of heat required to raise the temperature of 1 pound of water by one degree Fahrenheit.

per man-hour and percentage recovery of coal in the seam. Independent coal operators regarded research as irreligious and when they were forced by stockholder opinion to adopt a more stylish attitude, their notion of reporting research progress was to show in the annual report a photograph of a portly man in a laboratory coverall squinting at a piece of coal, as if wondering whether it was animal, mineral, or vegetable.*

The American coal mining system was and is what is known as room-and-pillar. One digs, makes a labyrinth, and leaves half of the coal hopefully to hold up the roof, which is bolstered precariously with roof bolt plates, the affixing of which is possibly the most dangerous job on earth (next to jumping over lines of trucks in a motorcycle).

The collapsing of roofs and the explosion of methane gas are responsible for most of the horrifying casualty lists of American coal mining. In the early 1950s, after most of the coal industry had been taken over by petroleum and steel companies and other people more receptive to new ideas, the continuous miner was developed—a $400,000 machine that looks like a thousand-toothed monster with headlights for eyes. With the manipulation of 23 different levers its teeth gnaw the coal loose without picks, shovels, and explosives. After the introduction of this chewing engine the work force in the country's underground mines shrank from 400,000 to 120,000 with a high point in productivity (precisely the 16 tons of the song, per man-shift) in 1969. But the continuous miner did not stop the human carnage; if anything it made it worse, since the machine-mined coal created more dust and more sparks to set off methane explosions. Pneumoconiosis (black lung) came to public attention, and on November 20, 1968, the Farmington, West Virginia, explosion, killing 78 coal miners, was the culminating disaster that caused Congress to pass the Coal Mine Health and Safety Act of 1969.

There was and is so much squawling and screaming on the part of coal-mine owners because of this legislation that one has to accept with some reserve the exactly similar output of noise concerning the 1974 Strip-Mining bill. It seems that if one had to make mines safe, one would go bankrupt, just as one would also go broke if one were not allowed without restrictions to chew up the delicate Western grasslands with shovels big enough to hold a high-school band. It is true that productivity decreased from 16 to about 11 tons per man-shift in 1974, but this can hardly be blamed on the Mine Safety Act, since very few miners (unless heavily unionized) actually observed the act, and the carnage continued almost unabated. The Pop-and-Uncle-Dan mines in such places as Northwestern Virginia and Tennessee could not afford to buy spark proof machinery. For lack of a $20 guardrail (required by law) a man could be caught in a conveyor belt and torn to pieces, and in fact this happened many times. It is notable, as pointed out by Congressman Ken Hechler of West Virginia, that the safety records of large

---

*It is a curious thing that the great English industrial innovators of the seventeenth and eighteenth centuries did not regard research as a systematic occupation and did not report anything on paper except to get patents. Most of their crucial experiments were written up, not by themselves, but by envious Swedish and French observers.

captive mines, such as those owned by U.S. Steel and Bethlehem Steel, are excellent, and in fact there are fewer deaths and injuries in the deep mines of these companies than in the surface mining operations of such outfits as Consolidation Coal, Eastern Associated, and Pittston. Year in, year out the same companies rated highest and the same ones rated lowest. Probably one reason for the smoother, safer functioning of the captive mines is that they are part of a larger economic whole (the steel industry) and, as mines, do not have to show a dramatic profit by cutting corners and dashing about.

Representing, like good little soldiers, the most brutal and cynical of coal concerns, such as Duke Power Company, Senators Howard Baker and Marlow Cook and others of the coal brigade draw nearly metaphysical distinctions between gassy and nongassy mines, and they propose to loosen the restrictions of the 1969 Safety Act on the nongassy ones. It is a dogma (one could almost label it a superstition) that mines located above the water table are nongassy and should not have to observe the precautions required by the Safety Act. What Howard Baker and others fail to mention is that in the provisions of the 1969 bill, nongassy mines were given a 4-year grace period in which to buy nonsparking equipment. During the grace period there were at least 12 explosions in mines previously considered nongassy. One was the Hayden, Kentucky, disaster in December 1970 which killed 38 men.

The truth is that there is no such thing in nature as a nongassy mine, for methane seems to be associated inevitably with bituminous coal. In fact, the Bureau of Mines has recently come up with the sensational estimate, based on careful samplings, that there are about 250 trillion cubic feet of methane trapped in the nation's coal seams, which is about the same as the nation's known reserves of natural gas (natural gas is methane). There is an element of tragic irony in this discovery. The same gas that was causing half the deaths in underground coal mines was also, as a competitive fuel from a different source, driving coal out of business.

The Bureau of Mines proposes to recover methane from the coal deposits and at the same time to lessen the mine-explosion peril by drilling shafts from the surface hundreds of feet down into the coal, then to burrow out 8 tiny horizontal shafts like spokes from a wheel into each seam. In terms of safety this process would be best applied to virgin coal beds so that most of the gas would be removed (and sold) before mining begins.

Even if the explosion danger were removed, we would keep on killing miners by cave-ins or what is more politely called subsidence. Subsidence can scare the hell out of people and even kill them on the surface, long after a room-and-pillar mine has been abandoned. What happens is that the pillars are eroded, sometimes by water and air attacking the coal or pyritic shale associated with it to form sulfuric acid, and the roof collapses. Houses at the surface lurch as in a San Fernando Valley earthquake; the subsidence shuffle is not confined to rural areas. Streets and buildings have been wrecked by subsidence in old mines under cities such as Scranton or Wilkes-Barre.

According to a bold 1968 study of the environmental deficits from deep mining made by the Bureau of Mines but never officially released by the secretary of the interior, some 6 million acres of the country—an area larger than the state of Massachusetts—have been undermined in the process of getting coal and are rendered as unreliable as land over active earthquake faults. Unless all this honeycomb of holes is stuffed with gob (rock separated from coal) piles from the mines or permanently filled with water, the sins of the past can still send us reeling against our bathroom walls through the next century.

Both the killing by cave-ins of miners and the frightening of and injury to their great-grandchildren have been completely unnecessary, because a method of mining exists called longwall that avoids accidental subsidence and at the same time recovers nearly twice as much coal per deposit as the antiquated room-and-pillar method. It has been used successfully in Europe for several decades and in Britain 92 percent of the coal is recovered by the longwall technique. That less than 1 percent of American mines use this modern system underscores the fact that American coal operators are not only "fossil fools" but are appalling skin-flints. Just as they automatically blame all mine accidents on the carelessness of miners, so they recoil in reflex terror from any new concept of getting coal out of the ground, in particular, if it means an additional capital expenditure.

Longwall mining involves shaving or shearing the coal away from the seam rather than gnawing it out, but the really innovative feature is that controlled subsidence occurs with the progress of the machine along the coal wall. The operators are protected by a thick canopy supported by a hydraulic jack that advances by remote control with each pass of the shearer. The deliberate and gentle cave-in behind this mining operation avoids any accidental present or future subsidence. Mine safety is increased also because there is never a sufficiently large void to accommodate a big explosion. Longwall is like a mole that eats its way through underground dirt, leaving no passage behind, while room-and-pillar is like a gopher that digs a permanent tunnel. At least 87 percent of the coal in place is recovered compared with about 50 percent for the average room-and-pillar operation.

However, the greatest challenge for longwall may be the prodigious seams (sometimes 100 feet thick) often found in the underground coal deposits of the American West. There is no way known at present to mine coal in this form, although one suggestion is to drill it full of holes like a Swiss cheese, then to start a controlled fire (*in situ* partial combustion) to recover energy in the form of a gaseous mixture of carbon monoxide and hydrogen. Essentially the gasification of coal, either in an underground mine or as a conversion process topside, is a waste of chemical energy since in the process of gasification part of the heat content of the coal is used up to form less energetic gaseous fuel.

Although underground mining is regarded by such environmentalists as Russell Train as much better housekeeping than surface mining there is room for argument here, as there is also room for argument as to how much coal we have and what proportion of it has to be deep mined. A classically accepted figure is that the United States has over a trillion tons of coal, 97 percent of it deep underground and 3 percent surface strippable. This 32/1 ratio of underground to surface minable coal has been highly publicized by the anti-strip-miners.* Unfortunately these reserve figures are completely false, since they include such impossibly uneconomic resources as 14-inch seams, 4,000 feet down. When you eliminate the Mickey Mouse stuff, the figures look about as follows:

Total Reserves (in billions of tons)

	U.S.	East	West of Mississippi River
Underground	293	168	125
Surface	135	35	100
Total	425	203	225
Reserves containing less than 1 percent sulfur	105	30	75

SOURCE: Bureau of Mines, May 1974.

Thus the proportion of strippable coal is more like 31 1/2 percent than 3 percent and this amount in energy units is more than the world's proven reserves of oil.

As to land pollution, there are more acres of damaged land from deep-mining subsidence and wastes than there are from the effects to date of strip mining. Millions of tons of gob have accumulated over the years to form hideous mountains in coal communities. Most of these trash mountains are smoking from bits of coal on fire and not only the gob piles but the abandoned mines (those at least not fully buried in water) are sources of sulfuric acid formed either by reaction of air or water with pyritic shale or with organic sulfur in the coal itself.

The consequences of this is that long before strip mining became popular, the constant flow of acid had made thousands of miles of Appalachian streams absolutely lifeless—no fish, no worms, no bugs, not even any mosquitos.

One of the greatest of all coal-mine-related disasters happened on February 27, 1972, at Buffalo Creek, West Virginia, where the Pittston Coal Company got to fooling around with its gob pile, using it to impound water to wash the coal. In a downpour, this impoundment burst at eight o'clock on a Saturday morning and loosed a 30-foot wall of coal sludge and water to crash down on the houses below, killing 125 men, women, and children. As Ken Hechler bitterly relates, you can still climb to the top of the Buffalo Creek gob pile, where you will find a sign that says "No Dumping." In the area around the smoking gob the people are fined $25 for burning trash in their own backyards.

Ex-Senator Fred Harris in a description of conditions at the Eastover Mine

---

*Ken Hechler proposed a House bill that would have outlawed strip mining. In answer to the objection that we need coal faster than we can dig new deep mines, he quoted Marshal Lyautey, who wanted a big tree planted in his yard, and when told by his gardner that the tree would take 75 years to attain full growth, said, "In which case, there is not a moment to lose. Plant it this afternoon!"

in Harlan County, Kentucky, owned by the Duke Power Company and not unionized until 1974, has mentioned another hitherto unpublicized way to die underground—by electrocution. Miners there say they often have to stand knee-deep in water while handling 440-volt cables for the continuous miner. When the fuses blow, the cable is spliced or hot wired around the fuse. Breaks in the cable are often merely wrapped with masking tape and exposed again to the water. "If you don't like it," says the foreman, "you can always get your [lunch] bucket and get your ass outa here. We gotta cut coal."

This is typical foreman talk in a nonunion mine. If and when the union takes over, the men absolutely refuse to work in a sloppy, dangerous mine, and in fact one reason that productivity tends to drop is that the foreman becomes the safety inspector.

THE GREAT STRIP-MINING FIGHT

For some time more coal has been produced in this country by strip mining than by deep mining. The destruction (or euphemistically in the language of government reports, the disturbance) of land by this surface attack has left some of Appalachia looking like the back side of the moon. What the surface mining equipment consists of is a drag line, including a monstrous power shovel, a 300-foot boom, and a central buggy as tall as St. Patrick's Cathedral. The super scoopers, known as "Big Muskie" and the like, are not used, however, for digging coal but for removing overburden. Somewhat smaller shovels, still huge, follow in Big Muskie's jaw marks to excavate the coal and dump it into trucks. The spoil, or rocky overburden, bitten out in 75-cubic-yard mouthfuls, is laid down to form hillocks called highwalls. Highwalls and spoilbanks are dirty words to land conservationists, and they are dirty sights.

No other living orator is so eloquent as Congressman Ken Hechler in describing the ruin that comes with strip mining in Appalachia—the bleeding hills, the mucked-up glades, the streams befouled and stinking. From Shakespeare's *Julius Caesar* he quotes,

> O, pardon me, thou bleeding piece of earth,
> That I am meek and gentle with these butchers.

Hechler is not gentle with the butchers but he is frank to admit that he is a freak, a politician from West Virginia who escaped the establishment. At the state and county level, the coal barons run the show and local restrictions on strip mining would be unthinkable. He himself explains the successful development of reclamation laws that surround strip mining in Pennsylvania and Ohio by the fact that these two states are rich and versatile and not, as is his own state, obsessed with the sole subject of coal mining.

It is a dramatic of lachrymose experience to hear Ken Hechler read letters from his constituents and from sad people in other parts of Appalachia. Listen to Mrs. Prige Ritchie of Knott County, Kentucky, whose baby's grave was ruthlessly violated by Big Muskie, the casket thrown on the hill and piled over with boulders and dirt. "My heart is broke," writes Mrs. Ritchie.

To the west, now embarking tentatively in the strip-mining adventure, Hechler cries, "Don't let them Appalachianize you!"

And this is what the shoot-out in Congress has been about. The exclusion from strip mining of land where the federal government owns the mineral rights, known as the Mansfield Amendment, passed in October 1973, when the Senate leader could appeal more effectively to ranchers and lovers of the Big Sky than he could later when the energy crunch became more of a gut issue. In states, such as Montana and Wyoming, the early homesteaders in most cases left underground rights to the government, so Mike Manfield's amendment would have checker-boarded out of production an amount of coal equal in energy value to more than the entire oil reserves of Saudi Arabia.

In the House, the contentious HR 11,500 was passed on July 25, 1974. This called for complete reclamation of all land subjected to surface mining (including restoration of the original contour of the land); it required the permission of the surface owner (which in most cases made it necessary for the coal producer to buy or lease the underground property twice); it forbade mining in forest or grasslands run by the Forestry Service; and it provided, in the McDade Amendment, that previously disturbed or orphan land be reclaimed out of monies reserved by the government from leasing rights to oil drilling on the outer continental shelf.

The joint decision on the part of Morris K. Udall (Arizona), chairman of the subcommittee on Environment of the House Interior Committee and of Patsy Mink (Hawaii), chairwoman of the subcommittee on Mines and Mining to get with HR 11,500 a workable compromise between coal production and land conservation faced some terrible challenges on the part of nature—especially nature as she makes herself known in the arid states around the Rocky Mountains or even in the hilly coal states of Appalachia.

For many years coal of various grades, including lignite, has been strip mined in the Ruhr Valley of Germany with such punctilious reclamation procedures that one would never have guessed that the lush, green meadow that one looks at had once been carefully excised, the underlying coal removed, and the top soil and even the turf put tenderly back in place. This is possible at a cost of $5,000 an acre on smooth land with an ample rainfall. Would it work in the semideserts of the American West, where the meager topsoil and the vegetation are so delicately in balance that the laying of interstate roads has often resulted in ecodisasters? In New Mexico there are patches of ruined land, where no vegetation has grown for 5 centuries: They are the sites of little turquoise mines dug by the Indians in the fifteenth century.

In Montana, Wyoming, North Dakota, New Mexico, and sister states a $5,000 per acre cost of reclamation would be less than peanuts since the average yield of surface coal per acre is in the neighborhood of half a million dollars' worth. The question, rather, is whether reclamation is possible. In Rosebud

County, Montana, Peabody near the site of its Blue Sky* mine has a demonstration orchard of 3,000 cottonwood, pine, plums, willow, ash, and crabapple trees grown on reclaimed land. The reclamation director of the company has also grown 5 or 6 grasses along with alfalfa and sweet clover. Western Energy Company has a similar show place, but the ranchers in the area are frankly skeptical. They point out that the experimentally reclaimed grassland gets more water sprayed on it than a lawn in Beverly Hills, while one rancher reports that his land after mining has been reclaimed 3 times but still looks pretty puny. They didn't use so much water.

Water. That's the rub. Pending further study, Montana, concerned that its farmers would run short for irrigation, has declared a 3-year moratorium on any new commitments of water from the rivers of eastern Montana, such as the Yellowstone.

Professor Robert Curry of the University of Montana is profoundly pessimistic about reclamation, without special irrigation, in the West. The ground surfaces of the Big Sky state, according to him, once disturbed, could not be expected to resume their normal procession of vegetation without very long periods of geologic time—many times longer (he apocalyptically observed) "than we might expect men to inhabit the earth."

There are no sulfuric acid troubles in the West, since there is no pyritic shale and the coal is low-sulfur. Trouble with water drainings (assuming enough water to drain) would be with alkali rather than acid. The water problem is made immensely complicated by the fact that the great coal seams are themselves often aquifers. Thus if you scoop up the coal, you may have screwed up a complex underground water system that is tied in with water balances throughout giant geologic structures, such as the Powder River Basin which dips westward from South Dakota to high altitude in Wyoming. This is shaped like a bowl with the sides made up of many layers, shading down to a bottom layer of granite which surfaces in the Black Hills at one extreme and the Big Horn mountains at the other, while in the middle the hardpan may be over 20,000 feet deep. Aquifers of sandstone (such as the Flathead) and of limestone (such as the famous Madison) may shade into deep veins of coal that act as important links in the ground water complex.

Many hydrologists believe that industrial water in the West (whether used in mining or in coal processing or whatever) should always be drawn from impounded or surface runoff (rivers) and never from underground aquifers. Otherwise in any given year of drought, one can trigger the irreversible desert cycle and dry up forever the western grasslands.

The consensus of experts and presumably neutral observers seems to be that there is enough rain in the northern Rocky Mountain states and the Northern

*One of the most curious things about the coal business is that it runs to fancy even fairylike names such as Meadowlark Farms and Magic Window. Ralph Nader wrote a sharp letter to an unscrupulous British owner of coal-rich land in Kentucky whose name was Sir Denys Flowerdew. In this industry the hand of Dickens appears like the hand of God.

Great Plains (15 inches per year or more) to insure successful reclamation after strip mining but not enough also to supply large power plants or coal gasification plants. In Arizona, Nevada, and New Mexico there is not even enough rain to make reclamation of strip-mined land feasible.

This consensus was naturally not accepted by the coal companies, the utilities or by their vocal supporters in Congress, such as Craig Hosmer of Long Beach, California, the expert on nuclear power who turned himself overnight into a sort of know-it-all on Western coal. Although in his district none of the young people had ever seen a piece of coal,* in preparation for the 9 days of fierce debate in July 1974 he had published in the *Congressional Record* for months a series of memoranda all headed "11,500 Bananas on Pike's Peak," ending each memo with the pronouncement that producing any coal under legislation such as H.R. 11,500 would be as fantastically difficult as growing banana trees on Colorado's mountaintops. Congresswoman Patricia Schroeder, who represented the Colorado area encompassing Pike's Peak, finally became incensed enough to insert in the *Record* a scathing piece entitled "11,500 Bananas in Long Beach."

To tell the truth, Hosmer's blasts against H.R. 11,500 and his cheers for his own bill (which, among other blatant features, provided no protection against swindling the Crow, the Cheyenne, the Navajo, and other Indians who had coal lands; and which exempted open-pit mining from all control) were in the best tradition of snappish, no-holds-barred congressional fracases. If we had not had a Hosmer, we would have had to invent him. In a moment of candor, he mused aloud on the floor, "H.R. 12,898 [his bill] must be a good bill because it seems to make everybody a little unhappy. But H.R. 11,500 has turned into such a bucket of snakes that amending it is about impossible."

Hosmer had all kinds of new names for the environmentalists, who had joined up with the ranchers to fight western strip mining, setting up a hard-hitting magazine called *The Plainsmen.* Hosmer called Congresswoman Patsy Mink the leader of the "green bigot brigade" and urged the consideration of any epithet that rhymed with "Mink." Environmentalists were also "deep breathers" and they were people who "set more value on three-toed salamanders than on ten-toed babies." Supported by the National Chamber of Commerce, Hosmer, gave innumerable radio addresses and wrote uncountable letters. (When Udall was asked whether he got more letters from constituents for or against strip mining, he answered that he got more letters from Craig Hosmer than from all the rest put together.) Hosmer was a terrifically hard worker and along with his tempestuous lawyer temperament he had a good deal of the engineer in him. He published in the *Congressional Record* "Hosmer's Data Book," a very useful tabulation of conversion factors, heat units for coal and petroleum, and the like.

*In order to insure that members of the House could know what they were talking about, he brought in a large chunk of coal and displayed in on his desk.

But the coal barons and their lobbyists did not support Hosmer's bill, because they regarded it as too restrictive! They wanted no federal control at all, no federal guidelines whatsoever. They were willing to fight it out on the state level. The lure of strip-mined Western coal was so irresistible that no delays were to be tolerated. "We don't want to have more lawyers than miners on our payroll," they said. In 1973 already, coal produced by strip mining had passed in quantity deep-mined coal, and the companies slavered for the thick Western seams, the high sales appeal of the low-sulfur subbitumen and lignite. There were other appeals. Because of the lack of underground safety restrictions and the thick seams, operation in Wyoming and Montana could strip about 120 tons per man-day of labor, compared with 11 tons in an Eastern deep mine and 35 tons in an Ohio strip mine. At the same time, operators avoided the average $1.50 per ton cost of adhering to the 1969 Coal Mine Health and Safety Act. Much Eastern coal is tied up by the steel industry. But in the West, coal land ownership is concentrated in the hands of the federal government, of Indian tribes, and of individual ranchers, enabling industry to sign long-term contracts with single owners. Although the government temporarily halted lease transactions in 1974, pending congressional action and resolution of the environmental problem, it had already leased 682,000 acres to Exxon, Texaco, and Arco. And, going a step farther, 30-year contracts had been signed by Detroit Edison and American Electric Power for 150 million ton quantities of Montana and Wyoming strip-mined coal, from Decker Coal Company and Carter Oil Company, respectively.

Western strip-mined coal is not only cheaper to deliver into unit trains (100 hopper cars each carrying 100 tons per car) but the union labor situation was also (at the time of writing) beatific for the operator. In the West the strip miner either belonged to the International Union of Operating Engineers or to no union at all. Thus the industry could avoid the 80 cents per ton royalty to the United Mine Workers' Welfare fund and presumably the constant threat of strikes. The man sitting up there 400 feet in the air at the console of a Big Muskie may draw down the salary of a vice-president, but there are fewer of him than there are vice-presidents, and he has nothing to strike about—certainly not the monotony of the job, for each giant gulp may come up with a nest of rattlesnakes or the skeleton of a dinosaur.

After prolonged conference meetings between House and Senate figures, during which among other changes the Mansfield Amendment was thrown out, a bruised but workable and reasonable strip-mining bill came out. With great imprudence President Gerald Ford pocket vetoed it.

THE BURNING OF COAL

In Chapter 16 on Pollution we shall go a little deeper into that subject, but because of the crucial fact that most of the low-sulfur coal in America is west of the Mississippi, certain facts of life in air polluted by burning coal have to be considered in mapping out the probable course of big wheelings and dealings. Seventy-five percent of the fuel used by the electric utility companies of the United States is now surface-mined coal. In order to meet the Clean Air Act requirements, these utilities must decide whether to use low-sulfur coal or to use high-sulfur coal and to scrub the sulfur dioxide out of the stack gases. All the utilities, including the Tennessee Valley Authority, but with the singular exception of the Louisville Power and Light Company, claim stoutly that scrubbing sulfur dioxide out of stack gases is an impossible mess. The various chemical solutions proposed for scrubbing corrode the equipment, they complain. In a month or so or one comes up with impossible piles of "throwaway gunk" from the reactions that would soon add up to the greatest garbage disposal problem in the country.

Strangely enough, one of the first full-scale scrubbing plants in operation was a double-alkali scrubber developed by General Motors, a company that is so big and impassive that it prefers to go ahead with its own private power plants. Blandly it announces the cost of $10 per ton of coal burned. It uses the throwaway gunk as landfill. (This is, of course, a standard fate for garbage, but the country is running out of convenient places to fill and in the meantime the collection and hauling away of gunk has got to be one of the most expensive operations in cities and industry. It costs 35 cents per can to collect empty beer cans beside Michigan highways—more than the price of the beer—and the street cleaners in San Francisco get a minimum of $17,500 a year.)

Immense pressure, as enormous as the tides of Jupiter, is being exerted continuously by the utilities and by all big coal-burning outfits, and for that matter by all producers of high-sulfur coal, to get the Clean Air Act relaxed or to get an indefinite moratorium on it. But the emotionalism tied up with this question is too steamy to be contained in this chapter, and we shall reserve further discussion on the sulfur dioxide problem until Chapter 16.

One other factor should be mentioned here however: A new and more efficient process for getting electricity by burning coal might automatically clean up the sulfur dioxide.

MAGNETOHYDRODYNAMICS—ELECTRICITY FROM HOT FLAMES

The magnetohydrodynamic generator is no harder to understand than a dynamo itself, but then a dynamo is pretty hard to understand. Magnetohydrodynamics (MHD) depends on the fact that if you run a lot of electrically charged particles between the coils of a magnet you get a unidirectional electric current produced in the particle flow, which can be tapped off at suitably placed electrodes.* The charged particles (ions and electrons) are produced when any-

---

*Electrons in a very hot gas are analogous to the electrons, frozen but potentially mobile, in a good-conducting metal like copper or aluminum. If you move such a metal in a magnetic field you get a current—the electrons stream in an orderly way—and this is the secret of the dynamo, which

thing (including coal) is burned at very high temperature, and such an ionized gas mixture is called a plasma. How do you get the very high temperatures? You have to preheat the air or you have to use oxygen instead of air or at least air enriched with oxygen.

In order to encourage the ionization, you add to the feed for the furnace tube a small amount of seed material such as metallic potassium or potassium carbonate. This is filtered from the stack gas and recovered to be used over again. But for people who want to burn high-sulfur coal, another delightful thing happens. Sulfur dioxide (which is in equilibrium with sulfur trioxide) in the hot plasma reacts with the potassium feed to form potassium sulfate, which is simply filtered out by running through a dry cloth or an electrical precipitator. There is no wet chemistry—no mess or gunk, but a dry powder which, if desirable, can be electrolyzed to regenerate potassium seed particles.

Since the plasma, which has generated a direct current in the take-off electrodes, still contains a lot of energy, it is run at lower temperatures through a gas turbine or under a boiler to generate steam for a steam turbine to get more electricity. The gas can also be used for preheating the air fed to the MHD burner. The combination of MHD with the conventional gas or steam turbine results in an efficiency of conversion of chemical into electrical energy of 1 1/2 times as much as with the most advanced steam turbine alone.

Although MHD in this country was first stimulated by studies in the Avco Everett Research Laboratory, using a facility originally designed to study re-entry conditions for ballistic missiles and space vehicles,* the United States has been singularly sluggish in following up with large pilot or demonstration plants and we have been outengineered in this field not only by the Russians but by the Japanese, although the Russian plant near Moscow is run on natural gas rather than coal.

As a rough measure of relative efficiency, a modern steam turbine generating plant has an efficiency of 40 percent, a nuclear fission plant 33 percent, a first-generation MHD plant 55–60 percent. The over-all efficiency of an MHD plant can be increased greatly by cutting back on the amount of power needed for energizing the electromagnetic coils. The Japanese experimentally have accomplished this by using a superconducting magnetic coil; that is, by operating the electromagnet with special alloys at such low temperatures that the electrical resistance is close to zero. Since the notion of superconduction is crucially important to the future of many strategies of energy production and distribution, we shall go less superficially into the matter in a later chapter.

converts the kinetic energy of motion through a magnetic field into electricity. In the magnetodynamic generator the electrons are formed by the very high temperature and the movement is caused by gas expansion away from the flame at the feeder end of the tube.
*The friction of the high-velocity of space vehicles as they re-enter earth's atmosphere is so great that the air hit by the vehicle becomes plasma, and the electromagnetic radiation from the moving electrons interferes with radio signals. That is why the returning Apollo rockets underwent a period of radio silence before the parachutes opened.

MAKING GAS AND LIQUID FUEL OUT OF COAL

The gasification of coal, although the phrase has a deceptively modern ring, is an old art and to anybody born before World War I there should be a sense of *déjà entendu* when it comes to the ears. Before natural gas became the glamorous giant of the fuel family and before the technology of welding pipe to transport gas thousands of miles became available, gas came from coal. Did you ever hear of the gashouse gang? There were gashouses in every city and in a goodly portion of towns. As a young boy I can even remember a gashouse in Los Angeles. As one drove by it hastily (for a gashouse neighborhood was always a kind of ghetto) one caught the not unpleasant stink of aromatic chemical compounds from the roasting of coal.

Most of the old as well as the new gasification processes take place by the partial reaction of air or steam or steam plus oxygen with beds or suspended cyclones of coal, the main products being hydrogen and carbon monoxide, both of which have the same heating value per unit of volume. Depending on the amount of inert constituents such as nitrogen and carbon dioxide, such gases vary from about 150 to about 300 Btus per thousand cubic feet (Mcf). By methanating them (that is, catalytically reacting the carbon monoxide (CO) and hydrogen (H_2) to form methane (CH_4), the heat content is raised to the neighborhood of 900 Btus per Mcf, and the synthetic natural gas can then be pipelined long distances for high-grade uses, such as residential heating. Methanation so far has not been accomplished on a commercial scale, but is being studied vigorously in Wakefield, Scotland, with funds provided by a consortium of American power companies.

The old gases from coal such as producer gas made by airblowing were being used as boiler fuel as early as 1836 and in some countries, including Turkey, India, South Africa, Scotland, Morocco, Yugoslavia, and Korea, coal is still gasified by the old-fashioned methods. Gasifying with oxygen plus steam yields what used to be called blue water gas, but is now better known as synthesis gas. This is because it is suitable for making large amounts of pure hydrogen for the synthesis of ammonia for fertilizer or, by the Fischer-Tropsch process, reacting pure hydrogen and carbon monoxide for making gasoline, as the Germans did in World War II and as the South Africans do today.

The low Btu content of power gas (or modern producer gas) made by air blowing is deceptive, since in such purposes as heating boilers to drive steam turbine electric generators, it is better to compare it with natural gas on the basis of heating value per unit volume of combustion products (which includes hot nitrogen from the air used for combustion). If you look at power gas through these spectacles you find that the worth of power gas at the boiler fuel feed value is only about 15 percent below that of natural gas.

Such considerations as these are especially important for a new concept in power generation known as the combination unit. After passing through the boiler heating system, the gas is still hot enough to run a gas turbine and obtain an additional slug of electric power. For this purpose, however, the gas must be free of sulfur-containing combustion products, such as sulfur dioxide, which would quickly chew up the turbine blades. Since the sulfur in synthetic gas is in the form of hydrogen sulfide, the removal of which is easy and is routinely practiced in all refineries and natural gas plants, the whole air pollution problem is readily solved with synthetic gas. Another advantage is the relatively small volume treated in comparison with the burned products containing the difficult sulfur dioxide. Thus the combination unit and sulfur removal go together like ham and eggs.

Although ambitious plans are underway by El Paso Natural Gas Company and others to gasify New Mexican coal, and to upgrade the synthetic gas by methanation in preparation for shipping high Btu gas to California, probably in mixture with natural gas, there is grave question as to where the process water is going to come from. A 250 to 500 million cubic foot per day gasification plant gulps up 20 million tons of coal and swallows with it 3 billion gallons of water per year. That is not a lot of ocean water but it is a lot of New Mexico water.

The liquefaction of coal to produce, in effect, synthetic petroleum is in the laboratory-curiosity stage. The indirect method via the Fischer-Tropsch process in which the coal is first gasified to a fixed ratio of hydrogen to carbon monoxide, and then these 2 gaseous products are catalytically condensed, with the elimination of water, to form liquid hydrocarbons is known to be feasible; otherwise, the Germans could not have fueled their *Panzer* divisions and *Luftwaffe* with virtually no petroleum during the war years.

Alternative methods are lumped under the term *solvent extraction,* although this is a misnomer. The Bureau of Mines Synthane process involves passing powdered coal mixed with oil (previously produced from coal) along with hydrogen at very high pressures over a fixed bed of catalyst pellets. About 3 barrels of low-sulfur heavy oil can be produced in this fashion per ton of high-sulfur coal.

5 Shale Oil and Tar Sand—
The Powerful Cousins

If a man cheats the earth
The earth will cheat the man.
—CHINESE PROVERB

THE ROCK THAT BURNS

Incredible as it may seem, during and right after World War II there was another short panic about the self-sufficiency of the United States in petroleum reserves. Enormous amounts of heavy fuel oil from Venezuela had been lost to the Atlantic Ocean between Maracaibo and New York or Boston because of the German submarines, provoking the same cry of "Independence!" that had echoed so squeakily in 1918 and the early 1920s. In the post-World-War-I era the company that later hired me in the 1930s had taken the false emergency quite seriously and had bought up considerable acreage of oil shale land in Colorado. When I became research director in the 1940s we decided to see what we could do with this fairly rich Mahogany shale. A sharp chemical engineer who worked for me designed a simple retort that worked so well that before we realized it the whole pilot plant area was smelling like stale fish.

This was my first acquaintance with this American heritage. The boys put some freshly run shale oil distillate in a pyrex cylinder on my desk. It was as clear as water but smelled like an overused fish bowl. After being interrupted briefly, I found that the liquid in the cylinder had in a few minutes turned as black as coal.

The fat shale itself is peculiar, rubbery stuff. If you get mad at it and hit it with a hammer, the hammer will most likely bounce back and strike you a painful blow on the nose. It is certainly a kind of petroleum or coal but it is much higher in nitrogen compounds (source of the fishy odor and cause of the blackening in sunlight) than any oil you can pump out of the earth, and indeed these are the sort of nitrogen compounds you might expect to get by steaming a corpse for a month or so.

The term *shale oil* is a most deceptive one, since before retorting it is not oil and the rock is not shale, but marlstone. The organic material called kerogen is tightly, almost chemically bound to the rock and can only be released from its frantic embrace by heating or retorting the shale at temperatures high enough to crack the kerogen into lighter, petroleumlike fractions. When you do this, the spent rock has still managed to hang on to some carbonaceous residue, so enough heat can be recovered by burning this to be useful in a continuous process of retorting.

There are several continuous retorting processes that have been tested over a period of years and there seems little doubt that the problem of making useful gas and liquid fuels (and chemicals, for that matter) out of oil shale has been technically solved. The problems remaining are more massive ones: how to mine the shale, how to dispose of the spent rock,* how to get enough process water, how to avoid grievous water and air pollution, how to cope with an influx of thousands of people into a mountain wilderness inhabited mainly by the greatest mule deer herds on the continent and by golden eagles.

THE WAY IT WAS

East of Edinburgh there are still huge piles or bings of red spent shale that loom on the Scottish countryside, where the oil shale industry was born over 120 years ago. Indeed, it was Scottish oil produced from cannel coal (Scottish pronunciation of candle coal) and later from oil shale that fueled the lanterns for America's prairie schooners. James Young, a chemical engineer nicknamed "Paraffin," invented a batch retort for distilling oil out of shale and this simple pattern of iron not only gave him a successful production business but made him rich from patent licensing. In the 1850s and 1860s, he got over $100,000 a year from 2-cent-per-gallon royalties paid him by some 60 American companies who used his process in recovering fuels from oil shales in various parts of the United States, especially by the Mormons in Utah. The discovery of petroleum in the Drake well in 1859 put a fairly definite end to the lives of these little corporate entities, however.

Historically the shale had been noticed by several scouts and explorers, including the Lewis and Clark expedition, usually because when a campsite was close to an oil shale cliff, the campfire would set the cliff to smouldering. High up, one would see a glow in the night and sometimes be mightily impressed, if not terrified.

Even today, as for scores of years, some 25 million tons of oil shale are mined each year in Estonia, over half of it for burning at mine-mouth power generating stations rather than for conversion to oil.

In the face of the near-panic that it had caused by its thoroughly amateurish inventorying of American petroleum resources, the U.S. Geological Survey in

---

*Intrinsically the nub of the oil shale problem lies in the fact that, on the average, 1 1/2 tons of shale has to be mined, moved, and cooked to recover a barrel of oil.

1918 erected the first twentieth-century retort in DeBeque, Colorado. Although later the Bureau of Mines labored in its steady, heavy-handed way on studying oil yields and improved processes, it was not far from this site on its own property near Rifle, Colorado, that the Union Oil Company in 1957 tested a large pilot plant. The complex produced and refined oil from up to 1,000 tons per day of shale and in fact actually marketed motor fuel made by the process; but it closed down in 1958 because of the low price for crude petroleum and also because the government at that time did not promise a depletion allowance corresponding to what Union Oil management expected. The original Union Oil process used special rock pumps to carry crushed shale to a continuous retort where hot off-gases burned to make the shale release its oil, which was drawn out the side as spent shale was forced out the top in the form of clinkers.

At another spot along Parachute Creek only 75 miles from the plush ski resort of Aspen, the Colony Development Corporation (a consortium of Arco, Oil Shale Corporation, Ashland, and Shell) owns 8,000 acres of Mahogany-grade deposits and has spent $55 million on a large pilot plant feeding 1,000 tons of shale per day. In the Colony or Tosco process, ceramic balls are heated, then mixed with very finely crushed oil shale to break down the kerogen. Because the contact is between two solids, rather than between a hot gas and a solid, the heat transfer is very efficient. Colony has completed the design of a plant to produce 50,000 barrels of oil per day, which is scheduled to go on stream in 1977. If no unexpected hitches develop (such as attacks en masse by armed members of the Sierra Club), Colony will almost certainly be the first modern company to make American shale oil commercially.

Union will probably be next, since with an improved retorting process, called SGR (steam gas recirculation) and its exceptional know-how in catalytic hydrogenation for refining such sour, smelly stocks, plus its previous mining and retorting experience in the area, it is back in the catbird's seat and may be the only company willing to risk putting together a 50,000 barrel a day facility on its own.*

How much property like those parcels that were to be exploited separately by Colony and by Union is there? An enormous amount, most of it lying along the Green River as it meanders its way through Utah, Wyoming, and Colorado. In the three-state region there is believed to be about 1.8 trillion barrels of shale oil, some of it deeply buried, some at the surface, but a considerable part in shales probably too lean to exploit. If we draw the line at shales containing much less than 30 gallons of oil per ton, there are about 600 billion barrels (still comparable to the total known world reserves of petroleum) and a large part of it is in 30-foot thick seams in the Piceance Creek basin in Colorado, northwest of the Union Oil property. With a few exceptions, such as the private holdings of Colony, Union, and Occidental Petroleum, practically all of the oil shale lands belong to the U.S.

*Since writing these two paragraphs, the darkening stagflation has made doubtful the survival of either the Colony or the Union projects. The Colony group has definitely announced a postponement.

government and can be leased, at its pleasure (but subject to the buzzing and stings of Congress) by the Department of the Interior.

The leasing is usually on the basis of 20-year-renewable contracts, and the results of a leasing program by Secretary of the Interior Stewart Udall in 1968 are most instructive in pointing up the difference between then and 1974. The 1968 leasing show was an absolute and complete flop. Nobody showed up. Nobody bid, until belatedly an offer of $500,000 was made for 5,000 acres of the best and fattest Colorado deposits—an offer which Udall regarded as so insulting that he promptly canceled the whole leasing program.

In the winter of 1974 the same 5,000 acres went to a Gulf-Standard-of-Indiana partnership bidding team for a bonus bid of $211,305,600. The Colony group bid nearly $118 million on another 5,100 acres to add to their private holdings, while Phillips-Sun bid $75.5 million and Phillips-Standard and Ohio-Sun offered $45 million on similarly sized tracts in Utah. The Interior Department also put up chunks of Wyoming property, but nobody was having any of it, since it did not appear workable by conventional mining and the yield of oil per ton of shale was very skinny.

HOW TO GET THE STUFF OUT OF THE GROUND

Among the more important motives for the government's modest leasing program in 1974 was to see how various mining methods were going to affect the Green River region and the water equilibrium, before putting up for grabs any really substantial part of its vast holdings. Some hydrologists are not even sure there is enough surface water to handle more than 2 50,000-barrel-per-day shale oil complexes if at the same time strip mining for coal and coal gasification plants are going on. Already, there seem to be commitments that threaten to dry up the tributaries of the Colorado River and, by reducing the flow of this master stream, to increase automatically its salt content in irrigation reservoirs such as Lake Mead behind Hoover Dam.

In general, the oil shale deposits lie much deeper than the Western coal seams and therefore are not so easily surface mined with a dragline. One question is whether open-pit mining of the type practiced for copper ores is more appropriate than conventional underground methods such as the room-and-pillar technique. Sun Oil Company has been awarded a contract by the Bureau of Mines to make a technical and economic study of single-pass* open-pit mining of deep shale deposits in the Piceance Creek basin. The open-pit systems have the advantage of recovering nearly all the shale while, as in coal mining, the underground methods would get back only 50 percent (although the European longwall technique described in Chapter 4 might do a lot better than this).

The trouble is that, unlike coal mining, what you are digging out is mostly

---

*Under the single-pass concept, after an area is once mined, it would not be disturbed again.

a bunch of rock that has to be dumped somewhere after the oil has been cooked out of it. Typically, on the Colony project, spent shale will fill a nearby canyon to a depth of 250 feet in 7 years, leaving about 700 acres on top. Each layer is compacted and, according to Colony, the hill won't start to slide unless a slope of 3/1 is reached. However, experts at Colorado State College point out that snowfall destroys the compaction and that, unless the top is protected with soil and vegetation, catastrophic slides are likely to occur. Unfortunately the Tosco retorting process that Colony plans to use yields a spent shale that is powdery and entirely exhausted. After 2 years with watering to saturation, only a few little weeds straggled up on an experimental pile of this compacted spent shale.

This is the kind of news that mining companies hate to hear about, because they know that the Sierra Club and other environmentalists are watching with the eyes of eagles. As expected, the Sierra Club came out with one of its cordial blasts: "We think the oil shale program is far more damaging than any off-shore drilling program, and all for maybe 500,000 barrels per day 10 years from now!"

Other spent shale samples, such as the clinkers from the Union process, seem to offer more hospitality to the native vegetation, but even testing is fraught with difficulties. Where do you get the native seed? For example, who is in a position to sell you four-winged saltbush seeds?

There is another possible but not very probable way of getting energy out of oil shale: drive the oil or valuable gases out by so-called *in situ* partial combustion, an approach that we referred to in the section in Chapter 4 on the gasification of coal. The leases in Utah and in Wyoming were believed by the Interior Department to be especially suitable for this kind of energy recovery. On a small scale the Bureau of Mines had found that after chemical explosion and hydraulic fracture had been used to open up the extraordinarily tight and nonporous structure, a fire flood (that is, maintaining by air injection a burning front that advances across the seam, driving gas and distillate ahead of it) can yield perhaps 40 percent of the total energy locked in the rocks. The Bureau of Mines, however, had not been able to apply this *modus operandi* with any success to deep-lying shale formations. Edward Teller and others proposed that 130 kiloton nuclear blasts would shake up the tight shale formation to an extent that *in situ* partial combustion would clean all the fuel values out of the seams, but the vague and disturbing results from Project Rulison and Project Rio Bravo on stimulating natural gas production had dampened the ardor for using such big bangs, and there was already enough air and water pollution to worry about.

It must be mentioned, although with delicacy, that Armand Hammer of Occidental had managed to get enough publicity to nudge his stock up a few points by describing in lavish terms in a speech at Long Beach, California, a sort of *in situ* process that Oxy had proved out in conjunction with the Stanford Research Institute. The irrepressible Armand Hammer (who thinks nothing of chatting up $10 billion deals on one thing or another with Brezhnev and other high honchos of the Soviet Union) claimed that the Stanford Research Institute regarded the Oxy process as better than anything they had seen and estimated that one could produce shale oil for $1.18 a barrel, an absolutely preposterous figure that would not even pay for the water used.

Although the details of the Oxy mining process are secret in the sense that a circus in rehearsal is secret, the noise, heat, and fury associated with it are such that at least an outline is available. What Oxy does is to tunnel horizontally into a shale bank (so-called stoke mining), hollow-out a low room, and blast down the ceiling. Then the room is sealed off and the combustible gases are burned with injected air. The shale oil drains out through a trough previously cut in the floor. Once ignited, a room could burn for several months.

Oxy has produced oil from 2 rooms 30 feet square and 70 feet high, and is now said to be at work on a room 250 feet high. To extract 30,000 barrels a day by this mining scheme at the claimed yield of 60 percent, one would have to complete and ignite at least one such room each week.

The apparent advantages of such *in situ* processes are that you don't bring out any rock but according to Charles Prien of the University of Denver, a long-time oil shale savant, *in situ* recovery may simply hide the environmental problems underground. What he is most worried about is the effect on precious underground water. For example, in the region of Piceance Creek, which eventually flows into the Colorado, there are 2 major aquifers for the return of water to the creek. In the north half of the basin, 1 of the aquifers is above the shale zone and 1 is below it. Mining could create communication between the 2 aquifers, and the water passing through the hidden spent shale could leach salts out of it. Problems such as this could better be controlled by conventional mining than by *in situ* partial combustion, especially since you can never be sure in what prevailing direction the burning front is going to go.

One other method of separating the kerogen from the shale, possibly in an *in situ* manner, should be mentioned, although it is only in the early flushes of adolescent research. This is the use at the University of Southern California of the sulfur-oxidizing bacteria, thiobacillus, which produces sulfuric acid from organic sulfur. Since the singularly powerful bonds that cement the kerogen to its rock lover are believed to involve sulfur, the introduction of a thiobacillus plague into an oil shale deposit might eventually result in a mixture of acidic oil gunk and rock which could be separated by solvents or worked out with water at modest temperatures.

Unless some such entirely new approach to the recovery of oil from shale emerges, the whole shale oil dream appears a delusion. It may founder simply on the principle of net energy; i.e., with all the pumps to run, the new people to house, the water to find and transport and to clean up, more energy may be expended on mining the shale and getting the oil in a tank as a refined product than it is capable of returning as a fuel. It is evident that such big corporations as Exxon, Texaco, and Mobil have managed to restrain their enthusiasm on the subject, since to my knowledge they have not spent a nickel to buy their way in, and I am informed that Texaco, at least, took a long hard look at oil shale and turned it down on the grounds that there was simply not enough water in the region to support a mature industry of some million barrels of oil per day.

I am inclined to agree. Furthermore, simply as a source of petrochemicals, we need to have something in safe underground storage for the far future when we have burned up all our petroleum and all our coal. It is possible to make a lot of our plastic, rubber, and essential organic chemicals by a long way around using the cellulose of green plants, but shale oil would be better and reserving it for these more expensive but essential purposes makes a good deal of planetary sense.

SAND TAR—OR HEAVY OIL, IF YOU ARE KIND

When we take up the job of estimating resources of fossil fuel that have only recently been regarded as of any technical interest, we are in the twilight zone of pure guesswork. This is particularly true of tars, heavy oils, and natural bitumens. In some cases the material may represent ecologically a finger from a larger pool of deeper, more conventional petroleum. This is true of the La Brea tar pits in Los Angeles famous as a trap for relatively recent although prehistoric animals. It is probably true of a kind of heavy oil that at one time barely oozed out of the casing in Oxnard, California, and which I recall with nostalgia since it had, for an oil man, the singular distinction of showing a sulfur content higher than its API gravity.*

Most of the tar or heavy oil available in the world for exploitation lies in immense, relatively shallow deposits, of which the most famous are the Athabaskan tar sands lying in the north central part of the Canadian province of Alberta, and the Eastern Venezuela tar belt which extends some 375 miles along the north bank of the Orinoco River. For purposes of further argument, it can be tentatively assumed that each deposit contains nearly 700 billion barrels of tar. (quite recently the Venezuelan Ministry of Mines, for public relations reasons, changed the name from Orinoco Tar Belt to Orinoco Heavy Oil Belt) or, at any rate each, deposit contains somewhat more energy than the total proven reserves of conventional petroleum in the world but probably not as much as the total shale oil resources. Furthermore, there are mini tar deposits in many places, including Utah and New Mexico, and there is a curiously baffling pool of about 160 billion barrels of heavy, unpumpable oil that underlies some 42 counties in southeastern Kansas, southwestern Missouri, and northeastern Oklahoma.

If the figures—actually mere guesses—are right, this is more than the proven reserves of normal petroleum left in the United States (excluding Pet Four of Alaska), but nobody knows how to persuade the stuff out of the ground. It has refused to respond to steam injection, water flooding, or even fire flooding. It is

*The API gravity is a rather simple-minded measure of density. It is measured by putting a calibrated spindle in the liquids. The farther it sinks, the higher the gravity and the lower the density. An oil of 10 degrees API has the same density as water. The Oxnard crude oil would sink in water, since its gravity was 8 degrees API and its sulfur content 8.5 percent.

too deep for mining. The Bureau of Mines with commendable doggedness plans to recover enough to prove out its Sol-Frac process, which combines chemical explosive fracturing to open up some channels in the giant formation with solvent extraction of the oil.

Prehistorically, as in the case also of the Orinoco tar, the Alberta deposits some 120 million years ago were the bottom of a shallow sea, having accumulated from the bodies of microscopic marine organisms, when the world was warmer. Tar formation probably took place after fairly sudden glaciation put deep ice over the whole region, which includes deposit areas not only at Athabaska but at Watasco, Cold Lake, and Grace River. Beneath some of the shallower deposits, paleobotanists have discovered huge, perfectly preserved branches and trunks of primitive pine trees similar to those in Florida and Australia today. Not so long ago Indians paddling down the Athabaska River in the summer used to grab handfuls of the gummy soil from the banks to patch their canoes.

Because of the movement of the North and South American continents northwestward, after the breakup of the supercontinent of Pangaea, the Orinoco region at the time of fossil fuel formation was much farther south, probably within the range of glaciation fingers from the South Pole. It is now in the midst of a tropical jungle, while its nearest counterpart is close to the Arctic. You pick a green hell or white hell, and it is by no means certain which will be really conquered first. If talking about actual deals and even cheering from the side lines is a criterion, Athabaska will get the biggest play.*

STICKY, MESSY, EXASPERATING

Until the Sun Oil Company, led by that indomitable and forbidding old man, the late J. Howard Pew, formed Great Canada Oil Sands, Ltd., and tackled head-on the lower and more accessible part of the Athabaskan deposit at Fort McMurray, there had been only experimental nibbles at the vast formation here and there by people at the same level as pipe fitters. Pew was impressed by the fact that here was a great lot of oil you could see—you knew it was there.† He was willing to take a chance at making and selling it. This was in 1967 and his 50,000-barrel-a-day plant lost a total of $90 million until the first half of 1974 when it showed a gleam of a profit of $2.1 million.

It is not hard to separate the tar from Athabaskan tar sands, since as long as the oily fraction is lighter than water (and it can always be made lighter if necessary by adding distillate back to the tar-sand mixture), the tar can be floated off as a froth from hot water. (The basic process was invented by a native Alberta scientist, Karl Clark, over 50 years ago.) Unlike oil shale, there is no passionate

---

*Herman Kahn, the futurist of the Hudson Institute, has suggested a $20 billion multinational crash program to build 20 100,000-barrel-per-day Athabaskan plants within 3 years.
†So confident are the Venezuelans that the Orinoco heavy oil will be exploited that their leading oil official, Dr. Perez Alfonso, is already proposing a new tax, a secure-source premium. Even if it is like black toothpaste and nobody knows how to produce it, nevertheless, nobody can deny that it is there.

attachment between the sand and oil as in the case of marlstone and kerogen. Nevertheless, in an average strip-mining operation one winds up by handling over 2 tons of sand and 1 ton of overburden for every barrel of bitumen—a higher ratio of mineral waste than in the case of average-grade oil shale.

It is fortunate that Fort McMurray is way out in the boondocks, since on Great Canada Oil Sands' 4,000 acres small mountains of earth are rising from discarded overburden (the swell factor, caused by fluffing up of the ground, means that an acre of earth and sand put back where it came from would be 100 feet higher than the original plot). The tailings, consisting of water and suspended sand and clay from the flotation process, cannot easily be clarified for recycling of the water so they are simply dumped around in lowlands at the rate of about 5 million gallons a day. Since the recovered oil is essentially nothing but contaminated asphalt, it is run through a coking and hydrodesulfurization process to yield synthetic crude oil, before it is moved to Edmonton, then southward to disappear into the vast maw of the Chicago fuel market. By-products are 300 tons per day of sulfur and 2,300 tons of coke, little of which is sold. They just stand around.

Who would like to work in this place? It is flat country, a wilderness of black spruce and tamarack, a muskeg swamp. Muskeg itself is something you wouldn't want to be buried in. In the summer it is a stringy floating mass of decaying vegetable mush. Below it at depths varying from 4 to 20 feet in the workable areas is the overburden and below this the jet black tar sands. A dense miasma is common in the hot summer and sometimes the stranger is not sure whether he is seeing a fog or a cloud of mosquitos, because the foul, melted muskeg breeds uncountable billions of them, along with black flies, no-see-ums, and bulldogs (a devilish breed of flies that bite and won't let go).

The muskeg is fought like some weird vegetation on a strange planet, and the muskeg fights back. Big DC-8 caterpillars often falter, break through the half-frozen crust and sink into the horrid mush. Although Great Canada Oil Sands (GCOS) tries to drain the muskeg every 2 years, it is still like the pea soup you take out of cans, to which you are supposed to add water. Working with it in the summer is like trying to pick up soup with a fork. Working with it in the winter is treacherous but more practical.

The company has fleets of special 150-ton trucks costing over $300,000 each (the tires alone cost $20,000). The business of digging out the tar sand is the job of running 1,800-ton bucket-wheel excavators, custom-made in Germany for $6 million a piece. Each bucket takes an incredible cut of 120 by 70 feet, unloading to the trucks 10,000 tons per hour. Before special alloys were developed, the 120 teeth (each weighing 100 pounds) on the bucket wheel would last about 4 hours. Many of the teeth would be torn out of their sockets by the frozen tar sand, which is tougher than concrete. The teeth glow red from friction on a dark winter's day. But it is the summer that excavator managers hate worse, for the giant machines tend to sink suddenly and without warning into the deposit.

The mixture of sand and tar is probably the most exasperating mess a mechanic will ever meet up with. It can manage to get in and clog up a truck radiator in one 8-hour shift and wear out the underside of tractors in one-fifth the usual time. And it will eat away in a few weeks the $9,000 tires used by the dump trucks. GCOS, in the course of bitter experience, has found that strip mining in the summer is not worth the gamble (a fact which argues against the cheaper recovery of oil from the Orinoco tar belt) so the hot weather is now spent in clearing the land of brush and trees and dynamiting the ground to break into the minable structures.

In spite of the dismal tension of this kind of environment, men will come and even bring their families wherever the pay is good; hence Fort McMurray has grown from a village of a few hundred, before GCOS came in, to a town of 10,000, and the population is expected to double in the next few years.

With the abrupt increase in the international cost of energy, many powerful people who had for years played rather idly with the idea of Alberta tar deposits suddenly put their money on the barrelhead. Shell Canada got the approval of Alberta's Provincial Energy Resources Consumption Board to build a $700 million, 100,000-barrel-per-day recovery unit, also near Fort McMurray. Syncrude Canada (a consortium composed of Imperial Oil, Cities Service, Arco, and Gulf) will begin building nearby a 120,000-barrel-per-day complex costing $1 billion. Still another deal has been worked up by Petrofina, the Belgian oil firm, including Continental and Murphy Oil Company among other faces strange to the frozen north. There is even some talk of Japanese money possibly supporting a separate effort on the part of the Alberta government.*

Neither the newcomers nor Great Canadian Oil Sands is likely to remain satisfied with the clumsy strip mining plus flotation techniques for tar recovery. In the first place, only about 12 percent of the bitumen in the Athabaskan field is close enough to the surface for strip mining (including, however, all of GCOS's 4,000 gently rolling acres). Although Syncrude, Shell, and Petrofina will start with strip mining (and in fact pay GCOS handsome fees for the 7-year know-how it has acquired in its stubborn agony), they are experimenting with steam injection and with *in situ* partial combustion (to recover cracked distillate and salable gas instead of tar). Shell has spent $25 million in pilot tests at a 750,000-acre lease site in the Peace River tar sands region west of Athabaska, while Imperial—Exxon's Canadian company—has a mysterious and well-guarded experimental operation going on in the Cold Lake area. It is predicted by some tar sand engineers that the first large *in situ* combustion plants will be in operation by the mid-1980s and will have taken over entirely by the turn of the century.

We have mentioned that men can be found to tackle the harsh Alberta climate and the mind-shattering exasperation of the job. But how many? Alaska and Yukon gold attracted more than enough, but digging for one's own fortune

*Canadian provinces are proud and greedy. They are just as likely as Arab kingdoms to take whatever steps are necessary to insure them the lion's share of profit from any resource that lies within their boundaries.

and fighting the muskeg on a salary represent different orders of incentive. For construction purposes Syncrude alone will require about 3,000 skilled workers. It seems very doubtful that when the same types of skills are needed in building up a coal strip-mining and processing industry in the Western United States, there will be enough men to build three new tar-sand complexes at the same time in Alberta. The world has grown old and there are not so many adventurous young men any more. No longer can one rely on the floods, as regular as the ocean's tides, of Irish and Italians and Bohemians to take up the slack; and besides, for these new jobs in the wilderness, we need not strong backs for shoveling but alert and trained minds. The peculiar and rather thrilling thing about the shale oil and the tar sand and the Western coal adventure is that it devours smart young men as the dumb and the sluggish men wind up in the aging assembly lines of Detroit.

Again, an epilogue is appropriate. The brave new consortiums tremble before the thunder of engineering and hardware inflation of a monstrousness never dreamed of. Companies fall out and are sued and in turn sue. I dare not attempt an incisive summary, but as I write, only Sun's valiant GCOS is sure of continuing the unspeakably bitter battle against muskeg and the freezing of the heart.

6 Energy Storage and Fuel Cells

There is more art in saving than in getting.
—BENJAMIN FRANKLIN

At this point in our review of energy and power problems, it is time to stop between the dimensions of 2 aspects of the way we get energy from the sun. In the first 5 chapters we have looked at energy that the sun stored in the form of once-living organisms—fossil fuels—that survived sufficiently to yield us their final soul, so to speak, when we put them to the torch. In later chapters we shall look at the energy that the sun continues to bestow upon us in the form of atmospheric and oceanic movements, which we could put to useful work, and in the form simply of sunbeams that we can catch if our hands are clever enough.

But in the way we use or hope to use both the sun that shone millions of years ago and the sun that is shining today there is an incredibly foolish flaw in our technology—one that costs us billions of dollars a year and, unless we correct it, can make some of the future ways of using not only the sun but the nuclei of heavy atoms basically too expensive to help us much in the long run.

The flaw is that we do not know of a good way to store energy. For example, right now well over 99 percent of the electricity we use is generated virtually at the instant we use it. If we were going to heat a house solely by the energy of the wind, we have no good answer to the question, what happens when the wind dies down?

THE ELECTRICAL STORAGE DILEMMA AND SOME PARTIAL ANSWERS

Since energy storage is an immediate and desperate problem for the electric utilities, let us look in more detail at the fix they are in. Let us look specifically at a small city in the prairie (call it Prairieville) whose power is furnished from a single plant which contains various generators. Since Prairieville is no Las

Vegas, its power demands fluctuate almost as regularly as the ocean tides. When the sun comes up, factories start turning their wheels, offices open, families begin to turn on the furnace or the stove or the lights, preparing for work or school, and there is a sharp peaking of demand for power in Prairieville. During the night, basic power has been maintained by the use of the most efficient power source, perhaps a modern fossil-fuel steam turbine or even a nuclear generator that cost so much that one can only get it to pay off by running it all the time at full load. But during the morning peak and at times during the day and through the early evening hours, when more electric lights go on, the basic power units are not enough. The utilities crank up their second string—older generator units that use more fuel per unit of power distributed. And to avoid brown-outs on a very hot day or a very cold day a third team of still less efficient generators is switched into service; often these are stand-by gas turbines or diesel engines.

The utilities would save a lot of money and fuel if, instead of these second-or third-string substitutes, they could run modern power units at full capacity day and night, shunting the power that is unneeded at the slack hours to some kind of storage system that would return it to the power grid during the hours of peak demand.

There is one delightful way this can be done, but it is not for any of the Prairievilles of the world, because it depends on the proximity of a mountain reservoir and a river. What one does is to use the excess power at times of low demand to pump water from the river up to the mountain reservoirs. During peak demands the stored water falls down through turbines (which, as motors, may be the same ones that drive the pumps), generating additional electric power. The efficiency is about 66 percent; that is, for every 2 kilowatt-hours that one gets from the artificial waterfall, 3 kilowatt-hours have been expended in pumping the water up hill; but there is not a utility in the country that would not prefer this means of handling peak loads to the use of second- or third-string low-efficiency steam plants or diesels. Unfortunately there are not enough mountain reservoirs adjacent to large communities. In the whole country there are in fact only about 25 situations suitable for pumped storage, and in some of these the economy is dubious because the mountain is too far from the center of demand; one fast loses efficiency in the act of transmission by a long cable.

The largest pumped storage system in the world is owned by Consumers Power and Detroit Edison in Luddington, Michigan, costing $300 million dollars to construct and holding 27 billion gallons. TVA will soon top this with its immense facility atop Raccoon Mountain near Chattanooga, where four reversible turbine units can furnish 1,530 megawatts at the cry of need. (This is enough as a hydroelectric plant to furnish a large city, if the water source were permanently renewed by rain rather than by laborious pumping from the river below.)

Even when this lucky concatenation of a mountain, a river, and a power plant makes pumped hydroelectric storage feasible, the project may be blocked by large landowners, who believe that the river belongs to them, because they have vast estates and polo fields and private golf courses and what not along the iver prospect. This has happened to the much harassed Consolidated Edison (Con Ed) of New York, which for 10 years has tried to get a 2,000-megawatt storage plant (the Storm King project) on the Hudson River near Cornwall, New York.*

COMPRESSED AIR

If you don't have a mountain, do you have a leak-proof underground cavern? Then you are in the energy-storage business. All you need is a gas turbine. In a normal gas turbine, fuel is mixed with air compressed in a compressor stage and burned to generate mechanical power which is converted to electrical power. About two-thirds of the energy produced by the turbine is needed to run the compressor. If you have a way to store compressed air, however, you can disconnect the fuel injection stage and use excess power to run the compressor to pump high-pressure air into an underground cave. When you draw in this pressurized air during peak power demands, all the turbine power gas goes into the generation of electricity, because the air is already compressed. You get the bonus of a highly enhanced power output per unit of fuel consumed.

Most investigators regard the economics of compressed air storage as hopeless unless you have a natural cavern on hand. In my estimation, these investigators are incurable romantics. There are fewer natural air-tight caverns than there are concatenations of mountains, rivers, and cities. This idea of storing compressed air is too good, it seems to me, to be allowed to depend on a sort of Tom Sawyer dream which does not exist. What is obviously necessary to make the compressed-air storage idea workable is to learn how to form large, leak-proof underground caverns cheaply by special mining, tunneling, and leaching. It is possible that Ted Taylor's idea of a shaped-charge atomic explosion that would drill an almost geometrically, exact round tunnel as much as half a mile into a hillside would be the best answer.

Just for the record, but not to be taken seriously until the next century, is a method of energy storage that has been suggested at that citadel of dreams that often come true—Los Alamos Scientific Laboratory. There it is called the Great Solenoid and it depends entirely on the development of superconducting wires, a development which by itself would revolutionize the energy situation of the world. A direct current started in a loop of superconducting wire would theoretically continue to circulate forever and would generate a correspondingly eternal magnetic field. This sytem, once charged, could be short-circuited and shut in a storage closet. It would be as much a source of electricity, when needed, as an idealized storage battery.

*In view of my record as an environmentalist, made clear in my books *The Breath of Life* and *Death of the Sweet Waters,* nobody can accuse me of fronting for big power against the public. If you have the power needs of the City of New York (relatively modest on a per capita basis because of the paucity of large power-consuming industries) endangered by a few large property owners (Professor Irving Kristol calls them "upper-class malcontents") who feel that the scenic wonders of the Hudson are somehow ruined by pumping water to the top of a mountain, I must put myself on Con Ed's side.

CHEMICAL STORAGE

Storage battery? You will have said to yourself—and justifiably—how about a lot of storage batteries? They store energy, don't they?

If you look at chemical batteries from this lofty and exacting standpoint, you find to your astonishment that no practical storage battery has yet been developed which would stand up under the constant cycling between fully charged and fully discharged states—and that is what you need in the commercial power business. The familiar lead-acid storage battery, so successful in automobiles, endures as well as it does only because its charge level is kept nearly constant by the car's generator. It is possible that the lead-acid battery could be modified in the direction of cycling durability, but it has other disadvantages. It is such a clumsy article with so high a ratio of weight and volume to power capacity that somehow it has the aspect of something left over from the last century of steam locomotives and illuminating gas.

Experiments are being carried out with large arrays of new sorts of batteries such as the molten sodium-sulfur cell with a solid electrolyte of beta alumina. The battery is operated at the high temperature range of 575–650 degrees Fahrenheit necessary to shake loose sodium ions to conduct electricity across the solid matrix. Even more promising are the lithium-sulfur cells with molten salt electrolyte, such as a mixture of lithium and potassium chlorides. These operate at a still higher temperature, but the low weight conferred by the use of lithium makes them attractive for use in electrically powered vehicles as well as for storing power at a utility station. But none has yet proved out in large-scale power operations.

Perhaps the ultimate in chemical energy storage is the idea proposed by the great biologist and mathematician, J. B. S. Haldane, at least 40 years ago: Use the excess energy of a power plant to electrolyze water to yield hydrogen and oxygen gases, then store them in separate tanks, to be reacted when needed in any suitable combustion engine (steam turbine or gas turbine) to generate peak-demand electricity.

Instead of storing the hydrogen in a tank, more prudent use of space can be made by reacting it with certain metals, especially a mixture of titanium and iron, to form hydrides. This is equivalent to having solid hydrogen, as it is supposed to exist in the case of the planet Jupiter. By warming slightly, the hydrides decompose to yield hydrogen gas at any rate desired.

A modern version of this idea which we are not quite ready to discuss is to react the hydrogen and oxygen in a fuel cell, thus producing electricity directly and painlessly. (Since fuel cells were for several years a research obsession with me, I am fidgeting to describe them, but I have first to discuss what seems to me the most profound and effective solution to the energy storage problem.)

BACK TO THE FLYWHEEL

The best answer to energy storage turns out to be one of man's earliest machines, the flywheel, used first as the potter's wheel and later in smoothing out the motion transferred to a drive shaft from reciprocating engines. Storing energy in a heavy, freely rotating wheel is not a new idea, but up until the age of space flight, men have been so obsessed with iron or steel as materials of construction for everything that the heavy flywheels could store little energy for they could not revolve fast enough without the hoop stress exceeding their tensile strength, resulting in the wheel flying apart and causing as much damage as a flock of hand grenades. Engineers were too hypnotized by the notion that a flywheel should be heavy, for they imagined mass to be its most important characteristic, while on the contrary the kinetic energy is crucial and this varies with the square of the speed and only as the first power of the mass.

Contrary to the naïve guess, what one wants in an energy-storing flywheel is the lowest-density, strong material available. Let us see if we can understand this.

At equal speeds of rotation the light flywheel feels much weaker centrifugal stress and hence can be speeded up still more before it reaches its limit of tensile strength. At the limit, the light flywheel at its higher speed may, let us say, be storing the same amount of mechanical energy as the heavier one at its lower speed. Now let us also say the light, fast flywheel is only one-tenth the density of the heavy wheel and assume also that both have the same tensile strength. The important thing practically is that the light flywheel will require only one-tenth as much mass to store the same amount of energy as the heavy wheel, which is too clumsy, too expensive, and too difficult to fabricate.

Where do we get high-strength light materials? Fortunately they are a spin-off (perhaps the most important one) of the space program and they consist of fiber composites. Nylonlike fiber materials, made by Du Pont and Monsanto, when properly stretched and compressed together, can store 7 times as much energy per unit of weight as steel. Fused silica fibers may be even better, perhaps by a factor of 15 times the energy-storage capacity of the most expensive steel alloy.

Another advantage is that when the fiber composites are overstressed they fail by shredding or powdering rather than by breaking into deadly chunks of metal like a bomb in an oil drum.

For the storage of off-peak energy in a power plant, the flywheel would be connected to a motor that can also operate as a generator, and in order to reduce losses from air resistance, both would be enclosed in an atmosphere of helium or hydrogen below atmospheric pressure (a semivacuum). For power station use the flywheel would be about 12 feet in diameter and weigh from 100 to 300 tons. Each unit would be able to store some 20,000 kilowatt-hours of energy at full charge (a rotation speed in the neighborhood of 3,000 revolutions per minute). A good-sized utility system would probably use more than 100 such units, preferably located at the substations.

In charging or drawing down flywheel systems, there is no problem, as in electric batteries, of cycle fatigue, because the rotating wheel is never stopped and started; it is simply slowed as power is withdrawn through the generator and speeded as power is added through the same unit acting as a motor. The transactions are typically of very high efficiency, as is the conversion of water power to electricity.

It is obvious that smaller versions of the flywheel storage system can be used for other forms of energy, where either the energy source or the energy demand fluctuates. Flywheel storage would be perfect for trapping wind power and direct solar energy. But it is as a prime mover for an electric automobile or bus that the super flywheel has attracted the most attention. Although we shall discuss this more thoroughly in Chapter 17, the idea is exciting enough to try to infect the reader with the enthusiasm that infuses me, in case he gets too discouraged ever to reach Chapter 17.

One would simply spin up the flywheel (perhaps this time to supersonic speeds of 12,000 or more revolutions per minute) with the motor running off an electric outlet; thus the flywheel would drive the car with the motor operating as a generator to supply power to smaller motors, one on each wheel.

This device shares the advantages of the more conventional electric car in being free of pollution and representing a link in a much more efficient energy chain starting at the power plant than the internal combustion engine. The over-all efficiency in terms of auto mileage per unit of fuel burned at the power plant is about 3 times the efficiency of the gasoline engine which is only 10 to 15 percent. Any new national demands for electric power arriving from the use of flywheel electric automobiles could thus easily be met within the present reserve of fossil fuel or of nuclear resources.

Compare the composite-fiber flywheel with a lead-acid storage battery system. In order to provide the same amount of power (for a range of 200 miles at a speed of 60 miles per hour) one would need for a small car over 2,000 pounds of batteries, compared with a superflywheel containing only 130 pounds of fused silica or 280 pounds of nylon-type fibers. There are other advantages that we shall discuss in Chapter 17. However, I cannot resist the temptation to emphasize the stability of this magic wheel. Suppose you and your family have a flywheel car and want to spend the summer abroad without it. You can leave it at the airport, wheel spinning away, and when you come back 3 months later, it will still have ample spin energy to get you home. (The rundown time for a flywheel in an inert semivacuum is from 6 to 12 months.)*

---

*It should be noted that the Swiss were the first ones to use flywheels to run vehicles. In the 1950s a Swiss-designed bus, called the Electrogyro, operated in Europe and Africa for a number of years. Since it was constructed of steel, it was extremely inefficient and could power the bus only about 7 or 8 city blocks before it had to be spun up again by power from an overhead trolley cable.

THE INCREDIBLE FUEL CELL

In a fuel cell, a fuel (say, hydrogen) is passed over one electrode of a cell which contains an electrolyte; and at the same time an oxidizing substance, such as oxygen (which would normally react chemically with the hydrogen) is passed separately over the opposite electrode. What happens is that the hydrogen loses an electron and goes into solution in the electrolyte as hydrogen ion while the oxygen picks up an electron to go into solution as a negative ion. Electrons make a useful circuit as in the conventional battery. The only product is water. The process emits some heat but not nearly as much as when hydrogen and oxygen react directly (and often explosively). What's more, the efficiency of direct conversion of the potential chemical energy of the hydrogen and oxygen to electrical energy is much greater than the efficiency of a furnace or of an internal combustion engine in converting the heat of the explosion of hydrogen and oxygen into mechanical, then by a generator into electric energy.

If the fuel cell would work on cheaper more complicated feeds than hydrogen, such as gas oil or coal gas or even natural gas, it would be a much more efficient and much less polluting way to generate electricity than combustion to heat the boiler of a steam turbine. Intrinsically it possesses a precious advantage over most other energy sources in that it can be scaled down without losing efficiency. A 1 kilowatt unit is as efficient as a 1,000 megawatt giant. This is a much rarer form of virtue than it sounds, for practically all other kinds of electric generators (including those depending on the nuclear heating of steam boilers) have an optimum size for most efficient operation, and this size is usually in the megawatt range. This makes the fuel cell almost unique in effectiveness as a means of providing power for separate homes. The fuel can be pumped over 3 times more cheaply than electricity can be transmitted and as an oxidizer the air is free. The fuel cell has the additional virtue of operating at high efficiency at part load, again a nearly unique property.

In the late 1950s and early 1960s there was a powerful epidemic of research on fuel cells and I must confess to having participated unsuccessfully in it. Everybody remotely concerned with an energy business was in this field, and the main object of investigation was to find a catalyst or a set of conditions or a gimmick that would make it possible to use cheap hydrocarbon fuels, rather than pure hydrogen, to generate fuel-cell electricity. Yet even the simplest of hydrocarbons, methane (CH_4), the chief ingredient of natural gas, refused to work. On the other hand, along with hydrogen, ammonia and methyl alcohol would work, but these were considered too expensive. There was an element of progressive hysteria in the universal discouragement which grew, as year after year nobody could make the stubborn methane give up its electrons to a catalytic electrode. One by one and finally by the dozens, people dropped out of fuel-cell research and development. Only one outfit, the Pratt and Whitney Division of United Aircraft, energized by one man, Bill Podorny, remained stubbornly at the plough. And only 5 or 6 years ago they discovered the secret. They found that it is practically if not theoretically impossible to make hydrocarbon molecules sit down in such a way on a catalytic electrode surface that they can, without a nasty argument, give up electrons and form ions which react with oxidizing ions from the opposite electrode to yield carbon dioxide and water.

What you have to do, according to Pratt and Whitney's core notion, is to first form hydrogen from whatever hydrocarbon fuel you are interested in. Pratt and Whitney's great technical contribution was to develop attached reformers—reaction chambers in which the hydrocarbon fuel (including methane or even heavy fuel oil) would be broken down catalytically in the presence of steam to form a mixture of hydrogen and carbon dioxide. The hydrogen would then gracefully undergo the classic fuel-cell process and the carbon dioxide would go along for the ride. Although this technique considerably lowers the over-all efficiency of producing electricity compared with the reactions that work only on paper, it is still of such great interest to utilities that nine of the most important ones in the country grouped together to support the Pratt and Whitney development. In 1970 a 12 1/2 kilowatt fuel cell operating on natural gas was installed in a large house in Wethersfield, Connecticut, and has accumulated over 300,000 hours of field-test time. Other demonstration cells have been installed in residential, commercial, and industrial sites in the United States, Canada, and Japan.

With the growing scarcity of natural gas, one of the big questions is whether the Pratt and Whitney type of fuel cell will operate on power gas from the gasification of coal; that is, essentially mixtures of hydrogen and carbon monoxide. Will the carbon monoxide efficiently undergo the fuel-cell reaction?

Pratt and Whitney has one minor competitor, which, however, takes a different approach and aims for a different market. Engelhardt Mineral and Chemicals Corporation, a specialist in platinum and other noble metals, designs fuel cells for use in remote locations, such as the Arctic and Antarctic or Greenland, using ammonia or methyl alcohol as fuel.

When we later come to look at what have been termed the hydrogen economy and the methanol economy we shall see that in these power complexes fuel cells, without the Pratt and Whitney complications of reforming, are as ubiquitous as power steam boilers are today.

The fuel cell fits nicely into the hydrogen mode of energy storage referred to above, especially for the solar energy plant. Electricity from the photovoltaic process (discussed in Chapter 12), being low voltage and direct current, is ideal for electrolyzing water to form hydrogen and oxygen. The recombination of these in a fuel cell is so efficient that the incremental peak power is much less costly than from other stand-by sources such as pumped hydroelectric storage or gas turbines.

One unexpected disadvantage of fuel cells is their high volume requirement. As Podorny says of his darling, "A gas turbine is very graceful in size, but the fuel cell is a clod, a volume-eating machine." If you use it to provide the power for a home or an apartment complex, it has to have the equivalent of a room of its own, but this is no less than we expect for a good and faithful servant.

7 Nuclear Fission— The Light That Failed

You who are younger cannot imagine the mixture of desperate hope and protesting despair in which we who could believe in science lived in those years before atomic energy came.

—H. G. WELLS

THE POWER, THE GLORY, AND THE POOP-OUT

To a naïve but perceptive soul from another framework of time, nothing could appear more dramatic than the story of the genesis of man's use of nuclear energy: the stately intensity of the march of findings and the cavalcade of events; the Faustian bargain that we were suddenly faced with; the registry of gentle, complex intellects in the business of the annihilation of whole cities. As a matter of fact we were more conscious of the drama at the time than we are now (an unusual switch) because like all brilliant stories it has been told so interminably that at length we are heartily sick of it. Yet, basically, from a scientific (or perhaps we should say a science-fictional) point of view, it is an even more bizarre story than would at first be apparent to the layman. In the splitting of heavy atoms with the conversion of a small mass fraction to energy, we had something brand new, a local, a provincial accomplishment, so to speak, that depended on certain special chemical resources of the planet that we live on.

As an understanding of the sun grew more sophisticated, it became clear that the energy of nuclear fusion (the hydrogen bomb and controlled application of hydrogen fusion) was, on the other hand, the *lingua franca* of the whole universe. Uncountable billions upon billions of stars, with a family resemblance to our own sun, use nuclear fusion as a means of livelihood, as a way of staying in business; and in that sense, nuclear fusion (although we cannot yet control it) is the most commonplace of banalities. But nuclear fission is a peculiar planetary property —like beds of coal.

During the days of what I later came to know as the Manhattan Project, I was a research director on the Pacific Coast, and I began, mysteriously, to lose outstanding chemists to some unsuspected limbo that existed somewhere in the

Chicago area. This annoyance came to a head when it turned out that one of my ex-chemists was, in turn, trying to lure to Chicago one of my best young-woman chemists. I got a telephone number and finally a connection with my ex-researcher, whom I started to denounce for allowing his libido to overcome his sense of wartime urgencies. But he was the one with the cosmic urgency. "I can't tell you what it is, but it's the greatest thing since—since the *discovery of light!*"

He probably meant to say "the discovery of fire" but it was obvious, even over the telephone, that there were stars in his eyes. The next time I got to Chicago I took the shortest bridge between two scientific continents. I knocked on the door of Dr. Arthur Compton's private residence and spent nearly a whole afternoon drinking tea with his gracious wife, until his return. After getting his story, I persuaded him to visit my rooms at the Palmer House that evening where I would have responsible representatives from all the big petroleum companies on hand, to be assured, as I now was, that their inexplicable losses of high-caliber technical personnel were in the interests of a lofty cause. For some reason after that I got the reputation for being a know-it-all in this field (whereas I knew practically nothing until the Smyth Report came out) and my pocketbook was full of top-secret clearance cards received gratuitously from the various military services, as well as a Q-clearance from the Atomic Energy Commission. As it happened, in the field of nuclear energy, these clearances were only of use to me several years later when I became familiar with the first attempt to construct and operate a small breeder reactor.

I found out, also much later, that although Germans, Italians, and Hungarians were the most active on the purely scientific frontiers of uranium and plutonium fission, while American money and enterprise built the bomb, the idea of an atomic pile and a critical mass had occurred in nature and that she had evidently carried out a massive experiment nearly 2 billion years ago in West Africa in what has come to be known as the fossil nuclear reactor. This is a most peculiar scientific detective story.

Natural uranium ore, usually in the form of the oxide U_3O_8 or yellow cake, contains the spontaneously self-splitting isotope uranium-235 only in the amount of 0.7 percent, the rest being essentially uranium-238. This isotope percentage is invariable; until recently all ores found had precisely the same isotope composition, and there are stringent theoretical as well as experimental reasons to believe that whenever uranium occurs naturally in the universe it is always in this ratio of isotopes. This is an important technical fact as well, since with careful removal of nonuranium impurities and with suitable design of neutron reflectors it is possible to get a chain reaction (although not an explosion) with natural uranium containing 0.7 percent uranium-235; and some modern power reactors (especially the French, Argentine, Canadian, and Indian units) are based on natural uranium, as they can escape commercial dependence on the American enrichment plants and for another more ominous reason we shall discuss later.

Unexpectedly the French found some uranium ore in Gabon, West Africa, that disobeyed the rules. It had only 0.4 percent uranium-235. It looked in other words like natural atomic fuel that has been partly burned up (since in nonbreeder reactions only the uranium-235 is consumed, and that only partially). No other explanation remained except that an extraordinary and rather frightening concatenation of geologic circumstances had resulted in the formation of a gigantic atomic pile underground in which the critical mass of the self-refined ore deposit had been exceeded, and a chain reaction had resulted in the consumption of enough uranium-235 to bring the percentage throughout the deposit from the normal 0.7 percent down to 0.4 percent. How long this took can only be guessed. Probably a second or two. But in those moments the Gabon of 1.7 billion years ago must suddenly have been a very hot place. Elementary creatures must have swum about, figuratively screaming from the scorchings of hell.

Since in order to have a self-sustaining chain reaction, there must be a total absence of neutron absorbers such as cadmium and others, this happening had such total improbability as the AEC was wont to claim for the blowing up of a commercial power reactor. Yet it happened. When one thinks of probabilities, we as living things share an improbability as great as any other imaginable (the vast improbability of life itself), and it ill-behooves us to deny even to our part of the universe any peculiar and unforeseen combination of events.

After World War II, the American talent for the tolerance of nervous strain impelled us in a rather extraordinary way to continue the wartime extension of the nuclear phenomenon rather than to focus on civilian use. Thus, instead of building nuclear plants for producing electric power, as the British did, we thought immediately of nuclear powered submarines, and in January 1954 we launched the *U.S.S. Nautilus.** Six months later it was the Russians who built a small nuclear station for civilian power, the first of its kind in the world. And in October 1956 Great Britain put Calder Hall into action, the first full-scale plant. It was not until 1958 that the United States built its first civilian power plant at Shippingsport, Pennsylvania. The AEC could not seem to get advanced ideas untracked from schemes of achieving military superiority. (This was in spite of a hearty and prolonged fight in 1946 that saw Chet Holifield and others of the newly formed Congressional Joint Committee on Atomic Energy win the battle for civilian control of the AEC and its great national laboratories.)

The little breeder experiment I was familiar with in 1951 became, apparently, the basis for the liquid-sodium cooled breeder on the *U.S.S. Sea Wolf,* launched in 1956; and today we are still philosophizing about large breeder reactors for the production of electric power, after Britain, France, and the USSR have all long since gone on stream with them.

What we did next on a large scale in nuclear energy was also typically American: We came out with a sort of Model T power generator—the light-water reactor (LWR), so named to distinguish it from the heavy water or deuterium

---

*Although the *Nautilus* and *Sea Wolf* are commonly ascribed to the noble insistence of Admiral Hyman Rickover, the truth is that (aside from Rickover) both the Navy and the Department of Defense were so afraid of using fully enriched uranium in a submarine engine that the AEC had to pay the bill.

oxide model developed in Canada. Like the DC-3 airplane, the LWR nearly swept the world market. It was cheap, even rather tacky, and probably dangerous in comparison with other reactors, like a Saturday-night-special pistol. But it worked more often than not, and there were two large and energetic American companies to make and sell two different versions of it: Westinghouse the pressurized-water and General Electric the boiling-water system.

What exactly are we talking about? In the first generation of nuclear reactors, where the flow of neutrons is heavily moderated, so that the main source of energy is the breakup of heavy fissionable atoms struck by relatively slow rather than by fast neutrons, the heat is absorbed in a working fluid such as water or carbon dioxide or helium and normally transferred to a boiler which drives a steam turbine. From the boiler on, the nuclear power plant is the same as an ordinary plant running on coal or petroleum, and the thermodynamic efficiency is in the same ball park.

In the light-water reactors the design requires a slightly enriched uranium fuel (that is, a mixture of about 97 percent uranium-238 and 3 percent uranium-235). Normally the slow neutron system would use up the uranium-235 and convert part of the uranium-238 to plutonium-239, which is fissionable. Under the usual conditions of the light-water reactors, however, the efficiency is appallingly low, based on the uranium, and very little of the uranium-238 is converted to plutonium, while the plutonium that is produced for the most part escapes fission. That even with such tiny efficiencies we are able to come out with large power plants on the order of 1,000 megawatts or more is because of the incredibly high conversion factor of mass to energy. In the Nagasaki plutonium bomb ("Fat Man") the amount of mass converted to energy was 1 gram—one-third the weight of a penny.

The way we enrich uranium is by operating miles upon miles of diffusion cells, in which (because it is a little lighter) uranium-235 diffuses faster than uranium-238. It is seldom realized that the three different diffusion plants (at Oak Ridge, Tennessee; Paducah, Kentucky; and Portsmouth, Ohio) are themselves energy hogs. They use at least 6,000 megawatts of power, which is 1.5 percent of the total electric power in the country, for the most part furnished by TVA generators operating on strip-mined Appalachian coal. We begin to see emerging what was shrugged off as a "sick joke" by the AEC in the last decade. With the recent unbelievable amount of down time, repair jobs, and unscheduled shut downs, the average percentage of on-stream time of the total of some 40 to 50 nuclear power reactors in this country (practically all LWRs) was 61.9 percent in 1973 and at the darkest month of the energy crisis, January 1974, it was even worse: Nuclear power plants were operating only 47 percent of the time. Since even when running at design capacity of 80 percent, these reactors would furnish only about 4 percent of all the electric power used in this country (less than the total amount of energy the United States gets by burning firewood) it is possible that we are actually putting more total power into atomic plants and fuels than we are getting out of them. This is the sick joke, but it can no longer be tittered at or shrugged off.

It is a symptom of something so wrong about our society that it is a dozen times more frightening than the scares dreamed up by the Union of Concerned Scientists, the Friends of the Earth, and a dozen other groups who are hypnotized by the aura of Hiroshima that surrounds every American reactor. One fact that makes it more rather than less disturbing is that a large proportion of the breakdowns are occurring in the steam side, where both nuclear and conventional power plants are similar. As the recently dismissed Milton Shaw, former head of AEC Development and Safety,* said, "Basically the hardware industry in this country isn't in good health." Under these circumstances, it is difficult to agree with Chet Holifield's urging that nuclear plants be "turned out like automobiles," since in 1971, for example, the car manufacturers had to recall more vehicles than they produced (8.8 million compared with 8.6 million).

Among the "unscheduled outage" problems (the AEC is as fond of euphemisms as it is of acronyms) are valves that simply don't work; and it doesn't seem to matter which of the 10 major valve manufacturers in the United States the valves came from. This problem, like others, has ominously accelerated. During the late 1960s the AEC would find 2 defective valves per plant per year. In 1972 the average had climbed to over 8 per plant, and today the figures are apparently classified, which certainly does not mean a decrease.

Milton Shaw used to point to the fact that the Navy has the power to impose standards on manufacturers who make parts. Until the AEC (or its 1975 version the Nuclear Regulatory Commission) gets such a power, Milton suggests that policing the industry with routine inspection is "like pushing a brick around with a wet noodle."

Some of the troubles seem to be associated with mistakes that could only be made by men who are drunk or drugged or so absent-minded that they don't belong to the world of the late twentieth century. Control rods (rods that are pushed into the reactor pile to moderate the rate of the chain reactions and are thus designed chemically to provide a very precise amount of neutron-absorbing capacity) were found with the components dangerously assembled upside down. A mysterious vibrator problem developed with General Electric boiling-water reactors that occupied the full time of many trouble-shooting crews. While a crew had the massive head from the Vermont Yankee reactor removed, a local technician accidently pulled out 2 control rods at the same time. This is like starting a fire when you are inside repairing the fireplace, and the AEC promptly fined Vermont Yankee $15,000 for this diddle. The technician confessed he simply didn't know why he had done such a foolish thing. So frequent are these diddles (such as the one at Hanford that allowed the escape of a large amount of plutonium from a tank) that some people are convinced that making our Faustian pact was a mistake because the Devil is now busy at work confusing the souls of the faithful.

---

*Milton is a hard-boiled engineer of the type of Lockheed's "Kelly" Johnson of the "Skonkworks," but Dr. Dixie Lee Ray, then AEC head, found that he was too abrasive to talk with tender souls like the Harvard and MIT professors of the Union of Concerned Scientists and with Ralph Nader.

One example of the many atomic lemons is the Millstone Point Power Station owned by Northeast Utilities. This one doesn't seem to want to work at all. Certain key parts were defective when installed, but the replacement parts also promptly failed. This can be discouraging. A steam valve blew at the Virginia Electric Power Company plant, killing 2 men. (It had nothing to do with nuclear power.) Another steam line ruptured at the Florida Power and Light Company, again traced to an engineering fabrication failure. Operating licenses of 6 reactors are restricted because of fuel problems.

It is all too easy to go on with an index of horrors, but most of the same kind of accidents are happening at conventional plants (and indeed, as we shall see later, the safety record in terms of fatalities and injuries is much better in the nuclear plants). What I am complaining about is not nuclear technology but the degradation of American technology and craftsmanship in general. If one lives or works in the Chicago area, one will be impressed by the fact that everything in fact seems to be coming up roses. The state of Illinois through the great Commonwealth Edison utility, had more operating nuclear power reactors (7) in 1973 than any other, and an incredible 25 percent of the Chicago electric load is furnished by atomic fission. The Commonwealth Edison people are quite pleased even with an on-stream time in the 50 percent range, since they are in an area of high sulfur coal and expensive petroleum fuel and figure they save 62 percent in operating costs compared with conventional fossil-fueled plants.

But even for optimists such as Commonwealth Edison, who would like to put more fissionable atoms to work, there is, as for everybody else, the exasperating problem of delays.

THE GREAT AMERICAN STALL

If poor workmanship and sloppy operators have become a dismal instance of some sort of fundamental malaise in our technological society, the delay problem is even more disheartening: It shows a body-technical afflicted with all manner of arthritis and phlebitis and atherosclerosis; it cannot move without creaking and groaning and whining for more money.

Of 98 planned reactors 70 are up to 5 1/2 years behind schedule. According to a survey carried out by the Atomic Industrial Forum, one can expect a reactor to be delivered ready to go, within 4 years of placing the order—in Japan. Here is a frantically crowded little island nation whose memory of past atomic events are not pleasant ones, but it is likely under present circumstances to have even an advanced breeder reactor before our great luxurious land, where the customer is lucky to get a delivery of a Model-T light-water reactor in less than 10 years. How can we reduce the constipation, or are we really serious about the whole thing?

Much of the delay is caused by lawyers, and here it is not difficult to identify the imps of the cloven hoof. The modifications imposed by licensing requirements arising from unreasonable local governmental authorities and by the innumerable and lawsuit-loving hordes of environmentalists represent the happy hunting grounds for lawyers, and delay is for the legal mind not an abomination but a way of life. The problem of siting, which means that your reactor design depends upon where you put the reactor, is a sticky one and has inspired some experts to suggest a siting bank; that is, a file of sites previously approved with standard requirements, so that the customer does not need to go through the agony of finding that his Old Southern Comfort Power Station is located over an earthquake fault or that the site is the only one in the whole world where the roseate pileated wood warbler likes to nest.

Other causes of the stalled atomic assembly line include late delivery of components and materials; a shortage of craft labor and the shockingly puny productivity of this labor; and perhaps more fundamentally than these, a shortage of engineers. (We shall review in a later chapter this theme that runs like a bone-destroying cancer throughout the skeleton of modern energy technology.)

Without doubt, design standardization would help. If one had a Model-T LWR, of any color providing it is black, it would please Westinghouse and General Electric no end, but it might also saddle the country with a thousand obsolete reactors that would use up the available ore in a few years and call for immense extension of the power-gobbling enrichment plants.

IN THE FOG, SOME HOPEFUL SIGNS

Of all the streamlining strategies recently proposed, however, it must be admitted that Westinghouse, along with its partner Tenneco (which has some shipbuilding experience), has come up with the boldest and at the same time the most reasonable idea.* If the goal is to cut production costs and license delays, one should build reactors—standardized, but not frozen in design forever—in a factory, coming up with a nuclear plant too large to be shipped by land but readily shipped by water and in fact located in water.

The Offshore Power Systems Corporation (the merger of Westinghouse and Tenneco) plans to build at least 16 floating power plants in a highly specialized factory in Jacksonville, Florida. Upon completion they will be towed down the St. Johns River and thence to ocean sites, where they will be located just within the 3-mile limit. Protection against high winds, 50-foot waves and the accidental impacts from tankers will be provided by massive breakwaters, the construction of which, along with the conducting cables, will be the responsibility of the purchasing utility, such as Public Service Electric and Gas Company of New Jersey, which has contracted for 4 1,150-megawatt units, costing $375 million each, to be moved near Atlantic City by 1980. Breakwaters cannot be allowed to float but must be anchored in firm rock structure, which on the Atlantic coast is not a formidable chore because of the great breadth of the eastern outer continental shelf. The 3-mile limit for the location is primarily based on the fact that the Price-Anderson Act (which in the case of nuclear accidents would limit

*I trust that by the time this book gets in print, the notion will not have been squashed by some marine environmentalists' lawsuit or paralzyed by stagflation. In fact, since writing this, Tenneco has retired from the venture, and the money for the off-New Jersey project may or may not be available.

the liability of private insurers and the government to a total of $560 million) applies only to accidents occurring within the United States.

Offshore Power Systems Corporation is interested in floating nuclear plants (FNP's) not only off the Atlantic Coast but in locations on the Great Lakes, coastal areas abroad, and even mooring points in the Mississippi River, near Baton Rouge, for example. The standard assembly line FNP would be 400 feet square, have a 32-foot draft, rise 177 feet above the water line, and bear a displacement of 160,000 tons. Each FNP would have a 4-loop pressurized water reactor (naturally, since Westinghouse makes them). It would contain quarters for 112 operating personnel—a crew roughly the same as that of a nuclear submarine.

The manufacturing time per unit is expected to be only 26 months by the time the eighth unit is assembled, which compares with about 80 months now required to build a custom-designed plant of the same power rating. This sounds fine, as far as cutting delays is concerned, but, as might be expected, the whole notion is repugnant to the Union of Concerned Scientists, who point out that it's bad enough if an atomic plant melts down on land, but it's worse off-shore, because then you poison the whole ocean with stuff like strontium-90.

OTHER ATOMS, OTHER COOLANTS

Before we return to what has become the major vortex of argument about nuclear power plants (their supposed dire threat to the environment), we have a few technical roads to travel, and one of them involves the discussion of a power plant which bids fair to overtake the Model-T LWRs as the modern Chevrolet overtook the Model-A Ford automobile. Going back to acronyms, this is the H T G R, or high-temperature, gas-cooled reactor. If we are optimistic enough to assume that commercial development will escape the tentacles of sloth and incompetence that has held the LWRs in thrall, this is perhaps America's most promising contribution to nuclear power.

Reactors cooled by gas were actually operating in Great Britain commercially before the United States had got around to building any industrial-scale units whatever, but the modified Calder-Hall design, the Magnox, used by the British until the 1960s, operated on natural (nonenriched) uranium, which meant that it could not attain high temperatures and was therefore comparatively inefficient at the steam end. The British had buoyant hopes for their AGR (advanced gas-cooled reactor) which operated on enriched uranium, and thus attained high temperatures, and was cooled with carbon dioxide. What they had not realized was the terrifying corrosiveness of very hot carbon dioxide. By 1971 the prototype plant at Dungeness was already 4 years behind schedule and carbon dioxide was eating up component parts of 9 percent chrome steel like an elephant stripping trees. Moreover, zinc from galvanized wire was diffusing into the stainless-steel tubes of the heat exchanges, making them as brittle as dried bamboo. Because of such griefs after enormous overruns in costs—as much as $2 billion, or 70 percent more than the country invested in the supersonic Concorde airplane—

Britain still does not have a viable replacement for the Magnox.

At the same time, almost unnoticed and unheralded in this country, the HTGR experimental facility developed by General Dynamics (primarily an aircraft manufacturer always on the point of going broke) was demonstrating very fascinating performance properties. The subsidiary, General Atomic, that developed the unit was sold to Gulf Oil, then Royal Dutch/Shell bought in.

What the developers were prescient enough to realize was that if you were going to use a gas coolant the best choice, because of chemical inertness and peculiar advantages in heat transfer, was helium. From the standpoint of the hard-boiled utility manager, the primary selling point is that the efficiency of the General Atomic HTGR is about 40 percent, compared with 32 percent for the LWR. This does not express the full superiority of the hot, gas-cooled system, for it puts out heat at a greater power level. Power being the rate of energy delivery, this means that you get more kilowatt-hours for your dollars' worth of fuel—as much as 18 percent more electricity per day. The gas outlet temperature is around 1,400 degrees Fahrenheit, more than twice the 650 degrees Fahrenheit light-water coolant temperature. It is true that the HTGR operates on highly enriched uranium (nearly weapons-grade: 93 percent uranium-235 plus thorium) but the efficiency of use is very satisfactory.

This new glamour toy has other extremely crucial advantages. Because of the high temperature and noncorrosiveness of the helium outlet gas, it probably can be used directly to drive a gas turbine rather than heating up a boiler for a steam turbine. If the spent helium from this can be cooled sufficiently in air coolers before recycling to the reactor, one has the perfect desert power plant: No water at all is needed. This is of compelling interest in regions like Southern California, where the recently formed Coastal Land Committee has made it very tough to expand old nuclear plants, such as San Onofre, or to build new ones that are located near tidewater.

General Atomic signed an agreement with the powerful utility complex, American Electric Power System, to deliver a 1,500-megawatt plant. This is suddenly a hot ticket. Utilities from Chesapeake Bay to San Diego have bought one or more units and the foreign market is interested.

One more extraordinary plus is that the Union of Concerned Scientists and other safety and environmental watchdogs think the HTGR is as dependable as an old water mill compared with their favorite objects of hate, the light-water reactor and the liquid-metal-cooled breeder. All in all, in the long run, the HTGR may prove a better answer to American energy shortages than the breeder, which we must now discuss.

HOW TO MAKE A PERPETUAL MOTION MACHINE

Theoretically the breeder concept results in more available energy being stored in the fission process than energy taken out of the process in the form of heat. We need not worry about conservation laws, since in Einstein's world of the interconvertibility of mass and energy, no laws are broken, but in the breeding system, energy that would otherwise stagnate for eternity is made accessible for immediate use. Moreover, the breeder as an actual construction of hardware does not live up to its theoretical reputation (which is always the case, since dreams on paper are never realized in material form because of a sort of sludge factor or a second law of practically everything). In the classical breeder, the load is 80 percent uranium-238 and 20 percent plutonium (both of them all too available as waste products of standard nonbreeding reactors and uranium-238 additionally stockpiled as tailings from enrichment plants producing uranium-235). In the breeding process neutrons from the splitting of plutonium-239 convert uranium-238 to additional plutonium-239. You get more plutonium atoms formed than you split. How can you lose?

The breeding process is not all cake and jam. It represents an entirely different reactor regime and one that is as close to an incipient bomb as we can safely come. Breeders are nearly all fast reactors, and in nuclear physics this has a very special meaning. In conventional nuclear plants, control rods or moderators are used to slow down the average flux of neutrons to a level where only fissionable materials such as uranium-235 or plutonium-239 are affected by neutron hits. But if you are going to add a neutron to a merely fertile, not fissionable atom such as uranium-238 to produce the fissionable plutonium-239, you have to hit it hard with a fast neutron. A fast reactor refers therefore not to the reactor's speed but to the fact that it is not moderating fast neutrons but using them.*

In order to get the heat efficiently out of the breeder reactor fast enough, one has to resort to highly pressurized gas or to liquid metals, such as liquid sodium. The United States has chosen the latter expedient, so our number one breeder candidate is called LMFBR (liquid-metal-cooled, fast breeder reactor). It is in a hell of a mess, drowned in money but battered by hate mail. (Ralph Nader calls it "maniacal.") And getting nowhere fast. The incentive nevertheless is considerable in view of the fact that the breeder uses from 60 to 70 percent of the available uranium, compared to 2 percent burn up in conventional reactors, thus saving nearly 2 million tons of uranium ore over the course of 50 years.

In 1973 Great Britain and France started up prototype breeders, while the USSR, starting in 1972 built 2 breeders. One of them at Sheschenko on the northeast shore of the Caspian Sea was the first large fast-breeder to achieve a self-sustaining nuclear reaction, and it definitely re-established Russia's primacy in the nuclear art. It is now at work producing desalted water from the Caspian.

*Another kind of breeding process, but one which is not so efficient involves a moderated thermal reactor (the opposite of fast reactor) in which thorium-232 is converted to uranium-233, which is fissionable, like uranium-235. Because this involves slow neutrons, it produces energy at a slower pace, but in the long run it may prevail, because of the greater availability of thorium compared with uranium ore. Still another possible breeder model is the molten salt reactor in which the uranium and plutonium fuels are in the form of liquid salts.

It appears that both West Germany and Japan will probably also beat the United States in getting a large breeder on line. West Germany (with some help from Belgium and Holland) and Japan, with the Monju, will have 300-megawatt plants—hardly prototypes.

The British and French designs call for a tank or pool in which the liquid sodium coolant circuit and the heat exchanger (more liquid sodium) are contained within the reactor vessel, protected by massive steel and concrete. On the other hand, the United States, West Germany, and Japan will rely on a loop design, in which hot sodium coolant is exchanged outside the reaction vessel. Russia is trying both types.

Progressing at the pace of an old, sick elephant, the United States plans first to try out various breeder components in a so-called Fast Flux Test Facility at Hanford, Washington, then to build a demonstration plant at Oak Ridge, which may come on stream in 1985—at least 10 years later than the European and Japanese breeders.

There is something maniacal about our breeder program, it is true, but not in the sense that Ralph Nader meant. The whole project seems to have been designed by a committee of tired and goofy giant sloths.

The so-called Demo 1, the LMFBR, programmed for Oak Ridge, was subjected to the professional criticism of Professor Hans Bethe of Cornell and his panel representing the greatest nuclear scientists in this country. They concluded at once that, whereas an economic breeder must be able to double its plutonium content in less than 10 years, Demo 1 would not replenish itself in less than 60 years. Demo 1, the panel reported, "was not a useful breeder at all." (This conclusion appeared in the record draft of the Bethe report, but was deleted by the AEC from the final published document.)

At the time of writing it appears likely that, although it might be better sense to spend money on perfecting the efficient and proven General Atomic's HTGR, perhaps with the idea of converting it later to a breeder by pressurizing the helium coolant, the AEC is hypnotized by the liquid-sodium-heat-transfer system and may be forced in the end to license from the Europeans. Requests to the British and French to allow us to test experimental components in their breeders have met with icy refusal, although the Russians have not given us an unqualified nyet. It would be high and bitter irony if in the end we had to buy breeder know-how from the Japanese.

BRINGING ENRICHMENT UP TO DATE

If we cannot develop a sensible breeder program (and it is by no means certain that our international competitors are going to make the breeder work effectively enough to justify the grave risks in plant safety), one road to improvement of the over-all economics of fission energy is to lower the cost of uranium-235 for feeding to very efficient reactors such as the General Atomic's HTGR. As we have noted, our 3 huge diffusion plants are 30-year-old power-slurping hogs, gulping nearly as much energy as we expect to get out of the refined product. There are other enrichment processes that look better. Exploration of these processes or even of the diffusion process itself is a popular activity in Europe, since nobody wants to be either confined to a reactor that uses natural uranium or to come with hat in hand to the United States to beg for increasingly overpriced uranium-235.

There is a curious and ominous exception to this. Both India and Argentina preferred to buy reactors—India from Canada and Argentina from West Germany —that operate on natural uranium.* The obvious reason is that natural uranium produces plutonium in a form ideally suited for making a bomb, while the reactors using enriched fuel wind up with plutonium in an isotopic mixture that causes a lot of trouble for bomb makers. One specific disadvantage is that more plutonium-240 is produced as an impurity from enriched fuel. This is fissionable, in fact too fissionable, for it tends to give premature detonations. Basement nuclear bomb makers would find themselves in about the same dilemma as early terrorists who fooled around with pure nitroglycerine: They blew themselves up more frequently than they did their enemies. India's excuse that she wants to use atomic explosives along the line of our Project Ploughshare—for earth moving and the like—is possibly the most disingenuous international statement ever made. Argentina, being more frankly ferocious, does not pretend it is going to explode beneficent tunnels through the Andes. This method of obtaining weapons-grade plutonium is expensive but easier, I suppose, than stealing.

The French have apparently decided to go with an improved diffusion process and have formed a cartel with Belgium, Italy, Spain, and Sweden (Eurodif) to build a large plant at Pierrelotte in the southeast of France. The immediate European competition is the gas centrifugal process, which depends on the fact that when uranium isotopes in the form of the hexafluorides are spun at extremely high speeds, the heavier portion (uranium-238) tends toward the outside of the centrifugal fans.

The Urenco cartel consists of British, Germans, and Dutch, and a prototype plant will be located in Holland.

In our country the enrichment situation is somewhat muddled by the fact that in new process development, especially in centrifuging, the field has been thrown open to private design and construction as well as operation. Two whale-size teams were at one time considering enrichment programs, one composed of General Electric and the Exxon Nuclear Company, and the other, called Enrichment Associates, Inc., consisting of Bechtel, Union Carbide, and Westinghouse. (Later these fell apart because of the horrible inflation of hardware and the indefinite length of pay-out.) If stagflation doesn't permanently delay all such programs, the AEC† estimated the potential foreign exchange from enrichment to be between $50 and $70 billion and that out of 12 new separation plants it recommended for U.S. design by A.D. 2000, actually 7 would be for foreign customers. Dr. Ray thought that we had something that Urenco didn't know

*Brazil became a German customer quite recently.
†Now the Nuclear Regulatory Commission.

about and that whereas a Urenco enrichment plant would need hundreds of thousands of centrifuges, we would only need tens of thousands.

Another process, commonly believed to have been invented by E. W. Becker, et alia in West Germany in the mid-1950s, uses a high-speed nozzle to squirt uranium hexafluoride into a low-pressure tank. The nozzle is aimed at a small paring tube on the opposite side which captures the central portion of the jet stream, which is enriched in uranium-238, since the lighter isotope tends to stray to the outside. This process is in use in a sizable plant in Durban, South Africa, where there is a lot of coal around. This is the only kind of situation in which the nozzle separator could survive even temporarily because, unlike the centrifugal method which is fairly modest in power requirement, the Becker process apparently gobbles up about 2 1/2 times as much electricity as the prodigal American diffusion plant.

We save, as usual, the most glamorous process for last. This involves differential stimulation of the uranium isotopes by means of a finely tuned beam, emitted by so-called dye lasers—dye solutions that are capable of narrowing a laser beam to a very small range of frequencies. The uranium-235 is preferentially excited, then ionized by a second beam system so that it can be separated as the hexafluoride by a simple chemical reaction or even by an electrostatic precipitator. The calculated efficiency is high and power consumption so low that this enrichment system might revolutionize the economics of atomic power; for example, it might make the breeder reactor unnecessary for several centuries. A variant of the laser technique would greatly lower the cost of heavy water, so that the Canadian heavy-water moderated reactor might suddenly become more than competitive.

There is an international mystery of rather somber implications involved in the laser enrichment process. In October 1973 Exxon Nuclear, Inc., revealed that a joint research venture with Avco Everett Research Laboratories had succeeded in enriching small amounts of uranium by the laser technique and it noted that two Israeli scientists appeared to have duplicated this feat, judging by a patent taken out in the name of I. Nebenzahl. The part of the patent abstract that chilled the weapons establishment world-wide was the description of a laser experiment reporting that in a period of 24 hours, the manipulation had resulted in a "yield of 7 grams of 235 U of 60 percent purity." A sophisticated designer would need less than 60 kilograms of 60 percent uranium-235 to make a powerful fission bomb. This tantalizing laser-enrichment episode has compounded the mystery (at the date of writing in the winter of 1975) of whether Israel is, or even wants to be, a nuclear power. They don't need the Nebenzahl patent to join the club. Israel's reactor at Dimona, built by the French in the mid-1960s, surely has produced enough platonium by now for a bomb or two.

TOO DANGEROUS?

Senator Domenici of New Mexico has made a profound observation: If the first form in which gasoline was introduced into the world had been napalm, we would still be riding around in horse-drawn carriages. As previously noted, the aura of Hiroshima hovers over every nuclear power plant. Because of our supposed sins at Hiroshima and Nagasaki, we have raised 2 generations who regard the splitting of the atom as a simple extension of unique sin and whenever a nuclear power plant is erected, the Puritans of these generations see over the city around it the mushroom-shaped cloud.

I repeat, the fact is that experience with nuclear power plants to date shows that there have been far fewer fatalities and injuries per megawatt-hour produced than in conventional power plants, and those accidents occurring in nuclear power plants have almost without exception involved that part of the train of energy that is common to any plant that generates steam to run a turbine; in other words, the overwhelming majority of accidents in nuclear power plants have nothing to do with the fact that nuclear fission is involved.

The National Safety Council each year presents an award for the best safety record. This award has been won every year since 1962 by the AEC and its prime contractors, representing over 100,000 workers. But this does not seem to impress Ralph Nader.

Speaking quite personally, as an author of books on air and water pollution and various other pollutions,* I believe that the Union of Concerned Scientists, Ralph Nader, Senator Mike Gravel of Alaska, Barry Commoner, Margaret Mead, and other outstanding anti-nuclear-power leaders are seriously endangering the future health of the country.

Take the matter of coal versus nuclear energy. Is it generally known that a large part of the so-called universal background radiation that one measures and discounts in the evaluation of radioactive hazards is due to the burning of coal? In other words, that we now receive more radioactive damage from the 100 million pounds of radium, uranium, thorium, and the like spewed into the world's atmosphere from the burning of the (roughly) 3 billion tons of coal used every year than from any other radioactive source? In addition we have to cope with some 200 million pounds of sulfur oxides as well as hosts of carcinogenic and otherwise toxic hydrocarbons. The American share of the pollution from coal has been conservatively estimated to cause directly or indirectly about 19,000 deaths per year. This is equivalent to a rate of 6 reactor catastrophes per year, using the so-called Wash 740 table, beloved of atomic-energy-phobes, which describes the dire results of a hypothetical release of instantaneous fission energy that has since been shown to be impossible.

There is a singularly cogent point that has too seldom been stressed in comparing pollution from the burning of fossil fuels with radioactive pollutants: We know much more about the medical effects of radioactivity than we do about the medical effects of auto emissions and of power plant effluents. Professor Hannes Alfven's portentous statement that the nuclear power industry relies on a level of perfection in which "no acts of God are permitted" is romantic drivel.

*See *The Breath of Life* (1965); *Death of the Sweet Waters* (1966); and *The Deadly Feast of Life* (1971).

Nuclear power plants are designed to be lightningproof, earthquakeproof, tornadoproof. It is precisely the opposite case. Unfortunately these plants are not proof against acts of man.

Although a large percentage of the caveats of the atom-phobes have been addressed to the supposed deficiencies in the emergency cooling systems of light-water reactors, raising the specter of a reactor melting in place and distributing its contents like an exploding witch's caldron,* the more sophisticated criers of doom now point to the terrible toxicity of plutonium, not to the danger of its exploding uncontrollably but of it leaking into air or water unmanageably.

If there were any evidence that such leaks occurred with any frequency, this propaganda would be justified. Plutonium is indeed a strange substance. As it lies there in the very small proportions occurring in wastes from a reactor, it is harmless. You could even handle a ball of it without risk, if you had a good gas mask. Its alpha radiation cannot penetrate the skin of even a thin coat of paint. Once, however, it is ingested orally or by breathing, it is by far the most poisonous material known, perhaps 100,000 times more toxic than cobra venom and 10,000 times worse than nerve gas. It forms immediate cancer in the lung and the bone tissue.

From the standpoint of cost-effectiveness and simplicity the use of the nerve gases will probably be pursued by terrorists before plutonium. A quart of VX costs about $5 to prepare and with proper apportioning will kill several million human beings. It doesn't have to be breathed. Merely a drop of the heavy oil on a man's skin will kill him before he becomes conscious of any pain.

Twenty years ago in a consulting capacity under secret clearance I visited a nerve gas factory in Tennessee and with tedious formalities learned the formula and the astonishingly simple processes associated with making it. Since that time, however, the United States and the United Kingdom have declassified the formula for VX and patents disclosing in every detail its manufacture were released by the British government. (They tried subsequently to recall the patents, but it was too late.)

Although the presently favored technique of handling VX is the binary method, whereby 2 otherwise harmless constituents are mixed to deliver the active toxin, the now widely diffused information about the binary system plays even more into the hands of the terrorist. It is like handing him a canister of gasoline and a box of matches.

The various isotopes of plutonium (plutonium-239, plutonium-238, plutonium-240, plutonium-241, and plutonium-242) have different degrees of toxicity and various half-lives, but plutonium-239 is the most common isotope, the most useful, and the most dangerous. The innocuous plutonium-238 is being used by thousands of people to power cardiac-assist devices (pace makers). For very small amounts of ingested plutonium-239 the only therapeutic agent known is the

*In AEC circles this is known as the China syndrome. The molten reactor burns a hole down through the earth, emerging in the confines of the Forbidden City in Peking.

so-called chelating reactant, diethylene triaminepenta-acetic acid (DTPA) which forms a complex with the heavy element that is eliminated in the urine. Jack rabbits near the Nevada Test Site have accumulated plutonium in their bones equivalent to 5 times the concentration of plutonium in the soil where they live. On the other hand, none of the residents studied at Palomeres, Spain, where plutonium was dispersed following the crash of a U.S. bomber, showed any detectable lung burden or significant amounts of plutonium in the urine, even though the ground was highly contaminated.

DISPOSAL PROBLEMS

Plutonium-239 has a half-life of 24,500 years, hence the basic problem in disposal or management of atomic power wastes is to insure that wherever the wastes are put they do not hang around to contaminate the creatures of a more naïve species or generation than our own, since there is considerable pessimism about the endurance of man, at least in his present political form for another 50,000 years. Perhaps the most ingenious of the proposals is to sink the wastes in canisters in the mile-deep Antarctic or Greenland ice, allowing them through their own heat emission to melt their way slowly down to bedrock. Another still more positive though very expensive means of atomic garbage disposal is to shoot the wastes in rockets into the sun. At one time, salt domes seemed to be the answer, but they are out of fashion because of leakage problems and a paucity of salt domes at appropriate locations and of sufficient size.

Favored at present is what is known as the mausoleum system. This means that you maintain the wastes in carefully guarded storehouses until, in effect, you can think of something to do with them. It is purely a holding action, as temporary as a championship football team. Hopefully the reactors of the future will be able to recycle all these wastes, so that at least the mausoleum storage doesn't take up an inordinate amount of parkland area.

THEFT AND SABOTAGE

Perhaps the biggest scare the AEC ever had was on November 11, 1972, when three skyjackers threatened to bomb the Oak Ridge reactors. The whole plant was shut down and evacuated.

When we reach (if we ever do) the age of breeders, or even if we go for plutonium-239 recycle for slower reactors, we are going to have a lot of plutonium around: in storage, in transit, in solution as the nitrate salt, and, of course, in weapons, the theft of which is not inconceivable.

The fact is that, in a sense, every reactor is a kind of breeder, in that it produces plutonium, at least part of which splits to give fast neutrons which will in turn convert fertile material such as uranium-238 back into more plutonium. The average thermal reactor can be looked at as an atrociously designed breeder, but the point is that it is always producing plutonium-239, which is the bomb maker's delight.

Any country that has a power reactor automatically has a source of plutonium, and is thus a potential bomb maker. When we give Egypt or Iran or Israel a thermal reactor we are giving them the makings of an atomic bomb.

What Ted Taylor and others have recently emphasized* is that one does not need to be even a small nation to develop a bomb. A gang of terrorists can steal the ingredients (plutonium nitrate, for example) and, with information available in any well-stocked public library, can put together something that could topple over the World Trade Building. Even a bomb that professionals would regard as a fizzle is horribly destructive. As Taylor has pointed out, nobody that set out seriously to make an atomic fission bomb has ever failed. When Taylor himself was designing small tactical bombs that could be shot out of a gun to destroy a brigade or so of troops, Enrico Fermi congratulated him on one that finally failed to go off. "Now you're making progress," said the great physicist.

Moreover, one can threaten to poison the inhabitants of a whole city by dumping plutonium in the water supply. One could kill 20,000 people by introducing a mere whiff of plutonium into the air-conditioning system of a great office building. When you can steal something like plutonium-239, the mutations and variations of terrorism are almost infinite. And so are the terrorists: the Ulster Freedom Fighters, the IRA, Black September, Al Fatah, the Tupamaros, the Japanese Red Army, and others, adding up to 50 known terrorist groups in the world (5 in North America, 5 in Latin America, 5 in Europe, 10 in the Middle East, and some 25 others scattered around the world). Such groups have shown no compunction in putting plastic bombs in baby carriages or of indiscriminately shooting everybody in sight at a civilian airport or of blowing the legs off of hundreds in a crowded pub. With a fizzle dropped from a private airplane they could kill 100,000 people at a soccer match.

There is really no defense against organized terrorism. That such groups have no superstition about playing around with radioactive gimmicks is demonstrated by the little publicized attempt of a group in Austria to poison everybody in a railroad car with radioactive iodine.

What is the most vulnerable link in the chain of atomic-reactor technology? Possibly the movement of spent fuel elements to the reprocessing plants. Here there is temporary storage of plutonium which requires, as Sam Fox has pointed out, a "priesthood" of storage maintenance people. Even more sensitive are plants that are producing bomb-grade materials. In a recent survey of the security arrangements of such places, the General Accounting Office found no priests; instead, the agency found a group of Keystone Kops who were armed with 38s that they had never been instructed on how to use. (One man did not even know how to manipulate the safety adjustment.) Whereas sensitive atomic materials in the Soviet Union are shipped only with a sophisticated military guard, we casually send it through the mails or in random truck and airplane shipments.

In the thefts of fissionable and toxic material for organized terroristic pur-

*See especially John McPhee's brilliant reporting job, *The Curve of Binding Energy*, containing information mainly obtained from Ted Taylor, master fission bomb designer.

poses, one must realize that it is not necessarily the terrorists who will do the stealing. At present, plutonium is worth about the same price, grain for grain, as pure bootleg heroin. When you are up in that money league you attract not merely fanatics but the so-called Mafia. And the Mafia knows how to buy skilled thieves.

All in all, the safeguarding problem is so serious in the kind of political world we live in that I am personally convinced that industrial nuclear energy will never make it big in this generation. The delays, the skyrocketing costs, the hopeless deterioration in craftsmanship, the deep slump in productivity, the growing popular appeal of the unreason of the Henry Kendalls and the Barry Commoners —all these combined with the unthinkable disasters of sabotage and illicit use by both small, fierce countries and large, fierce gangs make fission power suddenly a bad and dangerous investment. As all great challenges are, it was fun while it lasted. But I do not believe we were up to the challenge.

8 Nuclear Fusion—
The Tenuous Dream

Anything constructive in relation to atomic energy must inevitably be novel and immensely interesting.
—INTERNATIONAL CONTROL REPORT ON ATOMIC ENERGY

STARS DO IT

The energy of atomic fusion and the term *plasma* are connected in our minds with the densely mathematical and (even now) mostly classified information concerning the hydrogen bomb. Nuclear physics of this type is about as understandable to the average human being as are ancient Persian dialects. Yet, if one were to talk with an old spirit who had been taking trips around the universe, perhaps one of God's lieutenants, she (or he) would perhaps have to strain her angelic mind to recall that there was any kind of energy other than that resulting from fusion and that there was any kind of matter other than plasma.

At least 99.9 percent of the energy transactions in the universe involve the fusion of hydrogen, and an equally large percentage of the matter of the universe consists of plasma, that is, the matter of the stars, which is mostly hydrogen and helium in the form of ions (i.e., stripped of their electrons) and free electrons at exceedingly high temperatures. The hard, rocky, nonionized matter which makes us feel at home is so rare in cosmic chemistry that a textbook for cosmic children could be quite acceptable (physically, if not morally) if it skipped over the occurrence of earthlike planets and chemical reactions taking place at temperatures of less than, say, 1 million degrees.

On our strange little planet Earth we are absolute slaves to our own star, the sun, unless we can learn to generate energy the way the sun does, unless, that is to say, we can imitate in a small way the awesome behavior of the plasma of the stars.

It turns out that this is a very difficult thing to do. In order to accomplish a burst of fusion we have to use trigger forces that are quite peculiar to small

111

agglomerations of matter on small planets; that is, we had to use our peculiarly provincial fission energy—from splittable isotopes of uranium or plutonium—in order to achieve momentarily the conditions in which the energy of the stars (fusion) could be released. It is by no means certain, but it seems probable that this will always be so; that hydrogen bombs cannot be made to work without a fission explosion as an ignition source.* Actually there is some comfort to be had from this, since it means that if all nuclear energy plants were converted from fission to fusion (without explosion), terrorist thieves could not lay their hands on anything destructive enough to constitute any immediate danger to other human beings. As we shall see later, some rather complex sabotage could unloose modest amounts of tritium (a sort of triple-sized hydrogen as deuterium is a double-sized hydrogen), but although tritium is radioactive and slips easily into compounds that normally contain hydrogen, such as water and foods and living matter, it has a half-life of only 12 1/2 years and has no such frightful toxic effects as plutonium-239.

Historically, as might have been expected, the fusion process was first observed in the laboratory in high-energy accelerator beams some years before the fission of uranium-235 by slow neutrons was confirmed.

It is important straightway to make it plain that we cannot use hydrogen itself. It is only the isotopes of hydrogen—deuterium and tritium—that we intend to use, but both of these are available in practically inexhaustible amounts, deuterium from heavy water (deuterium oxide) from the oceans and tritium as a breeder product in a reactor cooled with liquid lithium. The nuclear equations involve the evolution of protons, neutrons, and X-rays.

For the present we will be more than satisfied if we can show a positive gain of energy in the form of heat compared with the energy we have spent in triggering the reaction, purifying the reactants, and building the plant. The heat, mostly from the exceedingly energetic neutrons, is absorbed in a blanket of molten lithium, which is in heat exchange with molten potassium, which in turn is used either as a vapor to drive an electricity-producing turbine or in heat exchange with water to drive a steam turbine. An all-important point is that it is in their contact with the lithium that some of the neutrons change this very light metal into tritium. That is the way to make tritium. Lithium is used up and is therefore not simply an energy absorbent but a crucial partner in the whole process. Happily there is enough lithium on earth to last a million years.

The big question is how do we get the ions of deuterium and tritium to fuse together to give off neutrons and helium ions plus energy? There are two vastly

*In spite of the expostulations of Professor Edward Teller, main inventor of the hydrogen bomb, the design of this ignition process is still highly classified. Teller points out, however, that at least 100,000 and probably 1 million people know the secret anyhow, so its formal concealment from the public is quite silly. While all the techniques of making a fission bomb are as available as the recipe for vichyssoise, the hydrogen bomb technology is clutched to the enormous breast of the Department of Defense and what used to be called the Atomic Energy Commission.

different ways, one involving magnetic containment and the other pulsed explosions triggered by laser beams. Both of these are too complex to describe in this book, which is just as well since any reader will have passed to his reward long before either process becomes commercial.*

If fusion plants of the microexplosion type work, we are going to see peak pulse powers of almost inconceivable magnitude. The peak rate of fusion energy production will be at least 10^{18} watts or a million terawatts (a terawatt is a trillion watts). This power (which, to be sure, is intermittent) is a million times greater than the power of all man-made machinery put together and is about ten times greater than the total radiant power of sunlight falling on the entire earth.

There is some disagreement about what the ultimate step in fusion would be, but the exceedingly bright workers at the Lawrence Livermore Laboratory believe that it may be the fusion of ordinary hydrogen with boron to form 3 atoms of helium. This is a peculiar reaction since it is a mixed fusion and fission process in that more atomic particles are produced than are consumed, although the total mass, of course, decreases. It has the tremendous advantage that neither David Brower, Ralph Nader, nor their descendants could throw rocks at it because neither the reactants nor the products have any radioactivity and there are no neutrons to induce secondary radioactivity. The reaction yields only the 3 energetic ions of helium.

In the meantime, however, possibilities that would be exceedingly unpleasing to environmentalists are being investigated. It seems likely that the fusion neutrons can also be used to convert nonfissionable isotopes of uranium or thorium to fissionable isotopes, just as in fission reactors of the breeder type that we discussed in the last chapter. In fact, the neutrons released by microexplosions are energetic enough to release 20 to 50 times as much energy in the form of fissionable uranium or plutonium isotopes as was released in the original fusion reaction. The Lawrence Livermore people believe that such hybrid fusion-fission reactors may make their commercial debut before pure fusion systems become economically realistic.

I sincerely hope this is not so, because there has already been established in the mind of the energy-sensitive public a distinct suspicion of fission processes, especially the breeder, whereas the crucial public sector has not yet been alarmed by the possibilities of electric power from fusion.

These are important things for the scientists to bear in mind. Even multiples of research and development cost do not counterbalance fearfulness and insecurity in the public mind. I would myself feel much more comfortable if we were outresearching the Russian Lebedev Institute in fusion rather than spending so

---

*Since we do know how to make hydrogen bombs, it has been suggested that we set them off regularly in great salt domes half filled with water. The resulting steam could be used to drive turbines (Project Pacer). This is not so crazy as it sounds; but it is still crazy, and it has been dropped.

much of our money on the fission breeder. I must admit that part of my prejudice may be (how shall I put it?) theological. A method of energy production that is used by the whole boundless universe of flaming stars must be more natural than one that depends upon the existence of a few extraordinary heavy atoms infecting like skin cancer the soil of a pretty planet.

9 Wind

It is an ill wind that blows no man profit.
—THOMAS FULLER

In scientific space excursions to date nothing has given us so much feeling of togetherness, of planetary brotherhood as the vast winds of Mars that for a time prevented our getting a clear sneak preview of the surface of this forbidding world. That atmospheric movements of superhurricane velocity can take place when there is scarcely any atmosphere to move seems odd, in fact would be odd were it not for the bizarre topography of the red planet, where gigantic volcanic peaks are rimmed with dead, meandering river beds giving the sun places to radiate with heat and leaving shadows which are colder than Greenland at midnight. On any planet with any atmosphere, the sun will cause winds, but if one could locate a planet surrounded by suns rather than the reverse, the planet would be windless. This is because, in order to produce wind, the sun's heat must be unevenly distributed.

The impenetrable dusty storms that periodically afflict Mars are an example of a centrally important thing about wind. Although its power varies with the density of the atmosphere, it also increases with the cube of the wind's speed; hence the thin, sneaky, fast streamings of gas on our sister planet have power enough to lift huge numbers of stony particles and swirl them across lands as wild and ruined as an iceless Antarctica.

The law that makes it possible for storms to tear at the peaks of Mars, with its tiny veil of an atmosphere, also decrees that the recovery of wind power on earth is more fruitful at high altitudes because the winds blow faster there. At the extreme, in the troposphere, we have the ceaseless jet streams whipping around the earth as much as 7 times faster than those close to the surface; and these winds rule most of the world's weather.

The urge of a mass of air molecules to move together from "here" to "there" is founded on the fact that "there" is less crowded than "here." "There" has been more heated and dispersed by the sun so that the pressure is lower, and all molecules like to go from a place of higher to a place of lower pressure. In some instances the sun acts by a less direct mechanism. Its heat causes water vapor to come off plants (transpiration) and to evaporate from bodies of water, and the heat is thus stored in the atmosphere. This creates a period of suspended storm and sometimes ominous silence until the heat is released by rainfall, and the winds then pick their way nimbly through patches of heat and cold, high and low pressures, dancing sometimes into the hideous contortions known as tornados. This is not the kind of wind the power companies want to imagine.

Luckily there are global wind systems that can be relied upon for steadiness, simply because the earth rotates steadily—the trade winds, the westerlies and the polar easterlies, the equatorial doldrums. In different parts of the globe there are also local wind systems extensive and regular enough to have been given names. There are about 52 such pet winds (some of them with evil reputations), such as the sirocco, the monsoon, the mistral, the foehn, the helm, the transmontana, the simoom, the southerly buster of New South Wales, the Santa Anas of the Los Angeles Basin.

WINDMILL HISTORY

In spite of vague references to the use of windmills in ancient Egypt, the earliest specific manuscripts refer to a Persian millwright in A.D. 644 and to windmills in Seiston, Persia, in A.D. 915. These early machines were true mills, in that they were used to grind grain; but there was a peculiarity about them, to our eyes, in that they had horizontal sails on a vertical axis, a configuration that might seem puzzling to us, but which contains advantages, in that there is no need to rudder the windmill, since it uses winds from all directions without prejudice.

When Genghis Khan's Mongols swept through Persia, contrary to popular belief they did not spend all their time stacking up heads and drinking blood, but through a period of many years they studied what the Persians had to offer. The windmills so impressed the Mongol observers that captive millwrights were taken back to China, where to this day windmills are used mainly to pump water for irrigation.

When windmills appeared in Europe in the eleventh century, the axis was no longer vertical but inclined at an angle of 30 degrees to the horizontal. The Dutch and Danes ultimately brought the axis up to straight horizontal with the vertical sails that we are familiar with. By the seventeenth century the Netherlands had become the world's most industrialized nation through the extensive use of wind power in ships and windmills. The sails gave way, in the course of three centuries, successively to hinged shutters, like venetian blinds, and then to the propeller or air screw.

The first windmill designed to produce electricity was working in Denmark in 1888 not long after electricity was first understood as a power medium. Prior to World War I, Denmark had developed a network of well-designed windmills with a total generating capacity of 100,000 kilowatts. They abandoned an ambitious plan to augment this system in favor of buying electricity at discount rates from Sweden, which had a surplus of hydroelectric power but needed customers to justify its development. The good Danish mills are still working, having run trouble-free for 60 years with virtually no maintenance.

During World War II the Germans, like the observant Mongols, spent much time wondering what they could loot from France—in addition to art treasures. They were strangely fascinated by the Eiffel Tower, not because they considered hauling it back to the fatherland, but because they noticed that the top of the tower is almost continuously swept by strong winds even though Paris is not a particularly windy city. By 1944 Germany had decided to construct a series of extremely high towers with 400-foot diameter propellers* capable of generating 10 to 50 megawatts of electricity each. That, however, was the year that the Third Reich not only ran out of steel but ran out of luck as well.

Following 8 years of very fruitful research after World War II on the Welsh and Cornish coastlines, where wind patterns and seacliffs offer a sort of wind-power utopia, the British got cold feet about windmills and spent their money instead on the premature promise of nuclear fission.

On the other side of the Atlantic Ocean wind power was as natural to the American pioneers as the long rifle. By 1850 the use of windmills in the United States represented about 1.4 billion horsepower-hours of work, the equivalent of burning 11.8 million tons of coal. But by 1876 the use of wind power had been cut in half, for the steam engine, with its fossil fuels, had come to stay.

Nevertheless, in the America of half a century ago, farms all across the United States, but particularly in the Great Plains, used windmills to generate electricity as well as to pump water for washing and drinking, for irrigation, and for watering livestock. However, the federal government brought in the rural electrification program (which in hindsight may have been one of the most colossal mistakes ever made), relegating windmills in the footnotes of textbooks to "other sources" of energy.

Yet during World War II in the United States, a strange thing happened. The biggest windmill ever built was set up and produced power. S. Morgan Smitto, a hydraulic turbine manufacturer from York, Pennsylvania, became determined to make electrical power with a 117-foot-high windmill on Grandpa's Knob in Vermont, near Rutledge. After generating power for less than a month in 1940 for the grid of the Central Vermont Public Service Corporation, it ground to a halt, having burned out a bearing. It was repaired, but some years later a second breakdown—this time a fatigue crack in one of the 87-foot metal blades —shut the big machine down for good. Materials were scarce, repairs would have been expensive, coal prices had dropped, and the nation had excess generating capacity. Some useful lessons were learned, however, about the metallurgy of windmill blades.

Something more constructive could have come out of Grandpa's Knob. In

---

*The power recoverable from the wind in a single device varies with the square of the diameter of the swept area.

about 1943, Vannevar Bush, director of the Office of Scientific Research and Development, had become worried about the nation's fuel reserves.* He installed wind-power advocate, Percy H. Thomas, as staff consultant to the Federal Power Commission and got the War Production Board in 1945 to sponsor wind-power research at New York University and at Stanford.

Percy Thomas was a zealot (much in the pattern of William Heronemus about whom we shall speak later) and he kept arguing until he had convinced the Federal Power Commission that the Department of Interior should build a large prototype wind-power plant—something along the proportions of the Empire State Building. As so many lovely ideas do, this concept died in birth in the House Committee on Interior and Insular Affairs, ostensibly a victim of the Korean War. But then as always, the House Interior Committee was overpopulated with stubborn congressmen from Western oil-producing states.

NASA ENTERS THE SCENE

Although there was not even room in the 1973 Master Research Plan (put out by Dr. Dixie Lee Ray) for windmill research and in recent reviews of alternative energy sources the windmill seldom even rates an asterisk, this must be a matter of prejudice, because there is more wind than we thought. The average American thinks of a windmill as a joke, something on the order of an outside toilet, and he associates it with wooden shoes. American oilmen and coalmen do not suffer from these misconceptions, but nevertheless in trying to shoulder wind out of the money, they advertise it as a farce. In late 1973 and early 1974 the TV commercials sponsored by oil companies commonly showed a picture of a huge Dutch windmill, but always wound up with the question, "But what happens when the wind dies down?"

This is the number one technical problem, but it is not unique to wind power; it is simply the energy storage problem in another guise. If one considers wind as a prime source of power for a national grid, one would turn the problem upside down. When the wind dies down, other power-source stations would be started up to fill the gap; that is, until a method is devised of storing the excess energy produced during gales or even during hurricanes. If we take this attitude toward wind as a primary source of power, and other things such as fossil fuels as supplemental sources, we find we are getting a cheap ride.

Unlike tidal energy, in world wind energy we are in the realm of very big numbers. How much of the air's kinetic energy is available to windmills (thinking in terms only of ground-based structures)? In 1954 the World Meteorological Organization, using a superconservative approach, calculated that 20 billion kilowatts are available for harvest at specially suited sites around the world—bald mountain knobs and seacliffs, for example, in regions of very high average wind

*Our psychic history as a country is one of schizophrenia in regard to energy. Either we have too much or too little; but somebody of importance has always worried about it, while nobody else would listen to him.

velocity. Other estimates range as high as 80 trillion kilowatts in the Northern Hemisphere alone. According to the Federal Power Commission, in 1970 the total world electrical generation capacity was 1 billion kilowatts, of which the United States generated and consumed nearly one-third. We have 5 times as much easily available wind power as the country needs for generation of electricity. If one includes the jet streams in the tropopause, the energy in the winds that cavort around our planet represents a virtually illimitable resource. Like the sunlight, it will last as long as the solar system.

For this grandiose resource the government has been willing to spend only $865,000 over 2 years (probably the most ridiculous "farthing to soverign" ratio in the budget). This tidbit will go to a space-age windmill work by the NASA Lewis Research Center at Cleveland. The experimental generator will use a 125-foot rotor mounted atop a tower 125 feet tall to generate up to 100 kilowatts at Sandusky, Ohio. It is designed for 18 miles per hour wind. The blades— probably 2—will be able to change pitch, like those of a helicopter, and where the winds get over 18 miles per hour the blades will merely spill excess wind, maintaining a constant voltage.

Until we know more about the aerodynamics of windmills, this may be a reasonable approach, but it would seem to deserve more of an investment. Since it is an aerodynamic problem, and we are virtually in the position toward high-technology windmills that we were in during World War I toward airplanes, it is logical for NASA to take on the job. All the airfoil data they have accumulated in wind tunnels may, when looked at through different spectacles, be appropriate for windmill blades.

In the NASA prototype the blades are automatically feathered completely when the wind speed reaches 60 miles per hour, to prevent possible damage. But surely in the windmills of the future—which I picture as devouring storms with gusto—this will be regarded as a waste, for with the power varying as the cube of the speed we are at 60 mph just getting into the real action.

Also located on top of NASA's Sandusky tower are an alternator and transmission equipment. The latter boosts the 40 revolutions per minute (RPM) of the propeller to 1,800 revolutions per minute in the vertical shaft, giving an electric output of 460 volts at 60 cycles. Also in the enclosure atop the tower are sensors and servomechanisms that keep the rotor aligned with the wind direction.

The current NASA plan is to have 6 wind generators experimentally operating at different locations in the United States by 1979. Although NASA is somewhat bashful about their larger plans or hopes, the implication is that ultimately (or perhaps within 2 decades) a grid system of wind machines would cover the most appropriate regions of the country, providing at least half the nation's electrical demands. NASA believes it has the aerodynamic expertise to devise a very efficient wind scoop or blade and to collect enough full-scale data by 1980 for the final design by electrical companies that know a lot about power generation, like General Electric, Westinghouse, and Allis-Chalmers. John Serino, director of NASA's Lewis Wind Energy Program, says, "If the Danes could get 200,000 kilowatts from the wind back in 1908, we should be able to get the power we need right now."

NASA's machines supposedly are designed for the use of private and public utilities; but, as in the case of direct solar power, we are faced with a conflict of interests, affecting both design and economics. Just as in solar energy, we have the 2 options of designing self-sufficient solar homes or central power stations; the direction of wind-power application could go toward relatively small, private, single-home windmills or toward central collection by huge wind machines. Or we could split the middle and go after medium-sized units designed in groups for condominiums, buildings, senior-citizen retirement villages, and the like.

As an example of residential windmills, Point Richmond, a fancy suburb overlooking San Francisco Bay, is equipped with 35-foot machines copied from a $4,000 Swiss windmill that had served ski resorts in the remote areas of the Swiss Alps. Direct current from a battery-storage unit must be converted to alternating current for most home appliances but is all right without conversion for the lighting circuits. This is a very unusual case, for on Point Richmond the wind blows at least 320 days a year and at an average of 20 miles per hour.

OTHERS IN THE BUSINESS

For the condiminium crowd, the Grumman Aerospace Corporation is building a modest wind generator that has a semirigid airfoil design developed at Princeton by Thomas F. Sweeney. It is based on a high-performance light-aircraft wing. Called *Silverwings,* the windmill generator has a 25-foot-diameter rotor and an aluminum mast; it weighs only 300 pounds. NASA may come up with something better, but they will have to extend themselves to equal the ingenuity of Sweeney's semisolid blades that deform in the wind, thus feathering themselves automatically.

Boeing-Vertol is another millwright outfit relying on experience in aeronautical engineering to design windmill blades which are better than the fat, slow-moving, and clumsy arms ordinarily used. They are working on a design that calls for fiberglass blades 150 feet long. This material is stronger than metal and can better withstand the rather complex eddy forces at the blade tip. With this design they expect to reach a rotary speed of 200 miles an hour, compared with the 80 miles per hour of the best Danish windmills. At the higher speed the blades could spin a 1,000-kilowatt generator in winds averaging 20 miles per hour.

In an attempt to solve the storage problem, Boeing-Vertol and the Southwest Research Institute are planning to hook a 1,000-kilowatt windmill and its generator to an air compressor which, in off-peak hours, will pump air into an abandoned mine. During peak demands for electricity, the compressed air would be released to drive gas-turbine generators. (Although the advanced flywheel energy-storage concept discussed in Chapter 6 had not become familiar enough to wind-machine engineers to be considered earlier, it is obvious that in practically all cases the flywheel will do the best job and should be preferred in place of batteries, pumped high-water, chemical storage, or caved air storage.)

The rather pedestrian approach of NASA is discouraging in that too much energy is wasted in maintaining a constant rotor speed by varying the pitch. Professor William R. Hughes and his associates at the electrical engineering department of Oklahoma State University have taken a more imaginative approach with their field-modulated generator—a device that produces a constant voltage despite variations in speed of the shaft. This system is coupled with a daring storage technique involving the electrolysis of water at high pressure.

Historically, as mentioned, the old Persian windmills operated on a vertical axis—like a merry-go-round. The modern Darrius and Sovonius rotors go back to this design, as does the remarkable Atomic Energy Commission prototype from the Sandia Laboratory at Albuquerque, which is shaped much like a gigantic egg beater.

Favorite places for windmill location are being nominated every day. Aerodynamic students at West Texas University now claim the Texas Panhandle is the windiest area in the United States and that the potential electrical output from wind in Texas averages 250,000 megawatts or about 8 percent of the nation's demand for electrical power. Donald Grace of the University of Hawaii favors the mountain areas of his home islands, where the wind averages 20 to 30 miles per hour and where there are numerous sites surrounded by steep cliffs that give a funneling action to accelerate the wind.

Utility companies in Oregon, now perhaps the most progressive-minded state in the union, are interested in wind, under the inspiration of Professor E. Wendell Hewson of Oregon State University. Hewson insists that the coasts along the Pacific Northwest are perfect spots for giant windmills. The winds sweep right in off the ocean, unobstructed, strike the coastal range, and are uplifted with a corresponding increase in velocity. Hewson calculates that it would take an average wind velocity of just over 12 knots to make 10,000-kilowatt generators feasible, and this speed is attained up and down the Oregon coast most of the hours of the day and most of the days of the year.

Hewson has another idea: Use wind power to augment the sometimes drought-haunted water-power energy reserves of the Pacific Northwest. He suggests that the windmills drive pumps to lift water up to already existing reservoirs. One would need additional water-power generators to utilize the higher water level and more dam capacity would be required. Hewson has attracted not only the interest of several utility companies, but their money as well for development projects.

Unfortunately the utilities of New England (in spite of the brief but respectable history of Grandpa's Knob) have been curiously resistant to one of the most remarkable wind enthusiasts and technologists of all, William E. Heronemus, professor of civil engineering at the University of Massachusetts (Amherst), undisputed pretender to the throne of King Aeolus, warden of the winds in Greek and Roman mythology.

Heronemus, who even talks and looks like an impatient but humorous wind sprite, thought at first that the way to go was to put up several hundred 150- to 300-foot windmills in the White Mountains of New Hampshire, where the winds could generate as much power as half a dozen nuclear plants. He was promptly advised that the Audubon societies would not accept the visual pollution of the White Mountains or the sacred Green Mountains either. Undaunted, Heronemus went in the other direction. He came up with the New England Offshore Wind Power System which he conceived as a huge network of windmills on floating platforms or concrete-pile Texas towers out on the Georges Bank and on the Nantucket and New York shoals. Central to Heronemus's concept is the use of the power generated to electrolyze sea water to produce hydrogen. Hydrogen would then be pumped ashore and converted by fuel cells or by combustion to electric power. (The by-product oxygen could also be pumped ashore to react with the hydrogen on shore or bubbled into the surrounding waters to enrich the fisheries resources.)

Heronemus's system, as blue printed, could generate 160 billion kilowatt-hours per year, which happens to be exactly the projected 1976–90 increase in electrical demand for New England. At a capital outlay of $22.3 billion, the Offshore Wind Power System (OWPS) is a bit steep for the average local electric utility. Yet the projected fossil fuel or nuclear costs are in the same range and Heronemus expects that notable improvements, both in the harvesting of winds and in fuel-cell efficiencies will make OWPS economically as well as environmentally superior to import-pump-and-burn power methods now in use.

Heronemus sent a copy of his proposal to all 48 New England electric utilities. He received 5 replies. Four indicated they would give the matter some thought, although he never heard from them again. One suggested it was a totally ridiculous idea. The only Heronemus convert appears to be Henry Q. Hutchinson, president of the Block Island Power Company, who has drawn up plans for a 250-kilowatt windmill for little Block Island off the Rhode Island coast. It would be economical, he says, if fuel on the island goes as high as 30 cents a gallon. That's below where it has since gone, and my most recent information is that at least 60 percent of Block Island's electricity will come by wind power by 1976.

Heronemus is reluctant to give up the New England scene. As he points out, nobody makes the hardware yet, but that's more plus than minus. "If New England would get with it," snaps Heronemus, "she could free herself from the fuel merchants, reassert her former independence, get all the energy she needs without pollution, and develop a new industry that could provide the jobs she so badly needs."

Looking beyond his tight-fisted native area, Heronemus envisages chains of windmills stretching across the Great Plains from Texas to Canada. One of his earlier versions would have 300,000 towers, each 850 feet tall and each bearing 20 wind turbines. More recently, in the interest of land conservation, he would build 800-foot-tall king posts straddling the highways at half-mile intervals with turbines slung from cables in between. He sees great farms of windmills set up along the Aleutian chain with tankers to carry liquid hydrogen to California.

When you get many large windmills spaced close together, there is some question about environmental effects. Some meterologists suspect this much absorption of wind might even change the weather. Although this seems a most unlikely thing to worry about, the most ambitious proposal of all would perhaps heighten this objection, for it would seize power from far above the clouds, from the very jet streams that are supposed to govern the weather below.

The distinguished Russian meteorologists, W. S. Lidorenko and G. F. Muchnik, propose windmills that hang from giant balloons anchored by electric cables to the ground. The wind-driven generators would produce electric currents in the balloon location and pulse it back to earth. In the tropopause, just below the stratosphere, at an altitude of 5 to 7 miles, where the jet streams rustle by, the air currents are ideal for extraction of power, for they are steady and very, very fast. The 60-miles-per-hour speeds at which NASA's rotors timidly feather their wings would be a lower limit at which the Soviet motors would only just be getting into stride. The amount of power up there is so huge that one need not have a vast proliferation of balloons and cables. The Soviet project is not an academician's dream; it is slated for the late 1970s and if successful will dwarf the present American plans. One might suspect it would bring a smile to the ghostly face of Ben Franklin.

10 The Waters of the World

Water—the element that knows no rest.
—LEONARDO DA VINCI

One rather complicated way in which the sun tantalizes the earth with its unbelievable strength is in powering the ocean currents and the evaporation process that gets water in high places so that in running back downhill we have the delicious kinetic energy of rivers and of waterfalls. The energy of tides is only partly due to the sun, but the fact that it is mainly the moon that rules our tidal behavior should not make us forget that the rather complex symmetry of tides on opposite sides of the earth depends on the fact that earth and moon both rotate around the sun.

The percentage of the solar energy striking the earth that goes into the actual performance of work, like moving the ocean and the atmosphere, is remarkably small, although its total in power units is impressive (about 370 billion kilowatts). But even a small fraction of an enormous number can seem huge when we are thinking as terrestrial brokers rather than in terms of the transactions of astronomical bankers. About half of the sun's radiation that hits the earth is converted to heat directly at the earth's surface. About one-quarter is reflected back into space and about one-quarter is spent in evaporating water. The unusual size of expenditure is because so much of the earth's surface is water and both the specific heat and latent heat of evaporation of water are enormously high.*

---

*Although H_2O seems a very simple substance with its deceptively naïve chemical formula, actually it is an extremely intricate material, containing hydrogen bonds, various polymeric forms, and peculiar behavior. What other substances, for example, can you think of in which the solid is less dense than the liquid form? It is a scandal that with so much water (so much in fact that beings from other systems would unhesitatingly name us the aqueous planet) we have not yet got a satisfying physical-chemical theory of this marvelous substance.

HYDROELECTRIC POWER

The use of running or falling water for modest chores, such as grinding wheat, is very ancient indeed and such small but significant hints as the commonness of the surname Miller or Mueller or Meunier or Molinaro are sufficient to persuade us that the use of water power in mechanical form is one of the most natural habits of the human race. Probably the mill wheel preceded the vehicular wheel as a human concept. It was only in the nineteenth century with Faraday's discoveries that the notion of recovering electricity from the kinetic energy of water was put to practice. It is an almost miraculously efficient transformation, as in practically all modes of converting mechanical into electrical energy. The converse process of converting electric to mechanical energy is by no means as efficient.

If one considers all the running rivers of the world, the earth's total hydroelectric power is about 3 billion kilowatts of which only about 8.5 percent is developed. The potential for water power in Africa, South America, Siberia, and Southeastern Asia is enormous; but in the United States (except Alaska) most of the feasible sites have already been developed.

This is by no means true of North America as a whole. One of the most colossal projects on earth is the $15 billion series of hydroelectric dams on the La Grande River flowing into the James Bay sector of Hudson Bay, some 550 miles north of the city of Quebec. When the 4 dams are completed in 1986, the project will provide 10,300 megawatts, more than enough for all of the province of Quebec. This undertaking has stirred up all the usual ecological dramatis personae: displaced birds, Cree Indians with no animals to trap, baffled caribou, forlorn moose, and the Canadian federal government slugging it out with the fierce provincial government of Premier Robert Bourassa. What the Audubon Society and and other environmentalists fear is an overwhelming technological triumph—which seems very likely—because this would be followed by an Ungava Bay project far to the north; another project on James Bay, using the Opinaca and Eastman Rivers, to the south; and Ontario, custodian of the western coast of James Bay, specially inspired to do something over there.

In Canada the provinces are very jealous of each other and the only thing that pulls them together is a common dislike of the United States. Clearly Premier Bourassa intends to make sure that hydroelectricity will do for Quebec what the petroleum industry did for Alberta.

In order to justify for the United States further installations, as in the periodically turbulent rivers such as the Stanislaus and Auburn of Northern California, the St. John of Maine, the so-called Garrison diversion in North Dakota, and a few others, the Corps of Engineers and the Bureau of Reclamation have strained credulity and common sense and, in some cases, in preparing the so-called benefit/cost ratio have resorted to rather stupidly obvious hanky-panky. For example, in fixing up the benefit/cost ratio for the proposed Dickey-Lincoln dam plus power plant on the St. John, the Corps of Engineers (which has such an unblemished record of getting caught with its accounting pants down that it never seeks solace in a blush any longer) used 3 1/4 percent as an interest in hiring money for the project and assumed zero inflation for the next 11 years. On the other hand, in calculating the cost of possible alternatives to the St. John hydroelectric project, the Corps assumed an interest rate of 8 3/4 percent.

It is only fair to state that most of the United States hydroelectric projects under consideration involve increasing the capacity of present dams. There is a sound reason for doing this, which gets at the very heart of the small, important role played by hydroelectric power in the electrical economics of a sophisticated nation. Hydroelectric power is intrinsically the best source of electric peaking power to supplement more massive units, such as those based on fossil fuels or nuclear fission. This is because all you have to do is press a button. The water is there—power in storage, so to speak—and can be increased simply by activating more turbines. The plans to increase the capacity of key dams simply by raising their height do not automatically increase the number of kilowatt-hours delivered steadily; they increase the ability of the dams to deliver more power over a shorter period.

TIDAL POWER

More nonsense has been published on this subject than on any other, with the possible exception of extrasensory perception. Some of the nonsense has come from the conservatives. For example, David Rose of the Massachusetts Institute of Technology makes the reckless statement, "If you built a low dike around the United States to harness all the tides, the resulting power would only satisfy the needs of a city the size of Boston." The inanity of this pompous, off-the-top-of-the-head remark is shown by the fact that from one estuary installation system alone (a combination of Passamaquoddy and the Bay of Fundy tides, in the region where Maine, New Brunswick, and Newfoundland join together) more than enough tidal power could be generated to satisfy the needs of not only Boston but Boston plus Portland plus Providence plus New Haven and all the other cities of New England.

Let us review briefly what we learned in the fifth grade about the tides. Since we have spent a lot of money sending men to the moon, it is at least poetic justice that we should consider harnessing the moon's great smooth shoulders to doing some work for us. As the earth rotates the moon moves forward in its orbit inducing a watery bulge or broad tidal wave directly under it because of lunar gravitation. But directly opposite, on the other side of the world, there is a similar moving bulge or tide mainly caused by centrifugal force, resulting from the fact that the earth and the moon are revolving around a common center, the sun.

To bring any meridian under the moon once, the earth must turn for nearly 25 hours, which means that the 2 tides at opposite sides of the globe cooperate to yield 2 high tides and 2 low tides within 25 hours at any meridian. The timing is a little awkward. Because of the fact that the 2 high tides and 2 low tides arrive

50 minutes later each 24-hour day, a continuous machine that extracts power from these tides is out of synchronous connection with our diurnal life style. If we relied entirely on the tides, as do some shellfish, we would change our life style to a 25-hour one, but the sun is much more important to us than the moon.*

Twice each month, at full and new moon, when the sun, moon, and earth are all in alignment, the gravitation is most intense. The flood tides are highest and ebb tides the lowest. These are called spring tides (it has nothing to do with the season of the year, just as steam in steam beer has nothing to do with the use of steam in its manufacture). Neap tides occur when the difference between high and low tide is smallest, because the sun and moon are situated at a right angle with the earth.

The total tidal power of the earth is estimated at 3 billion kilowatts, which happens to be the same as the total river or waterfall power. However, only a small fraction of the tidal power occurs in places, like narrow estuaries, where the tide builds up to heights of water whose potential energy can conveniently be extracted by special turbines. In order to be practical for exploitation, the tidal rush in small branches of the estuary must be faster than a man can run.

Historically it is known that the tides were used as early as 1066 in England by a miller in Dover to grind wheat. The Normans may have paused on their way to Hastings to strip this good man of his flour. A similar mill was built in 1640 near the mouth of the North River in Salem, Massachusetts. Yet the idea of harnessing the tides on a large scale was still a novel one when 2 Americans began to think about it nearly 60 years ago. These were Dexter F. Cooper, a Boston hydraulics engineer, and Franklin Delano Roosevelt, both of whom were accustomed to spending summers in Campobello Island in Canada where they could watch the sweep of the tides that poured through the Bay of Fundy into the smaller Passamaquoddy Bay that lies between Maine and New Brunswick. The "Quoddy" project was first proposed in 1919 and was authorized by Congress during the early 1930s at the urging of Franklin Roosevelt. Work was started during the Depression and halted before World War II. Although the dream of Roosevelt and Cooper seemed quite dead, lately Senator Edmund Muskie has been reviving it, just as many other ghostly and expensive projects of the past are gaining new life at a time when the cost of fossil fuels ascends heavenward.

Dexter Cooper's idea for the Passamaquoddy project involved 2 pools, a high pool (Passamaquoddy) and a low pool (the Cobscock Bay project) with a powerhouse between them. Separating these bays from the unconstrained ocean would be 7 miles of rock-filled dams. Cobscock Bay would open to the sea through 90 filling gates at Letite Passage and Deer Island Point. They would open when the tide rose in the Bay of Fundy and close when the pool had filled. The tides in

*In addition to the ocean, there are tides in the atmosphere (that is, regular ups and downs in barometric pressure that are not connected with the weather). Curiously enough these appear to be caused only by the sun; the reason for the moon's lack of influence is still something of a mystery. Lord Kelvin's theory is as good as any: Just as regular, well-timed pushes on a swing may drive it higher, so the sun's 12-hour tug may be better timed for earth's atmosphere than the pull of the moon.

Quoddy Bay would average 18 feet compared to over 50 feet in some branches of the Bay of Fundy. The expensive part of any project such as those proposed for Passamaquoddy or the upper estuaries of the Bay of Fundy is the necessity of anchoring the pool-forming dikes in deep bedrock. Designing turbines to operate at low heads of water is something of a problem, but they would turn only at about 200 revolutions per minute compared with over 3,000 revolutions per minute for the machines used for high-head hydroelectric power or fossil-fuel and nuclear power plants.

The price tag for the Quoddy project, which would have been $150 million in 1936, would now be $1.5 billion. In 1961 John Kennedy became interested in this warmed-over dream and assigned Stewart Udall to give it some further study. The Department of Interior concluded that the project was feasible but with a qualifier—that it be coupled with a dam and hydroelectric plant on the upper St. John River in Maine (to which we have alluded); otherwise the system would be essentially as Cooper had laid it out. Kennedy was enthusiastic but died 3 months later; whereupon everybody forgot about it.

Actually Canada is more likely to go ahead with the adjacent Bay of Fundy than we are with Quoddy. Study has progressed beyond the economics—which looks good at today's fuel prices—and includes a survey on what effect tampering with the Fundy tide might have on surrounding water—in particular, on one of North America's largest bird-feeding grounds. It is now estimated that Fundy power would cost 15 mills per kilowatt-hour, roughly comparable to the cost of nuclear power and lower than the 18 to 20 mills cost of power from fossil fuels in Canada. The Fundy idea has powerful moral and possibly financial support from Edmund de Rothschild of W. M. Rothschild and Sons, the London merchant bank, who organized the financing of the $950 million Churchill Falls hydropower plant in Newfoundland—the world's largest privately developed power installation. Rothschild in fact joined in the $350,000 study of the Fundy proposal and concluded that it was attractive. It would cost about $3 billion and faces the psychological handicap that Ottawa suspects most of the power would wind up in New England rather than in Eastern Canada.

The rhetoric on Passamaquoddy and Fundy continues and may last forever, but in the meantime the French, who are outstandingly creative when it comes to water, went ahead and built a big tidal power plant at the estuary of La Rance River in Brittany which in 1967 began to produce peaking power for Elecricité de France. Here the conditions are favorable with a range of 44 feet in tidal height. This single-basin, 240-megawatt plant was noteworthy in that the turbines were reversible, so that power could be obtained both on a rising and an ebbing tide. Although the low price of petroleum in the late 1960s did not make La Rance a favorable public pet, things are naturally quite different today, and in 1973 Electricité de France dusted off plans that call for a whopping 6,000-megawatt plant powered by tidal waters of the Bay of Mont Saint Michel, which is 230 square miles in area. The bay would be dammed up and divided into separate basins. As the tide falls, water collected in one basin would flow into an empty second basin, driving turbines in a divider dam. When the second is full, the water would be fed out at low tide through turbines in the sea wall, thus allowing the utility to come up with power continuously for almost 24 hours.

At the same time as the French, the Russians started on a much more modest scale but now have very large plans. Soviet engineers built an experimental 400-kilowatt, single-pool unit at Kislaya Guba, an inlet off the Barents Sea 600 miles north of Murmansk. They are now working on a feasibility study for a 6,000-megawatt project at Mezesskaya Guba on the White Sea t the Arctic Circle. This would help meet the peak loads of the north European sector of the Soviet Union.* The Russian engineers are also considering plans for a 10,000-megawatt tidal project on the Sea of Okhotsk, possibly as a joint venture with the Japanese. Only immense projects make sense to the Russians, and they scoff at estimates of cost. Lev Borisovich Bernstein, tidal expert at the Hydro-project Institute in Moscow says, "Small tidal projects are absurd—a blacksmith forging an insect. . . . As for cost, did you ask about the cost per mile of the first airplane?"

Most engineers believe that future tidal power stations will be based on the Soviet model rather than the French. The French temporarily dammed La Rance River estuary and built the plant on the dry river bed. The Russians built their experimental plant at Kislaya Guba by floating prefabricated sections of the plant out into the bay and sinking them on prepared foundations.

South Korea has hired French engineers to make a feasibility study of a Yellow Sea tidal plant. Australia is thinking tidal power, but with the stubbornness of the inflation and the unreason of labor, the thinking remains a revery.

In Great Britain, Eric M. Wilson at the University of Salford and Thomas Shaw at the University of Bristol are pushing a notably reluctant government to support a 4,000-megawatt, double-pool tidal plant on the Severn River near Bristol. The estimated cost is $3.2 billion, but it would supply about 7 percent of Britain's consumption of electricity. The inclination of the people who would have to scratch up the money to pay for this is to wait and see what the Canadians do with Fundy.

The chances are very small that the Canadians will act at all. In fact, there is small hope that any ambitious program on tidal power will go ahead anywhere except where such projects have already proved themselves—in France and in Russia.

ENERGY FROM TEMPERATURE DIFFERENCES IN THE OCEAN

From the standpoint of a hydraulic engineer, the whole oceanic system of the earth can be regarded as a gigantic machine run by the sun. In the equatorial

---

*One enigma that constantly baffles a technical observer is that the Soviets have spent a good deal of horsepower in talking about the fathomless resources of Siberia, but when you come to add up their accomplishments in exploitation of this cornucopia, they are singularly paltry. Most of their efforts have been concentrated as near as possible to European Russia.

bands between the Tropic of Cancer and the Tropic of Capricorn, the surface of the seas runs as high as 80 degrees Fahrenheit; but vast rushes of water, larger than continents, submerge at the poles and make their way in deep currents in a continuous cycle toward the equator. In the tropical oceans this cold water provides a nearly limitless heat sink at about 40 degrees Fahrenheit and at a depth of about 1,000 meters. This 40 degree temperature difference, it must be emphasized, is purely the work of the sun. Here the earth machine in effect says "come and get it." There is far more potential energy in that 40 degree difference in temperature spread over billions of tons of water than will ever be consumed throughout the world.

There are certain obvious disadvantages but also some fat benefits for power plants built to subsist on this 40 degree differential in a water medium. The power stations should cost little more than conventional ones, since the sea acts as an engine for both the collection of sunlight and the storage of energy. One is faced, of course, with a fundamentally low efficiency because of the low temperature difference between the heat source and the heat sink, which means that very large amounts of warm water must be moved, yet the amounts are still comparable to the flow through a hydroelectric plant with the same output. The energy derived by allowing a kilogram of water to flow from a temperature of 80 degrees Fahrenheit to a temperature of 40 degrees is the same as the energy produced from a hydroelectric plant with the same kilogram of water falling 93 feet.

The French, with their extraordinary instinct for marine dynamics, were the first to realize the solar sea-power concept, initially stated by Jacques D'Arsonval, a physicist, in 1881. He had sufficient engineering insight to recognize that in an actual power plant an auxiliary fluid, such as ammonia, should be used to generate the turbine power in passing from the hot surface water to the cold, deep condensing systems. With volatile working fluids, including propane and freon as well as ammonia, the turbines do not have to be so enormous as they do with water vapor from the sea itself.

However in the 1920s another Frenchman, Georges Claude, went from one American and European college to another, demonstrating the workability of the straight water cycle. His props consisted of glass cylinders of warm and iced water with a toy turbine connected between the 2 free spaces above the water levels. The lights would be turned off in the auditorium or lecture room and the audience, upon seeing a wee electric bulb come feebly aglow from the handful of watts produced by the system, would wildly applaud and perhaps even sing the "Marseillaise." In 1929 Claude built a shore-based ocean-gradient power plant in Cuba that produced 22 kilowatts but was obviously an economic farce, since if one extrapolated the sizes required for a standard 1,000-megawatt plant, one would find that the turbine inlet would have to have an area of 10,000 square meters, compared to 1 square meter for a conventional fossil-fuel or nuclear installation and 10 square meters for an ocean-gradient turbine running on ammonia.

However, it is agonizing to give up the idea of using vapor from the hot surface sea water as the power fluid, because after it has run through the turbine and condensed, you have fresh water; and fresh water is becoming scarce as a world commodity. (The Food and Agriculture Organization of the United Nations has calculated that the global demand for fresh water will increase 240 percent by the end of the century.) Donald Othmer of Brooklyn Polytechnic Institute and Oswald Roels of Columbia University have come up with a blueprint for a land-based plant which recovers a modest amount of power from the difference in temperature at surface and depths of the tropical seas but which is guaranteed first of all to make the investor a lot of money. The power produced by the sea-water vapor turbine is used mostly to deliver fresh water to farmers and to pump up sufficient cold water to produce a fine mess of clams and oysters and what-not from the highly nutrient depths. If one is partial to shellfish, their prospectus reads like a menu from some famous Baltimore or Washington seafood restaurant. The mussels and cockles and other delectable mollusks not only grow quickly to giant size in the algae-rich cold water but they are peculiarly free of disease. And the fresh water produced from the turbine condensate is valued by these gourmet authors at several times the worth and the importance of the electric power. While I hope Drs. Othmer and Roels become as rich as Colonel Sanders and his pressure-cooked chickens, I am afraid they have added more to the literature of epicurean cuisine than to the chronicles of energy recovery from faraway places.

As in the case of wind power produced on off-shore locations, the cost of cabling the electricity to the consumer on land may be exorbitant. Heronemus's expedient, of electrolyzing ocean water by ocean power to transmit hydrogen gas rather than electricity shoreward, is being considered by several research teams who are responding to a revival of interest in power from the sea.

One of the most ingenious of all ideas, which sounds so simple that one feels there must be a bundle of bugs in it, is the osmotic marine pump described by Octave Levenspiel of Oregon State University and Noel de Nevers of the University of Utah. (Osmotic pressure is the pressure exerted by the dissolved salts of a solvent, such as water, on a membrane permeable to the water but not to the salts.)

Simply imagine yourself with a very long pipe open at the top but capped at the bottom with a semipermeable membrane. Now lower it into the ocean. Because the osmotic pressure difference between fresh and salt water is about 340 pounds per square inch, the inside of the pipe will begin to fill with fresh water when the pipe is lowered to over 230 meters—a little over an eighth of a mile—at which depth the hydrostatic pressure exceeds the osmotic pressure. Fresh water will rise in the pipe precisely to the level of 230 meters below the ocean surface. If you lower the pipe deep enough—to over 8,000 meters—the level of fresh water should actually rise above the surface of the ocean. Thus with an ideal semipermeable membrane and a very long pipe we get a perpetual fountain of fresh water from the ocean without doing any work.

An osmotic power plant derives from this shameless trick on nature simply by using two pipes plus membranes lowered to different depths in the ocean. Since the desalted water will rise to different levels in these pipes we can allow water to flow from one to the other and generate electricity by means of a turbine.

Why is this not a violation of the second law of thermodynamics? Haven't we made the marine osmotic pump into a sort of perpetual motion machine—obtaining work from a system in complete equilibrium? No, and that is the secret: The ocean is not in equilibrium. In an equilibrium ocean the ratio of salt concentration and density changes with depth so that in effect one never exceeds the osmotic pressure, no matter how deep one goes. The real ocean is somewhere between an equilibrium and a uniform ocean, but nearer the latter, and this is because the currents tend to mix the water. The currents are driven by the equivalent of a giant heat engine, in which the high-temperature source is the sun's energy in the tropics and the low temperature sink is the radiation to outer space near the poles. This engine overwhelms the natural diffusion toward equilibrium. Thus the osmotic desalter and the osmotic power plant, which seem to get something for nothing, do not violate the laws of thermodynamics. What they do is simply to harvest some of the sun's energy, as do windmills and hydroelectric plants and oceanic temperature-gradient machines.

The osmotic devices of Levenspiel and de Nevers would become of immediate practical interest provided that osmotic membranes far superior to those now available could be developed. That this is not unlikely is indicated by the large amount of activity that is being devoted by smart engineers, like the Israelis, to desalting brackish water such as the Dead Sea by osmotic techniques.

PUTTING THE OCEAN CURRENTS TO WORK

In steady purposeful currents such as the Gulf Stream (analogous to the reliable winds such as the Westerlies above the Pacific) the sun is showing off another way it can assume its kingship over the world's fluids. Although these ocean streams are slow compared with winds, they are of enormous momentum and size. The Gulf Stream, for example, approaches quite close to the southeast coast of the United States and carries enough warm water to supply the nation's power needs many times over, even if inefficient sea-power engines are used. The huge stream running northward from the equatorial waters is about 36 degrees Fahrenheit warmer than its surroundings, and the brothers Hilbert and James Anderson of York, Pennsylvania, have estimated that 182×10^{12} kilowatt-hours of electricity, or about 75 times the expected national demand in 1980, could be generated from the Gulf Stream which flows at the rate of about 2,200 cubic kilometers per day.

At the University of Massachusetts (Amherst), William Heronemus (the wind god) and his associates have prepared designs for a submerged plant to harvest this power, specifically in the Straits of Florida between the coastline and the Little Bahama Bank. They propose a modular configuration with 6 turbines in each of 2 hulls, hooked together to look like a submarine catamaran. Each hull would be about 480 feet long and 100 feet in diameter, probably made of reinforced concrete. The axis of the hulls would be at a depth of 250 feet, providing free space over the top for protection against wave motion and hurricanes. Heronemus is as proud of his dream of submerged turbine catamarans as he is of his regiments of gigantic imaginary windmills, and I do hope that this creative sprite sees some of his visions of natural power realized.

There is a peculiar sort of self-exalting feature in the process of extracting energy from the ocean that makes this resource not only inexhaustible but super-renewable. Both Clarence Zener of Carnegie-Mellon University, Pittsburgh, and the Anderson brothers predict that the effect of large-scale extraction of power would be a net increase in thermal energy stored in the ocean. The explanation for this is that the radiation absorptivity of the ocean's surface layer would be raised by the discharge of large amounts of colder water; hence solar radiation would more than make up for the heat extracted for power. This gracious bonus may not be important to twentieth-century engineers, but it has the aspect of good tidings and good luck, as if the universe were giving us a pat on the head.

11 The Hot Earth

Speak to the earth and it shall teach thee.
—OLD TESTAMENT, JOB 12:8
Verily the earth hath store of marvels for those who have faith to see!
—THE KORAN, 2:20

The older one gets the more one is charmed by the diversity and the mystery of the planet that one has been allowed to sojourn upon for a brief time in order to experience the universe. Geology has become a science for young adventurers to discover things that amaze and sometimes infuriate their elders, anxious to hold onto something solid and stable: the earth's flatness, or five centuries later the immutability of the earth's continents. As we send warm bodies or electronic spies to inspect our moon and the other planets, we become all the more aware of the utter strangeness of our own sphere; and the satellite ERTS (Earth Research and Technology Satellite) that keeps us advised of the shifting microgeography of crops and floods, that discloses unsuspected rifts, fissures, and jungle-hidden escarpments, brings us more thrills than the cruising snapshots of Mars or Mercury or Jupiter.

In spite of all our triumphs in applied astronomy, we are not sure how our own planet was formed. Presumably it was by the same process of accretion from the granular nebula that was the mother of the entire solar system. In this case we can claim to be roughly the same age as the sun. If the original source of the sun's thermonuclear brilliance is the force of gravitation, in pulling itself together, then the core of all planets, large or small, is hot, but not hot enough to trigger thermonuclear reactions. The larger the planet, the greater is the gravitational heat so that with mighty Jupiter we are dealing with a sort of subordinate sun that gives off more radiation than it receives.

We can assume that the earth when it formed from the mother nebula was so hot from gravitational contraction and from the accretion process that it was composed of liquid magma (melted rock). When there remained in space just a few isolated mineral fragments to attract, the earth began to cool and form a crust, but 4.6 billion years have not sufficed to lose enough heat for the core even to begin to solidify. It is believed to be molten iron and nickel, and will remain hot in its confinement as long as the sun's heat acts as a balance to prevent the earth's losing heat rapidly by radiation to a sunless outerspace while the core feeds heat up conductively to the radiating crust. Even under these conditions—with a sun that suddenly went cold—it would take several million years for our planet to become a hunk of ice and barren stone.

The Earth, then, has a heating system independent of the sun; in fact it has several heating systems, and it is difficult although important to distinguish one from the other. In addition to the constant heat of the molten core that slowly diffuses upward, the crust itself has heat sources of its own, consisting of radioactive minerals and the fact that the source consists of separate tectonic plates that are usually colliding frictionally with each other somewhere on the earth's surface. The fact that the movement of these vast rafts may be 1 inch a year does not eliminate the frictional heat created as the great surfaces slide over and under each other.

THE RIM OF FIRE

All around the Pacific Ocean, tectonic plates are bruising against each other, which makes the circum-Pacific countries geologically unstable. We think immediately of Japan, Indonesia, Hawaii, Alaska, and in fact the whole western part of the North and South American continental plates.

In the United States, the fact that the Pacific tectonic plate is wedging itself in an eastward direction underneath the shelf of the North American tectonic plate, melting granite with the vast release of frictional heat, explains some peculiar things that have been noticed for years by people like petroleum geologists who observe the drilling of deep holes. In that part of the country west of the eastern slope of the Rocky Mountains (the part that feels the collision with the brutal Pacific plate), the crust is thinner and hotter. Drilling at 15,000 feet one would find rock at 570 degrees Fahrenheit almost anywhere in this western region; but one would probably have to go to 19,000 feet deep and settle for 320 to 350 degrees Fahrenheit in the east. The fragility and instability of the western crust make it not only hotter, but more likely to crack and allow hot pieces of the mantle, even (some think) of the core to poke up here and there and come close to the surface of the earth. This is why we have fumaroles (dry steam leaks), hot springs, geysers—all indications of the intrusion of hot rocks much closer to the surface than would be normal in some more geologically respectable area, such as, say, Massachusetts.

These sources of heat within digging distance are like gold in the ground. Geothermal energy, at its cleanest, is the cheapest energy we know about. The trouble is we do not know about it. Our knowledge of geothermal energy is about equivalent to what our knowledge of petroleum energy was in 1900. Until quite recently, private corporations have been quite timid in investing money on the basis of a few snorts of steam and brimstone, because they did not trust the longevity of such a heat source. How long would Old Faithful remain faithful if you started to harvest the heat and impact from its jets?

We still do not know all the answers, but the events of the fall of 1973 impressed upon certain scientifically trained congressmen, such as Mike McCormack of the state of Washington, the advisability of paying federal money to find the answers. Since most of the western land that contains available geothermal sources of energy belongs to the government anyway—as in the case of oil shale —it took preliminary legislation, the Geothermal Steam Act of 1970, to authorize the opening of federal geothermal land to leasing, exploration, and exploitation. Even then the Bureau of Land Management was remarkably coy, and real deals did not start coming about until the Interior Department had established a sort of policy: Land in areas where the existence of geothermal energy had been established were to be subject to lease by public auction, whereas lands of unknown potential were subject to private negotiation. It was not until January 1974 that the auctioning of public land near The Geysers in Sonoma County, California, took place. The Shell Oil Company bid $4.5 million on 3,874 acres, where a decade ago private land in the same area was selling for 20 cents an acre. Veteran Bureau official Walter Holmes admitted, when he saw the Shell bid, "I almost dropped my store teeth."

HOW TO RECOVER GEOTHERMAL ENERGY

In order to explain why Mr. Holmes narrowly escaped toothlessness, we must review a little geological history and economics. As of today, there are roughly 4 kinds of geothermal sources of power. There is dry steam (a rare and obviously sweet investment); hot water or wet steam (by far the most common source); hot subterranean rocks which could be exploited if we had the technology; and a rather mysterious source encountered in deep drilling in the Gulf of Mexico known as geopressured zones (apparently these are very large hot traps of water containing absolutely enormous quantities of dissolved natural gas). Let us proceed from the money-in-the-bank steam fumaroles to the shadowy but great expectations of things to come.

The first dry steam deposit to be put to work by man was at Larderello, Italy, where in 1904 a small schoolboy turbine powered 5 light bulbs. For the last 45 years this remarkable resource has been exploited at the rate of over 500 megawatts through several government-owned power plants. The Larderello facility is not as large in ultimate capacity as The Geysers in this country, but its existence has been a comfort to geothermal people simply because it has gone literally full-steam for over 4 decades without noticeable depletion.

The Geysers is a steam engineer's dream. It was first reported upon by the grizzly-bear hunter, William Bell Eliott, who, stumbling across a hill in 1847, saw steam rising like a massive genie from a hole in a canyon. There, up in the lonely wilds of Sonoma and Lake Counties about 90 miles north of San Francisco, were all these steamy plumes (fumaroles) rising from behind trees and chapparal, a ghostly sight that for some reason or other failed to inspire the acquisitive eye of the energy industry until about 1955 when drilling started on privately owned property. Operators, such as Thermal Power and Magma Power and especially the Union Oil Company gradually and cautiously drilled and operated the wells; the Pacific Gas and Electric Corporation took the steam and ran it through turbines to produce electricity, which was enough at first to satisfy the power demands of most of Sonoma County and soon may be sufficient to power all of the metropolitan area of San Francisco.

The steam comes out of the ground typically at a pressure of 100 pounds per square inch and at a temperature of 205 degrees centigrade, as compared to 3,000 pounds per square inch and 550 degrees centigrade for the steam in some modern fossil fuel plants; and, furthermore, The Geysers' steam stinks slightly, like a dragon's breath, from traces of hydrogen sulfide, but it is nevertheless the cheapest steam in California. Because of the reduced temperature and pressure, the cycle efficiency is much lower than in conventional power plants. On the other hand the Geysers' plants cost immensely less to build and operate than fossil fuel or nuclear installations, making geothermal energy the cheapest source of electricity for Pacific Gas and Electric, a big and sophisticated outfit, which plays all octaves of the power spectrum. The Geysers, which now has some 15 separate power plants, probably has an ultimate capacity of well over 1,000 megawatts, but those numbers have been approached with everybody holding their breath, for who knows how long the dragon will live? Perhaps an earthquake could kill off the whole project. There is probably no danger of subsidence as there is when one recovers liquid (oil or water) from a formation. In the meantime farmers graze their cows by the quietly humming plants as the power whispers its way on its southward journey.

There is a definite minus point. With geothermal energy you have to use the heat at or near the source and, except in Iceland, there are very few fumeroles or hot springs located in the immediate vicinity of big cities or factory complexes. Lower electric transmission costs would be the same blessing for geothermal sources of energy that they would for low-grade, strip-mined western coal or shale oil.

ADD WATER AND GET HOLES IN YOUR PIPES

Except for Larderello and The Geysers, I know of only one other commercial source in the world that provides the industrial luxury of dry steam. This is at Matsukawa, Japan, where a 20-megawatt plant began operating in 1968 to serve the Tohoku Electric Power Company. All the other plants in actual operation are hot water or wet steam, and whether they go broke or not seems to depend on how corrosive the impurities in the water are.

The first hot-water or wet-steam source tamed to produce electricity was the Wairakei field in New Zealand, where a 192-megawatt plant is operated by the New Zealand Electricity Department. Other hot-water formations now producing electric power are at Kawarau (New Zealand), Otake (Japan), Pazhetska (USSR), Paratunka (USSR), Namafjall (Iceland), and Cerro Prieto (Mexico).

All of the hot-water fields feeding steam to turbines have to first separate the nascent steam and water, usually in a centrifugal separator. If the geothermal water has been double flashed, that is, if the water from the first separation has been allowed to boil at a lower pressure, then the water to be disposed of will have a temperature close to boiling and will amount to about 70 percent of the water originally produced. This is good, hot water and you can at least use it for heating any houses or buildings in the area, but in New Zealand it is dumped in the nearest river. If it is salty, it is commonly reinjected in the ground. In order to avoid subsidence, it is certainly safer in the long run to reinject. In some cases the geothermal wells will be located in desert country (e.g., the Imperial Valley of California) and here there is almost as much incentive for purifying the water for irrigation use as there is for getting the power out.

Many tender hearts have been broken by the corrosive salts in the geothermal hot water near the Salton Sea, but bidding continues for California and Nevada sites of proven geothermal prospects, in the Mono Lake-Long Valley tract near Reno and all over the Imperial Valley. It is only fair to state that no American company has yet been able to run the steam from such highly mineralized hot water through turbines without chewing up the blades and burning holes in the condensers. The San Diego Gas and Electric Company has worked fervently with Magma Power to develop new technology, so far unsuccessfully. In 1973 General Electric introduced a 135-megawatt generator designed especially for geothermal steams. It has short, stubby blades and corrosion-resistant alloys but, although it looks fine at The Geysers, it is no match for the fiery brines of the upper east mesa of the Imperial Valley.

Judging from the exhaustive research surveys of Professor Robert Rex of the University of California at Riverside, there is enough hot water under the Imperial Valley to justify intensive research and development programs. Rex has located some 8 thermal anomalies in the Valley and estimates the potential power reserves to be as large as 20,000 megawatts and over a billion acre-feet of water, much of it in the southern part of the valley where the water is expected to be less brackish than that near the Salton Sea.

One thing that has inspired continued leasing, as well as angry glints in some eyes, is the rather mortifying fact that in the southern continuation of the Imperial Valley, just south of the border at Cerro Prieto, Japanese engineers built a bonny little turn-key power plant for the Mexican government which has been running just fine, thank you, producing 75 megawatts of power since early in 1973. Cerro Prieto hot water has a salt content of 2 percent (sea water has 3.3 percent), while near the Salton Sea the hot water runs as high as 20 percent salt.

Desalting Imperial Valley underground hot water for irrigation use is an attractive proposition along with power extraction, if you can lick the corrosion, for the water is already hot enough to pay most of the costs of well-known methods of desalting sea water by distillation. The Los Angeles Metropolitan

Water District has in its future projects the possible blending of desalted Imperial Valley water with Colorado River water, which has now developed a salinity of 1,000 parts per million in its lower reaches. The trouble is salt disposal. Even for the less highly mineralized water near Cerro Prieto, geothermal plants equivalent to 1,000 megawatts would yield 12,000 tons of by-product salt per day. What do you do with this? The pile builds up very fast, indeed. A possibility hopefully whispered by the Los Angeles Water District engineers is to separate the lithium salts from the rest, for there is enough lithium in these waters to sustain nuclear fusion plants (see Chapter 8) for a million years or so. The rest could be washed down a deep-injection well to avoid earthquakes from subsidence.

A proven way to minimize the turbine-blade corrosion is heat exchange of the hot brine with a fluid such as isobutane of lower boiling point than water, which is then run through a closed-cycle gas turbine to generate electricity. The corrosion problems are thus confined to the exchanger joints and baffles rather than extending to high-speed moving parts. A plant of this type is successfully operating in the Soviet Union. As we shall see later, the secondary-fluid turbine concept is likely for other reasons to be a necessary part of the expanded technology of obtaining power from the earth's heat.

In the last few years and accelerating rapidly with the scaldingly inflated price of oil and coal, hot-water formations are coming under engineering scrutiny in places all over the globe, especially near active or even decrepit volcanoes. The Hellgafiell Volcano is now Iceland's answer to the energy crisis. A new, volcano-heated town is now rising on the hot ashes from the latest eruption of July 1973. On the Kamchatka peninsula holes nearly 2 miles deep are being bored to the heart of the Avachinskayaspoka volcano. Water from a nearby river will be pumped into some holes while others will serve as steam outlets. The Soviets rate a small volcano like this one at about 300 megawatts.

The Philippine government has been conducting mapping and feasibility studies in preparation for the construction of a geothermal power plant. They don't know where they will drill but they want to get into the act. El Salvador, Guadeloupe, Taiwan, and Turkey are digging or planning or both. It would not be surprising to hear of geothermal developments in the very kingdoms of oil, in the Middle East, since the geology is somewhat misshapen and there certainly is enough exploratory drilling going on.

Our beautiful fiftieth state, Hawaii, is rocking with geothermal fever and has been experiencing unsatisfied power hunger since long before the energy crisis of 1973. *Wela Wela Popeleu* (hot rocks) has long been an industrial symbol, like the rock of Gibraltar for life insurance. The Magma Power Company of California (one of the participants in The Geysers bonanza) made an unsuccessful attempt to drill wells for steam in 1961 on the "Big Island" (Hawaii) but the devotees of *Wela Wela Popeleu* believe this was aimed too shallow.

In another typical example of bad luck or poor planning, a drilling attack on the crater of the active volcano of Kilauea turned into a sort of farce. Lava frequently emerges from the somber, wounded mountain at 1,200 degrees centigrade, so the drill hole was pointed toward the predicted location of a hot pool of underground magma. In the first 500 meters the temperature proved to be lower than at the surface where the geologists were drinking hot coffee in the cold wind. At about 400 meters above sea level the drill encountered rocks fully and revoltingly saturated with water saltier than sea water. When they angled down below sea leavel the hottest water they found was only 137 degrees centigrade. Engineer John Shupe of the University of Hawaii reports that there is still a lot of enthusiasm on both the Manoa and Hilo campuses and something useful will be found either on the Big Island or on the others. Hawaii did not become the first state to earmark money for geothermal development, says Professor Shupe, for nothing. In fact, Hawaii is regarded as an ideal spot for simultaneous development of solar, geothermal, oceanic, and wind energy resources.

Back in the continental states, recent drilling by the Union Oil Company has discovered a promising thermal pool in Sandoval County in New Mexico at 6,700 feet. The water is more benign, reports Union, than that of the Imperial Valley and there is probably a lot of it.

Peculiar things have been going on in the deepest well in the world in the Anadarko Basin in Oklahoma. The Lone Star Producing Company, down to 31,441 feet (nearly 6 miles) found no oil and no hot water but nearly had a volcano of hot liquid sulfur. The bottom-hole pressure gauge was "kicking like crazy" and cement was hastily pumped in to halt the mud flow at 14,100 feet. Nothing like this had ever been seen before and, in fact, no sulfur had ever been encountered in the Anadarko Basin. Although this experience does not add much to the annals of geothermal energy, it proves that when you get down there far enough the mineral world starts to play wild tricks and anything that can melt wants to escape to the fresh air of the surface.

KLAMATH FALLS, REYKJAVIK, AND A PARIS SUBURB

A tour of occasional uses of geothermal heat for other than spas and imaginary cures of the gout* discloses a charming versatility.

California is not the only geothermal state on the West Coast. The Klamath Basin, a high, rolling prairie on the top of the Cascade Mountains in Southern Oregon is now the focus of a new American land rush. Geologists, such as Dick Brown of the Oregon Department of Geology and Mineral Industries, believes that the Klamath region sits on top of one of the richest stores of geothermal energy.

Geothermal wells in Klamath Falls (population 16,000) provide heat for some 500 homes, schools, and businesses along the Hot Springs Belt—an area of

---

*The slight, evil-smelling concentration of hydrogen sulfide in the water of many hot-springs resorts has no therapeutic significance whatever and in fact may be somewhat toxic. It is true that you can reduce your gout-causing uric acid content in the blood by drinking a lot of water, but it does not have to be hot or smell like overripe eggs.

several square miles that outlines an immense hot-water reservoir, beginning at only 400 or 500 feet down. By city ordinance, inside the town the geothermal system takes no water out of the ground, for fear of depletion. Instead, there are down-hole exchangers: Cold water is piped down a well, heated to near boiling within the pipe by the hot ground water, then piped back up and into the home.

The city of Reykjavik (population 90,000) in Iceland is the first in the world to be heated 99 percent by geothermal energy. The capital stands directly over deep reservoirs of hot, nearly salt-free water, but between these reservoirs and the surface lie thousands of feet of lava. The water was apparently trapped in gravel and other permeable material left by the ice ages and later was covered by a lava flow from the Atlantic riff that runs south through Iceland all the way to the Antarctic. The Icelanders have bored some 32 holes down through the lava to hot sweet-water level. Each successive penetration is announced in Reykjavik to the surrounding residences and department stores by a window-shattering roar. The fire department quenches the eruption with cold water long enough for pipe fitters to cap the flow with a wellhead.

Sophisticated Icelandic housewives use the hot water for dishwashers and washing machines and baths and space heating but for washing silver and copper-ware they are smart enough to avoid the slight halitosis in the dragon's breath (hydrogen sulfide) by switching to heated water from the cold water tap. Ar-cheologists tell us that for centuries the Icelanders washed their clothes in the hot springs and baked their bread by burying a loaf-sized oven in the ground.

About a mile underneath the Paris suburb of Melun (population 42,000) there is hot, brackish water in sufficient amount comfortably to heat the homes and shops. Since the water is only 160 degrees Fahrenheit, it is not of much interest for power extraction but it is useful in the home, being heat-exchanged with regular city water and reinjected at a point only 35 feet from the original drill hole. This indirect extraction of heat is necessary since the French, unlike the Icelanders (who have a nonchalance bred by life "under the volcano"), worry about subsidence and want only the heat not the salt from this geothermal nest egg.

PROBLEMS

Probably the most serious financial problem for an enterprising driller who wants to find hot water as well as oil is that, if he finds hot water there is no clear depletion allowance. Although the Internal Revenue Service has recently decided that geothermal steam meets the standards for a depletable resource, nobody can find a respectable protocol for a depletion rate. The producers don't yet quite dare to demand a bold and brutal percentage of revenue, as in the petroleum gimmick (which, as mentioned, has no real connection with physical depletion itself, since the allowance will often compensate for using up the resource 15 to 20 times over) and yet they don't know how to tie it honestly to the lifetime of the hot-water well, since nobody has yet exhausted a geothermal property.

This is one of those ticklish questions that may make all the difference commercially as to whether geothermal operations attract specific investors or remain part of the agenda of oil companies or of public utilities. While the venture matures as a serious and standard way of obtaining energy, one has to assume a much closer collaboration of petroleum companies and public utilities than they have been used to in the past. Between the two of them it is possible to imagine the issue of a financial depletion incentive not only bringing them together but making them sweethearts. After all, it is the law in the United States that only a public utility may sell electric power, and there is no unifying sentiment stronger than a mutual desire to profit at public expense.

One other problem oddly enough is air pollution. As long as hydrogen sulfide is merely a disgusting flavor in the hot springs, whose water thousands of people quaff to try to cure months of overeating or booze, the danger is minuscule. Hydrogen sulfide is extremely soluble in water, but as a dry gas it is one of the most dangerous air pollutants one can imagine. I can remember during a strike in a California oil company, in which the research department was housed within the refinery limits, the research scientists volunteered to run the plant as scabs. A Ph.D. chemist, a friend of mine, in charge of research in petroleum analysis, took on the job of tank gauger. On top of a tank of sour crude oil (i.e., containing hydrogen sulfide) he was overcome by leakage of that gas on the graveyard shift (12 midnight to 8 A.M.), staggered, and fell off the edge of the tank to break his neck. Of all common effluents from energy installations, with the exception of plutonium-239, hydrogen sulfide is probably the most toxic. In the geothermal plants it can most easily escape during the cooling process.

The most recent and sophisticated estimates indicate that the amount of sulfur released in one form or another (hydrogen sulfide or sulfur dioxide) at The Geysers is equivalent to that emitted by a fossil-fueled plant of the same power capacity burning low-sulfur oil or coal, and that at the hot-water plant at Cerro Prieto, the sulfur releases might exceed that of comparable fossil-fuel plants burning high-sulfur coal. When the plants become much larger they will have to be cleaned up and, indeed, at that time the necessary restrictions on sulfur release might provide a good incentive to use the secondary fluid systems, in which the emissions are easily controlled, since the primary fluid goes through a closed circuit, returning (after giving up its heat) to the ground.

If we limit our survey to natural steam and hot water (neglecting even the shadowy geopressured zones in the Gulf of Mexico) how much geothermal energy do we have in the United States?

The National Petroleum Council has estimated that American geothermal resources can be developed to supply 1,900 to 3,500 megawatts by 1985. (This is surely superconservative, since the lower figure is quite likely to be reached at The Geysers alone.) However, the Hickel Conference in 1972 estimated the development potential as 132,000 megawatts by 1985, which would be roughly 20 percent of the electric power needed in the United States by that year. About

60 percent of the wells drilled can probably be classified as producers. With this success ratio the total number of wells required in the United States by 1985 to produce 132,000 megawatts would be about 42,000 or 3,800 per year, starting in 1974. This can be compared with the yearly total of on-shore petroleum well completion in the United States, which has been around 30,000 or about 8 times the number of geothermal wells needed. Looking at the future pragmatically, it would appear that, before the end of the century, from well-established sources of geothermal heat we could recover 10 percent of our total electrical power this way, which is twice what we recover from hydroelectric dams.

UNDERGROUND MOUNTAINS OF ENERGY

The required number of geothermal wells for hot water probably will not be drilled. What is more likely is that an entirely new technology, combined with a new exploration technique, will turn the geothermal world around and what we will be looking and drilling for are large hot hunks of dry granite. Here the amount of potential energy may conceivably almost overnight come to be seen as larger than all the fossil fuels and uranium combined.

The *hot dry rocks* is a term for bedrock at depths of 12,000 to 20,000 feet normally, but this prosaic concept has been shattered by the occasional intrusion of granite magma at high temperature into much shallower zones. In other words, the accidents that happen—the intrusions of the substance of the mantle or even possibly of the core into the high altitudes of the crust, like giant meteors falling upward—now lend the whole geothermal picture a certain brilliance of vast, haphazard power. It suddenly seems possible, in other words, that under the western earth there are hundreds, perhaps thousands of volcanoes that never made it to the surface.

New ways of looking at and looking for hot rocks have become the specialty of a group of young scientists located at the Atomic Energy Commission's facility, Los Alamos Scientific Laboratory in New Mexico, a complex run by the University of California, brother to somewhat similar groups at the Lawrence Livermore National Laboratory and the Lawrence Berkeley National Laboratory, all three of which have fortunately interested themselves in various aspects of geothermal energy.* At Los Alamos, they have not only done a lot of thinking about hot rocks, they have done some inventing and some experimental drilling.

How best to exploit a hot dry rock? At Los Alamos the doctrine is to shatter the rock so that a large surface of interlacing cracks is available to heat cold water injected from the surface. Depending upon how hot the rock is, the shattering process is accomplished either by simple dousing with cold water or by the process known in the oil business as hydrofrac, that is, fracturing under high water pressure, possibly with the introduction of grains of sand along with the water to keep the cracks open. (In petroleum fields the rocks are normally

---

*A little-noted congressional amendment to the Atomic Energy Act in 1972 gave the AEC authority to undertake research in nonnuclear energy.

sedimentary rather than the igneous granites that Los Alamos is interested in, so it is still a matter of conjecture as to whether the hot rocks will crack obediently and regularly.) After establishing a hot, cracked source of energy, Los Alamos keeps the injected water under pressure so that it doesn't become steam. You recover more heat with water than with steam. Since the Los Alamos experiments are in desert country, you have to be stingy with your injected water. As it comes up hot, you run it in heat exchange with a secondary fluid, such as isobutane, that drives a gas turbine to produce electric power. You do this not because the water comes up full of salts but because you do not want to waste water to the air, as they do at The Geysers.

In their first drilling experiment Los Alamos drilled 800 meters into rock at the edge of the huge volcanic Valle Grande *caldera* in the Jemez Mountains of northern New Mexico. The results showed not only that crystalline rocks like granite can be hydraulically fractured, but that only modest pressures are required. The water in the test well began to penetrate the rock when the pressure at the wellhead reached 8 million newtons per square meter.* Even drilling into the granite—expected to be the most expensive phase—turned out to be relatively easy. The engineers at Los Alamos have invented a bullet-shaped, molybdenum-tipped, electrically heated drilling bit, called a subterrene that reaches temperatures of over 1,800 degrees centigrade. It can bore equally well through unconsolidated soil, forming behind it neat tunnels of obsidianlike glass, or through granite, in which case most of the rock melted by the bit passes into a hole in the tip of the penetrator and back through the innards of the subterrene for removal at the opening of the tunnel.

While the scientists of Los Alamos were cranking up and experimentally drilling and rapping in all-night sessions, a young man from Texas, a Ph.D. candidate at Southern Methodist University named David Blackwell, discovered in Montana the geological equivalent of a new planet. At Maryville, not far from Helena, his measurements of heat flow in mines and wells proved the existence of a vast rock more than 8,000 feet in radius and about 6,000 feet beneath the surface, at the extraordinary temperature of over 900 degrees Fahrenheit. A cubic mile of heat at this temperature is worth a billion dollars. The energy in the Marysville "object" is estimated to be approximately equivalent to that contained in the oil in the Alaskan North Slope.

Financed by the National Science Foundation, the Battelle Memorial Institute of the Northwest hopes to drill into this still cooling mass of lava that apparently boiled up into the earth's crust about 80,000 years ago. Paralleling the Los Alamos studies, Battelle will examine ways of fracturing the Marysville type of hot igneous rock with chemical explosives.† More importantly, money will be

---

*A newton is a unit of force capable of accelerating a mass of 1 kilogram 1 meter per second. It will be used universally as American engineering converts to the metric system.
†In spending money for such research, Congress has specifically forbidden the use of nuclear energy, mostly at the insistence of representatives from Colorado and Nevada, who have had their bellyful of Project Ploughshare.

spent both in the Helena-Great-Falls-Butte-Anaconda geothermal axis and in the southwest to develop methods of scouting for such bonanzas. The Marysville Empire Creek Valley had not even been listed as a probable geothermal area by the Geological Survey, and who knows how many Empire Creek Valleys there are left undiscovered in this country? There is some reason to suspect that the existence of large masses of relatively shallow hot rock can be detected by patterns of low-intensity shallow shocks; in other words, earthquakelets. Several exploration companies are technologically based on this assumption.

Congress also wants some money spent on investigating the geopressured water fields or zones of the Gulf of Mexico, far beneath the ocean beds. As far as is known, these immense, queer domains consist of uncompacted sand and clays in which water has been trapped. They were formed presumably by successive deposition of sediment carried down the Mississippi and the Rio Grande Rivers during the past 40 million years. The trapped fresh water has become geopressured by the enormous weight of the millions of layers of sediment. Since water is a poor thermal conductor, it has absorbed the heat emanating from the earth's mantle and simply sits there at extraordinarily high pressures and temperatures.

The incredible extra bonus of such of these zones as have been outlined is the fact that the water contains natural gas in dissolved form. (Pressures have to be high indeed to cause water to dissolve methane and other gaseous hydrocarbons, especially at the temperatures involved.) It appears that for one zone examined cursorily the natural gas content may be 40 cubic feet per barrel of water, or for this particular zone as a whole, about 2,700 trillion cubic feet. For comparison, the known United States reserves are about 300 trillion cubic feet and our natural gas consumption during 1973 was at the rate of 23.6 trillion cubic feet. Although we are speculating mainly on the basis of Texas enthusiasm, just one such geopressured water field would possibly provide enough gas for over 100 years at the reckless consumption rate of 1973, not to speak of vast reserves of nonfuel energy in the form of high-pressure hot water.

These gigantic and mysterious depth bombs are planted very deep and must be approached with the utmost caution. If you plunged into one of them willynilly you might find half the Gulf along with the cities of Houston and New Orleans up in the air in a mushroom-shaped cloud the size of all Mexico. Such an apocalyptic vision may be exaggerated, but in a sense it is truer than the scattered numbers of the U.S. Geological Survey. It gives us the well-justified feeling that beneath the breast of our Mother Earth lie wild, rock-confined treasures of energy that we simply forgot about.

12 Face to Face with the Sun

The sun never repents of the good he does.
Nor does he ever demand a recompense.
—BENJAMIN FRANKLIN

Contrary to the beliefs of certain young engineers, who have suddenly realized that the sunlight is free and strikes the earth in glorious multiples of any conceivable total world demand for energy, the idea of directly employing sunbeams for useful application is not a new one. Before these young engineers were born, in fact, there was considerable stir in the air about using solar collectors for heating water and residential space; and such activity in this country not unnaturally focused in Florida. As early as the 1920s Florida was using its ample sunshine to heat water in homes, and even today Eric Ferber's solar energy laboratory at the University of Florida is one of the most advanced and versatile in the world. Ferber and his collaborators are eager to demonstrate how to use the sun not only to heat and to distill water but to run engines and to pump and to treat sewage.

The early fervor about solar energy in the Florida of 5 decades ago was extinguished when cheap natural gas came by pipeline into the state.* Today there is a strange reluctance on the part of Florida banks and engineering companies to re-enter the solar energy field, because (as they say, as reported by Florida Congressman Bill Gunter) solar energy is to them "old-fashioned," a "flapper-era phenomenon," with pipes on the roof and lukewarm water on cloudy days.

Resurgences here and there of interest in using sunlight occurred in the 1950s and early 1960s. The Solar Energy Laboratory of the Institute of Atmospheric Physics at the University of Arizona, under James J. Riley, built and tested a solar house in Tucson. Later it experimented with the solar desalting of sea water at Puerto Penasco, Mexico; and still later it established a $3 million

---

*Here again the unforgivable error of the Supreme Court decision of 1954 (controlling interstate prices of natural gas at drastically low levels) muddied up not only the economic past but stymied a rational entrance into energy's future. On all technical fronts, alternative to petroleum and natural gas, save for that decision, the United States would be a quarter-century ahead of where it is now.

solar desalting plant and commercial greenhouse in the sheikdom of Abu Dhabi on the Persian Gulf, now a fountainhead of low sulfur petroleum. (We shall have occasion later to discuss more recent goings-on in Tucson with another research team.)

Throughout these pre-energy-crisis decades certain dedicated scientists, such as the late Farrington Daniels, continued unflaggingly to preach the solar gospel, and his 20-year-old book *Direct Use of the Sun's Energy,* reissued in paperback, remains perhaps the most inspiriting essay on the subject. In 1961 at the United Nation's Conference on New Sources of Energy, Harry Tabor of Israel's National Physics Laboratory demonstrated with direct sunlight the same kind of delightful toy that Georges Claude had 50 years before used in his lectures on obtaining energy from the temperature difference between the surface and depths of the tropical ocean—a tiny turbine running on a low-boiling fluid such as butane. A lonely but productive project on solar houses was carried out by the Massachusetts Institute of Technology between 1938 and 1958. Test houses were built, the last one of the series in 1958 in Lexington, Massachusetts.

In 1964 Hubert Humphrey introduced solar-energy legislation in the Senate and made a good many typically exuberant speeches, as did California's then ubiquitous congressman from Long Beach, Craig Hosmer (now retired); all to no avail. The world's excess of petroleum seemed eternal, and the low price of interstate natural gas discouraged anybody whose interests were in a quick buck rather than the future of the country and of the world.

Of course, we need not merely review the earlier twentieth-century past of our own country to discover man's keen but baffled engineering interest in the sun. Even now, as Sir George Porter, a Nobel laureate, has pointed out, if one could use sunbeams as weapons of war, the problems of direct solar utilization would long ago have been solved.*

The 1,000 kilowatt solar furnace at Odeillo in the French Pyrenees differs very little in essential design and purpose from one exhibited in the Stockholm museum, made in 1612 by somebody in search of the philosophers' stone. Napoleon III extended the demonstration of a solar steam engine in Paris in 1866. This 1 horsepower engine, invented by Auguste Monchot, required 172 square feet of solar reflecting surface to operate. (As we shall see later, the so-called Stirling cycle engine with a quartz cylinder head has been recently designed to run on sunlight.) Before he became interested in the relaying of solar energy from artificial earth satellites in the form of microwaves, Peter Glaser now of Arthur D. Little, Inc., demonstrated in the early 1960s that famous American instinct for rejuvenating junk by building a 5,000 degree Fahrenheit solar furnace with used army searchlight mirrors at an out-of-pocket cost of $37.40.

As for what is now known as solar climate control (or air conditioning of

---

*Sir George forgot that sunbeams were once used as weapons of war; that is, if we are to believe the story of Archimedes at Syracuse. He is supposed, in 212 B.C., to have repulsed a Roman fleet by lining the harbor with soldiers holding highly polished shields to concentrate the sun on the sails and in the eyes of the invaders.

houses by the sun's energy) the Greek historian Xenophon noted about 400 B.C. that "we should build the south side [of the house] loftier, to get the winter sun, and the north side lower to keep out the cold winds." The most illustrious of the architects of ancient Rome, Vitruvius, devoted much of his *Ten Books on Architecture* to suggestions on building design for various climates and locales, with emphasis on trapping the sun inward in wintertime and blocking the sun out in summer.

Except in Japan and the Soviet Union, the solar energy dream never materialized. Basically it was up against some tough facts of nature. The total insolation of the earth is huge but diffuse. The atmospheric absorption of the sun's rays by water vapor, carbon dioxide, and oxygen is responsible for reducing the energy flux from 2.0 calories per gram centimeter per second at the top of the atmosphere to 1.40 at sea level. For every 100 watts of incoming solar power, 24 are reflected by clouds, 7 are scattered back into space by the atmosphere, and 4 are reflected back by the planet's surface.

Still, in the United States alone, 9 quadrillion watt-hours of sunlight are received annually, the equivalent of the energy from 1.15 trillion tons of coal, which is about all the coal we have. The energy contained in the sunlight falling on Lake Erie on an average day is more than the total energy used that day by the entire United States. The power in sunlight falling on one acre is about 4,000 horsepower; that on each square yard of your front lawn is 1 1/2 horsepower.

In still other terms, the maximum energy received at the earth's surface is 290 Btus per hour per square foot in clear air, but only 200 in New York City on an average day. Around typical cities of our country the insolation (measured this time in million kilowatt hours per acre per year) varies as follows: El Paso 9.5, Fresno 7.8, San Diego 7.0, Miami 7.0, Salt Lake City 6.7, Lincoln 6.3, Cleveland 6.1, Washington 5.8, Seattle 5.4, Boston 5.2, New York City 4.9.

Obviously El Paso would be a more favorable place to install a gigantic sun factory than New York City. The Southwest would be a fine place to locate new generators. With all that desert and all that sun, one could set up enormous collectors to run steam turbines and send electric power all over the country. Right? Wrong! This would be impossibly expensive for the simple and depressing reason that the cost is so high and the efficiency so dismally low for the transmission of electricity at great distances that before we had a breakthrough in the design of solar collection, we would need a still more spectacular breakthrough in the transmission of electricity by cable.*

If, instead of thinking big in terms of the extensive solar farms needed to trap

---

*Kraft Ehricke of Rockwell International, in order to get around this fundamental dilemma, has proposed a power relay satellite that would provide cheap transmission of electric power over distances of 3,000 miles or more. Electric power from a desert generator would be transmitted by microwave to a satellite in synchronous orbit, then beamed down to any one of several sites close to a center of large power consumption (e.g., Arizona desert to New York City, Chicago, or Seattle; Sahara desert to London; Gobi Desert to Shanghai). An exceedingly important advantage of this system would be the lack of necessity for energy storage.

the sun for central power generating stations, we limit ourselves to things we can do with our own houses, we come up against a social or psychological problem, first clearly stated by Marjorie Meinel of the husband and wife team at the Optical Science Center at the University of Arizona. In her own experience, putting in and maintaining a solar roof collector and the various gadgets that go along with it is simply too much of a nuisance for the average American family. A solar house is fine for a retired plumber. He can fiddle around with it every day of the year and even make it work. But for people who are busy (even busy, like the Meinels, at research on the utilization of solar energy) the nagging leaks in water pipes, the constant presence of Murphy's law (which decrees that everything that can possibly go wrong will invariably do so) make the care and feeding of a solar house an impossibly exacting sideline, maybe like raising turkeys.

There is another, purely economic angle that argues against private, do-it-yourself or kit-type solarization. As Marjorie Meinel points out, the "heat-pump" type of home air conditioner became popular in the Phoenix area. In new subdivisions, installations priced as low as necessary to sell, the average lifetime to failure of a major component, either the pump or the motor, was 18 months. In solar installations, which are highly capital-intensive, the temptation would be to lower the price by making them tacky. Solar climate control, like the heat pump in Phoenix, might get a bad reputation it could never live down. The Meinels have even arrived at a sort of law of their own: Solar utilization is only practical when enough associated consumers are involved to require full-time professional operation and maintenance of the system. Since there has been a trend toward condominium and apartment living, this criterion still takes in a lot of people; in fact, enough people to justify a review of the whole subject of solar climatic control.

THE GREENHOUSE EFFECT

There are 3 absolutely distinct methods of collecting solar energy: (1) classically to use the heat content of the light to raise the temperature of a fluid such as water; (2) chemically to store the sunlight energy, a notable example being the process of photosynthesis on which all plant life depends; or (3) to use photovoltaics, which in the case of the so-called solar cell so widely exploited in the Apollo and other astronaut programs, involves the ability of certain materials to convert sunlight directly into electricity.

The first method—that of storing light as heat—depends on the greenhouse effect, an optical phenomenon which is by no means confined to the properties of glass and which is exemplified in a rather horrible way by our sister planet Venus. On that tortured world there is an extremely dense atmosphere but virtually all of it consists of carbon dioxide. Now carbon dioxide has the property of absorbing that part of the solar radiation or reflected radiation from the planet itself which is in the infrared or pure heat-ray end of the spectrum. The result is that energy can escape from Venus only when the surface temperature becomes high enough so that more reflected energy is concentrated in the lower, visible wave lengths which are not so completely gobbled up by the stifling blanket of carbon dioxide. In other words, the surface of this poor planet must be about 900 degrees Fahrenheit, which is above the melting point of many metals, including lead, to enable it to escape still further incineration.

Glass has an effect in a terrestrial greenhouse similar to that of carbon dioxide on Venus. You will have experienced the greenhouse effect unpleasantly if you have left your car parked in the sun with the windows rolled up. The glass lets through a broad spectrum of sunlight but reflects back into the interior the infrared radiation from the objects heated inside the automobile. Neither Venus nor the automobile on a sunny day are any longer associated with the act of love. In order to incorporate the greenhouse effect into a house the simplest thing to do apparently is to cover with glass some blackened pipe through which one circulates water.

But it turns out that this is not the simplest thing to do. Since the invention of the water bed, something even more primitive has been developed. The so-called Atascadero house developed in California by Harold R. Hay is the ultimate in simplicity, involving neither fluid circulation nor glass collecting systems; but it should be emphasized at the start that it is a very small, compact residence, preferably for a dwarf bachelor. You put the bags full of water, which look exactly like water beds and, indeed, depending on the water-holding durability of the same plastic, on your roof, you insulate the rest of the house (floors and walls) in a modern way and use double-glazed windows; hence the roof is a sort of naked thermal valve for a perfectly insulated box. In the winter the water bags heat up, if the sun shines, and at night an opaque panel is drawn above the bags so that the heat stored in them is directed downward into the house rather than radiated outward to the night sky. In summer the bags would be covered during the day by the panels, so that instead of absorbing the sun's heat they absorb the heat from the house, then radiate it off, with panels open, at night. With no forced circulation of air, this may or may not cool satisfactorily a mere hatbox of a house. Atascadero, in northern California, was selected as the site for this almost absurdly simple living machine, since the temperature ranges from 20 degrees to 110 degrees Fahrenheit in the course of the year.

There must be some bugs in this system, but I have not found them and HUD has become sufficiently interested to finance further study with engineers at California State Polytechnic University at San Luis Obispo. It is a question to me whether the probable deficiencies of the Atascadero house are worse than the quite obvious vulnerabilities of any house that has glass on the roof: destruction by hail, for example, or even stones thrown by small boys.

A more typical solar residence is located in a suburb of Washington, D. C. It is Harry Thomason's house in District Heights, Maryland. Thomason even has a romantic story to tell reporters about the genesis of the idea. In 1956, during a hot afternoon at his future wife's home in North Carolina, a sudden thunderstorm blew up. As he dashed into a barn for shelter, drops of warm water dribbled off the rusty, sheet-metal roof, pelting his bare head. Thomason was impressed by the heat of these drops and when the sun reappeared, he held a thermometer under the metal roof. Ping! It broke as the mercury passed 140 degrees Fahren-heit.

Nearly 20 years later he designed his house in Maryland. The solar collectors that cover one side of the roof are blackened metal sheets of corrugated roofing, much like the Carolina barn of his courting days, but they are covered with glass. Water pumped from the basement trickles down the corrugated metal, is warmed by the sun's rays and is recollected in the basement in a 1,500-gallon tank surrounded with several tons of fist-sized rocks. As the rocks warm, a blower passes air over them into the central forced-air heating system. Harry Thomason can heat his house (important in a Maryland winter), but unlike Harold Hay of Atascadero he has no way of cooling it, and in a Maryland summer the water bags of Atascadero would not be up to the cooling job either.

For cooling houses and buildings in the hot wet summers of the Eastern seaboard and the Midwest and the South, as well as the blistering dry heat of the Southwest one needs a more potent amount of power than one gets from a shallow greenhouse on the roof. The fact is that no simple, inexpensive, and at the same time powerful mechanism for cooling a simple house exists using the sunbeam method. Without going into parabolic mirrors or lenses or vacuum-pipe insula-tion plus special pipe-covering compounds (all of which cost like the very devil) the individual home owner is now forced to be satisfied with water at the tempera-ture of breakfast coffee. This is not enough to imitate the simplest of air-cooling systems, in which, in effect, one burns a flame to heat a fluid that in the act of expansion or of evaporation cools its surroundings.

THE DELAWARE HOUSE

The limitations for the simple house whose climate is controlled by simple photo-thermal methods do not exist when one goes to the alternative technique of converting sunlight directly into electricity. This is being demonstrated by Profes-sor Karl Böer of the University of Delaware in an experimental home which should demonstrate technical, although at this stage certainly not economical, feasibility.

The Bell Laboratories (G. C. Pearson, C. S. Fuller, and D. M. Chapin) demonstrated the first practical solar cell in 1954. They discovered that if two different types of silicon alloys, doped with boron and arsenic, were connected with pure silicon and exposed to light, direct electric current would be generated and would flow through the system. The first solar cells were mounted in an array the size of a cigar box and would provide enough power to run a transistor radio. Later, using solar cells coated with a thin sapphire layer as protection against strong radiation, Bell used these photovoltaic converters to power radio and television relays in the TEL-STAR satellite. Solar cells of the silicon type were used as sources of electric power in all later space adventures.

This kind of solar cell is enormously expensive, perhaps on the order of

$100,000 per kilowatt, but there is some hope of getting the price down to mortal rather than the astronomical levels that NASA was willing to pay for Project Apollo and other space shots. For example, instead of forming single crystals of silicon into a cylindrical boule that has to be sliced, wafer-thin, Bruce Chalmers of Harvard and A. F. Miavsky of Tyco Laboratories have been able to form continuously 6-foot-long ribbons of perfect crystallinity from molten silicon. If the quality is satisfactory, this would be the answer; but there always seems to be a fly in the jam and in this case it is the flabbergasting fact that molten silicon is the most perfect solvent known. It will dissolve anything except pure graphite. If the graphite used for the dies in the ribbon process contains any impurities they will wind up in the ribbon and the silicon will be useless or hopelessly inefficient as a solar cell. Another approach lies in improving the efficiency and working lifetime of other photovoltaic solids, such as cadmium sulfide or germanium arsenide.

In his concept for the Delaware House in Newark, Professor Böer selected a mixture of cadmium sulfide and copper sulfide. Of Swiss extraction, Karl Böer is an eminently practical man and he realized that the climate-controlled house had to be surrounded by certain nontechnical posies to attract the capital of investors or the interest of architects. (That he has wrapped a tempting package is indicated by the fact that Shell Oil Company was willing to invest $3 million in Böer's private company, Solar Energy Systems, Inc.) Böer figured that for market acceptance his system had to (1) have low first cost—less than 10 percent of the total cost of the home; (2) the solar energy should be no more expensive than any other form of energy; (3) the system should be as reliable as conventional ones; and (4) there should be some incentive for at least one member of the "builder/consumer chain."

The last proviso is the shrewdest, for specifically it attracts the support of the local utility, first of all by making the system supplemental rather than substitutional and, secondly, designing a feedback into the local-utility electrical grid of any temporary excess of energy from the Delaware House. Böer hopes, indeed, to have the utilities interested to the point of a fond and fatherly attitude toward the experiment—perhaps even a subsidy.

Böer's design in the end included both photothermal and photovoltaic elements. Heat is picked up from the open ends of the solar cells under glass on the roof and is transferred by air into a heat processing unit and heat storage. The solar cells are connected to an electric power processing unit that contains a means for electric storage (e.g., storage batteries) and an inverter to change direct current to alternating current. A heat pump is used in conjunction with a base heat reservoir operating in the 70 to 75 degrees Fahrenheit range.

On a clear summer night the base reservoir will be cooled through air from the collectors, the air being cooled by radiating its heat content to the night. The heat pump will operate mainly during the night and coolness will be stored in a secondary heat reservoir near 50 degrees Fahrenheit.

The electrical energy from the cells on the roof will be used as direct current for certain appliances (e.g., the kitchen stove, the heating coil of the clothes dryer, the auxiliary house-heating motor fans, and the permanent light fixtures. Individual converters will apply the home-made juice as alternating current to run the heat pump and the refrigerator.

On paper this looks very elegant and Böer has calculated that the total cost of installation of his solar electrical/thermal system would exceed that of a conventional installation by only about $3,000 for a three-bedroom house. His system would produce heat energy at a cost of $1.50 per million Btus and electrical energy at 2.7 cents per kilowatt-hour, figures that compare favorably with the current energy prices in Delaware.

There is not enough experience with this crucial design to know whether it is "going to fly" or not. It may be, from Marjorie Meinel's practical standpoint, too clever. There are so many things to go wrong—beginning with the eutectic salt heat-storage systems, which have a bad track record. In my own experience sometimes the salts fail to crystallize because of incidental impurities or pure cussedness and have to be seeded. One visualizes sleeping in such a house and having a perpetual nightmare of electrical engineers, chemical engineers, plumbers, electricians, and haggard professors dashing in and out, charging up and down the stairs, and falling off the roof. I hope this is not a prophetic dream and I wish Professor Böer and his Delaware House many happy calories.

LARGE-SCALE SOLAR INSTALLATIONS

If one uses the Meinel criterion that the consumer energy load (whether it be a condominium, a big apartment house, a school, a hotel, or an office building or a whole city) has to be large enough to justify full-time professional operation and maintenance, the outlook is more practical and correspondingly, in spite of stagflation, the competition is fiercer. For central power plants one can justify (or at least one can consider) optical concentration with lenses or mirrors—the burning-glass principle. The large elliptical furnace in the French Pyrenees produces a temperature of 5,000 degrees Fahrenheit, high enough to melt through steel armor plate. One of the most practical designs for this method of solar enhancement is the use of a parabolic trough to heat a pipe containing water or air or some other heat-exchange fluid which can be used either to heat a boiler for a steam turbine or can be fed directly into a gas turbine. The Meinels of Tucson experimented several years ago with such a trough but were shocked at the cost, the deterioration of the mirrors because of dust, and with the frequency of cloudy conditions even in the desert winters of Arizona.

The parabolic-trough collector concept perhaps has reached a sort of four-minute-mile phase in the tenfold concentration achieved by a design originated by Richard Winston of the University of Chicago and developed by John Martin of the Argonne National Laboratory. The basic unit of the Winston collector is an elongated, steep-sided trough lined with a thin, reflective, polished film of aluminum. A number of these units would be put together in a bank. As the sun passes in an arc over the troughs the light is reflected from the sides and concentrated on the bottom where it is converted to heat in a blackened fluid-carrying pipe. The particular tilted parabolic design of the trough, as Winston found later, had been invented by evolution over 300 million years ago in the receptor units (ommatidia) of the compound eye of the horseshoe crab *(Limulus).*

A very powerful but expensive light-concentrating design is the one-point focus system, where a field of tracking heliostats (mirrors automatically following the sun in its path) direct reflected sunlight on a central tower absorber, where some fluid is heated continuously to high temperatures. The Martin-Marietta Company is working on one version of this concept in which a hillside is used to house the mirrors and the receiving station is at ground level. The McDonnell-Douglas Corporation one-point focus system requires no special terrain, but the center of focus may be a tower 1,500 feet high (taller than the World Trade Center skyscrapers in New York).

The line-focus includes the parabolic trough already mentioned. Among people working on various versions of it are Honeywell of Minneapolis plus the University of Minnesota, Gulf-General Atomic, Itak, and Helio Associates (Meinel's Company). In the original (Meinel) design, focusing was onto a stainless-steel or ceramic pipe covered with a selective coating that re-emits only about 5 percent of the radiation absorbed and this pipe is itself enclosed in an evacuated glass chamber to reduce conductive and convective heat losses. Nitrogen gas is pumped through the pipe at 4 meters per second to transfer heat to a central storage unit, probably consisting of eutectic mixtures of salts, mostly sodium nitrate. As needed, the heat would be used to produce steam for electric generators.

Ernst Eckert of the University of Minnesota and Roger Schmidt of Honeywell also conceive of a central power station, but their parabolic reflector concentrates sunlight into a heat pipe, a device that transfers heat along its length efficiently without fluids or pumps. As in the Meinel design, the pipe's outer surface would be a selective coating and the pipe would be enclosed in an evacuated chamber. A small heat-storage tank is attached to each reflector-heat-pipe combination but there is no centralized heat storage. An underground conduit brings water to each storage tank and returns it as steam directly to a turbine, thus reducing pumping costs compared to the Meinel system.

One of the more cunning ideas in line focusing is that of John Russell of Gulf in which the parabolic mirrors are fixed in a trough on the ground and the absorbing pipe is moved to follow the sun. Another novel concept is that of Howard Palmer of Pennsylvania State University, who uses graphite in the collector. As a thin slab in a long, well-insulated glass pipe, the graphite absorbs heat and transfers it to a stream of helium gas which, at about 1,100 degrees Fahrenheit, would drive a gas turbine electric generator. Palmer's scheme is appropriate for dry areas, because it requires no water.

Much less expensive than the point and line focusing collectors are so-called afocal systems, where no lenses or mirrors are needed, and where medium-high

temperatures are obtained by the use of novel and extremely selective surfaces.*
In taking this option, as the Meinels have recently done in designing an installation for use in some commercial buildings in Tucson, one foregoes the glamour
of "Big Heat" and has to be satisfied with temperatures from 400 to 500 degrees
Fahrenheit, hot enough to provide space heating, refrigeration, and the like, but
not enough to run an efficient steam turbine. What one sacrifices in intensity, one
gains in flexibility. The collectors do not need to focus on the sun and, indeed,
they can operate in diffuse light. But to accumulate a lot of power, they need a
lot of space, perhaps about as much space, if one is going to run the country on
sunlight, as would be strip mined in digging for Western coal.

But what appears to be the natural progression of solar power is first the
installation in big, separate buildings. For example RCA plans to build a $6
million conference and dining room onto its Rockefeller Center skyscraper that
would use solar energy for lighting and heating. The Environmental Quality
Laboratory of Cal Tech, along with the Jet Propulsion Laboratory and the
Southern California Gas Company, plans to install demonstration solar heating
systems in 3 new apartment buildings in the Los Angeles area. The University
of Tulsa is working with engineering firms on the solar climate control of a new
shopping center. Plans for a new building in Pittsburgh with solar heating and
cooling were reported to be completed by a combination consisting of Standard
of Ohio, Alcoa, PPG Industries (a big glass company), and the architectural firm
of Oliver Tyrone. The roof will be slanted to catch the sun in collector cells of
coated aluminum filled with water and antifreeze. The windows on the east and
west will be angled to collect a maximum of sunlight, while the southside windows will be shaded by solar collector cells of the same type as those on the roof.
The three largest contractors for the National Science Foundation—General
Electric, Westinghouse, and TRW—have revealed encouraging results of studies
on the feasibility of solar heating and cooling two large skyscrapers. Perhaps the
largest heating project under way is that of the classroom center at Denver
Community College. There have, in addition, been numerous proposals for the
application of solar heating and cooling to separate schools here and there and
to churches.

I cannot help mentioning again the Meinel team. They combine an impressive combination of self-confidence and common sense. What Aden Meinel now
emphasizes is the principle of commingling for power utility companies; that is,
the initial high cost of electricity from solar units is buried in the total costs from
burning natural gas or coal or from hydroelectric installations, so that in the
whole mix of therms or energy units delivered by the utility, the effect of introducing high-cost solar therms is relatively painless and, as further development
makes the solar contribution more than competitive with the conventional

---

*Research by IBM has shown that tungsten, although ordinarily a poor absorbent for sunlight, can
be surface-treated in a remarkable manner so that it will retain solar heat at temperatures as high
as 500 degrees centigrade. A vapor-deposited tungsten film has a surface covered with microscopic
dendrites, which absorb sunlight and refuse to let go of it.

sources, the customer gets a bonus, like the fond kiss of gentle sunlight on a bald head. There is ample precedent for this method of accounting in the recent proposal to mix initially expensive synthetic natural gas from coal with native natural gas in large pipeline deliveries, as from plants in New Mexico to Southern California.

In estimating the future costs of solar collecting hardware, Meinel, although a professional astronomer, does not believe in transposing costs at the level of practical astronomy to the level of solar collectors. A good source of information is the Sears Roebuck or Montgomery Ward catalogues, where hardware similar in materials or construction (for example, kitchenware) to solar plants averages about 80 cents a pound, compared with telescopic equipment at over $30 a pound. This would average out around $4 per square foot of collector-working surface or about $10,000 per kilowatt of electricity. The Meinels estimate that by the time the thirtieth solar power farm of 100-megawatt size has been produced, the cost will be down to $1,500 per kilowatt. This is more expensive than nuclear fission power, but (as discussed in Chapter 7) energy from uranium ores relies on a nonrenewable source, and there are growing qualms about the safety, not only of the fast breeder, but of the indefinite multiplication of standard light-water reactors.

One should not overlook the dreams of those who place their bets on the photovoltaic (solar cell) way to go rather than the photothermal techniques we have mentioned. A real breakthrough here could change everybody's plans overnight in regard to big solar electric installations. For example, never underestimate the power of a very large research entity such as Exxon Enterprises. Working with the Solar Power Corporation, they put on the market 2 years ago a 1 1/2 watt solar cell module made in a new way from silicon, but they are now aiming their guns at something perhaps a thousand times cheaper—an organic photovoltaic system. With all the technical clout in this particular electronics area (which verges on the semiconductor domain) the United States with Bell Laboratories, IBM, and a dozen other world leaders in fundamental electronic research could be expected to come up with something vastly more efficient than cadmium sulfide and enormously less expensive than crystalline silicon.

And, in spite of stagflation and a general feeling of glumness and disenchantment about space adventures, I believe that Peter Glaser of Arthur D. Little, Inc., has the most magnificent idea of all. He would build huge power stations outside the atmosphere at the altitude (22,300 miles) necessary for synchronous satellites (where, like the communications satellites, they revolve at the same speed as the earth). These would weigh some 25 million pounds each and each could generate 5,000 megawatts, enough to meet the needs of about 10 million people. In Glaser's Solar Satellite Power Stations (SSPSs) electrical power would be generated by 2 large panels—each about 10 square miles in area—consisting of millions of lightweight solar cells and surrounded by reflecting mirrors. The electricity produced by the solar cells would be converted to microwave radiation and beamed back to a receiving antenna on earth of about the same scale. The microwaves would then be reconverted to electricity, these conversions being of surprisingly high efficiency.

The problem of getting the SSPSs into orbit would hopefully be solved in the course of, perhaps as the chief goal of, the great space shuttle program now in the advanced planning state by NASA for the 1980s. It would take some 500 shuttle flights to get the components of each SSPS in place. It would cost more billions of dollars than one wants to think about, but perhaps not as much as the Apollo program, provided that the cost of the solar cells could be greatly reduced.

It should be noted that the satellite power stations, since out there they have available more powerful, ultraviolet-containing sunlight, could introduce more solar energy into the earth than it would normally receive. There has also been the objection that the intense microwave beams around the receiving stations on earth would cause people to go off their rockers and to roam around howling at the moon. It seems to me that the complaints have been niggling. The excess energy criticism has no merit whatsoever, since we started introducing excess energy on earth when we first split the atom. There is no evidence that even very intense microwave radiation causes maleficent side effects on human brains that happen to be in the general vicinity. With all the giant challenges it presents, I truly believe Glaser's concept, if not within our reach, will be within the reach of our grandchildren. Indeed, if Glaser's brilliant dream could be accepted as part of the space shuttle program, the 1980s might see mankind pull itself out of its paralysis and depression and become truly human again.

CHEMICAL TRICKS

As a lifelong chemist I have been disappointed at the paucity of chemical dodges investigated in the utilization of solar energy. It is true that some important but unspectacular work has been done at Tulsa University on increasing the rate of heat exchange from sun-heated surfaces to water and other fluids by the addition of surfactant dyes, but I am amazed at the lack of credit and publicity afforded the outstanding work achieved at the Naval Research Laboratory under the direction of Talbert A. Chubb, which evolved into the so-called Solchem process.

What Chubb and his fellow chemists realized was that a good deal of the engineering grief of changing solar energy into heat energy at a high enough level to run a turbine, to heat or cool a building, and the like was the insufficiency of transporting energy as sensible heat: Why not transport it as potential chemical energy? They chose the simplest system: $SO_3 \rightleftarrows SO_2$ and $1/2$ O_2, in which sulfur trioxide is decomposed to a mixture of sulfur dioxide and oxygen in a small reaction chamber at the focal point of a parabolic mirror at about 800 degrees centigrade. The decomposition is a strongly endothermic reaction; that is, energy is absorbed and the mixture of sulfur dioxide and oxygen leaves the reaction chamber at a relatively low temperature, perhaps 110 degrees centigrade. Very little energy is lost in transmitting this gaseous mixture to where it can be used to heat a boiler or a space heater or cooler by catalyzing the reverse (exothermic, energy-emitting) reaction of sulfur dioxide and oxygen to sulfur trioxide, probably over a platinum catalyst. After giving off its very large heat of formation, the SO_3 is recycled back to the solar furnace, and again the temperature at transmission is low so that energy losses are minimal.

This, indeed, is what makes the process such an engineering pet: Heat losses don't have to be avoided by vacuum bottles and superinsulation, because the useful energy is not in the form of sensible heat but of chemical potential. The solar furnace operates at an efficiency of about 60 percent (extremely high in comparison with pure thermal absorption and photovoltaic utilization of sunlight), while the catalyzed heat-exchange process operates at over 90 percent efficiency. The technology of this particular chemical reaction (coping with the corrosiveness of the reactants, especially) has been well and widely known for over a century, for it is the basic process for making sulfuric acid, the highest tonnage heavy chemical in all world industry.

This process deserves immediate attention and I understand it will be tested on a fairly large scale at the Army's solar furnace at White Sands, New Mexico, sometime in 1976 or 1977.

When one begins to think of this cycle—absorbing sunlight by an endothermic reaction into materials that later release energy by an exothermic reaction —the realization dawns upon one that this is exactly what the tandem processes of photosynthesis and burning of photosynthesized organic matter (wood, dry leaves, coal, petroleum, all other fossil fuels) consist of. Evolution learned the first step of the tandem process perhaps 4 billion years ago, and man learned the second step in the discovery of controlled fire, perhaps half a million years before the present.

Are we smarter chemists than organic evolution itself? Why should we suddenly neglect a process of solar energy utilization that is responsible in the long run for all life on earth?

George C. Szego, president of the Intertechnology Corporation, and his coworkers have been the most pressurizing and sparkling-eyed exponents of "energy forests" and "fuel plantations." What their capital cost comparisons boil down to is the following tabulation:

Process	Capital Cost	
Photovoltaic	$100,000 per kilowatt plus cost of storage	
Photothermal	$5,000 per kilowatt plus cost of storage	
Photosynthetic	0.6 acres per kilowatt (0.7 percent energy conversion)	$ 130
	Other capital costs	$ 50
	Power station	$ 200
	Total cost less than $1,000 per kilowatt	

When Szego's critics (e.g., the Atomic Energy Commission) point out that we don't have enough land to raise crops or forests for power fuel (that we need the land for raising food), his reply is, then why don't you shut down the paper pulp business in the South? About 350 square miles of pulpwood forest is required to support a 1,000-ton-per-day kraft paper pulp mill. An area about this big will support a 400 megawatt electric generating station even if only 0.4 percent of the solar radiation that falls on the land is converted to fuel value.

Besides the great desirability of increasing the rate and efficiency of photosynthesis itself and the ratio of burnable calories to empty calories in the plant (both are botanical or genetic problems), there is no technical difficulty associated with the conversion of wood chips, bagasse,* or even dried cornstalks into electric power. Wood-burning boilers that generate 800,000 pounds per hour of steam at 1,250 pounds per square inch pressure and 950 degrees Fahrenheit are commercially available. Such a boiler will support an electric generating capacity of about 80 megawatts. Because unfossilized vegetable matter generally contains less than 0.1 percent sulfur, energy-plantation fuel is nonpolluting. It has another basic advantage over fossil fuel. The combustion of fossil fuels not only causes an increase in the carbon dioxide content of the atmosphere, which may eventually turn the planet into another Venus, but it uses up oxygen. The growing of the live fuels uses up more carbon dioxide than it gives off when burned and produces more oxygen than it destroys when burned.

Szego concludes that the area for an energy plantation big enough to supply a modern-sized generating station is of the same magnitude as the blocks of forest land now being managed for each of 2 dozen large pulp mills. His estimates suggest a price, including freight, of about $1.25 per million Btus for fuel value derived from chipped pulpwood currently grown in the American Southeast. The energy can probably be produced from a farming rather than a forestry operation using Middlewest cornstalks for about $1.00 per million Btus at a solar conversion rate not beyond achievement within the next few years.

If solar radiation conversion can be increased to an efficiency 2 or 3 times that already fortuitously achieved in forestry operations, the fuel value can probably be sold for between 70 cents and $1.00 per million Btus on forest growth cycles between 5 and 15 years.† This is lower than the average price of synthetic natural gas from coal and lower than modern prices for energy in the form of petroleum and most coal.

From the standpoint of tree or plant culture, it is already known that sugar cane gives nearly 10 times the photosynthetic efficiency as a pine tree and, even from the standpoint of paper manufacture, a type of hibiscus, kenef, that looks like a marijuana plant, gives some 7 times as much pulp per acre as Southern pine. It takes only 120 days to grow to maturity. One cannot overlook the achievements in experimental forestry by the paper companies. International Paper has recently

---

*In the Philippine Islands today most of the electric power is obtained by burning bagasse (dried, extracted sugar cane).
†In the referee's note to the classic paper by Szego and Clinton C. Kemp, published in *Chemtech*, May 1973, it is stated that independent calculations put the cost of wood fuel as now grown, at just under $1.00 per million Btus, corresponding to coal at $25 per ton.

specialized in supertrees or "Marilyn Monroes"; for example, strains of Eucalyptus that now grow to 85 feet in 5 years or less.

Then from the advanced chemical standpoint, we must keep an eye cocked toward the extraordinary research at the University of California and at the Lawrence Berkeley National Laboratory. If God had never invented photosynthesis, Berkeley would have done the job.

Some far out work at the Lawrence Berkeley Laboratory includes a project relating green-plant photosynthesis to the direct generation of electricity. At the University of California in the summer of 1974 the Nobel-prize-winning Melvin Calvin reported the development of a chlorophyll semiconductor cell that produced an appreciable amount of direct current. He hopes eventually to incorporate the plant cell-molecules responsible for this biogenesis of electricity into a solar cell assembly. Even further out in the blue (and gold) is the Berkeley notion of modifying photosynthesis to produce hydrogen gas. In this case the enzyme hydrogenase generated in green plants decomposes water to yield hydrogen, a heretofore incredible reaction.

To the south at the University of California at San Diego, John R. Benemann and N. M. Weare have discovered that a certain, gifted species of blue-green algae, *Anabaena cylindrica,* in the right chemical mood, will proceed to produce hydrogen from water and light.

THE BIOSPHERE

When reconsidering a modern use of photosynthesis as the easiest way to use solar energy, one is conscious somehow of a *déjà vu* feeling, similar to the Florida identification of solar water heating with the days of the Great Gatsby. As the mind does its shuffling act, one suddenly realizes that we are back to much before the 1920s; we are back to the middle-class English of the Victorian and Edwardian eras, the gentle folk who doted so passionately on vegetation that they had a conservatory (a greenhouse) attached to the parlor or the kitchen.

An M.I.T. engineer of British extraction, Sean Wellesley-Miller, and a physicist, Dag Chadroudi, have designed an impressive solar-heated structure that they call a biosphere, which would contain a greenhouse for growing and flowering plants. An 800 square foot greenhouse could provide almost all of a family's fruit and vegetable needs in the Northeastern United States. The M.I.T. biosphere would be constructed with a south-facing wall of a transparent plastic membrane that turns opaque in certain temperature ranges. In winter the plastic surface would remain transparent only when the sun was shining and would turn opaque at other times to reduce the loss of heat. The process would be reversed during summer. Wellesley-Miller believes the biosphere can be produced for about $5,000 and would pay for itself in about 3 years in reduced food and heating costs.

Here we have something that could make a deep appeal to the American heart. Until the stringencies of World War II, the American was not only uninterested in conservatories or greenhouses, he was bored by kitchen gardens. The great food inflation has changed all that. Unless the farm lobby can get Congress to pass some law that makes it a criminal offense to grow your own food, I predict that the M.I.T. biosphere or something like it will be the next big innovation in both urban and suburban living. If, as the M.I.T. calculations indicate, this means of avoiding some of the economic insults of the supermarket and the winter heating bill costs only in the neighborhood of a new automobile, people will buy biospheres instead of new automobiles—in itself a brilliant cultural and ecological accomplishment.

13 The Hydrogen Economy

Oft expectation fails and most oft where most it promises.
—WILLIAM SHAKESPEARE

THE HINDENBURG SYNDROME

One of the first TV shows to profoundly shock everyone who saw and heard it, begins May 6, 1937, with interior shots of the big, luxuriously appointed dining room of the *Hindenburg*, the Atlantic-crossing Zeppelin. Happy people—some 97 of them—are drinking champagne toasts to the view of the New Jersey shores as they approach the landing port at Lakehurst. The commentator, now viewing the dirigible from the side as it prepares to hook up for delivery of the lucky luminaries who have enjoyed this fine, vibration-free ride from Frankfurt, talks with the rapid-fire, supersalesman rhythm that was so popular in those days. Suddenly, before your eyes, the *Hindenburg* explodes. Gigantic gouts of flame and vapor fill the screen. The commentator becomes hysterical and sobs, "Oh, no! . . . They're all gone. . . . The Hindenburg is gone. . . . Oh God . . . How . . . can . . . we . . . stand it . . . ?" With the majesty of a dying dinosaur, the glowing aluminum frame of the dirigible folds in the middle; the holocaust apparently has burned up everybody on board, as the commentator begins actually to blubber. Fade out. Finis to hydrogen-inflated dirigibles and balloons. Beginning of an age of hydrogen fear.

In retrospect, we realize that we have been conned to a certain extent. Actually less than half of the 97 passengers and crew perished. The holocaust, which looked as if it had devoured every living and combustible thing within the volume of a cubic mile, was actually the flash of a few instants and the rapid diffusion of hydrogen carried it away to the heavens. Indeed, an equivalent amount of natural gas or gasoline would have caused more fatalities, because flames would have been anchored for a longer time.

Perhaps the most curious fact of all is that the people who shuddered at the

Hindenburg collapse in 1937 were unaware that the coal-derived town gas which many were burning in their kitchen stoves that very day was over 50 percent hydrogen. It is true that town gas (as we have mentioned in Chapter 4) gave way to natural gas. This was not, however, because of the element of safety, but the element of price. Now we are on our way back to town gas or something not too different from it for the same reason, and we may be heading toward a world body of energy in which pure hydrogen plays the role of the body's blood.

The curse was removed from the hydrogen syndrome with the success of the Apollo flights, in which hydrogen was used as rocket fuel and also in fuel cells which provided all-purpose electricity during the moon flights and in the Skylab. Hydrogen had become a giant-scale chemical reactant in the 1960s with the development of the hydrocracking process of producing high-octane gasoline from heavy petroleum fractions; for other refinery processes such as hydrodesulfurization, hydroforming, and so forth; and equally important in producing nitrogen fertilizers essentially by the old Haber process of reacting atmospheric nitrogen with hydrogen to form ammonia. Hydrogen is produced in the United States at the rate of about 15 billion pounds per year. It is very big, but if the hydrogen boosters have their way it could become the key medium in all energy transactions.

A sort of patriotism for hydrogen grows (isn't it strange the passionate alliances the heart of man is capable of?). At an American Chemical Society meeting in April 1972 an *ad hoc* organization was formed called the H_2indenburg Society (H_2 is the symbol for the molecular form of hydrogen gas).

THE NUCLEAR PLUS ELECTRICAL PLUS HYDROGEN ECONOMY

Most of the visions of a hydrogen economy are based on 3 factors: (1) hydrogen can be piped, especially at distances of greater than 500 miles, much more cheaply than electricity can be transmitted; (2) as a fuel, hydrogen produces little or no residue except water; and (3) hydrogen is the perfect fuel for the fuel cell. Whereas hydrogen is now most commonly made by the steam reforming of natural gas,* or by the partial oxidation of any hydrocarbon, these routes obviously become antiquated as the fossil fuels are exhausted. What then is left? We could still obtain hydrogen by the electrolysis or the thermal decomposition of water.

We are back, as we always seem to be, to one of Jules Verne's ideas presented in 1874 in *The Mysterious Island*. When the hero was asked to predict the fuel of the future he replied without hesitation, "Why, water, my friend."

In our century the idea of large-scale manufacture of hydrogen from off-peak electricity was suggested by J. B. S. Haldane, the English biologist, in the 1920s

---

*The reforming step, which results in the production from methane and water of a mixture of hydrogen and carbon monoxide, is followed by another catalytic reaction with more steam but at a lower temperature to yield additional hydrogen and carbon dioxide from the carbon monoxide. Pure hydrogen is obtained by absorbing acidic carbon dioxide in an alkaline scrubbing solution.

and in more engineering detail by Rudolf A. Erren, a German inventor living in England in 1933. F. T. Bacon, the Englishman who revived the fuel-cell concept and was killed in a laboratory explosion, always had as his true goal the development of a hydrogen storage and pipeline system using the fuel cell reversibly to electrolyze water.

The notion of using nuclear energy for the electrolysis of water, yielding hydrogen and oxygen, which are then stored or separately transmitted to give on-the-spot electrical power, by way of either a fuel cell or a turbine, is admittedly glamourous. Hydrogen as an energy carrier in place of high-voltage electricity is cheaper than overhead cable transmission at long distances by a factor of about 8 to 1. And the pipelines, built for natural gas, are there in the United States, in Europe, and in Russia. In our country we have over 250,000 miles of high-pressure gas underground pipe which with slight overhauling of the compressors should be suitable for carrying hydrogen.

The trouble is that electrolysis is an inefficient and expensive business.

SNEAKY WAYS TO MAKE HYDROGEN

Chains of thermal inorganic reactions by which hydrogen is obtained below the very direct decomposition temperature of water at about 2,500 degrees Fahrenheit are as intoxicating to chemists as is catnip to a cat. These methods have been labeled by General Electric as "closed cycle" processes, since ideally they use only water and heat and produce only hydrogen, oxygen, and the degraded heat of reaction. The chemical steps involve total recycle of intermediate reactants. General Electric has devised several closed-cycle chains which they are so impressed with that they call the best ones by women's names, like hurricanes. Thus "Agnes" involves a first step at about 500 degrees centigrade to react ferrous chloride with steam to yield ferric chloride, hydrochloric acid, and hydrogen. "Beulah" yields hydrogen from the reaction of hydrochloric acid with copper and hydrogen plus oxygen from reacting chlorine with magnesium hydroxide. "Catherine" is the most likely of a family of processes based on iodine.

The Argonne National Laboratory has described a process somewhat similar to Catherine, except that the hydrogen-evolving step is the decomposition of hydrogen iodide at 425 degrees centigrade. This is within the reach of present-day nuclear reactors and probably even solar heat. Because of the possible applicability of the HTGR (high-temperature gas-cooled reactor) to water-splitting, General Atomic, in collaboration with the Northeast Utilities Service and Southern California Edison, has examined a large number of published and unpublished closed cycles and has come up with 24 schemes that it considers useful but is too shy to specify in public (or over the telephone).

In the far future it seems possible that we will obtain some hydrogen by biological processes of the kind described in the last chapter. But in the meantime, everybody who roots for hydrogen hopes intensely that Catherine or some other relatively low-temperature thermal rather than electrolytic process will work, for look at what the latter would require: If we had to produce today from water an amount of hydrogen equivalent to the total production of natural gas in the United States, we would have to duplicate every year the fuel values of 22.5 trillion cubic feet of gas or 22.5 quadrillion (10^{15}) Btus. This corresponds to 70 trillion cubic feet of hydrogen which would require an electrolytic power of over a million megawatts. The present total electric generating capacity of the United States is only 360,000 megawatts.

As mentioned, we have enough installed pipelines to handle all the hydrogen we would be able to make for a long time (say, 10 trillion cubic feet per year) but another question comes up in regard to storage. At some 348 locations in the United States natural gas is stored in underground, porous rock formations with a total capacity of about 5 1/2 trillion cubic feet. We don't know for sure whether these formations will hold hydrogen. However, we are comforted with the fact that about 30 billion cubic feet of helium gas with leakage and diffusion characteristics similar to those of hydrogen, is now safe in an underground reservoir near Amarillo, Texas.

Assume we can make it transport it, store it, what can we do with it? Why is hydrogen so clean, so powerful, so lovely, so desirable?

THE MANY DELIGHTS OF HYDROGEN

Consider hydrogen as a fuel. Its dangers lie in one single property—its low ignition energy. In the *Hindenburg* disaster, for example, the explosion was probably started by an atmospheric spark from thunderstorms in the area. Since that time, with the proper precautions, billions of cubic feet of hydrogen have been safely pumped and millions of gallons transported in thermos-type tanks as the cold liquid. In one notable accident a tank-trunk of liquid hydrogen ran off the road, splitting the tank. The hydrogen evaporated almost instantaneously without ignition. Hydrogen is so light and diffuses so fast that if you get through the first microseconds of any crisis, you probably have it made.

Because it burns without noxious exhaust products, hydrogen can be used without vents. You can burn hydrogen in a furnace without a flue, saving the cost of the chimney and adding 30 percent to the efficiency of a gas-fired house-heating system. In fact, each room could be separately supplied by unflued heating devices, operating independently of one another. Since water is the only product, you have beautifully humid heat. With a ceramic catalyst, you can have true flameless gas heating, with the catalyst bed being maintained as low as the boiling point of water. This promises all kinds of new domestic heating and cooking techniques and the absolute absence of even traces of nitric oxide, which is formed in high-temperature flames of any kind.

There are only 2 precautions that the seller of pure hydrogen fuel for space-heating has to observe: He has to add not only a squinch of odorant, since hydrogen like natural gas has no smell, but a squinch of illuminant, because hydrogen burns without color. The odorant and illuminant may be the same squinch, as long as it contains carbon, because things with carbon always give visible radiation when they burn. A mercaptan, a chemical of the same class as that added as odorant to natural gas and invented for his own purposes by the skunk, is probably the answer.

Perhaps the greatest immediate interest in hydrogen as a fuel has been shown by developers of improved engines for automobiles or for airplanes. (Unfortunately, as usual, one has to make an exception of the Detroit people. If they have been interested, there is extraordinarily little sign of it.) The most advanced work on the use of pure hydrogen for an auto engine has been done by Roger J. Schoeppel of Oklahoma State University and by Roger Billings, president of the Billings Energy Research Corporation of Provo, Utah, who in 1972, when still at Brigham Young University, won first prize in the Urban Vehicle Design Competition with a Volkswagen modified to burn hydrogen carried in liquid form. As might be expected, the exhaust from this car was much cleaner than the air in the proving ground where the competition took place. As Billings says, the exhaust is "fog instead of smog."

Hydrogen has an extremely fast flame speed and a very high flame temperature, which is why hydrogen welding (at 5,000 degrees Fahrenheit) is competitive with acetylene welding. In an unmodified engine the low ignition energy of hydrogen often results in preignition. (You may have noticed preignition in your own car if it has collected enough carbon. Preignition is evident when an engine keeps stubbornly running after you have turned the spark ignition off. Auto mechanics call this dieseling, because a diesel engine runs without a spark. The gasoline is being ignited by glowing deposits of carbon on the inside of the cylinder heads. Roger Schoeppel found that preignition could be suppressed by excess air and by injecting the hydrogen through a diesel-engine-type valve.)

Since the hydrogen flame is nonluminous, it radiates less heat to the cylinder wall and the engine runs cool. Extremely high compression ratios can be used because the octane value of hydrogen is so high as to be off the scale. However, carrying liquid hydrogen or high-pressure gaseous hydrogen around in an automobile tank is not an assignment that appeals to anyone who proposes to drive over 10 miles an hour or on a crowded freeway. We may have made an excellent recovery from the *Hindenburg* syndrome, but we are not quite ready for nonchalant collisions while carrying the *Hindenburg* fuel.

The best answer appears to be the formation of hydrides, as developed at the Brookhaven National Laboratory, the most feasible being the mixed hydrides of iron and titanium. The powdered metal alloy is contained in a bundle of tubes like a steam boiler. Hydrogen is readily absorbed to form the hydrides and, indeed, by this conversion more hydrogen can be stored than if the fuel were in the form of the liquid. The loose hydride bonds are broken to let the gas evolve, by gently heating in exchange with the water from the radiator.

As a gaseous or liquid fuel, hydrogen, because of its tiny density, has a lower volumetric heating value than gasoline or liquefied petroleum gas; thus without the expedient of storage as the hydride it would require very large automobile tanks. On the other hand, the heavy metals used to form the hydrides are a weight disadvantage. It seems evident that even though 20 percent of the stock of the Billings Energy Research Corporation was bought early in 1975 by Winnebago Industries (the largest maker of recreation vehicles or campers), there is quite a lot of work to be done before the hydrogen economy extends itself to the cars of Joe Doakes and Mary Doakes on the American roadway. Specifically the hydrides of lighter metals would be helpful.*

What seems a more likely way to go at least in the near term, is the sensationally good idea proposed and quickly acted upon by the "little old lady of Pasadena"—the famous Jet Propulsion Laboratory of Cal Tech. The idea is to divert a proportion of the motor fuel to a portable steam-reforming unit in the car, to make hydrogen as you go along, and to use this to improve the performance of the engine, not only as regards air pollution but fuel economy as well. In two classical tandem papers presented in late 1974, the Jet Propulsion Laboratory described first a practical way of generating hydrogen on board and, second, the results obtained with the hydrogen enriched gasoline.

When the gasoline is enriched with the hydrogen mixture, the greatest benefit obtained is the ability to run at extremely high ratios of air to total fuel without misfiring. The excess air improves the fuel economy in several ways: It increases the ratio of specific heats at constant pressure and constant volume (I need not go into this thermodynamic measure of engine-cycle efficiency); it decreases heat losses to dissociation; and it greatly reduces thermal losses to the engine's cooling system. From the standpoint of exhaust pollutants, the lean scheme of operation would be fine, especially in meeting the fiercely harsh restriction on nitrogen oxides (a maximum of 0.4 grams per mile) in the EPA 1977 standards. But you can't run a car lean enough on gasoline to come within shooting distance of these restrictions without misfiring, an engine misfortune which pours hydrocarbons out the exhaust, thus simultaneously constituting an act of polluting and of ruining fuel economy. The hydrogen enrichment gets you over this hurdle. If you run on the pure hydrogen-carbon-monoxide mixture itself while starting and idling, you eliminate another source of pollution and of fuel wastage, especially the excess hydrocarbons resulting from a hard start in cold weather.

As to actual numbers, the Jet Propulsion Laboratory found that its on-board hydrogen enrichment would immediately increase economy by 40 percent at 55 miles per hour and would reduce emissions to 1.5 grams of carbon monoxide per mile, hydrocarbons to 2.3 grams per mile, and nitrogen oxides to 0.5 grams per mile. These values are well below the 1977 EPA specified maximums, except that the nitrogen oxides exceed the 0.4 grams per mile marginally. In view of the fat increase in mileage, which would bring a Datsun B210 to the absolutely unheard-

---

*When weight is not a problem, as in electric power plants, the iron titanium storage system, in connection with a fuel cell, is already being looked at as an excellent source of peak power. At off-peak periods the nuclear plant, for example, would use part of the electricity to produce hydrogen from water.

of highway cruising economy of 55 miles to the gallon, the slight overage on nitrogen oxides would be waived, I am certain.

Since the on-board manufacture of hydrogen as required should cost little if any more than the present catalytic exhaust systems for handling emissions, I do not forsee any undue production cost hike on cars modified according to the J.P.L. plan. For simultaneous conservation of fossil fuels and reduction of air pollution until we need, definitely in the next century, to go to electrical vehicles or to hydrides or to nonpersonal transit, I can see no better answer than the one that has come out of Pasadena. It remains to be seen whether Detroit will catch the pass that Pasadena has thrown or whether it will remain in its usual posture of sulking on the bench.

The fact that hydrogen has a low heat of combustion per unit of volume is not so important in aviation fuels as the fact that hydrogen has a very high heat of combustion per unit of weight. When you're in the air, it is the weight that counts, except perhaps in the case of highly streamlined supersonic fighter airplanes. Lockheed has a contract with NASA for studying the use of hydrogen in subsonic passenger and cargo aircraft, and throughout the airframe industry research is being sketched out on improved aerodynamics and hydraulics of hydrogen as a gas or conceivably as a liquid.

Boeing's Lloyd T. Goodman says that once the problems of handling liquid hydrogen are overcome, it would develop 3 times the thrust of conventional jet fuel. The upper-lounge lobe of the Boeing 747 could be extended the full length of the fuselage to provide a 24,000 cubic foot tank. With 90,500 pounds of liquid hydrogen, the airplane would be able to go farther than the current 747 with 268,500 pounds of standard fuel. The Space Shuttle program of the 1980s will provide a long, tough, and expensive tryout for all new aviation and rocket-fuel concepts, certainly including hydrogen.

This brings up a strange question. Is it possible that we might return to a hydrogen-fueled, lighter-than-air ship? In other words, to a new *Hindenburg?* My guess is that we might, except that it would be a double dirigible in which the propulsive gas—hydrogen—is stored in an interior bag, surrounded in entirety by a bouyancy bag or envelope of nonflammable helium.

Hydrogen is being looked at by the Naval Ship Research and Development Center as a shipboard fuel for gas turbines. Also the hydrogen-oxygen fuel cell is being tested as a power source for deep submergence rescue vessels.

And not least, I must mention some mysterious goings-on in regard to monatomic hydrogen as a rocket fuel. Monatomic hydrogen is quite different from the hydrogen ion which has no electron. Monatomic hydrogen has a lonely, unpaired electron, which makes it in modern chemical parlance a free radical, the simplest and at the same time the most active of all known free radicals. Because of their unpaired electrons, free radicals are hungry and snatchy, erratic and demon-fast. (By astrophysical spectrometry, free radicals have been detected in outer space where their low concentration—perhaps one per cubic mile—guarantees probably an eternity of unrequited yearning and loneliness.) All organic reactions with which we are familiar, including combustion, take place by some-times very complicated mechanisms involving sequences of free-radical reactions called chains. This is true of such seemingly simple processes as the burning of natural gas and probably of such extremely complex processes as growing old.

The desire for the free-radical monatomic hydrogen to unite with itself to form the stable diatomic molecule (H_2) is so frantic that a fantastic amount of energy is released when the reunion occurs. Any reaction that releases so much energy is of interest to, among others, rocket designers, and it is not surprising therefore to find Gerald V. Brown and his associates at the Lewis Research Center of NASA investigating the possibility of producing monatomic hydrogen, storing it in some way, and then letting it recombine to give a jolting thrust to a rocket body.

They have a notion of 2 different ways of storing monatomic hydrogen, once it has been produced by some decomposition process, such as electrical discharge. First, they would lead the normal hydrogen gas into the electrical discharge region of an apparatus in which the resultant mixture of H_2 and H would condense on walls cooled with liquid helium and would be subjected to a terrific magnetic field. Theoretically a magnetic field of this strength will, like an inflexi-ble drill sergeant, align the magnetic moments of the electrons in the hydrogen atoms. As long as that alignment is preserved, the hydrogen atoms cannot reunite for a reason too recondite to bore you with. Once released from the clutch of supermagnetism, however, the reunion will occur.

Another way to make monatomic hydrogen is to freeze a mixture of tritium and hydrogen to 0.1 degrees Kelvin;* the tritium will radioactively decay and the energetic electrons from that decay process will go ripping through the hydrogen crystal lattice, breaking the strongest chemical bond known to make monatomic hydrogen.

Hydrogen as a metal created by pressure of over 3 million atmospheres (44 million pounds per square inch), as it exists in the interior of the great outer planets such as Jupiter, would store the same amounts of energy as spin-aligned monatomic hydrogen, and since it would be 15 times as dense, it would be still more interesting as a rocket propellant.

In a way it is too bad that we cannot reach Jupiter because the availability of solid hydrogen there, mined by some industrious disembodied spirit, would undoubtedly allow us to study this material as an electric superconductor. In that role it has even more potential interest than as a rocket fuel. Today the highest temperature at which superconductivity is known to exist in certain exotic metal alloys is 23.2 degrees Kelvin. Metallic hydrogen theoretically will show supercon-ductivity up to over 100 degrees Kelvin, a temperature that would require nothing more unusual than boiling nitrogen (77 degrees Kelvin) to maintain. At Cornell University Professors J. N. Ashcroft and J. A. Krumhausl are trying to determine

---

*The Kelvin or absolute temperature scale starts with a zero corresponding to -273.11 degrees centigrade. The incremental degrees are the same as in the centigrade scale.

the transition pressure at which liquid hydrogen turns into a metal, and they are also studying its metastability (will it remain a metal for some time after the pressure has been released?).

It is evident that the hydrogen economy in the centuries to come may be as far-reaching as man's dreams of power and beauty. Yet there are many engineering aspects of this simplest and most prevalent of all the elements of the universe that remain to be clarified. We still do not know all we need to know of hydrogen's behavior and of its seemingly boundless possibilities.

14 The Alcoholic Fuels

Our wasted oil unprofitably burns like hidden lamps among sepulchral urns.
—WILLIAM COWPER

In Saudi Arabia about 5 billion cubic feet a day of natural gas is flared—simply burned to get rid of it. In this one kingdom of oil—to put it in different terms —5 trillion Btus of energy in a form which would command a million dollars in the United States is simply thrown up into the sky every day in the year as carbon dioxide, water vapor, and wayward heat. This nonchalant manner of flinging away energy which it took the earth hundreds of millions of years to accumulate is deeply shocking to conservationists but it is also very tantalizing to energy merchants.

Although there has been a tendency, especially in Iran, to stuff the gas back into the ground in order to maintain the formation pressure and thus to increase the total recovery of oil from a given pool, the amount of flaring from the Middle East, Libya, Indonesia, Nigeria, Gabon, and other oil-rich places remains unreasonably high. But what can be done about it?

By expensive compressive and cryogenic equipment you can store the gas in liquid form, ship it in special tankers designed like floating thermos bottles, and sell it after an expensive voyage for twice or thrice the price of normal natural gas in the gas-spoiled countries such as the United States.

There is another thing you can do with this orphaned methane. You can convert it into methanol (methyl alcohol, wood alcohol, methyl fuel, CH_3OH). This is an excellent liquid fuel and needs no special transportation equipment. In a peculiar chemical sense it can be regarded as the equivalent of synthetic natural gas or town gas, since one can visualize it as made up essentially of 2 molecules of hydrogen and 1 of carbon monoxide,* and upon catalytic decomposition it

*The standard way of making methanol from natural gas is to catalytically reform the methane with steam to yield carbon monoxide and hydrogen; then combine these gases over a copper catalyst in the ratio of 2 molecules of hydrogen to 1 of carbon monoxide to yield the alcohol.

yields these gases back. Thus, if you want a substitute for natural gas rather than a liquid fuel, by this expedient you have saved yourself the trouble of buying cryogenic tankers and other elaborate equipment. You can even go one step further and make the substitution complete by developing a methanation process (such as is now being done in the coal gasification industry) to react the hydrogen-carbon-monoxide mixture to form methane and water. For this you need a little more hydrogen than you get from decomposing the methanol.

There is another, even simpler noncatalytic way that the Germans have found to get to methanol from the methane of natural gas. This is to react it under pressure with insufficient oxygen to burn it. At 450 degrees centigrade at a very short reaction time, one obtains a yield of 70 percent methanol, with 15 percent formaldehyde, the rest carbon dioxide and water. This is not a bad way to go since the oxidation of methanol to formaldehyde accounts for 40 percent of methanol consumption in the chemical industry.

Because methanol can also be produced from coal and by the dry distillation of wood (hence wood alcohol) there has been traditionally an American protective import duty of 7.6 cents per gallon; but this was repealed in 1974. Depending upon the degree of inflation of plant construction costs (usually enormous but varying from place to place) the Houston Natural Gas Company may or may not go ahead with its original plan to build a methanol plant in Saudi Arabia, in partnership with Petromin, the Saudi national corporation. In the summer of 1973 the methanol was to be sold on the American East Coast for $1.10 to $1.20 per million Btus or for 6 to 7 cents per gallon, which was then lower than the East Coast price for propane or butane, with which it could expect to compete as a domestic heating fluid.

Methanol is a good clean fuel but is a little low on heat content. Since it burns without any noxious pollutants, it would be well suited as fuel for gas turbines used as auxiliary peaking-power units of electric power plants which otherwise rely on nuclear reactors or coal-burning steam turbines for the steady load.

There will always be a fuel use for methanol, for like hydrogen it possesses one priceless attribute: It can be made to work in a fuel cell with no trouble at all, and at high efficiency. From this standpoint, methanol substituting for natural gas in pipe delivery to buildings and homes has the same advantage as hydrogen: Without the elaborate Pratt and Whitney reforming accessories, it could furnish homes their electric power via home-installed fuel cells and could be used to burn as one burns propane or butane for stoves and space heaters. In this sense one could even speak of a methanol economy.

We started this discussion, however, putting to good use the flared clouds of natural gas in foreign countries. Methanol is a good way to package this gas, so to speak, and make a shippable and marketable commodity out of an otherwise tragically wasted planetary asset. But as long as we have coal, we do not have to regard a methanol economy only as a way to salvage the surely temporary though gigantic excesses of methane in the Middle East. Instead of our present course of making coal into synthetic natural gas, we could take a look at making coal into methanol. Then it becomes a liquid fuel that remains with us as long as our coal holds out. But it is, of course, not in the more or less eternal category of hydrogen, which in the last analysis can always be made from water.

METHANOL IN AUTOMOBILES

During the several remaining centuries of access to coal, can we use methanol as a motor fuel? This is a good way to start an argument and possibly a fist fight.

Recent testing by Exxon Research and Engineering, by the Bureau of Mines, and by the Continental Oil Company seem to point toward a not always clearly stated consensus. Methanol by itself, with a special carburetor and with a large enough tank to make up for the low heat content per unit volume compared with gasoline, is a very satisfactory fuel. Dick Tallman of Continental heretically calls it "potentially a *swell* fuel." It solves the present air pollution problem, in fact better than hydrogen, since it burns very cool. Its high heat of vaporization apparently eliminates peak flame temperatures that are responsible for nitrogen oxide formation and that occur even in the case of hydrogen enrichment (see last chapter).* Thus, if it were at a price advantage, methanol could take on the job of substituting for gasoline in fleets of cars or trucks, and take it over right now.

Of course, it could not now displace gasoline entirely, and the question is, how much of it could be blended with gasoline?

Here the fist-fighting starts. It looked pretty good on earlier tests at M.I.T. and other places with cars of the vintage of 1967 or older, and the reason seems to be that the older generation of cars generally ran with rather rich-set carburetion; that is, the ratio of fuel to air, before the age of economy and emission-control, was much higher than for 1973 or 1974 models, which ran much leaner. (In 1975 models, and presumably as long as we have catalytic exhaust treatment, the mixture will be somewhat richer than 1973–74 but not as rich as 1967 and earlier.) What the addition of 10 percent by volume methanol to gasoline did was to automatically make the mixture leaner; since the methanol contains oxygen, its addition is chemically equivalent to burning the same amount of gasoline that is contained in the blend with an extra amount of air. The effects on economy and on the emission of pollutants (hydrocarbons and carbon monoxide) are what one would expect from using a higher proportion of air in the carburetion. On the rich-running older cars the effect is to improve both economy and emissions. On the lean-running newer cars the effect on economy and emissions is either harmful or hardly perceptible (except for an anomalously low nitrogen oxides figure, which may be due to the effect of methanol in lowering flame temperature). On the 1975 exhaust catalyst cars the effect is intermediate but the improvement, if any, is miniscule.

However, Exxon and Continental have both concluded that the blends are

*Exxon Research and Engineering, which on the basis of 3 test cars has undertaken to assume the role of hatchet-man in derogating the possible usefulness of methanol as a motor fuel, points out that methanol may give excessive amounts of formaldehyde in the exhaust.

unsalable, but for unforeseen reasons. Methanol is so unlike gasoline that it is not entirely miscible with it, and just a few drops of water (with which methanol is completely miscible) cause the alcohol to separate as a bottom layer. Without an enormous increase in housekeeping efficiency in the merchandising of gasoline, the methanol would be separating constantly. If you add the gasoline and water separately to the customer's tank, the onus is upon him. A few drops of water condensing in his tank and he has to cope at one time or another with a slug of wet methanol for which his carburetor has not been adjusted and which may cause complete engine failure.

Again, because methanol in gasoline finds itself in alien company, it has a very strange effect upon the volatility and evaporating behavior of the hydrocarbons. Even 1 or 2 percent methanol greatly increases the vapor pressure and alters the distillation performance. This is because methanol forms with individual hydrocarbons in the gasoline loose couplings which are called azeotropes, and which boil at lower temperatures than the boiling point of the hydrocarbons or the methanol by themselves. An excess of low-boiling constituents, even though artifically present as azeotropes, will give vapor lock in an automobile engine— a condition in which the engine misses or simply refuses to fire, because the cylinders have too much fuel vapor and not enough air.

In order to avoid vapor lock, the gasoline must be stripped of its lighter components, butanes and pentanes, before mixing with methanol. This defeats the purpose of the whole exercise, since the loss of energy in the form of butanes and pentanes more than counterbalances the gain in the form of methanol. What do you do with the discarded butanes and pentanes? One might suggest that you use them as bottled domestic fuel. A much better alternative is to use the methanol as a bottled domestic fuel and burn the butanes and pentanes in the gasoline.

Even when, by cutting out butanes and pentanes and substituting methanol, you have prevented vapor lock, you have a mixed fuel that is unpleasing from the standpoint of acceleration and other driving features that the car-savvy public has become used to. In particular, the blended fuel shows with newer cars what Detroit calls stretchiness. This is an exasperating hesitation in responding to your foot on the accelerator. It is probably connected with the fact that modern cars operate on the ragged edge of the lean limit of fuel-to-air ratio and the additional leaning effect of the oxygen-containing methanol may carry the carburetor mixture over this ragged edge.

ETHANOL

Ethanol (ethyl alcohol, grain alcohol, C_2H_5OH) is a more basic and eternal material than methanol since it's so easy to make from any sugar or starch; and, in fact, nature insists upon making it at the slightest opportunity, given the sugar or starch and the yeast (fermenting) organisms, which are everywhere, even in Antarctica. As we shall see in the next chapter, a discovery by Army scientists at Natick, Massachusetts, that the enzyme from a mutant species of mildew will quickly transofrm cellulose into glucose, a readily fermented sugar, has overnight revolutionized the availability of ethanol. It now has all the earmarks of the perennial fuel, inexhaustible as long as we have cellulose, that most renewable of all earth's natural organic chemicals. It is comforting to know that this astronomically vast source is waiting in the future for us, but at present the ethanol is also readily available from grains. Although for the time being, ethanol can certainly be made more cheaply from petroleum-derived ethylene than from grain, the demands for ethylene in plastics are so astonishingly huge that there is still a sound argument for grain alcohol as a fuel; that is, providing there is enough grain.

The grain states have blown hot and cold on this issue, according to the wheat and corn market. In the period 1935–39, service stations in northeastern Kansas, Missouri, Nebraska, and Illinois sold an alcohol-gasoline blend called Agrol, but the Agrol people went out of business because gasoline was so cheap. In those days you could buy 10 gallons of gasoline and a pack of cigarettes and still have change on your dollar. Now there is renewed interest in gasahol (the Nebraska term for a blend of 10 percent ethanol and 90 percent gasoline) because, even though the price of grain remains high, the price of gasoline is rising faster. The Nebraska legislature passed a bill for a 3 cent reduction in the state tax for gasoline sold in the state containing 10 percent *grain* alcohol. (The accent was on the grain, because the Nebraskans did not want petroleum-derived ethanol to get into the act.) The most active gasahol research is that carried out at the University of Nebraska at Lincoln.

Ethanol looks good, both as a motor fuel in the neat form ("Vodka for your Volkswagen") and as a blend. Since it is much more miscible with hydrocarbons than methanol, the blends suffer much less from such troubles as water sensitivity, vapor lock, and stretchiness. Ethanol has a very great advantage in heat content over methanol (ethanol: 89,000 Btus per gallon; methanol: 57,000 Btus per gallon). The carping criticisms directed at ethanol and its blends are political in nature.

I think such criticisms, even when pseudoscientific, represent a fundamentally wrongheaded, Detroit-centric point of view; namely, that motor fuel should be tailor-made for a certain standard kind of Detroit engine, presumably for the best-selling Chevrolet. In a time of motor-fuel crisis, this is the wrong way to look through the telescope. The car engine should be designed for the economically most available fuel. It is my belief that the Natick discovery will, within a decade, make ethanol or ethanol-gasoline blends by far the most economic fuels, not only for this country but for any country that has enough green or trash cellulose.

That grain alcohol will not go far enough is shown by a few numbers. Roughly 100 billion gallons of gasoline were sold in 1973 in the United States. Thus, if the nation were on a total gasahol automobile diet, something like 10 billion gallons of ethanol would be required, corresponding to 4 billion bushels of grain. Conversion of the nation's entire wheat crop in 1973 would have yielded only 6 billion gallons of ethanol. However, maybe this might make sense at that, for the following reasons: We use only the starchy part of any grain to make alcohol. Actually from a nutritional standpoint, for the fourth world particularly, it is the protein part that is more essential. The Far-Mar-Company, a big cooperative in Hutchison, Kansas, has developed a process to separate grain into starchy and proteinaceous fractions. They plan to sell the protein as human food and charge the carbohydrates to fermentation for alcohol. Current techniques enable Midwest Solvents, Inc., the largest producer of grain alcohol, to obtain 2.5 gallons of ethanol per bushel of wheat or milo and 2.6 gallons per bushel of corn.

Only one recollection of my young manhood gives me cause to worry about gasahol fuel. Presumably the blend would contain no tetraethyl lead. When I first started to work as a chemist for a California petroleum company, just before the repeal of Prohibition, I made the acquaintance of a big Swedish youth who worked in the inspection lab, a part of the refinery where the petroleum raw materials and products were analyzed. Natural gasoline (casinghead, as it used to be called, for it would condense on the casinghead of the well) came into the laboratory in metal bombs—one-quart containers shaped to withstand several pounds of vapor pressure. When nobody was looking, the Swede would shake the casinghead gasoline up with milk and drink it as an emulsion. He claimed it was much better than schnaps or aquavit or vodka. Although he smelled all day something like a gas well in production, I noticed no apparent physical disabilities. He never fell on the floor. Later I found out that drinking lead-free gasoline was a common practice, which continued long after the repeal of Prohibition and bothered service station operators who had to arrange for special security for tanks containing third-grade or lead-free motor fuel.

I must admit that I have not stayed awake nights worrying about the problem, but will gasaholism become another drug disease? One never knows what the people of Nebraska, let alone Los Angeles, will take to drinking.

15 Food and Energy

The death of a single individual is of consequence and pathos
but the death of millions is a matter of statistics.
—JOSEPH STALIN

AMERICAN FARMING

It is true that American farmers grow more grain per acre and more soybean crops per year than any others in the world. That is because American farms are run on a deluge of gasoline and diesel fuel for a supershed full of expensive machinery, and the big grain crops are saturated with fertilizer. Whereas a prudent farmer in the past would have rotated his corn with a soil nitrifying crop such as alfalfa or some other legume, the present-day agronomist no longer bothers with that, not even with planting legumes between corn rows. Instead he forces the soil, by use of hybrid seedlings and enormous amounts of fertilizer, to yield umpty-six bushels an acre of corn and umpty-nine bushels an acre of wheat.

In realizing these yields the American farmer has been heralded as the new miracle man. Not only is his produce exported to feed a skinny world but his techniques, transferred to the less-developed countries, are intended to teach them how better to feed themselves. The green revolution for Asia was based on this idea of transferring cultivated high-yield mutants of wheat and rice to well-fertilized and well-watered soils. But the green revolution has helped only the already rich farmers of the Punjab plain of Pakistan and of Northwestern India —one of the great breadbaskets of the world; it has done no good for the poor of Bengal, Bangladesh, Sahel (the sub-Saharan countries), Honduras, Burma, Northeastern Brazil, the Philippines, or even Mexico. The reason is plain: At least until recently the rich farmer of the Punjab could afford the fertilizer and machinery and could also afford diesel fuel for irrigation pumps when the monsoons failed. On the other hand, no matter what seeds they are given to sow, the poor farmers of Asia and Africa and South America could not, and perhaps never will be able to, afford the energy-lavish practices of modern American agriculture.

If we look at farming from the standpoint of calories of food crop delivered to the American table compared to calories of energy expended in the form of fuel, electricity, chemicals (including pesticides as well as fertilizer), energy tied up in the manufacture of farm tools, transportation devices, supermarket refrigerators, etcetera, etcetera, we come to the appalling conclusion that the American food system devours over 9 times as many calories as it produces. Instead of being the most efficient system, it is energetically by far the least efficient system of agriculture that has ever existed or that we can imagine.

Although we could have realized vaguely, looking at the popularity in the Western World not only of highly processed foods but of strings of purveyors of ready-to-eat processed foods that we had unbalanced our energy equilibrium in regard to food retrieval,* it took 2 gifted and incredibly assiduous teams of investigators to add up all the figures and show us why the food industry is the worst energy wastrel in our society. These teams were David Pimental and his colleagues at Cornell and the Steinharts (John P. and Carl E.) of the University of Wisconsin. Some of their findings, often mined from records and archives that one never suspected were in existence, underlined for the first few years of the 1970s (before the great inflation of 1973–74) some startling and disturbing facts.

For instance, the curve in the United States for calorie input per unit of food calorie output has increased from less than 2 in 1910 to over 9 in 1970 and the curve is not leveling off. Fragmentary data for 1972 suggest the increase continued unabated and, with the sharp increase in fuel and fertilizer costs, certainly the dollar input per calorie of food in edible condition skyrocketed in 1973–74 as never before in any civilization.

Yet a still more significant generalization comes out of these surveys: The energy expended in raising and harvesting crops in the United States was in 1970 about 526.1 trillion kilocalories, but this was far less than a third of the total energy including the transportation of the food, gathering it, processing it, refrigerating it, exhibiting it, packaging it, bringing it home, refrigerating it again, cooking, and so on. The intermediate energy, up to the time of the retail sale, amounts to 841.9 trillion kilocalories and the final customer's energy expenditure 804.0 trillion kilocalories. The total energy involved with producing food was thus 2,172 trillion kilocalories or about 15 percent of all the energy consumed in this country in the year 1970.

We imagine that because the number of American farm workers has greatly decreased in the last 40 years and because farm-working animals (horses, mules, and oxen) have virtually disappeared, we have turned a large proportion of hicks into city slickers; but actually the number of jobs concerned with food has greatly increased. Yesterday's farmhand is today's canner, tractor mechanic, and fast-food carhop. And most of these jobs pay better than a hired hand used to get.

---

*The gasoline for automobiles in going out to dine or even in driving a private 2-ton car to the supermarket twice a week to fetch 30 pounds of food, make up a surprisingly large percentage of American eating costs. Great energy savings are realized if the market or grocery delivers by car or truck to the private homes of its customers.

On the farm it is obvious that some of the peculiar and dangerous food prejudices of the American people are responsible for the large energy imbalance. For example, every red-blooded American expects to sicken and grow pale unless he can frequently eat steak or roasts from prime or choice beef. Now, what these designations refer to is essentially the fat content of the meat—the more fat the more prime and the more choice. The fattening process is realized by taking 400-pound calves out of pasture and stuffing them with grain—mostly corn and sorghum until they weigh over half a ton.*

As calculated by the Steinharts, feed-lot beef requires over 10 calories of input energy per calorie of beef on the table compared with only a half calorie for range-fed beef. For the extra fat, white rather than yellow in color (because of the pasture's carotene) the Americans are expending 20 times as much input energy and, incidentally, exposing themselves to about that multiple of increased likelihood of atherosclerotic heart disease. Luckily, we need to use very little irrigation, except in California for fancy truck crops, for if we had to water the bulk of our staple grains and soybeans we would nearly double the already nonsensically onerous and complex energy burden of our agriculture.

To pretend that this hugely cumbersome and immensely expensive agribusiness, leaky and glowing with excess energy demands, could in conjunction with new strains of wheat and rice be the basis for a green revolution among farmers who can afford only a bent stick to plough with, is to compound ignorance with folly.

We seldom truly realize that in comparing the subsistence farmers of India and China (where the people in the cities spend 80 percent of their $100 per year income on food) with the highly industrialized agribusinessmen of North America, Europe, and Australia, we are looking at 2 entirely different sorts of human creatures who might as well be different species. Their behavior, their ethology is as distinct as the ethology of tigers and rabbits.

To feed the rabbit nations (e.g., India) at the U.S. level of 3,000 calories per day (instead of their present 1,500) would require more energy than India now uses for all purposes. To feed the entire world with a U.S.-type food system, almost 80 percent of the world's total annual energy expenditure would be required just for this food system. There would not be enough energy for transportation or just keeping warm.

HOW NOT TO USE THE BOVINE STOMACHS

The systematic raising of cattle for eating is a relatively new thing in the world. It is, of course, not practiced by the natives of India and China and in Africa the cattle-raising tribes rarely eat beef since the herds are essentially for dairy purposes (although a Masai warrior also may suck blood from a temporarily opened vein of one of his creatures). In most foreign cattle areas, such as Argentina,

*In Japan the choicest of fat beef, fit for a visiting prince of industry, is attained by adding beer to the grain ration.

Brazil, Northern Mexico, California in the days of the great ranchos, one would never have dreamed of feeding grain to beef steers. At one time this would have seemed as unnatural as the Japanese practice of giving the animal beer with his meals.

The grain feeding of cattle *is* unnatural. What we do not seem to realize is that, if we want to eat the animal, he should be fed high-cellulose fodder (grass, hay, etc.) because that is what he can digest that we cannot. That is where he saves us money and energy and supplements us on the planet.

There is scarcely anything so chemically marvelous as the bovine 4-stage stomach. At Beltsville, Maryland, an experimental team of the U.S. Department of Agriculture has for many years been feeding cattle newspapers (like old copies of the New York *Times*) sweetened with a little molasses to take the curse off the editorials, and nothing else save urea. There is no problem at all with this feed. Out of the mixture of pure cellulose and one of the simplest of organic nitrogen compounds (urea is commonly used for fertilizer in place of ammonia or nitrate) the cattle digest and synthesize everything the bovine body needs to grow and thrive. One Beltsville bull is in fine shape after 9 years on this diet that one should have previously imagined would satisfy only a termite.

The absurd practice of feeding cattle grain unfortunately has been so textured into the American economy that it has caused an international inflation and depression of unprecedented ugliness. The almost vertical rise in all prices, especially that of food, in 1974 is often blamed on the OPEC decision to quadruple the price of petroleum. But a careful study of the chronology of the Great Inflation (as pointed out by the politically conservative London *Economist*) shows that American grain prices suddenly exploded several months before oil prices took off. Wheat at $6 a bushel preceded $11 a barrel crude oil. The wheat-importing, oil-exporting countries, such as Iran, found suddenly that whereas in the good old days of the 1960s one could trade a barrel of oil for a bushel of wheat (both at about $1.65) it took in the summer of 1973 at least 2 barrels of oil to swap for 1 bushel of wheat. Nothing so impressed the Arabs and the Shah of Iran as the elan and smoothness with which North American farmers had all of a sudden, as if by magic, become sharp, rich traders. As we have pointed out in Chapter 2, OPEC's decision was made with equal suddenness.

SAVING ENERGY IN AGRICULTURE

There seems to be very little doubt that we could save enough energy by abandoning our fat-beef complex, by the very simple expedient of banning feed-lot cattle, to help us on our way to energy independence. Suppose that is too much to expect.* Well, we could at least lower the total food energy bill by sending

*One of the reasons it is not likely is that, as pointed out by Frances Moore Lappe in her book *Diet for a Small Planet,* the food industry has blocked all attempts to establish a federal program of nutritional education in public schools. Later in the century when the starving people of the third world (now known as the fourth world) come to realize that the livestock population of the United States consumes enough grain to feed 1.3 billion people, it may be war rather than education that rectifies the small planet's balance.

produce to market in trains rather than in fuel-squandering trucks. There is also another trade-off possible. A large amount of tractor-fuel energy on the farm goes into ploughing. Now there is no magic in this operation. Turning over the soil does not of itself constitute an act of mysterious beneficence. The goal is simply to get rid of the weeds. Work is now being done to determine whether stiff jolts of advanced herbicides can do the job in so-called no-tillage agriculture. Another energy savings can be accomplished if the farmer substitutes natural manure and green manure (ploughed in grain stalks and leafage) for chemical fertilizer.

The chemical fertilizer shortage has stirred up unexpected animosities—and, indeed, in a depression one tends to snap one's neighbor's head off. According to Richard Nixon, Pierre Trudeau was an "ass-hole," and pillars of the agribusiness warn us not to expect fertilizer or petroleum help from Canada—don't expect any help from Canada, they tell us, "the land of the blue-eyed Arabs."

According to the Steinharts, plant breeders should pay more attention to hardiness, disease-and-pest-resistance, and especially to reduced moisture content to cut down on the use of natural gas or propane for drying. Biologic pest control should be substituted for the high-energy pesticides.

Does all this have a familiar ring? Indeed it does, for it outlines the philosophy of the organic farmer, who is commonly regarded in the agribusiness as a harmless amateur nut. Let me be quick to add that I do not share the biochemical notions of the organic foodster, including such fanciful ideas as that plants grown on chemical fertilizer somehow lack the zinginess and mineral virtue of organically grown vegetables. I have more faith in the ability of the plant to make what it needs out of simple forms of the essential elements than I do even in the cow's stomach. What I am emphasizing is merely that organic farming uses much less energy than modern intensive agriculture.

By far the most important advances in reducing the energy requirements of American agronomy would be expected in plant genetics. Suppose one could breed, for example, food plants that utilize much more than the fractional part of the sunlight that they now convert to chemical energy? Or what if one could breed a food plant that does not need large squirts of nitrogen fertilizer to thrive? This is, of course, a rhetorical question because we already have such a plant in the soybean, a legume.

THE SOYBEAN REVOLUTION

Until the early part of this century nearly all soybeans were grown in Eastern Asia, and the soybean is an essential, protein-rich part of the mainly vegetarian diet of China, Japan, and Indonesia. It was used in the West only for soy sauce in Chinese restaurants and for British ketchup. Attempts to raise soybeans in Europe failed because of the climate, which is troubled by early summer drought. But it so happens that large parts of the United States and South America are climatically ideal for this all-important legume.

Soybeans became interesting in the United States for a rather peculiar reason—the butter shortage of World War II. With soy oil going increasingly into margarine, the soybean acreage rose to 10 million in 1943, 40 million in the late 1960s, and 56 million in 1973, which puts the crop in a class with wheat and not far behind corn. Because of its modest fertilizer requirements (especially nitrogen) soybeans have actually surpassed wheat as an American cash crop. About three-quarters of the soybeans produced are grown in the United States and the bulk of the soybeans moving in world trade comes from the United States. If an Illinois farmer emerged as a ghost from a 1930 grave, his greatest sources of amazement would be the absence of farm horses and the presence of vast fields of soybeans.

In 1940 the ratio of butter to margarine in domestic consumption was 7 to 1. Now margarine is in the lead by a ratio of 2 to 1 (except in certain states such as Wisconsin, where anyone caught selling or eating margarine is surrendered to the hangman). Soybean oil accounts for three-quarters of the country's margarine production and, moreover, this ubiquitous oil accounts for over one-half of all the food fat produced in the United States. In the world as a whole soybeans have become the largest single source of edible fat, far ahead of butter and also far ahead of any other vegetable oil.

For reasons that are maddeningly obscure, agricultural scientists have been unable to increase the yield per acre of soybeans in this country, either by experimental genetics or by soil enrichment. On the other hand India seems a perfect place for soybeans, and certain varieties have turned out to promise 2 or 3 times the yield that they do in America. So isn't this the obvious ultimate solution for the Indian diet? A high-protein plant that requires no nitrogen fertilizer? One would think so, but as we pointed out earlier, we are confronted by people of the third or fourth worlds, in effect another species. Even in the agony of chronic starvation, they will turn up their noses at soybeans, because their noses are attuned to the smell of wheat or rice (or sewage on the Ganges). They will starve rather than consume a strange food. And starve they will.

If forced to eat nothing but soybeans, the North Americans might not sulk themselves to death, but they would surely raise hell. However, in effect they are being taught to like soy the hard and expensive way by cunning food chemists. Textured proteins of soy origin have been given the flavor of popular meats, such as bacon bits. Breakfast foods, biscuits, a variety of breads, sausages, and whatnot contain soybean meal in less expensive form than textured vegetable protein. As of the early 1970s, such foods consumed 10 times as many soybeans as the manufacture of textured vegetable protein. Yet consider the basic economics of soybean bacon. The production of natural bacon from corn-fed hogs requires 10 times as much cropland as the same quantity of imitation bacon from soybeans. Beef production, American style, calls for 20 times as much land as needed for soy protein.

Our irrational dependence on fatted beef has made soy meal a 2-year substitute for fish meal in feed lots during the temporary disappearance of the vast anchovy fishery off the coast of Peru. The anchovies are back but justifiable restrictions by the Peruvians will keep the yield down, so that fish meal will substitute for soy meal, if at all, mainly in proteinizing poultry and hog feed.

There is a growing feeling that fishing is basically too expensive to feed fish meal either to fowl or hog or man. The cheap coastal and Great Lakes species are disappearing, due to overfishing or to pollution, while pelagic fishing is so tied to the price of diesel fuel that it has become ruinously expensive, except possibly to the Russians, who do not run their bookkeeping in the same way that other countries do.

EATING BACTERIA

In the last decade or so a fever of interest has been warmed to the possibility of producing unlimited amounts of a food consisting of so-called single cell protein (SCP). This is composed essentially of the bodies of bacterial or yeast organisms that have been nurtured on petroleum fractions, such as paraffins or natural gas or on alcohols (methanol and ethanol) produced cheaply from petroleum. The technology, save for one dilemma, is well developed. It is easy to grow selected strains of bacteria or yeast on hydrocarbons and in fact hydrocarbon-eating bacteria are often found in oil pools and in oceanic areas where the oil has been issuing from natural underwater deposits for centuries or millennia, such as in the Santa Barbara Channel in Southern California. The rate of growth can be greatly accelerated by fertilizers, that is to say, supplementing the petroleum gas or oil or alcohol basic food with a nutrient solution containing other essential elements, such as sodium, potassium, phosphorous, and so on. The bacteria or yeast multiply so rapidly that one can in effect see a beefsteak grow up in a few minutes.

Being true splinters of life, the 1-cell organisms contain all the essential amino acids, and in this respect are superior to any plant protein which is usually unbalanced since the plant seed is not a true splinter of life but, so to speak, a fetus. After being killed, the mass of single cell protein organisms can be flavored and presumably fed safely to human beings. But to my knowledge, none *has* been fed to human beings. Endless experimentation with SCP as animal feed goes on but nobody dares take the leap from animal feed to human food. This is the dilemma. There is too much uncertainty about possible toxins in the killed bacteria. For this reason most of the SCP plants that are talked about or actually in operation use the petroleum bacteria or yeasts solely for feeding animals—a process which adds very little substance to the world food menu.

On a world market where soy meal is expensive (say, $500 a ton) the SCP may be competitive as animal feed protein supplement, but in the case of cattle the point I have tried so hard to make is that actually we don't need animal feed protein supplement. The bovine stomach can use the cheapest form of organic nitrogen, and this is true of all ruminants.* The great promise of SCP, its edibility

*The camel basically would be a superior source of meat in this country because of its greater range of diet, including desert shrubs. Being originally a North American native, it would have little trouble in thriving in the Southwest United States and in Northern Mexico.

for humans, would make petroleum overnight a standard source of food and more valuable as such, especially in the Asian countries, than as a source of fuel or fertilizer.

It is for this reason that by far the most interesting developments in SCP concentrate on making it in sufficient purity, that such grumpy and suspicious organizations as the Federal Food and Drug Administration and its Asian, South American, and African counterparts would quickly approve its direct consumption by people as well as by hens and swine. Evidently the purity depends not so much on the biological nature of the single cell organism as on the freedom of the primary feed from dangerous impurities. A barrel of crude oil, for example, contains carcinogenic fractions and other poisons. The bacteria or yeast normally will consume only the simple paraffin (waxlike fractions) and, indeed, this selective appetite has been experimentally used by the Russians to take the wax out of diesel fuels and light lubricating oil, so that they end up with the happy combination of low pour-point oil and animal feed. But in human food there is continual and probably justified suspicion that traces of poison from the original petroleum may wind up in the final SCP. The simplest way to get around this is to use petroleum fractions or derivatives that are easy to purify, such as natural gas (to be used in a Royal Dutch/Shell project) or simple, easily cleansed alcohols produced from natural gas or liquefied petroleum gas. Thus the Imperial Chemical Company of the United Kingdom intends to use methanol, made from natural gas, as a feed; while Amoco, a subsidiary of Standard of Indiana, will use ethanol, made from ethylene obtained in petroleum refining operations, feeding this to Tortola yeast organisms, explicitly designed for human consumption.

THE MAGIC OF THE ENZYME

But bacteria or fungi can serve other unexpected food purposes than simply to be eaten. One of the most spectacular and important discoveries of the century was made at the modest, not to say shabby, laboratories of the U.S. Army at Natick, Massachusetts, where a small team of biological chemists was studying the problem of how to preserve cotton cartridge belts worn by soldiers in the South Pacific. It seems that in tropical countries the fungus *Trichorderma viride* is such an avid eater of cotton (cellulose) clothes that unless one keeps a light burning in the closet, the morning may find one naked to the winds. The idea occurred inevitably to someone that the enzyme cellulase produced by the *T. viride* might be handy in cleaning up cellulose garbage, including old newspapers. Very few things, except the digestive juices of the ruminants and termites, will attack cellulose, but it was found by the little Natick group that a certain mutant of *T. viride* produces a kind of cellulase enzyme that converts cellulose almost instantaneously to glucose, a sort of universal life sugar easily digested by all manner of living things, including yeasts and the single cell protein bacteria. The glucose may also be efficiently fermented to ethyl alcohol.

In effect, the Natick mutant of a species of mildew makes it industrially feasible to make food out of garbage and trash. It is in the same class as the cow's stomach.

Municipal trash is composed of about 10 percent cellulose while livestock manure is 80 percent cellulose. There are 800 million tons per year of manure and 200 million tons of municipal trash collected in the United States. The fact that the *T. viride* mutant can transform this waste cellulose with almost magical speed and an efficiency of about 50 percent into the lovely, reactive sugar glucose may before the end of the century be recognized as one of the most significant findings in biology and conservation.*

From a long-term planetary point of view, the cellulase discovery is more important than the development of single cell protein from petroleum, for a quite obvious reason: While petroleum is a nonrenewable resource, we shall have cellulose with us as long as the sun shines and as long as rain falls.

THE INCONSTANT EARTH

But how long will the rain fall? In the long run, fresh water may be more critical than fertilizer and we may think in terms not only of energy efficiency of various styles of eating but of water efficiency. For example, in terms of water, 1 pound of beef is 2,500 percent more expensive than 1 pound of bread.

Very often our troubles with water come from sheer stupidity. During the past 2 decades the people in Bangladesh and Bengal cleared the Himalayan foothills to make room for crops. When the forests were cleared, the water from monsoons had nothing to hold it and it rushed down slopes, causing disastrous floods along with eventual famine.

Many climatologists of multidimensional vision believe that we are entering another period of enduring a cold planet, which has already driven the monsoon rains southward and caused severe droughts across Africa and Asia. On the whole, with a few exceptions, such as the American dust bowl of the 1930s, the planet has enjoyed a half-century of much more beneficent climate than ever could have been predicted. According to Professor Reid A. Bryson of the University of Wisconsin's Institute for Environmental Studies, the years from 1924 to 1974 world-wide have seen the most abnormally bonny weather the world has had in 1,000 years. We did not deserve and cannot hope for more of such an interlude.

But in a sense, the interlude is quite baffling because these 50 years have also seen the most critical stages of development of man-caused air pollution, which many meteorologists blame for changing the local climate, especially in the vicinity of major cities. As a specific example, take the new Washington suburb of Columbia. The atmosphere over that formerly almost rural area now contains 10 times as much particulate matter and from 5 to 25 times as much unnatural gaseous admixtures as before. As an apparent result the cloud cover has increased from 5 to 10 percent. The incidence of fog is 100 percent more in winter now and

*It is gratifying and significant that a woman biologist, Dr. Mary Mandels, was one of the leaders in this research.

30 percent more in summer. The rainfall has increased by 10 percent and snowfall by 5 percent.

Observations from the weather satellite or from Skylab dramatically show how, on the east coasts of the Asian and American continents, the large cities produce a long wake of cloud cover extending like tentacles over the oceans for hundreds of miles. Rainfall in and downwind of cities of a million or more population has gone up by 15 to 30 percent, depending on the particular city. Since over 40 percent of Americans live in these cities, that proportion of us now lives in a man-altered climate. In some respects the alteration is frightening since the suburbs share the growing severity of the central city, and thunder storms have increased by as much as 60 percent (more people are now being killed by lightning on a per capita basis than ever before); heavy rains, over 2 inches, are up by 80 percent; and hailstorms occur 5 times more frequently.

All this, however, can be categorized as minor inconvenience. The fact remains that the last 50 years for the planet as a whole are the best years of our lives and this may give us some humility, since it may show that compared with what we ourselves can do in emitting weather-changing influences, the volcanic power of the earth in a few shrugs of its shoulders can do immensely more. The major volcanic explosions of Krakatau in 1883 and of Mt. Pelie on Martinique in 1902 may have thrown more particulate matter into the world's atmosphere than would 1,000 years of our industrial spewing or our coughing engines of transportation.

If the mysterious periods of the earth or of the sun had received as much energetic attention as the insane mathematics of astrology, we might be in a better position to plot our future course of climate. Weather history needs more study. Some climatologists conclude that the world's climate as a whole—the average temperature—runs roughly in alternate 200-year and 50-year cycles and that the earth is now about to creep into an icebox phase comparable to the period from the sixteenth through the nineteenth centuries, which some geologists call the little ice age. It was during this period that the once lush fields of Greenland vanished and that England lost its capability of becoming a vine-growing country when the vineyards withered away forever.

Yet if one takes a longer view, in which a milennium measures merely an inhalation of the earth's rocky lungs, the curious and on the whole cheering fact emerges that for more than 90 percent of its existence the earth has been ice-free, even in the polar regions. Brilliant analysts, such as Wendell A. Moody, founding director of the Desert Research Institute and of the Hawaii Geophysics Institute, points out the growing evidence that naturally occurring variations in incoming solar radiation, which are over the course of the earth's lifetime the basic climate makers, result from the changed position and orientation of the earth in orbit around the sun. Fluctuations in insolation on the earth resulting from tilting of the Northern Hemisphere at perihelion toward the sun in summer in past geologic periods, or away from the sun in summer, as is now the case, have been calculated to be as much as 7 percent, that is $\pm$ 3.5 percent from the average. This crucial

3.5 percent variation has been enough to produce ice ages as well as the much longer ice-free intervals between. High insolation in the northern latitudes was unquestionably the most important factor in producing the warm interglacial periods. And it is of course in the northern latitudes where the concentration of man-made energy is occurring and where most of the food is grown. On this broader time scale we can expect sooner or later a slow swing back to the apparently more normal condition of an ice-free earth, in which case nearly all the coastal cities of the world will eventually be inundated by the melting of the incalculably vast icelands of the Antarctic, Greenland, and the Arctic.

If man as a master inhabitant of the earth can manage to prevent wars of annihilation between the hungry and the overfed of his own species, he might someday understand not only how to control the weather but how to control the climate, possibly by steering his mother sphere on an orbit and a tilt which never vary from the optimum amount of captured sunlight. With weather and climate control, man's food problems would be over.

Wendell Moody has suggested a different way in which the climate might be controlled. If one could create a Saturnlike ring of potassium dust around the earth, this would have the effect of producing a 12 percent increase in solar radiation incident on the earth, a more profound change (perhaps too profound) than by steering our globe by some method requiring astronomical expenditures of energy. If we had the amount of energy required to control the earth's orbit, as one corrects with rocket thrusts the position of a rocket satellite, we would not require the increased energy of sunlight that we achieve by such control.

On the other hand, the construction of a Saturnlike ring of potassium dust might demand less total energy investment than the placement in stationary orbit of solar-cell, power-relay satellites of the kind referred to in Chapter 12. But we would have to be awfully sure. It would be terrifying to build a ring around our world and then find that it caused some unpredictable and ineluctable obliteration of all man's loves and hopes and the loss of his future on this sweet, blue planet.

16 Pollution

Power, like a desolating pestilence,
Pollutes whate'er it touches.
—PERCY BYSSHE SHELLEY

During the time that it has taken to degrade the meaning of the once respectable term *ecology,* our emotional and political forces have so polarized themselves on different sides of an imaginary ecological barrier that the country might as well be in a state of civil war. Ecology is a science, in fact a quite abstruse one in which mathematical description of the effect of various independent variables on a given biological unit is the problem at hand. Ecology in the degraded, popular sense, however, is a religion in which one can have not only fervent practitioners but against which one can align roaring protestants and bellicose hooligans. Strictly speaking, one can no more be antiecology than antialgebra, but in the new theologized sense of the word, where ecologists may threaten the status quo, ecology is seen not only as a wicked religion but as a disreputable political doctrine, un-American, communist, in favor of ducks and coyotes over human beings.

The true ecologist, like any bonafide scientist, is surrounded more by doubts than by explicit messages from the burning bush. The things he studies, the vast, complex, and blooming, buzzing totality of the environment are very puzzling. He is glad to try to trace causes and effects, but the traceries are unimaginably complicated and very often he comes up with conclusions that agree neither with the brutish certainties of the industrial dollar men nor with specialized poets and preachers whose love of the environment is qualified by the proviso that the environment should contain no human beings.

We can perhaps best try to understand the state of civil war that now exists and the vast fuzziness of the issues involved by looking first at some of the problems of water.

WHEN IS WATER POLLUTED?

I confess immediately that I have been as guilty as any other propagandist in emphasizing the dangers of certain aspects of water pollution in my book *Death of the Sweet Waters*. Let me give an explicit example: I have been unreasonably horrified by the fact that a lot of human wastes get into both fresh and salt water. When I was a boy at Balboa Beach, California, I used to dig in the mud flats for cockles, and since the community's idea of sewage treatment was to dump raw toilet water into the bay through a screen capable only of filtering out things bigger than newborn babies, my cockle digging, especially at low tide, was punctuated by encounters with innumerable turds. I got 50 cents a bucket for the cockles but could not imagine why anyone would want to make chowder of these turd-haunted mollusks.

But why should I have been prejudiced against human feces? Except for considerations later to be discussed, human fecal matter is no worse than the fecal matter from aquatic animals. And consider the arithmetic. The 6 million metric tons of anchovies off Southern California produce as much fecal material as 90 million people, 10 times the population of the Los Angeles area; and the anchovies of course are only one of hundreds of species of marine life defecating in these waters. One can agree with C. E. Isaacs, the oceanographer, that the oceans are on the average starved for basic plant nutrients; and that the more sewage they get, the more plankton and other fish food they can support.

In Nöel Mostert's impressive book *Superships,* the author treats of the danger of polluting the fertile Southern Ocean with petroleum from spills or wrecks from the monstrous new oil tankers. But actually, from the standpoint of the true ecologist, do we know that these oil spills are doing any direct damage to the plankton? We are in a double dilemma. First, we do not have any proof that oil spills permanently damage the green algae that constitute the most basic link in the chain of food in the sea. Second, these same green algae in their astronomical masses are thought by many to be responsible for all the oxygen on earth. If petroleum spills destroy such plankton the plankton-eating organisms —and thus all fish life—are in danger of extinction, but we ourselves are apparently in double jeopardy, because we not only run out of fish food, we run out of oxygen to breathe. But the point is, we don't know this. Very accurate air analysis shows not even a change in the fourth decimal place in the oxygen content of air from year to year, and from decade to decade. It is not even certain that oxygen on earth is produced mainly from photosynthesizing algae.

According to a competing theory, oxygen is principally made by the decomposition of water vapor at altitudes sufficiently high to allow direct bombardment by ultraviolet rays, most of which are otherwise filtered out by the ozonosphere. If we boil down Nöel Mostert's nightmare of 400,000-ton oil slicks from the breakup of the supertankers, we are left with only one certain repercussion. This much oil would certainly kill a lot of seabirds, especially jackass penguins. And the loss of the guano from the birds might make for a poorer year for plankton and thus for fish—how much poorer, again we cannot say, because we cannot compare the relative contribution of bird excrement and fish excrement for the agronomy of the sea.

This sense of doubtfulness, of lack of proof, of contending alternatives is a hallmark of the scientific mind, but it is not good enough for planetary management, for we have continually to ask ourselves such questions as, suppose the oil spills do deplete all the oxygen on earth? When the proof is in, what do we do then? It is too late to do anything but compose requiems. We cannot take a banker's chance on world-wide trends beyond the control of local authorities.

On the whole our decision must simply be based on more knowledge, but in the meantime we could correct some of the leaks in our coastal refineries, administer sterner controls over tanker cleaning and bilge-water dumpings, and above all follow up promptly on the leads we have that derive from the fact that petroleum is a natural, biological product of marine organisms combined with geological accidents.

Because petroleum has been seeping into the ocean for hundreds of thousands of years in certain seismically unstable areas, such as the coast of Southern California, bacteria have evolved in these places which make a living off of oil slicks.* Since they are similar to the organisms which we discussed in the last chapter (single cell protein), they are inclined to feed selectively on the paraffinic fractions of the crude oil, which are those of lowest density and keep the oil afloat. When the petroleum bugs have eaten their fill, the oil slick becomes heavier than water, balls up into bituminous blobs and sinks. Thus the bottom of the Santa Barbara Channel over the millenia has become a kind of asphalt pavement.

Along with the jolly feminist suggestion that, as we have been naming hurricanes after women, we should name noteworthy oil spills after male politicians (Slick Ronald, etc), we should give serious thought to providing every oil tanker with a kit which includes cultured oil-eating bacteria, along with high-potency supplementary nutrients. Thus every cargo would be accompanied by the means for its own biochemical destruction.

There is another property acting against the preservation of oil slicks—their vulnerability to sunlight. Recent studies in fact seem to show that the sun causes more rapid decomposition, at least in the case of certain asphaltic petroleums, than bacteria; and happily the target of photochemical attack is complementary to the point of bacterial attack. While the micro-organisms prefer a diet of paraffinic hydrocarbons, the sun would rather aim its rapiers at asphaltic fractions, especially those with sulfur linkages.

This is a fact I know well since one of my first research chores was to develop a roofing asphalt of great durability from a certain crude oil, high in sulfur and

*Oil slicks were first reported in the New World in Havana Bay in 1508, and the survivors of De Soto's expedition used tar found on the beaches of Texas and Louisiana to caulk their boats. Asphalt was reported on the beaches of Galveston in 1541, while the early explorers of the California coast reported "rainbow hued" surface water in the Santa Barbara Channel.

of no apparent use for anything at all. Air-blown asphalt from the residium of this crude made coating for shingles of long life as tested in a laboratory weathering apparatus, except with certain types of granules (quartzite) that were relatively transparent to sunlight. The light had such a discoloring effect that a sort of profile photograph could be taken of an object placed between the light bulb and the asphalt panel. Moreover the water runoff after exposure to light and a rain cycle was acidic. Such roofing shingles result in corroded gutters and downspouts and stained driveways, because the chief constituent of the runoff (as in the case of high-sulfur coal tailings in the Appalachians) is sulfuric acid. We found and patented a way to stabilize such asphalts against decomposition by light, but it is also possible to add materials (photosensitizers) which accelerate the decomposition.

A combination of bacterial cultures and photosensitizers now looks like a good self-destruct kit for the tankers and as an adjunct to Coast Guard skimming equipment for oil spills. I freely donate this notion to whoever has the gumption to take it up and run with it.

But what about such questions as the drilling of the outer continental shelves? Here I must admit to a degree of geographic prejudice. The geology of North America is such that the Atlantic seaboard has a very broad outer shelf where drilling is relatively easy and relatively safe, except for seasonal hurricanes. Off-shore production at the present state of the art is the least of all the active sources of oil pollution. New England beaches, for example, should suffer less oil contamination from production wells 100 to 150 miles off-shore than from deep ports constructed to handle the 75-foot draughts of the supertankers bringing in oil from the Middle East or from Venezuela or Nigeria or Libya. Why should Louisiana, and in the future California or the Gulf of Alaska, bear the brunt of petroleum off-shore activity, when indications are strong that the shelf off New England (the Georges Bank) and off New Jersey (the Baltimore Canyon) are probably much more productive? There is the insinuation, which makes Westerners bristle, that somehow the sands of the Eastern coast are more precious or more delicate or that the people of the Eastern seaboard deserve more protection than other North Americans, presumably because they have more money. This indeed seems to have been the motive behind the extraordinary attempt on the part of Governor Russell W. Peterson of Delaware to keep the state as a kind of deer park for the Du Ponts and their relatives.

Even the eastern part of the Gulf of Mexico acquires sanctity, as compared with the Western coastal waters, and one of the more elaborate preliminaries to drilling off the Florida coast requires a survey by an archeologist, using underwater TV, divers, and sonic gear, to check whether some unsuspected archeological treasure, say, a sunken Spanish galleon, might not be impaled by the drill.

On the whole, save for the new grave problem of the effects of chlorination on drinking water, this country and the United Kingdom have made measurable strides in cleaning up key rivers. The Thames is clean enough to swim in and to support finicky fish such as salmon. The Detroit River, once considered hopeless, is sparkling blue again, and Lake Erie shows signs of reversing its progression toward a kind of American Dead Sea. The Willamette River that runs through Portland, Oregon, where I once put in some time as a cub reporter 50 years ago was such a horror that men refused to work on riverside construction because of the stench. Today thousands of people fish and swim in it. While we still have our problems of special chemical pollution on the great commercial rivers, industrial clean-up is no longer a cause for strokes of apoplexy in board meetings.*

Chemical companies and other chronic pollution-prone organizations have, I sense, been able to reverse the Tragedy of the Commons (which epitomizes the facet of human nature that encourages each individual to put an extra sheep on the public pasture because the gain seems to overbalance the common loss of available grass). If so, this is a great reversal indeed and I believe it may have been accomplished not by a gospel miracle but by the ever more obvious threat of perhaps the subtlest and yet the simplest measure ever conceived for the control of river contamination. This measure was invented evidently in Czechoslovakia and decrees that a user of river water must put his water intake pipes down river from his water effluent pipes. If you think this doctrine over a bit, I believe you will agree with me that it is endowed with the true stinging wisdom of Solomon.

Such an approach might even be applied to such problems as thermal pollution, although here I must again step across the bridge to the other side of the river and enregister myself under the flags of the sceptics and the energists. Thermal pollution is the kind of utterly phony issue that makes the public consider all environmentalists wacky. It is true that a change in river temperature by a few degrees may drive away for a few hundred yards one certain kind of fish or mollusk that the environmentalist is especially dedicated to; but on the other hand, it may attract other more desirable species. On some of the rivers and estuaries close to nuclear power plants, men of ingenuity have used the warm waters to grow luscious, oversized clams; and in Scotland the mariculture of expensive fish, such as plaice, has been greatly accelerated by the availability of such thermal pollution. The revivification of the River Thames in the center of London, which in 1957 was virtually lifeless but which today supports over 50 species of fish, took place at the same time that 3,400 megawatts of power plants used the river water for direct cooling.

Perhaps this is too kindly a remonstrance for the thermal-pollution criers. According to Irving Kristol's essay on the "Bugging of Con-Ed," the tribulations of this wounded giant of the industry have been caused by people in New York City who are not so much "pro-environment" as "anti-business." Professor Kris-

---

*While the United States and other highly industrialized countries have become water-pollution-conscious, it is all too evident that the developing countries cannot learn by example, only by experience. So polluted have the rivers of southern Brazil become that the vultures that feed on the small riverside animals are dying out from poisons and, according to toxicologist Paulo Roberto Delia, Brazilian vultures will in a few years be mere zoo curiosities.

tol draws an analogy between anti-Semitism, the "socialism of fools," and the New York version of environmentalism, "the socialism of upper-middle-class malcontents."

Let us now return to the question of human turds. How about pathogenic microbes? Raw sewage swarms with coliform bacteria, harmless residents of the human bowel, which moreover die rapidly in sea water often after about 2 hours' exposure. It is not known for sure whether pathogenic organisms, such as those that cause cholera, thyphoid fever, and hepatitis, are susceptible to sea water. Certainly they thrive in fresh water.

It is quite obvious that we cannot translate our problems with rivers and fresh-water lakes to problems with the oceans. One of our marked tendencies is to exaggerate our size and importance compared with the oceans. Usually enormous marine effects unfold before us in which we function only as worried spectators. When the conditions are right, for example, great blooms of algae develop suddenly and then die after a few days, in both cases depleting the surface water of oxygen. Within a few months the immense population of copepods, euphausids, and salps can change by a factor of 10. When the waters off California decrease in temperature or the current shifts a bit, red crabs of the genus *Pleuroscade* start floating by in utterly fantastic numbers, followed by hungry shoals of bonito and swordfish.

People who lived through the time of World War II will remember the California sardine, often a substitute for beef. When the sardines disappeared about 1950, this was blamed on overfishing. The geologic record shows, however, that sardines have a well-established habit of disappearing. They have come and gone many times before the arrival of man. The odds are probably good that the sardine and the haddock (also a periodic disappearer) will show up again, by the billion; just as the anchovies returned to the waters of Peru after a brief misbehavior on the part of the Humboldt current.

On the whole it appears that fish resist poisoning by trash (e.g., petroleum and solid waste) because most of the important species—all those of the trout and salmon family, for example—have the ability to cough. Coughing fish can discharge impurities from the gill system, and the incidence of coughing can be used as a very delicate measure of the concentration of trash in the water.

What should worry us more than natural pollutants, such as human wastes and petroleum,* are the synthetic chemicals, such as DDT, chlorinated biphenyls, and the like. The sudden decline of the brown pelican in California was attributed to DDT, which inhibits the metabolism of calcium and makes its eggshells so thin that the mother pelican breaks her own eggs by sitting on them. The source of the DDT was a single chemical plant in the Los Angeles harbor area. When it stopped discharging DDT wastes, the brown pelican came back.

---

*Most oceanographers are agreed that geologic seepage of petroleum enters the oceans at a rate of at least 500,000 metric tons per year. The total oceanic burden of petroleum from all sources is about 6 million metric tons per year.

THE MYSTERIOUS DOOMSDAYS

In all pollution problems we are realizing how little we really know, and it is this no-man's land of ignorance over which the battles are being fought. The reason we know so little is that there has not been enough time for the sciences of analytical chemistry and of medical epidemiology to catch up with the rate at which we synthesize new chemicals and throw things away. It was only a few years ago that we found out that asbestos was a fatal lung poison, although its effects might not show themselves in the human body for a score of years or so. Now we are faced with the practical circumstance that the Reserve Mining Company of Minnesota in connection with taconite (iron ore) mining has been discharging millions of tons of waste asbestos into Lake Superior and has no expressed intention of stopping this practice. Is raw asbestos in drinking water a poison? Who knows for sure and who can wait for the 20 or 30 years or so necessary to find out?

The attitude of the Reserve Mining Company, as is the attitude of all industrialists, is to assume no harm is being done, because there are no dead, asbestos-laden bodies strewn around Lake Superior. The industrialists' motto is "Prove it," but this is even before we know what we are trying to prove. Is it the fact that orally consumed asbestos is a poison at all, or that, like asbestos breathed, its fatal effects occur on a delayed doomsday? The natural instinct of the epidemiologist is also to respond with "Prove it," but he means quite the opposite. He means, "Since this is not a state of nature, prove that these huge asbestos effluents are not doing any harm." The industrialist replies that this would take 30 years. The epidemiologist responds, "Well, discharge the asbestos crap into a separate lagoon for 30 years until we find out." The industrialist says, "That would cost too much. We'd have to shut down the whole iron-ore project and that would put 2,000 men out of work, and it gets damned cold up here in the winter when you don't have a job." There is no answer to this. At least the epidemiologist has no answer, because he is not qualified to talk politics.

Let us not try to minimize the sense of helpless horror that has crept upon us, perhaps epitomized by the suspicion that chlorinated drinking water contains carcinogenic chemicals—absurdly simple things like chloroform or carbon tetrachloride which we have used for years in the various circumstances of modern civilization. We did not know they were cancer forming because, in the first place, we did not choose to drink them and, secondly (and most scarily), the lesions, as in the case of asbestos-poisoning, are delayed. What plutonium does in the lungs in a few minutes, some of these old false-friends take 2 decades to accomplish on other visceral organs. But you wind up just as dead.

The fearful suspicion of chlorinated hydrocarbons is of intense interest to a biological chemist with a taste for the evolutionary history of man. Chlorine itself or other oxidizing forms of chlorine, such as bleaching powder, are chemical artifacts; if man had not appeared on the planet, they would not exist. Viewed in this manner, all man-made chemicals are suspect because the human species has not had enough firsthand biochemical experience with them. (Man has been making new chemicals for less than 2 centuries.) If you expose hominids over hundreds of thousands of years to malarial mosquitoes, the evolving human beings—as in Central Africa—may develop protection in the form of sickle-cell blood. But the development of such exquisite and, indeed, hazardous immunization through the process of natural selection takes more time than man has left to him. In the case of malaria, modern man solves the problem by killing the mosquitoes through the trick of introducing a new chlorine-loaded chemical (DDT) that will probably turn out to kill man himself by slower means, as Aldrin and Dieldrin in drinking water kill.

In the recent discoveries of the carcinogenic properties of artificial foods, such as cyclamate and saccharin, and the dangerous effects now attributed to vinyl chloride, we come face to face with a question that sooner or later has to be answered: Is any artificial chemical compound, any chemical compound that did not exist on the planet before man became a synthetic chemist, *ipso facto* a dangerous material if given sufficient time to invade the secret tissues of the human body? Will we ultimately find aspirin to be a carcinogen? The barbiturates? The synthetic antibiotics? Tetraethyl lead?

In the unmeasured shadow of this horror we find ourselves setting up an index of time-on-earth compared with human toxicity (especially carcinogenicity). In this index, beer from spring water is obviously safer than chlorinated drinking water, because alcohol is the oldest poison on earth. Surely, if alcohol were carcinogenic, we would have known it by now, and besides alcohol is natural. Birds and monkeys can get drunk on fermented fruit.

When one comes to think it over, there are actually only 2 basic kinds of poisons: carcinogens, which may be ridiculously simple in chemical structure but a novelty on earth, and the toxins used by animals and plants for killing or defending against each other, most of them chemically complex beyond our powers of reduplication. The greatest war on earth for hundreds of millions of years has been the war between insects and plants and out of this endless conflict come most of the natural medicines that man has inherited (e.g., digitalis). These toxins are seldom carcinogenic, because cancer is too slow a way for plants and insects to fight to the death. It is true that some toxins, the alkaloids for example, may be carcinogenic in the long term, but they are designed primarily to knock an insect off his perch, not to subject him to an unhappy old age. Poisonous insects, venomous snakes want the action quick and certain, for in many cases they are preparing a meal rather than fighting for a cause.*

In automatically suspecting all man-made chemicals of carcinogenicity, we are exercising a sort of universal Delaney amendment (the law that makes all food

---

*The honey bee's sting, however, is a true case of dying for the great cause of honey-bee-hood. Her suicidal sting is meant to impress the stung enemy that honey bees are important and should not be molested.

additives or new food chemicals forbidden if they can be shown to cause in laboratory animals any kind of cancer at any dosage, however large), and perhaps recent events have justified the Delaney psychology. Perhaps they have also justified the organic farming technique, at least insofar as it dispenses with chemical pesticides and weed killers. Perhaps it is time for a massive and unprecedentedly ambitious re-examination of all the new chemicals on earth. Perhaps it is time to fire all synthetic chemists and turn them into analytical chemists. Perhaps it is much later than we think.

THE AIR IS FULL OF STUFF

Senator Hugh Scott, a gentle and surprisingly philosophic Republican from Pennsylvania, has pointed out that there exists in every person the eternal conflict between the *Han-Jen,* or civilized part of his nature, and the *Hsiung-Nu,* the barbarian part. The good senator hopes that in the face of the energy crisis, the American citizen will keep the dragon within him asleep.

A futile hope! Americans are not constructed so as to insure the quietude of anyone, let alone a dragon; and it is in the subject of air pollution that the *Hsiung-nus* make it a point to squawl on the fences night and day. The civil war that I referred to in the first paragraph of this chapter feeds most noisily on the issues that one thought innocently had been settled by the Clean Air Act of 1970. It turns out that in the face of an energy shortage, the poisons identified and targeted in that legislation are not poisonous after all. The federal legislators, it seems, had been made the victims of a gigantic hoax perpetrated by an evil conspiracy on the part of the Friends of the Earth, the National Audubon Society, the Sierra Club, the Wilderness Society, the National Wild Life Federation, the Izaac Walton League, and the American Forestry Association.*

It is not my thesis that the energy crisis really had any part in inspiring technical people to discover that air pollution was a phony issue. The polluters had all along been licking their wounded paws in their caves, waiting for another chance to charge.

Two problems of monstrous aspect evoked the long civil war: the sulfur dioxide effluents from power plants and the generous, fertile mixture of reactive hydrocarbons, nitrogen oxides, and carbon monoxide that is coughed out by internal combustion engines.

In an incredibly corkscrew turn of irony, the most popular means of detoxifying the auto emissions (by catalysts in the exhaust) has introduced instead a sulfuric-acid-type contamination that is virtually the same as the sulfur-containing destroyer that comes out of the stacks of power plants which burn high-sulfur coal. This is a long sad story, but since it is the sulfurous pollutants that are

*It should be mentioned that through the fact that contributions to such organizations are usually tax-deductible, the organizations are specifically prohibited from political lobbying. Their net influence on politicians, therefore, cannot be compared with that of the professional lobbyists of the oil, the auto, or the electric power industries.

known to have caused the death of thousands of people in the old disasters of London, Donora, the Meuse Valley, it is proper that we first have a look at this killer.

REQUIEM FOR SCRUBBERS

The American Electric Power System, perhaps the single most powerful privately owned utility in the world, has been spending its money not on pollution control, as one might hope, but on full-page advertisements in newspapers and magazines, blasting the regulations of the Environmental Protection Agency. The "requiem for scrubbers" means that this company disapproves of the suggestion that sulfur dioxide and soot particles be removed from the stack gases of its power plants, when the furnaces are fed with high-sulfur coal or fuel oil, by scrubbing with an appropriate chemical solution plus perhaps an electrical precipitator or cloth filter to remove the particulate matter.

The high-voltage copywriters for the American Electric Power System aim to persuade the reader that scrubbers set up to remove sulfur dioxide do more harm than good: They produce enormous piles of goop that can only be disposed of by burying, and so voluminous must be the burial grounds that in no time at all we would be surrounded not be countryside but by a "goopside." Whole troops of Boy Scouts and regiments of dancing little girls would disappear in goop, never to be seen again. Goop would conquer all, engulf all.

This makes a passable script for a horror movie but otherwise it makes no sense whatever. The goop nightmare applies only to scrubbers in which lime water is used to react with the stack gas. (If lime or magnesia is reacted before the burning, one has no goop, but a solid removal problem.) The fact is that modern scrubbing processes have been abundantly demonstrated in which the sulfur dioxide winds up not as goop but as commercial sulfur or as salable sulfuric acid.

There is no point in my acting as a salesman for these processes or comparing their technical merits. I have thoroughly studied a number of them and there is no question but that they work. In fact they are working commercially in Japan, which has suddenly become so pollution-conscious that the air standards for the present and the years to come are considerably more rigorous than those of any other industrial country. But it is apparently money in the pocketbook of the American Electric Power System to claim that the only available scrubbing process is one that yields intractable goop.

Yet even if we had to cope with goop, it would be worth it, for the modern epidemiology of sulfur dioxide is quite frightening. Although there is still an element of mystery in exactly how sulfur dioxide is transformed into a definitely more dangerous chemical missile, it is in the form of sulfuric acid absorbed on fine smoke or dust that the damage is done to human lung tissue and the breathing apparatus.

I want to emphasize this point, since it is easily the most crucial fact that has been established since the publication of *The Breath of Life* in 1965. When sulfur dioxide is released in dry weather and with very little dust or soot in the air, it is definitely harmful, especially to poultry, who are easily crippled by practically any air pollutant and it therefore would classify as a secondary environmental pollutant (harmful to animals, vegetation, statuary, etc.*). Under conditions of high relative humidity and a lot of metallic (especially iron) dust in the air, the sulfur dioxide rapidly becomes a primary pollutant—sulfuric acid aerosol—that is at least 100 times as dangerous to the human body as dry sulfur dioxide.

The situation with regard to the sulfur compounds is complicated by the fact that even very dry sulfur dioxide is synergistic with certain other powerful pollutants, especially ozone. That is to say, the effect of sulfur dioxide is multiplied manyfold by the simultaneous presence of ozone. In fact, there is so much absolutely unpredictable synergism involved in the epidemiology of air pollution that air ecologists sometimes despair to the point of giving up their jobs and studying something relatively simple, such as quantum electrodynamics.

One dire synergism is that of cigarette smoking and air pollution in respect to lung cancer. Old men in the Ecuadorian Andes can apparently smoke everyday the equivalent of 100 machine-made cigarettes and live past the century mark, but if they try to do that in a hopelessly polluted metropolis such as Mexico City, they seldom survive their sixtieth birthday. The lung cancer capital of the world is now probably Ankara which has everything going against it: isolation in a bowllike plateau surrounded by mountains, no winds, almost continuous temperature inversion, high sulfur lignite as the universal fuel for home and industry, a population addicted to smoking, enough auto traffic to provide a variety of synergists for a rich sulfur dioxide base, and overcrowding. When Kemal Ataturk made Ankara the Turkish capital, he was advised of trouble if the population exceeded 30,000. It is now over 2 million, and unless you are robust and a nonsmoker, I counsel you strongly to stay away from the place.

In 1969 and 1970 the Environmental Protection Agency in the United States brought together all experimental and epidemiologic data and established air quality standards for individual pollutants. It identified 24-hour standards, levels of pollutants that could be exceeded only once a year, and annual standards. Each state was supposed to achieve the standards by July 1, 1975.

Allegheny County in Pennsylvania, a very pollution-conscious area, measures sulfur dioxide and particulate matter and sets up an index, based on these all-too-compatible poisons, which had to be less than 25 to assure passing the EPA annual standard. In 1973 and 1974 the index ranged between 45 and 50, with episodes of over 100. At this level most lung specialists are now agreed that asthmatics or people with chronic bronchitis or emphysema would be hard pressed to survive in the open air. A report of the multi-million-dollar financial team known as CHESS (Community Health and Environmental Surveillance

*One century in New York City has done more harm to Cleopatra's Needle than 3,500 years in Egypt.

System) has also noted in episodes of sulfur dioxide particulate matter the almost instantaneous increase in croup and in susceptibility to influenza.

Despite such indications in Pennsylvania, Bethlehem Steel, among others, claimed that installation of scrubbers would make them go broke, and the residents of certain Bethlehem towns, such as Johnstown, alarmed at the possible loss of jobs, beseeched the steel company to submit proposals that would delay the cutbacks. The results were 3 controversial pieces of legislation (the Bethlehem bills) in the Pennsylvania legislature, which are more important for implication than for actuality, since they did not pass. One key provision would exempt older facilities of "limited life" from environmental laws for 12 years. A union leader of Johnstown summed up the hard-hat viewpoint on air pollution control: "I don't want to be the healthiest guy on the relief rolls." But the question would be more honestly put, "Do I want the steel company to get away with another 12 years of running a wheezy operation that ruins my children's lungs and kills my father?"

One of the extremely foolish alternatives to scrubbing that has been offered by certain industries and that was looked upon with favor by the Nixon Administration is the use of very tall smokestacks. This is simply a splendid way of transfering the sulfur oxide problem to the next county or even—in Europe—to the next country. Scandinavian crops, for example, have been badly damaged by sulfur dioxide or sulfuric acid aerosols blown all the way from the high stacks of Scotland. With tall plumes ripe with soot and sulfur dioxide, one encounters a bright, new, vicious problem—acid rain. Here the secondary pollution standards bear the brunt, for there is absolutely no doubt that a decade or more with rain, in which the acidity is as high as it gets with sulfur dioxide saturation, will reduce the net production of forests and agriculture. A 10 percent reduction in the New England states doesn't sound like much for we do not think of this area as a breadbasket or even as a forest; but in energy equivalents it would be tantamount to closing down 15 power plants of a 1,000 megawatts each. Acid rain from coal-burning or shale-oil-burning power plants in the Midwestern or Mountain states might actually cause a world famine.

The use of high stacks is guaranteed to convert a local problem, perhaps a failure to meet primary EPA standards, into a regional problem with a failure to meet secondary standards, along with an invitation to starvation.

THE FACTS TO DATE

Because of the synergistic effects referred to in the discussion of the most radical of all pollutants—sulfur dioxide and its derivitives—the automotive smog picture is deeply discouraging for medical systematists. The well-established primary toxins, such as nitrogen oxides (usually referred to in chemical shorthand as NO_x and pronounced popularly as Nox, as in the slogan "Knock Nox") and ozone, along with many derivatives, are known to be implicated in the same way the sulfuric acid aerosols are in respiratory diseases and coronary deficiencies.

The newer way of looking at air pollution, however, is focused on what kind of walking wounded are most easily finished off by air pollution episodes. The Chicago specialist Dr. Bertram W. Carnow, divides failure of resistance to pollutants under various categories.

Genetic Defects: Hypercholesterolemia, diabetes with atherosclerosis, asthma, cystic fibrosis, cystic lung disease, hypergammaglobulinemia, heart wall defects (atrial or ventricular), valvular defects, sickle-cell anemia, various allergies.

Development Defects: Hypertension with left ventricular disease, coronary insufficiency (with or without angina), rheumatic heart disease, congestive heart failure (secondary to atherosclerotic heart disease), chronic bronchitis, emphysema, tuberculosis, histoplasmosis, bronchiectasis.

Personal Habits: Cigarette smoking, heavy exertion.

Physical Condition: Aging or debilitation, newborn (especially premature) babies, preschool ages, obesity.

Living Conditions: Overcrowding, malnutrition, excessive cold. On the basis of his studies world-wide, Dr. Carnow has arrived at a rule of thumb regarding lung cancer: Regardless of smoking habits, an over-all reduction of 60 percent in urban air pollution would yield a 20 percent reduction in lung cancer. Of course, one cannot separate smoking habits from air pollution, since a large part of local air pollution is simply somebody else's cigarette smoke. This is especially true in Soviet Russia, where smoking is allowed in theaters, ballets, operas, and where the average individual smoking habit is heavier than in most other countries. The striking acceleration of lung cancer in the USSR may to some extent be correlated by an increase in alcoholism, since drinking and smoking are, so to speak, behavioral synergists; that is to say, people while drinking also feel like smoking.

Of all the pollutants considered, perhaps the sharpest change in attitude has been that toward carbon monoxide. It was previously regarded as something you commit suicide with in a closed garage, but it is now viewed very seriously at chronic rather than lethal levels. This is a change in viewpoint which I urged in *The Breath of Life,* emphasizing that we not only have little epidemiological data of our own on the effects of chronic exposure but we have overlooked the large number of direct observations made in Europe during World War II, when many countries were forced to use charcoal engines, for which the fuel was mainly carbon monoxide itself.

Accident frequencies in traffic can now be pretty well correlated (if one overlooks alcohol) with carboxyhemoglobin in the blood—the compound that is formed instead of oxyhemoglobin because carbon monoxide shoves the oxygen aside to react preferentially with the red blood cells.

The unexpectedly severe effect of chronic carbon monoxide poisoning on the cardiovascular system is shown by the increasing number of cases of hardening of the coronary arteries in young smokers. Striking changes in electrocardiograms and exercise tolerance are shown by men with heart disease after exposure to 30

minutes of Los Angeles freeway traffic. Carboxyhemoglobin counts rose to unexpectedly high levels. The changes in behavior of people whose jobs necessarily
expose them continuously to carbon monoxide (e.g., the classical surliness of New
York policemen and cab drivers) is now attributed to the reaction of carbon
monoxide with something other than hemoglobin, perhaps to an essential office
in the central nervous system or perhaps a still more deep-seated effect involving
the mitochondria of all nerve cells.

Recent surveys show a quite shocking situation that has crept up on us while
we were arguing about emission controls. On the whole, carbon monoxide has
so saturated the blood of Americans that nearly one-half of nonsmokers have
more carboxyhemoglobin in their systems than federal safety standards would
permit. Smokers in cities have 3 to 4 times more—so much that they should not
be allowed to donate their blood to heart patients. In this respect the worst of
American cities is Denver,* with Los Angeles second. From such findings the
opinion is becoming established that present and future EPA standards for carbon
monoxide levels and emission concentrations are too lenient. On the other hand,
the proposed NO_x levels may be unrealistically low.

THE LITTLE FIXES AND THE BIG FIXES

Even though emission control in automobiles has been of a sketchy and rather
blunderbuss nature up until the 1975 models, since 1961 (when crank-case venti-
lation was introduced), the total tonnage of hydrocarbon emissions has decreased
by 80 percent, carbon monoxide by 70 percent, and NO_x by 40 percent, in new
cars. Unfortunately the control techniques mainly were in the wrong directions
as far as fuel economy was concerned. One would think that reducing the hydrocarbon in the exhaust would automatically increase the car mileage, but automobile engines are not that simple. A combination of changes in air/fuel ratio and
spark timing in order to reduce hydrocarbons and carbon monoxide in the
exhaust does not automatically give better fuel efficiency; usually it gives worse,
sometimes much worse, because the conditions at minimum emission are such
that a smaller part of fuel energy is converted into torque.

In addition to changes in mixture ratio and spark timing, the pre-1975
American fixes included in some cases blowing more air into the exhaust manifold. When one was dealing with a large, heavy car (such as the 5,000-pound
monsters that the Big Three enjoyed selling), the combination of emission-control
engine regime, use of air conditioners, and the fact that at above 40 miles per hour
the fuel mileage decreases roughly as the cube of the speed in the case of big cars,
mileages in 1969–74 model cars took a sickening drop, from about 13 miles per
gallon (in the EPA urban-driving cycle) to as low in some cases as 7 miles per

---

*As pointed out by Congresswoman Patricia Schroeder of Colorado, the reason that Denver and other
high-altitude cities, including Salt Lake City and Albuquerque, are afflicted with bad air is that
automobiles fitted with the pre-1975-type emission-control systems all ran exceedingly fuel-rich, no
provision having been made at the factories for altitude correction.

gallon. When the price of gasoline nearly doubled in 1974, many eager entrepreneurs made a quick buck by specializing in decontrolling the engine; i.e., stripping off the control system in order to obtain better mileage.*

With the imposition of much stricter standards on emissions of hydrocarbons, carbon monoxide, and nitrogen oxides for the 1975 models, one could no longer stagger through the EPA tests by diddling with the timing and mixture ratios. The time for the Big Fix had arrived. Mr. Big Fix was the catalytic muffler and the exhaust gas recycle valve.

The catalysts were mixtures of platinum and palladium, either in the form of pellets (GM and American Motors) or monolithic honeycombs (Ford and Chrysler), and their function was to catalyze the further oxidation of hydrocarbons and carbon monoxide in the exhaust. The recycle valve was to introduce automatically, according to the phases of engine operation, a certain amount of exhaust gas back into the engine, so that the peak combustion temperature would be lowered, preventing the fixation of nitrogen from the air in the form of NO_x.†

The Big Fixes have caused a good deal of understandable petulance, especially among producers of tetraethyl lead, because the catalysts are poisoned by oxidized ingredients of the ethyl fluid—probably by the ethylene diobromide that is added with the tetraethyl lead to insure that the lead leaves the engine as the volatile bromide rather than crudding up the cylinder head as the oxide. The necessity for a lead-free or perhaps extremely low-lead gasoline (0.05 grams per gallon) for virtually all 1975 models has caused a great hullabaloo in which attention is called to the fact that the virtual omission of lead has a fearful effect on the energy balance. Either you have to go to a lower-octane gasoline (it is pointed out), in which case to avoid knocking you have to use a lower-compression-ratio, which lowers fuel efficiency; or alternatively you get your octane number by more deeply cracking or reforming the clear gasoline, thus losing energy efficiency in the refinery. Besides, if you run on lead-free gasoline you will burn out your exhaust valves.

The latter scare story probably needs no special testing to disprove, since Amoco has for many years marketed with success a premium high-octane, lead-free motor fuel. In fact Amoco (a division of Standard of Indiana) claims that the supposed $15 billion for increased refining costs on account of lead removal would be offset by savings in auto maintenance, mainly fewer replacements of spark plugs and corroded mufflers. Moreover tetraethyl lead is not produced

*The inclusion of secondhand cars in pollution standards in California has stimulated a competitive race of small business with precisely the opposite goal: the retrofitting of older cars with emission-control kits.

†According to my diaries, the first systematic use of recycled exhaust gas to lower NO_x was at the UCLA engine laboratory. When reported by the student researchers to the Society of Automotive Engineers, the seniors in the business laughed at such folly, but careful study, since described by engine chemists at General Motors, shows that this method of reducing NO_x is intrinsically very efficient, so far as fuel economy is concerned, because of a rather abstruse relationship involving the ratio of specific heats at constant pressure and at constant volume.

without an expenditure of energy nearly the equal, per octane increment, to the energy involved in more severe refining.

As to energy wastes, the fact is that the catalysts allow the car manufacturers to return to optimum spark timing and air/fuel ratios, thus retrieving the economy of, say, 1967 cars. EPA tests on all 1975 models in both urban and cruising cycles showed a 15 to 20 percent increase in mileage per gallon over 1974 cars, although the Ford line appeared to lag curiously behind the rest.* Further data on this problem is presented in Chapter 18.

I have mentioned the fact that sulfuric acid or sulfate mists have been detected in the exhaust from catalytic mufflers. John Moran of EPA's Environmental Research Center in North Carolina maintains that the deadly sulfuric aerosol is emitted from 1975 cars at the rate of 0.05 grams per mile, which is higher by at least an order of magnitude than similar emissions from noncatalytic cars. This does not sound like a large figure, but one must bear in mind that the sulfuric acid or sulfate aerosols are actually the only smog constituents that have been proved (in London, Donora, and elsewhere) to cause death in the streets. One could imagine that complete desulfurization of gasoline would be an easy answer, but the fact is that total, quantitative removal of organic sulfur is very expensive and perhaps impossible; and that gasolines are normally desulfurized to a maximum practical extent to increase lead susceptibility; that is, to boost the octane-number increase that one can realize by adding a given amount of tetraethyl lead.†

At the date of writing it seems quite possible the sulfuric-acid aerosol problem and the cyanide problem may result in the complete abandonment of the catalytic approach. This would be no great tragedy, because there is a much better, simpler and cheaper approach ready at hand.

THE BEST FIX

Although it had been known for years (and in fact loudly proclaimed by the Texas Company in its experimental Texaco Combustion Process) that a more subtle way of exploding motor fuel in the Otto cycle would greatly lower the concentration of pollutants, it is an almost incredible fact that the American automobile manufacturers appear to have done little or no work in this field, which is known as dilute combustion or stratified charge, or by the triumphant Japanese Honda Company as controlled vortex chamber combustion.

The Honda CVCC or Civic easily meets the Japanese 1975 standards, which are tougher than those of the United States; it has a higher fuel economy than

*Recent information on 1976 models indicates that Ford has recovered from this temporary engineering goof.
†Very recent work by R. J. M. Voorhoeve et al at Bell Laboratories (*Science,* October 10, 1975) has shown that drastic desulfurization (as required by California's Air Resources Board, for example) may change the situation from dangerous to catastrophic. They find that in the absence of sulphur dioxide in the exhaust, the platinum catalysts may reduce nitric oxides to hydrogen cyanide, the gas once used for executions. The conditions favoring this grim reaction are deceleration and coasting downhill.

most cars and can use tetraethyl lead to achieve any octane level desired since there is no catalyst to poison.

A complete explanation of either the Honda or the Texaco Combustion Process would require the discussion of many complex concepts, such as the difference between electronic and free-radical ignition, branched-chain reactions, and the like. In a simple-minded way I prefer to say that the stratified charge technique involves simply a foolproof way to ignite and burn a very lean mixture of gas and air.* Because the mixture is lean (high ratio of air to fuel) the stratified charge motor behaves more like a diesel engine than an Otto-cycle engine; thus carbon monoxide and hydrocarbons are more fully consumed. On the other hand, again because the mixture is so lean, the peak combustion temperature is too low to give much nitrogen fixation; NO_x also tends therefore to run low. The question is, how do you accomplish the smooth ignition and burning of lean mixtures without intermittent misfires, as would be the case if you tried to run an Otto-cycle engine like a diesel engine?†

In the Honda system you have 2 separate sets of carburetors. One set delivers a small amount of an extremely rich mixture (high ratio of fuel to air) into a small auxiliary chamber with a spark plug. The other set delivers the bulk of the fuel at a very lean mixture to the main combustion chamber. This lean mixture will not respond reliably to a spark. It will respond, however (for chemical reasons having to do with the propagation of free radicals) to the little explosion in the auxiliary chamber. The Japanese call the opening between the little spark-ignited chamber and the main chamber the torch, and that is really the secret to the whole thing. One can ignite and explode with a torch a mixture too lean to pay any attention to a spark.

Belatedly Ford has jumped on this band wagon and promises to have its version of a stratified-charge engine ready by 1978. They call it Proco, meaning programmed combustion. Like the Texaco Combustion Process, rather than the Honda system, it will not include double carburetors and prechambers but will rely on the precise timing of direct injection of a cloud of fuel so that the cloud is exploded by a spark in its center, where it is rich, with the explosion spreading throughout an over-all lean fuel/air mixture. Although General Motors and Chrysler have expressed a sour-grapes attitude, grumbling about other pollutants, such as aldehydes, being produced by stratified-charge combustion,‡ there is every probability that this method of operating an Otto-cycle engine will ultimately prevail.

*In other words, the same effect is achieved by design that the Jet Propulsion Laboratory obtained by the addition of hydrogen, as described in Chapter 13.

†In passing, it should be emphasized that the development of small, passenger-car diesel engines should not be overlooked as one answer to air-pollution and fuel-economy questions. The problems of excessive noise and roughness of performance have been skillfully approached by German firms, and the diesels may eventually devour as large a hunk of the passenger-car and pick-up truck markets as they now hold in the heavy-haul business.

‡Aldehydes have a sharp, characteristic odor but are not known to be toxic at small concentrations. It is noteworthy that the exhaust gases from diesel engines commonly contain aldehydes.

The fact that a small foreign company specializing in motorcycles was able to beat the gigantic dollar machines of Detroit to the punch is a most edifying example for the antitrust specialists.

THE ULTIMATE POLLUTION PROBLEM: ABOVE THE AIR

The worst trouble seems always to sneak up like a raccoon. Who would guess that the aerosol sprays that bloomed out as such a blessing for applying everything from sunburn lotion to pesticides would now loom as perhaps the most ominous pollution peril that we have ever faced?

When Congress turned down the idea of funding a supersonic airplane transport project like the Concorde, one of the chief and most easily justified reasons was that, according to calculations, a fleet of 500 supersonic transports would eject enough NO_x to encourage the reverse of the equilibrium reaction responsible for ozone in Los Angeles photochemical smog. In other words, it might eventually destroy the ozonosphere, which guards the earth from most of the dangerously energetic ultraviolet radiation from the sun.

We cannot reliably imagine and delineate what would happen to life on earth, if the ozonophere were to disappear. We are reasonably sure that life could not have evolved on land until the ozonosphere was formed. We are also sure that incessant skin cancer would become a more popular way to die than any we have now. But if even the most conservative estimates are anywhere nearly correct, by the unthinking use of aerosol propellants we may have already doomed the ozonosphere. It is simply a matter of diffusion time until the otherwise infernally stable chlorofluoromethanes that we squirt out into the air drift up into the ozonophere, where they are decomposed by the strong ultraviolet they find up there, releasing single chlorine atoms that proceed to destroy ozone.

The danger is more evident to a chemist than he can make plain to the layman, because the key reaction is a regenerative chain:

$$Cl + O_3 \rightarrow ClO + O_2$$
$$ClO + O \rightarrow Cl + O_2$$

Thus a relatively small concentration of the propellants will yield enough chlorine atoms to destroy a very large amount of ozone.*

It is a dreadful irony that the chlorofluoromethanes would long ago have photochemically decomposed at atmospheric levels if it were not for the steadfast defense of the earth's surface by the ozonosphere. Ralph Cicerone and his colleagues at the University of Michigan estimate that if the present usage level of

---

*According to Michael B. McElroy of Harvard, the bromine atom is as brutal an ozone assassin as chlorine and undoubtedly exists in the stratosphere, mostly from the huge total amounts of bromine-containing compounds (ethylene dibromide) used in ethyl fluid for motor fuels. If Professor McElroy's fears are well grounded, this constitutes unquestionably the best excuse for getting lead additives out of gasoline.

chlorofluoromethanes—about 800,000 tons a year—continues, the ozonophere will undergo complete obliteration by about 1985 or 1990.

Until we can find something stranger, this is the most serious pollution problem the world faces.

17 Transportation

I have seen the past—and it worked.
—HOWARD K. SMITH

The true history of the United States is the history of transportation.
—PHILIP GUEDALLA

LOS ANGELES: IT STARTED OUT SO WELL!

There are very few people living who have a nostalgia for Los Angeles and I am one of them. It is not for the present vast circus of vortices in an endless smog but for the strange merry little city in which I was born and brought up. My family lived on Mount Washington Drive and in another book* I have described the blessed canyon with its smell of eucalyptus trees, sage, honeysuckle, and Ragged Robin roses. School was on the top of the mountain—not on a peak, but on the edge of a high plateau, for Mount Washington was a small residential town in itself.

But this is a story of transportation and it is therefore immediately pertinent to ask how we children of the canyons made our way to our California-Alpine school. The answer is surprising: by cable-car, and on a slope much more protracted than the San Francisco line that goes up and down Nob Hill. To this admirable and extraordinarily safe and commodious 5-mile trip the alternative was a long and dangerous road that wound up the flanks of Mount Washington. Needless to say, the incline (as we called the cable-car route) was an essential part of the lives of us canyon children.

The incline was not a part of careful planning by the City of Los Angeles or of its school system. It was put in by the slightly nutty but rather grandiose hotel on Mount Washington, which stood right beyond the wheelhouse at the top of the ascent and beyond which one had to walk a mile or so to arrive at the school which perched on the verge of the steep canyon cliffs. When the old hotel (after spending its substance on expensive tennis tournaments and dances and liquor

* *The Breath of Life.*

and what-not), went broke, the beautiful incline system was abandoned, leaving only the hairpin curves of the Drive to get the canyon kids to school, most probably by flivver or early prototype buses which were about as safe as trying to arrive by glider-kite. So before I really got used to riding the "yellow car" trolleys to high school, I had seen an excellent mini-mass-transit system operated and abandoned. This in effect was my private prologue to the rise and fall of mass transportation in Southern California—a mournful story indeed.

The yellow car system—the Los Angeles Municipal Railway—crisscrossed the city most efficiently. For example, when the Los Angeles High School at Bunker Hill was torn down and, in a new avatar, appeared as a splendid structure* far, far out in the unpopulated meadows between West Adams and West Pico, the good, faithful yellow car line followed along, delivering scads of students to a school whose athletic teams naturally accepted the nickname "Pioneers."

In order to get from Mount Washington Drive to the place to which I felt bound with certain familial ties, since my father was an alumnus and my aunt still taught Latin and journalism there, I had to transfer from one long streetcar line to another; but I thought nothing of it. I did all my homework on the trolley and even had time left over for dreaming (all of which showed up later when the family moved temporarily to Mamaroneck, New York, and I matriculated at Andover, Massachusetts, where in the first semester I flunked all the courses I had been passing by the grace of soft-hearted teachers at L.A. High).

One took the yellow car for granted: One could get anywhere in town, which was even then was a rather extensive place. The limits of town were an arbitrary perimeter perhaps best defined in the public's experience as where the yellow cars stopped taking you and you then had to take the big red cars of the Pacific Electric Railway. I look back on this particular broad-gauge electric mass-transit system not only with nostalgia but with awe. I can certify that it took my family everywhere we wanted to go. I have a childhood memory of being carried by a big red car to the very foot of Mount Lowe in the San Gabriels whence we ascended by elevator to a jolly restaurant surrounded by snow. Big red cars whisked you on the north to the very head of the San Fernando Valley and on the south 60 miles to the lovely beach-and-bay town of Balboa, where my family built a house. As we stayed there a year or so, my father commuted. Since he was a journalist on the Los Angeles *Times,* a morning paper, his hour of return required the last scheduled Big red car, perhaps at 2:00 A.M.; but the service was impeccable and it never failed him.

We had a family automobile by then—an Apperson Jackrabbit—but my father would never have dreamed of using this to get to and from work. That was the job of mass transportation and it seemed to me (although my memories may be blurred by blind love for the Southern California of the 1910 to 1920 decade)

*Its comely Romanesque tower and main building have been seen in innumerable movies and TV shows, but alas, scores of years later it was so badly damaged in the earthquake of 1971 that it had to be destroyed like an old horse that has broken its leg.

that there was never such a time or place in which one could so simply get from one delightful spot to another.*

I should emphasize a point important to the theory of urbanization. I see nonnative Los Angeles experts explaining that El Pueblo sprawls because the automobile made sprawling possible. This is nonsense. The fact is that El Pueblo sprawled from the start because the Pacific Electric big cars made it so easy to get from the tacky little central city of Los Angeles to Pasadena, to Sierra Madre, to Santa Monica, to Beverly Hills, to Long Beach, to all the outlying subrubs which constituted at one time a new and precious kind of urban pattern, indeed, the makings of a kind of splendid supercity. It was electric mass transit that made greater Los Angeles (or made Los Angeles greater). It was the automobile that finally destroyed her.

But before we get into this vicious complot, one more memory to round out, like my aunt's electric car, the spectrum of transportation adventure that became familiar to me in my childhood: the jitney bus. Curiously this concept, even the name, is included in the kit that every up-to-date transitologist carries around with him; but in the Los Angeles of the 1910s the jitney bus was a flash phenomenon with little more planning and systematics than a dog fight. It came about because of a streetcar strike. Some people with automobiles shared the ride, but as the strike prolonged itself, some drivers decided to charge a nickel (a jitney) for a ride. In the course of several months the jitney bus (often a Model-T Ford) became a way for nonlicensed cab drivers to pick up money by delivering people in crowded cars from here to there, mostly within the confines of downtown.

Thus the informal, the rather merry jitney-bus craze got Los Angeles through the streetcar strike. But then the echoes of the guns of World War I were heard throughout the land and an enormous adventure was brewing in which gasoline for jitney buses would become scarce and the jitney coin itself would lose its potency until 15 years later its might would be restored for buying apples from pale, sick-eyed men in the years of the Great Depression.

Yet it was not until just after World War II that perhaps the most efficient mass transport system in North America (with the exception of New York) and the longest interurban electric railway system in the world were destroyed with a totality that reminds one of the salting of the fields in ancient Carthage.

THE CONSPIRACY

I have said that I do not hold with the conspiratorial theory of history. I must now retract that statement and reserve its validity only for alleged conspiracies that do not include the General Motors Corporation. This fabulous organism

---

*On special occasions, including about every other Sunday, we were visited at Mount Washington Drive by my teaching aunt (my father's sister) and his mother, who drove all the way from an apartment on West Washington and back in an electric automobile. Since this was at least a 35-mile round trip, I have been astonished and will continue to express my astonishment that 60 years later in 1975 auto companies claim that with a battery-operated car such a feat is beyond the power of human engineering.

seems in fact to have been born in conspiracy, to have multiplied by conspiring, to have dominated by conspiracy—in fact, to have dominated to the extent that no court in the land had the starch or guts to suggest even the possibility of GM's huge plot—so huge in fact that one can see a certain legal generalization emerging: If your conspiratorial trust is big enough, if it involves practically every citizen's pocket, then the courts will do little or nothing, because they come to accept it all as the directed circumstances of God in a God-fearing nation.

Although our focus is presently on Los Angeles and environs, one must recall that scores of other big and little cities throughout the country had developed electric streetcar systems, later supplemented with bus systems, after a fashion. (The case of New York is unique and its near downfall will be described later in a separate context.) Before General Motors could carry through its titanic plan to de-electrify the country's transportation, it had some technical chores to accomplish: For one thing, it had to make a good, salable diesel-powered bus.

If one can somewhat broaden the term *good* to include vehicles emitting such foul and corrosive exhaust chemicals that they dissolve the nylon stockings of young ladies standing behind them at the curb, GM succeeded admirably. In the first place it designed a bus that wouldn't tip over twice a week. While the older coach buses had been composed of wood or even canvas mounted on steel frames and essentially resembled covered wagons in design, GM developed the Monocoque body construction similar to that in modern airplanes with an all-metal stressed skin. In combination with the placement of the engine in the rear, this gave the weight distribution of one-third in the front and two-thirds in the rear that is critical for safety in steering, fast acceleration, and satisfactory tire life. In 1938 General Motors came out with a new 2-cycle diesel engine.* In the early 1950s it introduced air suspension for improved ridability.

By this time General Motors had a virtual monopoly of the motor bus industry, having knocked off Ford, International Harvester, Studebaker, Twin Coach, and Chrysler (Dodge).

The next step (in 1938) was the formation of a wrecking gang or political corporation called National City Lines which in addition to G.M., Standard Oil of California, Firestone Rubber Company, had as taggers-along Phillips Petroleum Company and Mack Truck. Subsidiaries, often more truculent and pitiless than the mother company, were formed for specific purposes; for example, Pacific City Lines operated in Los Angeles and started the monopoly campaign by buying up the Pacific Electrical Company (the big red cars) in Southern California and the Key System in the San Francisco Bay area. As early as 1940 the Pacific City Lines began to acquire and immediately to scrap the magnificent

---

*For petroleum-company research supervisors such as me, this was a challenge equivalent to that of the dragon to Saint George. To qualify for lubricating this little monster, one's superpremium oil had to undergo a 500-hour test in which the engine was run full out, so hot that it glowed. Very few brands qualified, and we succeeded only by doping the lube oil with a melange of additives which included a purple dye. Although the sales department was rather shocked, the advertising group saw no reason why the natural fluorescent green should not be replaced by a more imperial hue.

$100 million big red car system, including its crucial rail lines from Los Angeles to Burbank, Glendale, Pasadena, and San Bernardino. In 1951 the last big red car ran through Watts to Long Beach and might as well have continued right into the convenient oblivion of the Pacific Ocean, for along with its hundreds of brothers it would be stripped and burned. The unparalleled 1,164 miles of broad-gauge track was torn up and sold as scrap steel.

In 1944 another affiliate—American City Lines—was financed by GM and Standard of California to motorize downtown Los Angeles. Unlike the Pacific Electric tragedy, which had involved a nearly unique pattern of transportation and one which had, so to speak, made Los Angeles what it was, the dismantling of the yellow car downtown system had now become standard practice through-out the country. The Los Angeles Railway Company was purchased, its power transmission lines torn down, the tracks uprooted, and GM diesel buses pro-ceeded to fill the Los Angeles streets with their singular body odor.

National City Lines accomplished the same vandalization in 56 other previ-ously well-served cities throughout the land, yet a peculiar and fateful phenome-non must be noted. Although the trolleys and the electric interurban train systems disappeared, they were not replaced by a corresponding number of GM buses or by any buses (since GM had a bus monopoly).* What they were chiefly replaced by was an unprecedented swarm of automobiles.

The reason is easy to see. The arithmetic has the horrible simplicity of an execution by guillotine. One bus can eliminate 35 automobiles. One streetcar, subway, or rapid-transit vehicle can supplant 50 passenger cars. The train can displace 1,000 cars or a fleet of 150 cargo-laden motor trucks. Because of these displacement laws, GM's gross revenues are 10 times greater if it sells cars and trucks rather than buses, and 25 to 35 times greater if it sells cars and trucks rather than train locomotives. The inevitable result is that GM can maximize its profits by wrecking the rail and bus systems of America or of any other country. It has succeeded in doing so only in the United States.

In the specific case of Los Angeles, after the destruction of electric trans-portation, ridership in the city motor buses had declined since 1952 to 4.5 billion passengers per year and intercity to less than a million—a combined loss of 3.5 billion passengers, along with a drop in bus sales from 8,460 in 1951 to only 3,700 in 1972.

What were the antitrust people doing in the meantime? What ever happened to the antitrust laws? In 1962 Attorney General Robert Kennedy brought a suit against GM on the issue of monopolizing bus transportation. This suit was settled in 1965 with a consent decree, but by then the consent decree had degenerated into a sort of languid statement of probation. As Mayor Joseph Alioto of San Francisco, an illustrious antitrust lawyer, testified, by the time of Attorney Gen-

---

*As we shall see later, GM had also obtained a monopoly on diesel locomotives. After World War II, Alfred Sloan had insisted that GM, in addition, should get in and monopolize the airplane business "to protect our automobile situation," but fortunately for United Aircraft, Boeing, and the rest, the Federal Aviation Act had prevented this final incursion of Huns.

eral John Mitchell, consent decrees were being sold like bags of popcorn.

There had earlier (1949) been a criminal case brought against National City Lines for involvement in the destruction of 100 electrical rail and bus systems in 56 cities. A conviction was in fact obtained. GM was compelled to pay $5,000 and its treasurer, H. C. Grossman, the chief operator in the gigantic Los Angeles caper, was fined the sum of $1.00. (As I said, federal juries in the middle of the twentieth century, faced with established monopolies, were inclined to regard them as acts of God; indeed, if it had not been for the more robust jurists and veniremen of the 1900s and 1910s, we would still have Standard Oil running the entire petroleum business and the meat packers controlling all the retail meat outlets.)*

Rather pathetically the government tried to follow this up with a civil suit in the mid-1950s, seeking some more effective estoppel than elfin fines. By that time, however, motorization of the electric transit systems being virtually complete, GM and its allies had already sold their holdings in National City Lines. Furthermore, the judge of record, Julius Hoffman (more recently famous in the "Chicago Seven" trial), seemed impressed by the fact that National City Lines had conducted its takeover of the various transit companies by buying up their preferred (nonvoting) stock. Obviously this was *ipso facto* legal and even wholesome, though the tactic in every case nevertheless seemed to have the irresistable result of the transit lines being torn up and disappearing from the face of the earth. The civil suit collapsed utterly.

ALIOTO VERSUS REAGAN AND THE GANG

The case of San Francisco is similar in some respects to that of Los Angeles, although the events in time were displaced forward by a few years. When I attended Cal (the University of California at Berkeley) the only way to get across the bay was by ferryboat, of which there were hundreds; but once across, very efficient electric railway systems on both sides took you swiftly where you wanted to go. When the Golden Gate Bridge was built, the so-called Key System was in operation, connecting San Francisco, Oakland, and other areas in the East Bay with 180 electric streetcars and 50 electric passenger trains. The electric passenger trains took the place of the ferries, crossing the bridge on a lower level than the motor-vehicle tollway.

In 1946 the National City Lines gang bought up the Key System, announced they were going to convert it to GM buses, and in a few years pulled up all the tracks, including those across the bridge. Mayor Alioto believes this was done for a particular reason: to discourage the construction of BART (Bay Area Rapid Transit) which was being actively discussed as early as 1954. As the result of the pointless vandalism of tearing up the lower-deck bridge tracks, BART thence-

*As a matter of statistics, GM is probably bigger and more potent than the Standard Oil monopoly would have been if it had survived. GM's annual sales of $35 billion were larger than the revenues of any country in the world except the United States and the USSR (and Saudi Arabia).

forth had to plan on spending an extra $20 million to create the same corridor in the form of a tube on the bottom of the bay.

San Francisco itself was responsible for the approval of the BART project, and it was suburban motorists themselves who probably had the deciding votes, for they were fed up with commuting in to pay $5 per day parking fees in a city that was rapidly taking on the look and smog of Los Angeles. Alioto actually had done his best to help the motorists passing over the bridge by allowing cars with 3 or more passengers to cross toll-free in a special lane. But since World War II no share-the-ride plan has ever worked. What the peninsular commuters now do is to drive up to Daly City, park there at reasonable rates, and take BART on into the inner city. This park-and-ride pattern has become an easy transition for people used to commuter driving, since in fact it is simply a variation of the Eastern commuter train systems, where the wife drives her husband to the railroad station or, stepping up to the upper-middle class, where the husband drives his own car and parks it at the railroad station.

We shall have more to say of BART and its adolescent troubles later, but one more political note on San Francisco is worth making. Mayor Alioto, with a record of minor antitrust legal victories, was too dangerous a man to trifle with in an offhand manner. General Motors, Standard of California, et alia, apparently chose to enlist the anti-mass-transit help of Governor Ronald Reagan, a politician of extreme far-righteousness and pro-General-Motors leanings.

By a historical ploy of some obscurity the State of California had gotten in its possession the Port of San Francisco and Alioto wanted the port back. He was told by Lieutenant Governor Robert Finch that he could have the port back, maybe, if San Francisco would build a automobile freeway route connecting the San Francisco Bridge-Oakland Bay terminus with the Golden Gate Bridge terminus, right across the northern area of downtown San Francisco—in other words, take the first major step in turning San Francisco into a frank imitation of Los Angeles. When Alioto demurred, Reagan wrote a letter to the press accusing the mayor of endangering the traffic control of San Francisco by not giving in on the freeway.

NEW YORK EMERGES, IN SPITE OF MOSES

We should accept, I imagine, as the two outstanding villains of American transportation history, Robert Moses, the self-perpetuating and steam-rolling gray eminence of New York parkways and highways and freeways, and Alfred Sloan, the man who changed an honorable technology into a bloated, unprogressive, and wasteful industry.

Again, I have some personal memories. In the years before World War II, but when the Depression was lifting somewhat, I spent a good deal of time in New York City. I stayed at the Hotel Pierre and most of my business was down near Wall Street, 15 minutes and a nickel away by subway transit that was as smooth as cream and reliable as the elevators in my nice old hotel. I remember that year the song "Love Walked Right In" was popular and I would hear it from the depths of the hotel as I had my 5 o'clock cocktail at the old street-level bar. Another Californian used to show up at the same time to read his mail over his whiskey, and one day he told me, "Don, one more week and you'll never go away."

It was ridiculous, of course. My family and my career were in California. But I could see what he meant. New York's charm was in that frame of time almost overwhelming, all the more so since it was indescribable. The most curious fact was that, unlike its reputation, New York was not a city of wildly caroming people—like pool balls, all trying to get into the same pocket at the same time. It was a city of poise—even of ease. Either that has all gone or I have changed irrevocably. The last time I was there I could hardly stand it for 4 days. Just getting into and out of the airports is now a nerve-racking chore. The roadways are hopelessly congested, the subways all dirty, expensive, unreliable, and jam-packed.

In Robert A. Caro's awe-inspiring book *The Power Broker,* it is shown how Robert Moses nearly wrecked New York's life style by building highway after highway at the expense of mass transit. Yet it is a proof of the depth of the immense strengths of the old city that what mass transit it has left is relatively workable. The per capita consumption of gasoline in New York is less than in any other city or town in the United States. Although it exhausts in the form of heat over 6 times as much energy as it absorbs from the sun (resembling in this way somewhat the great planet Jupiter), only a small portion of this heat comes from the combustion of motor fuel.

In recent years even Moses could not prevail against the still stronger will of Governor Nelson Rockefeller who placed his friend William J. Ronan in charge of the world's largest transit agency, the Metropolitan Transportation Authority. It loses over $400 million a year hauling 34 percent of all United States transit riders. Its 2,324 miles of subways, bus routes, rail-bus combination lines, bridges, and tunnels handle 8 million people daily. In what came to be known as the "Wholly Ronan Empire" new grandeurs in public rather than private transit came about; for example, new equipment was put in to jive up the tired Long Island Railroad and construction was planned on the Second Avenue subway (since abandoned). But service breakdowns continued, along with pro-tracted strikes, while the subway and bus fares went from 20 cents to 50 cents, mostly to pay for costly labor contracts.

The trouble with mass transit is that it loses an abominably large amount of money. Nowhere have inflation and the intolerance of labor unions so badly bent any human enterprise. However, it is possible that mass transit became unprofitable, simply because the gasoline and highway lobbyists took away from it the economies of scale (which means in service industries that the more people you serve, the less it costs to serve 1 person). As recently as 1945 the U.S. bus, trolley, and subway systems returned a profit of 11 cents for every dollar dropped in the fare box. As ridership fell from about 19 billion in 1945 to 6.5 billion in

1973, the profit disappeared, and mass transit on the average now loses 25 cents for every dollar it collects.

This is not true of all cities. Philadelphia has a good system in the Lindenwall, a combination of subway, railroad, and bridge that services that part of New Jersey suburban to the big city across the Delaware River. It is almost unique in the country in being able to meet operating expenses out of farebox receipts, and this may partly be due to advanced automation. It has only 250 employees. Chicago is in fair shape. Atlanta is digging and at least on paper will solve its transport problems, but the present model for mixed transportation in North America is Toronto, which in less than a decade has, by careful planning, pulled itself out of dullness and sluggery (it was once known as hog city and even a weekend in nearby Buffalo was regarded as a treat) into the sparkle of great-city charm. Toronto has a combination of subway, trolleys, electric trains, and buses. There is a lot of park-and-ride with the consequence that the city is singularly free of traffic congestion. (South of the other border one can see the precise opposite in the huge, overmotorized, auto-stifled supermetropolis of Mexico City.)

It is not clear whether such well-balanced cities as Toronto come anywhere near breaking even on their public transit. Probably this is too much to expect in an interim period. The question really is, interim to what?

If one studies the developing structure of cities, the problem of living in a suburb takes on a somewhat more complicated aspect than simply getting downtown from the suburb and back again. The problem may be to get from the home suburb to another suburb. This indeed is quite common in Los Angeles which has been characterized as "77 suburbs in search of a city." In my high school days, my daily journey took me from the Mount Washington Drive suburb across a series of hills to the L.A. High School suburb, but the trolleys that I rode on went first downtown then out of town in a wholly different direction. As I have said, it took me long enough to allow completing my homework entirely en route, but this is far too much time for the modern temper. If Los Angeles is to have a successful mass transit system, it must include, structurally speaking, wheels as well as spokes. It is an amazing fact that decades ago the city of Edinburgh had the wheels-plus-spokes system in the form of electric trolleys and a fast electric train but abandoned the wheel component, much to the discomfiture of many Scotsmen who, in order to get from Newington to Morningside by public transit now require 2 or 3 bus transfers and an hour, while in the days of the circle route they could make the trip in less than 5 minutes.

THE RUBBER ALTERNATIVE: WHAT WENT WRONG WITH THE AUTOMOBILE?

Such otherwise well-meaning people as President Gerald Ford continue to express the opinion that the future of transportation in America does not lie with any fancy new people-movers but with the automobiles made in his home state of Michigan. But does the automobile have a future?

Of course it does. So does the snowmobile. So does the dune buggy. The point is that the automobile's future cannot be allowed to be the same as its past. We are all familiar with the elements of that past which can roughly be divided into 2 classical periods: (1) the first years culminating in the age of Fordism and the assemblyline concept of manufacture, and (2) the age of Sloanism, when only 4 manufacturers remained in an industry dominated by GM's concept of large cars in which there was a model change every year. The latter point is especially critical, since it meant in effect that depreciation of the purchased product became by far the highest expense item, in later years followed by insurance.

One result of going from a Model-T or Model-A system, in which the product scarcely changed internally or visibly over a decade or so, to a system in which economically if not technically the product every year became a new butterfly making the last year's model obsolete, was that depreciation became very high. The standard American cars have been such notorious gasoline hogs because the owner who could afford the monstrous rate of depreciation could also afford to drive fuel-wasting cars.

The Volkswagen Beetle (which was, in effect, a return to the Model-T concept) owed its popularity, especially among the young and nonaffluent, precisely to the fact that it did not follow the dictation of Sloanism; it did not come out with a new model every year, and its depreciation was therefore minimal. American compacts and subcompacts that sought desperately to take Volkswagen's business away were for the most part failures, not because of inadequate design, but because they could not remove themselves from the absurd Sloanistic annual model-change doctrine. It is possible that in the subcompact Vega and the Chevette, General Motors may eventually see the light and settle down to a low-depreciation vehicle, but so far the Vega is (how shall I put it?)—transsexual, a Volkswagen Beetle in drag. It is neither cheap transportation nor pleasant driving, in spite of the corps of "pleasability engineers" that Chevrolet trained for the Vega project.

One infuriating thing about American subcompacts is that from a merchandising standpoint they are mere hatracks on which to hang accessories. Optional equipment returns about 40 percent to manufacturers as profit. Even when extras such as radial tires or power steering are made as built-in standards, there is a 30 to 35 percent profit for the car makers. Thus it has become standard practice to send out a few basic or naked Vegas or Pintos and then flood the marketplace with more expensive models crammed with extras. An auto salesman on an airplane once told me, "You'll find that the basic Vega is nailed to the dealer's showroom floor."

The 45 years of Sloanism have been singularly unfortunate years for the American automobile, since the yearly model change (until 1975 with the advent of catalytic exhaust mufflers) did not involve any degree of technical modification. All the engineering innovations, such as power-steering, automatic transmission, synchromesh gearing, air conditioning, disk braking, and so on had been developed in the 1920s and 1930s, and since then the annual auto show change has been merely cosmetic—a new curve here, the erasure of an old curve there, the appearance and disappearance of fins, the burying of headlights, the various drapings of chromium. Some of the changes in fact have involved the elimination of useful and power-saving devices, such as the overdrive. I can recall the best handling, most economical car I ever bought. It was a Studebaker Champion of pre-World War II vintage and my wife and I drove it home from the factory in Gary to California. We averaged about 26 miles to the gallon through the life of this little sweetheart and we have never had a mechanical pet since that has given us such satisfaction. Studebaker and its Champions were driven from the scene by the big Impalas and all the other expensive and rouged and roaring fauna that made their yearly debuts on the highway circus scene.

What exasperates many people about the Big Three is that they will not even undertake such modest jobs as the production of a good taxicab, meaning a comfortable, short-wheelbase, low-power, easy-to-maintain, London-type cab. They persist in pushing their clumsy stock cars for use as taxicabs. It is just such lack of masculinity in Detroit that caused John DeLorean* to resign a $500,000 a year job. It is in fact such lack of masculinity that causes the intelligentsia of Wall Street to view the stocks of the Big Three as exceedingly unglamorous. As emphasized by Donald E. Weeden, chairman of the board of Weeden and Company, Wall Street abhors a monopoly just as nature abhors a vacuum. Weeden believes that splitting of the Big Three trust would allow for more precise investment. For example, those who believe in small cars should be able to pick 1 or 2 companies to back without having to buy into conglomerates which at the same time make big cars, dishwashers, and refrigerators.

As we saw in the last chapter, the 1975 catalyst fiasco showed that Detroit is intellectually bankrupt. The only new ideas that have come to market in the meantime have been the Wankel rotary engine, the Mercedes diesel passenger car, and the stratified-charge carburetor system—all developed by foreigners. These, in effect, constitute mobile proof that the American automobile industry deserves the slump that happened in 1975; that it has become so fat and stodgy that it is in immediate danger of dying of technical atherosclerosis. It is the kind of thing that happens, along with the disappearance of electric streetcars, when you have a massive, prosperous trust in which a great show is made of research in giant laboratories, but nothing comes out of the laboratories, or is allowed to come out, which might disturb the equilibrium of selling big, dirty, fuel-wasting cars at impious profits.

A good case can be made for the gas-turbine engine car, which Chrysler has been exhibiting for publicity purposes for 15 to 20 years. Yet Chrysler has not had enough warm blood to put it to the market test. Mercedes has shown how

*He was the gifted engineer-executive who changed the little-old-lady image of Pontiac and pulled Chevrolet out of a downspin that bordered on catastrophe in 1968, a crisis that GM successfully kept secret until *Fortune* broke the story in 1973.

to make an acceptably quiet, powerful, nonpolluting and fuel-saving diesel-powered car, but the American Big Three because of some enigmatic, possibly religious scruples continue to turn up their noses at diesels. Ford for years and years has played in the research show window with the Stirling engine (in which hydrogen is compressed, heated externally and expanded, recovered, and used over again in a closed cycle, the heating being accomplished by burning any clean fuel under such mild and steady conditions that no pollutants are emitted). Yet Ford's Stirling engine is obviously a doll-baby. After all the public-relations juice has been squeezed out of her, she will be put back in the playpen, along with Ford's lithium-sulfur batteries for an imaginary electric car.

The electric car! I have a multilingual file big enough to use as fuel for a trip to the moon about the electric car, which to all present indications will be marketed in all countries before the United States. Electrically driven buses (e.g., the Daimler-Benz), vans, small lorries, and variegated vehicles are being commercialized everyday in Europe and especially in Japan, yet the Big Three will refuse until the last gasp of the last emphysema victim to admit that the electric car is a commercial possibility. Too much battery bulk! Too little range! Too much, too little—too late! In Chapter 6, I have noted that an electric car without a battery is now feasible with the sophisticated storage and power delivery of the advanced flywheel. Moreover, there are perfectly practicable hybrid arrangements which have already been successfully demonstrated in Europe and Japan.

For example, there is the combination of a turbine stove with a battery. What one can do, as in the Stirling cycle, is use a clean, low-pressure engine as a source of nonpolluting hot air to pass through a turbine to store energy in a battery array which then discharges through electric motors to drive the wheels of the car. The fuel-burning engine's operation is intermittent and innocuous. This is the self-recharging, semielectric car.

The possibilities of the automotive steam engine depend on the same principle: The source of heat, since it need not be explosive as in the internal combustion engine, is harmless from the standpoint of air pollution. Its fuel-quality demands are modest. It doesn't have to have any octane number or cetane number or any other exotic combustion property; all it has to do is burn cleanly and steadily, as good kerosene burns in a lamp. Steam cars and buses, using a kind of recirculated freon rather than water, have been tried, notably by William Lear, the eccentric aircraft millionnaire, but so far his luck has been terrible because of lubrication problems in his turbine drive. Others have had better luck, such as the Scientific Energy System of Watertown, Massachusetts, and the Thermo-Electron Corporation of Waltham, Massachusetts. But this kind of cycle may be doomed on account of intrinsically poor fuel economy.

A Detroit philosopher, echoing the sentiments of his superiors, predicts that even in the year 2000 the American automobile will be just about the way it is today—only more so. It will use gasoline and will be able to accelerate to 100 miles per hour within 5 seconds and superhighways will allow it to cruise at 125 miles per hour; the only radical change will be the drivers: They will have smogproof artificial lungs.

The situation may become sunnier, the dead hand of Detroit may let loose of the American throat, or Detroit may unexpectedly undergo a second youth when, instead of suppressing new ideas, it opens the doors and lets in the young and the uninhibited so we can delight once again in something like the joyous ferment of the 1910s and 1920s when it was a pleasure to be a boy and to identify all manner of strange and variegated brands—the air-cooled Franklin, the Stutz Bearcat, the Overland, the Essex, the Locomobile, the Apperson, the Lozier, even the steam-driven Doble and the sedate electric broughams.

One cannot overlook the fact that before the triumph of Sloanism people had a genuine affection for a car, regarding it as a sort of member of the family. I recently came upon a letter to Ann Landers from an old man in Muskogee, Oklahoma, who asked whether it would be legal to be buried, not in a coffin but at the wheel of his 1937 Dodge.

THE LITTLE ENGINE THAT COULDN'T

On the whole, the large cities of Europe, South America, Asia, and Africa are as badly congested with automobiles as the cities of the United States, although they are doing more about relieving this congestion than we are. It is in fast, interurban passenger transportation—such as electric trains—that the United States is years behind such countries as Germany, France, and Japan. It is reasonable to blame this also on General Motors (and I shall proceed to do so), but in all fairness one can make a case for some peculiar knotheadedness on the part of the American railroad tycoons. Although they themselves would travel like sheiks in splendid private railway cars and every railroad had a famous luxury train (the "Lark," the "Super Chief," the "Twentieth Century Limited," etc.) there were signs that the railroad barons looked down upon passenger traffic as somehow ridiculous in comparison with the true mission of the rails: to carry coal, grain, chickens, and cantelopes to market.

Way back at the turn of the century James J. Hill, head of the Great Northern Railroad, remarked that a passenger train is about as useful and as decorative as a man's tits. How could he say such a thing? How, then, were people supposed to travel?

With this basic softness in the brain stems of railroad magnates, one can hardly be surprised that the American interurban passenger trains quickly gave up the ghost without a squeak as they were assaulted on the one hand by the airplane industry and on the other by General Motors. The importance of the GM attack consisted of the fact that, whereas the greater attractiveness of electric trains for passengers might have opened the way to continued competition with airplanes, GM was in a monopoly posture with respect to diesel locomotives. Furthermore, it was in a position to enforce dieselization rather than electrification because of its leverage as by far the biggest freight customer that the North American railroads possessed. So as Europe and Japan went electric, the United States went diesel. American railroads purchased locomotives that had one-half to one-third the power and which cost 3 times more than electric prime movers.*

As experienced travelers well know, there is an intermediate interurban distance (perhaps 300 or 400 miles) at which one actually can save time by taking a fast train rather than an airplane. This is because airports are almost invariably located in suburban areas from which it takes a long bus or cab ride to get to the central city. There are many ways to fight over this crucial 300-to-400-mile gap, and indeed also many ways to increase the gap to 600 to 700 miles, for example by very high-speed trains traveling nearly as fast as airplanes.

One way to fight the gap is to develop VTOL (vertical take-off and landing) or STOL (short take-off and landing) airplanes along with STOLports located in the central city. This has been a dream, especially in Europe, for several decades. The technology of the airplanes is there, but the enormous funds for the STOL-port systems, involving expensive inner-city real estate and hideously exacting public liability insurance rates, not to speak of a new system of close air-traffic control, are not there. There is not now and perhaps never will be enough risk capital to install this kind of air traffic.

The other way to travel 300 to 400 miles is by automobile or bus. About 20 times as many Americans travel in cars from city to city as travel in buses. But in Europe and Japan the modern electric train has made bus or interurban automobile travel obsolete, unless you are just out for a good time and probably a wreck on the *autobahn.*

The Japanese situation is especially interesting, since as occupying conquerors we asserted both positive and negative influences on the history of that country's modern transportation system. At the "suggestion" of General Douglas MacArthur, for example, the Japanese National Railways in 1949 became a public corporation independent of the government.

Today Japanese National Railways operates a network of 13,000 miles and is by far the biggest passenger railway system in the world. Twenty-five thousand trains carry 18 million passengers daily. Of the whole load of Japanese passenger transportation the trains handle 47 percent, automobiles 34 percent, and buses 16 percent. From the standpoint of traffic volume, two-thirds of the rail transportation is powered by electricity. (Japan produces no petroleum but has rich coal and water-power resources.) In 1964 the Japanese National Railways inaugurated the world's fastest train—the "Shinkan-Sen" or "Bullet Train," that makes the 320-mile run between Tokyo and Osaka in 3 hours.

The Japanese recall with some irony that after the war the Americans (or should we call them General Motormen?) strongly advised their wards to diesel-

*When at a critical time of railroad rebuilding in Great Britain, this shocking evidence was presented to Parliament in 1960, it was a unanimous Parliamentary decision to electrify rather than to dieselize.

ize the railroad lines. However, the Japanese adopted a compromise: They diesel-ized the local feeder lines and electrified the main lines. In retrospect the Japanese admit that just after the war they had taken to idolizing America as a technical wonderland and when they noted that railroading was a declining industry in the United States, they wondered whether on their rocky little islands they should spend their money on highways. Luckily for them, this mood did not survive the early 1950s, and Kenko Sogo, the president of Japanese National Railroads, insisted that the railroad was the most efficient mode of transportation in a crowded land for a very original and modern reason: Its operations could be easily computerized. Theoretically, trains could be dispatched every 3 minutes without a driver.

Japanese National Railways borrowed funds from the World Bank to put in the Bullet Train—probably the most productive loan this agency has ever made, since in 1974 the Shimkan-Sen yielded the incredible ratio of revenues to operat-ing costs of 4.6. There are more than 200 Bullet Trains daily, which means that one leaves every 10 minutes from 6:00 A.M. to 8:30 P.M., each train consisting of a 16-car unit. Since 1965 the Bullet Trains have carried over 500 million passen-gers without a single fatality. The Japanese are now experimenting with an ultra-high-speed train—300 miles per hour—which would complete the Tokyo–Osaka run in 1 hour.

Let us now look at Germany. In West Germany the German Federal Rail-way Board is responsible for the construction of railway lines, the procurement of rolling stock, and the operation and maintenance of both intercity and sub-urban traffic. This sounds like socialism, but the peculiar virtue of the German transportation situation is the multiplicity of manufacturers. Competing produc-ers of railway vehicles, for example, are Messerschmitt—Bolkow—Blohm, Wag-gon Union, Link Hofmann Burch, Talbost, Orenstein and Koffel, Man and Wegnam.

Similar variety and competition persist throughout Europe and in Japan. One has the picture of unified railway management drawing from a rich diversity of innovative designers and suppliers. In the United States we have exactly the opposite situation: a large number of rail lines served by 1 or 2 monopolies. And it is probably this that has done us in.

Poor Amtrak's struggles to preserve the passenger railroad concept with ancient, blood-stained equipment reminds me of a game I used to play with one of my granddaughters. In her home town in Nebraska, there was a junkyard containing (of all things precious to the childish heart!) an old Pullman car. We pretended in this noble, decaying remnant of a 1901 lounge car (outfitted even with the remnants of a bar and 2 johns) that we were traveling to great voluptuous cities, although occasionally this involved the misadventurous circumstances that the train would be stopped and the splendid lounge entered by uncouth robbers or Indians. (In fact the play ended for good one day when 2 local policemen entered with drawn guns, having been informed that a little girl had been impris-oned in the wreck by a child molester.) The old Pullman car disappeared the next year and I like to think that it is back on the rails in the service of Amtrak; that my precious granddaughter will ride in it and remember what fun it was once upon a time to play games of pure imagination with her grandfather.

ENGINES THAT THINK THEY CAN

In the European countries, in Japan, and even to a halfhearted extent at the Colorado testing station of the U.S. Department of Transportation, experiments with extremely fast trains are going on. It must be remembered that the United States has some 200,000 miles of track already built along established rights-of-way. In any revival of mass transportation or improvement of freight delivery, it would be senseless to overlook the reconstruction of this track system in comparison with starting from scratch. For supertrains the same beds could be used but there would be heavier rails, new fasteners, elastic pads, concrete tiers or slabs, continuous welded rails, and improved joints and turnouts. That would be in case you are interested in sticking with the old-fashioned idea of a steel wheel on a steel track.

In the track-and-rail exploration of the future the power plants may be gas turbines plus electric. The French National Railways (SNCF) combination turbine and electric train has already been clocked at 197 miles an hour. The same system has set the world record for a truck-and-wheel, straight electric traction train at 226 miles per hour in 1955. Although the track-and-wheel people have no intention of stopping here, they are disadvantaged at higher speeds by the load on the bearings. This load can be lightened by the so-called air-cushion effect, obtained by blowing air downward with compressors so that the train is in effect running on an air film rather than on steel. The big advantage is the distributed footprint; the load is spread over a large area, thus decreasing the need for a track of superstrength. Air-cushion suspension is often teamed up with propulsion by linear induction motors (LIM), which are essentially rotary motors unrolled to lie flat, so that they react with an electricity-carrying track rather than with an inner conductive core.

Instead of an air cushion, in which surprisingly low pressure (1.5 pounds per square inch) is demanded but a tremendous amount of air must be blown, the suspension may be by magnetic levitation. The West Germans are furthest advanced with respect to the actual hardware for maglev systems, of which there are 2: (1) electrodynamic, in which the levitation is obtained by a repulsive force exerted on a magnet moving over a conductive guideway; and (2) electromagnetic, which uses ordinary electromagnets that are attracted toward an overhead ferromagnetic rail, lifting the vehicle.

The most ambitious over-all program, advanced by MAN (Maschinenfabrik Augsberg-Nuremberg AG) and labeled Eurospeed is a breathtaking combination of a magnetic network with a conventional steel-wheel line, numerous pipelines, and cryogenic power transmissions.* These services would be carried jointly by

---

*Cryogenic transmission of electricity means using cables consisting of metal alloys (tin, niobium, germanium) which become superconducting (i.e., provide little or no electrical resistance) when the

an elevated superstructure, thus overlapping the sources of capital investment.

Although in comparison with the Germans and the Japanese, our people-moving innovations appear somewhat amateurish, we have in certain instances tried hard. The electrical system BART in San Francisco is running after a fashion, but had a long period of computer anguish when trains were suddenly stopping or refusing to stop; doors were opening when they should be shut, and brakes were mysteriously freezing up; passengers were being literally lost and forgotten in the algebra of the system. (One typical graffiti, "If speed kills, Bart will live forever." The idea of a computerized subway labyrinth so complicated that a train can disappear in it has appeared in science fiction and also in a fascinating song by the Kingston Trio.)

The personal automatic cab system at the gigantic Dallas-Fort-Worth airport, which is supposed to carry passengers from one airline terminus to another, went on a terrifying binge with people pounding on glass to get out or pounding to get in and missing their planes. It is said that a computer is only as good as the computer operator (the "garbage in, garbage out" doctrine), but perhaps some blame or credit is owing to the computer designer.

In November 1974 the Los Angeles voters turned down a $4.3 billion bond issue to construct a corridor (fixed-rail) mass transit system; but as a less expensive alternative, Aerospace Corporation submitted a study of a personal rapid transit (PRT) network for the Los Angeles Basin, which envisions 638 miles of one-way track carrying 64,000 small cabs between 1,084 stations for a total cost of $1.76 billion. A PRT system must operate cabs at intervals only a fraction of a second apart to achieve the people capacity required for mass urban transport. Although there is no PRT system with fractioned second intervals in operation anywhere in the world, companies in Japan, Germany, and France are getting close.

TENTATIVE CONCLUSION: THE BUS WILL TRIUMPH

For the United States, an over-all panoramic review convinces one that simply improved bus service will be the major answer for mass transportation. It is a fall from glamour but it seems to best fit the American temperament and the structure of most American cities. A nonpolluting bus, however, is an absolute necessity and before the end of the century I think we shall see hybrid self-charging, electric-powered buses carrying most of the urban transit load.

To make bus travel more tolerable, cities and towns around the country are putting in gimmicks such as reserved lanes for buses only, special nonstop express bus service from outlying areas to the central city, intersuburban lines, priority

temperature is lowered to that of boiling helium (4.2 degrees absolute) or, hopefully, boiling hydrogen (20.4 degrees absolute). The development of cheap electrical transmission by this technique, which is probably 20 or 30 years away from being made practical, would immediately revolutionize the energy planning and management of the entire planet, since it would for the first time make it cheaper to transmit electric power instead of gas or liquid fuel for long distances.

access to highways and tunnels, and bus-actuated traffic signals that allow buses to move swiftly in city traffic. Above all, more buses. If the customer owns an automobile and in giving bus travel a try during his working day finds that he has to wait too long, he will promptly go back to using his automobile.

Even with the poor present over-all service, bus ridership is increasing 2 percent annually, and this follows a long period of decline. But how the ridership could turn around and skyrocket is shown by such examples as the totally air-polluted mile-high city of Denver. "A conveyor belt for losers," was how officials described the privately owned city bus system before the voters in 1970 approved a public takeover. Now all that has changed. Passengers are whisked from suburb to office in new white, blue, and green express buses and tooled around the downtown area in minibuses called Darts (fare 10 cents). These are bargains for the elderly and for students, and the buses meet enormously more frequent schedules. The result is that ridership in the Denver system has grown at about 18 percent a year since 1971.

In order to keep the fares reasonable, such systems operate inevitably at a deficit, but one recent business event should not be overlooked. Ford Motor Company at the *Transpo '72* exposition displayed a new system of trolley cars built under government contract and Henry Ford announced that "entirely new public-transportation concepts" were urgently needed and should be financed in part out of Highway Trust Fund revenues. He said, "Today I am making the formal announcement that Ford is entering the public-transit-system business."

In the meantime the deficit should be paid by people who continue to drive their private cars to work, alone in solitary thought, and as in the proposal of Congressman Jerome Waldie of California, the users of public transit should be allowed to deduct their fares from their taxes.

18 The Lost Art of Conservation

Few will have the greatness to bend history itself, but each of us can work to change a small portion of events, and in the total of all these acts will be written the history of this generation.
—ROBERT F. KENNEDY

We were not always energy hogs. Without consciously being *conservationists* (a word invented by Gifford Pinchot for a different, more romantic doctrine that implied the protection of native animals and rural land and scenery), we in the reasonably comfortable middle class once were cautious. As a boy I cannot remember having beefsteak more than once a month or so, and it was no great delicacy, for Kansas-City, corn-fattened beef had not been invented; we were more likely to dine on Van Camp's baked beans. I can remember my father reproving me for using too much toilet paper. Our big leaky old house was cold nearly all the time, but people in California were not supposed to have a sense of cold and, indeed, positively courted it by indulging in sleeping porches, open to all the breezes, where diving into a well-blanketed cot was an indescribable act of shivery delight, especially if you had a dog or a cat or a Teddy bear to snuggle with. The electric lights were carefully policed and the only thing we were prodigal with was water for the large, complicated gardens that surrounded us, which were my mother's pride and joy.

As I have indicated in Chapter 5, in those days even in California coal was the staple fuel, both as a source of gas and as solid briquettes for the fireplace; but on the whole we used it sparingly. This was not a matter of our basic mettle and sagacity. It was simply that it never occurred to us to have a really warm house or to dream of things like air conditioning.

Eugene O'Neill's play "A Moon for the Misbegotten" takes place about the time of my early childhood. In one scene the drunken Phil Hogan bellows, "Down with all tyranny!" and then a line that always breaks up the house, "God damn Standard Oil!"

Such profanity—and against such a respectable bastion of corporate society —would have gravely shocked my father, who worked as star reporter for the Los

Angeles *Times,* whose building was shortly to be dynamited to pieces by the McNamara brothers because of the paper's extreme anti-labor-union politics. It was the day of the trolley, but the day of the automobile was dawning, coming up like thunder, in fact. However, even then, after World War I and the complete automobilization of the land, we were still not a nation of energy wastrels. The Great Depression, the highly successful gas rationing during World War II, the share-the-ride way of life that we got used to, these tended to throw a shadow of prudence for about a decade. Then the dam burst.

The 20 years from 1951 to 1971 were remarkable (or at least will seem historically remarkable, when our descendants look back upon them) as the years when the price of energy went down in comparison with all other things we could buy. We seemed to be bathed with energy. Technologists sat up nights dreaming of new things to run with electricity. There was a pogo stick that jumped on gasoline power. Anyone without a power mower might as well have wielded a scythe. Established in those 2 decades was the standard increase rate of 3.7 percent per year for total energy use. Then in the insane year of 1973, when unmistakable signs of fuel shortages and electrical brown-outs had already been visible for 18 months, the over-all increase rate topped out at 4.8 percent—the most power ever used by one nation in all history, so much more than other nations or than all of Europe, that it may well stand up as an eternal champion record of power swinishness.

Was it worth it? Did we reach a peak in the enjoyment and celebration of life? I am not an unprejudiced observer, but it seems to me that 1973, not simply because of Watergate and its sequelae, was a singularly listless and unhappy year. People had had more fun in the middle of the Great Depression. Maybe stuffing oneself with calories or kilowatt-hours brings on the melancholy surfeit that sooner or later inspires the inevitable hang-over question, "Is that all there is to it? . . . Then maybe we had best retire to a little stone-fenced farm in Rhode Island." And many did and are doing things like that.

Let us review some of the practices and contrivances that got us to the fevered peak of wasting 35 percent of the great gouts of energy that we consumed. Let us look at the things that we could do toward rebuilding a conservational society.

BUILDINGS AND HOUSES

Building a conservational society—the key word is *building,* for it is in architecture that the modern world has committed its worst sins and at the same time has occasionally, either by luck or brilliance, accomplished its most promising breakthroughs.

Consider the luck or instinct of the ancient builders of the cave dwellings in Mesa Verde, Colorado. They face south, and in winter, when the sun is low, it shines directly on the adobe back walls which store heat during the day and release it at night. In the summer, the sun strikes at the horizontal surface, where roofs of wood and grasses are set as insulation. Here is a dwelling built by men and women who knew the essential things to know about solar energy. They needed to go one step further: Heat water with it. But they probably felt no deep need, as we do, for what Rupert Brooke called "the benison of hot water." For this benison we now pay dearly, since the heating of water is the biggest single act of energy swilling in our homes.

Doubtless we could pull this demand way down by using cold water and the appropriate detergents for washing clothes; by using about one-tenth of the amount of water we consume in cooking vegetables (in fact, adopt the Chinese cooking style of rapidly heating small, relatively dry pieces of food); in using hot water in more clever ways; for example, as in modern English hotels, passing the hot water destined for the tub or shower first through towel racks that act as radiant space heaters for the bathroom); or, if you must consider it, take the counterculturist's advice, "shower with a friend." Personally the bath, alone except for some friendly literary companion, such as *Sports Illustrated,* is my notion of hot water's benison. Here I must confess in all humility is my most flagrant exhibition of energy-pigginess. I am a wretched sybarite, and as soon as feasible I will install solar water heating.

We shall return to homes and the energy that is secretly squandered there, but America has become essentially a collection of high-rise commercial buildings, and it is there that the real power spills take place. The operation of buildings consumes 50 percent of all the electric power produced in the United States, and of this power, over half of it goes into lighting. Let me emphasize in another way how big these numbers are. The commercial buildings of the United States consume the equivalent of 5.5 million barrels of oil per day.

One of the most baffling problems in biological chemistry is how the firefly produces cold light. If we knew the firefly's secret we would be out of the woods in energy almost immediately, since even the most efficient fluorescent lights or the Westinghouse prototype cerium iodide-mercury vapor lamps are absurdly inefficient in the ratio of lumens per unit of power consumed to the cold light of the animal world.*

The 110-story World Trade Center in New York is a positively weird array of electrical requirements (operating on the all-or-none principle of everybody being flooded in light or immersed in darkness). For such monsters of the regression of architecture, one is reduced to such simple-minded remedies as disconnecting every other row of fluorescent lights or unscrewing every other bulb. Even then the center demands as much electricity per year as the entire city of Schenectady (population 100,000).

As June Stein of the Smithsonian Institution has emphasized, one could start the campaign of energy economy in buildings at the cement mixer. Concrete gains strength for years after hardening, thus if early strength specifications were

---

*Although some architects are belatedly trying to catch the "heat of light" and pass it through conventional ducts and vents to help with the heating load in winter.

relaxed below the quite absurd standards now in force, an immediate savings of about 20,000 million kilowatt-hours per year would be achieved—enough to provide electric power for several million families. The relaxation of cement standards is of course associated in the public mind with city hall skullduggery, but the actual disasters that have happened because of rotten building materials occurred because the materials met no standards at all and were in fact never subjected to inspection.

Another unexploited area in so everyday a material as concrete is light-weight, air-bubbled material that acts as insulation, whereas normal dense concrete can get cold as a stone. Cement making itself is a hoggish industry, mainly because of the huge amount of heat needed to decompose limestone. The average fuel consumption in U.S. cement kilns is 1.2 million Btus per barrel of cement. In most European plants, heat rejected from the kilns is used to preheat the limestone, with the result that the total fuel requirement is more than halved to about 550,000 Btus per barrel. An even more economic "reinforced-suspension" preheater is used in Japan by the Onoda Cement Company. There is utterly no reason, save inertia and stubbornness why American cement companies cannot do better than they do.

Perhaps even more fundamental than cement making is the fact that in the United States the traditional way of financing buildings is based on first costs, what the owner pays at the time the building is completed and baptized with a drunken party. Yet in an energy-conscious society the building designer as well as the sophisticated bank should think in terms of life costs—what has to be paid out in cash or in net energy over the lifetime of a building to keep it standing and to keep it providing inexpensive comfort and light for the people who work in it or live in it.

THE GLASS MENAGERIE

Ever since Lever House was built in Manhattan in 1952, buildings consisting primarily of glass have sprung up all over the nation—an unfortunate example of the way architecture can go absolutely 180 degrees wrong because of a vague desire to be chic and trendy. As Frank Lloyd Wright, perhaps the most illustrious of American architects, once said, "A doctor can bury his mistakes, but the architect can only advise his client to plant a vine." There are, however, not enough vines to give the heat back. Glass is a notoriously poor insulator; as far as keeping the heat out in summer or keeping the heat in during winter, the glass building is virtually a thermal sieve. Special, high-metal, reflective glasses have been developed, but if you install them in your building windows, you increase your neighbor's air-conditioning bill, because you have, in effect, focused mirrors upon his building, which may be mostly glass too. Then if he also goes for high-reflectance glass, you engage in a sort of summer battle between two Archimedeses.

The answer is more expensive double-glazing, making every window of double panes, since the air sealed in between acts as a good insulator. (There is a limit to be discerned here too, unfortunately, because if the window is big enough, the air in the space between the panes has a sort of local weather of its own. If it gets to moving around, like an imprisoned wind, it transmits heat or cold by the process of convection.)

Office windows are seldom opened. Double-glazed office windows, one may say with some assurance, are never opened. This is a pity because as the architect Richard Stein points out, of the average 3,100 hours a year that an average office building is occupied, at least 900 of these are in the temperature range where untreated outside air can be used. Simply opening the windows would bring about a 19 percent reduction in the use of energy for handling building air. But instead of letting in outside air and the sound, perhaps, of birds as well as traffic, the modern skyscraper prefers to be sealed in and to substitute Muzak.

Some things have been done about designing even glass buildings more intelligently. There are some improvements visible and some obvious first principles still being applied. For example, it is axiomatic that a slab-shaped building will lose 20 percent less energy if the broad sides face north and south. Thus, in Tempe, Arizona, the new municipal building has its glass walls slanted at a 45 degree angle to reduce the amount of the sun's heat that enters. It is seldom realized that the weather at the top of a high-rise building is quite different from the weather at street level. The high winds up there not only produce 4 times as much pressure but may blow down the side of the building at rates of 30 miles per hour. Clever advantage has been taken of this fact in the new Qantas Airlines building in Melbourne, Australia, which is specifically designed to encourage air to rustle down and bring comfort to the street in the summer.*

Although one can argue about the design of high-rise buildings—how they use their lighting systems and how their huge capacities strangle a city's traffic and how we can say mean things about the way they look—there is no arguing about their essential superiority as energy conservers, especially if living in them is combined with working in them. High-rise population centers use much less energy than low-rise. (New York City uses only 138 million Btus per capita per year compared with an average of 255 million Btus for the United States as a whole.) High-rise apartments of the same living capacity use 58 percent less gas and 40 percent less electricity than single-family homes. Because of the much higher heat loss occasioned by the greater ratio of surface to volume, a row of ranch houses needs 2 1/2 times as much gas or heating oil as a residential tower with the same floor space.

Although most architects and all sociologists astonishingly agree that the gigantic high-rise, 2-dozen-building Pruitt-Igoe low-cost housing project in St. Louis was a disaster, it doesn't seem to me that it was the architects' fault.

*It now appears likely that the mysterious breaking of the panes of the John Hancock Mutual Life Insurance Company's all-glass building in Boston was caused by a mistake in design that did not take into account this aerodynamic effect which the Australians found useful.

This is energetically a sound way to house people. The fact that the people wrecked the buildings (which were eventually dynamited in order to get rid of the smell) does not seem *a priori* to eliminate this form of housing as somehow demoniacal.

In fact, with cleverly designed high-rise construction, we hear the first dawn noises of a new urban trend that would revolutionize life style as well as cut transportation energy uses to the bare bone. New York's first major project combining living and working space was the Olympic Towers on Fifth Avenue —a brilliant adventure that was massively pioneered by Chicago's 100-story Hancock Center. There one commutes (using a few watts of elevator power and producing zero air pollution) from, say, the ninetieth floor, where one lives, to the fortieth floor, where one works. Chicago's Sears Tower, the tallest in the world, is also suitable as a combination town-and-city where one needs no automobile in order to commute.

We are looking at the probable distant future because without some colossal breakthrough, such as fusion or solar satellite relays, this live-where-you-work system will be the only one that saves enough energy in the twin power-wasting giants of housing and transportation to wash the slate clean for a new start in Western civilization. However, that future is so far away that we must go back and review conservation at the miniature scale that may help save us not in one dashing architectural *coup* but in modest installments of common sense.

THE FACTS OF HOUSING LIFE

One of the silliest things I know about is that until very recently if you insulated your home or place of business you paid an ad valorem tax on the insulation, whereas the heating or cooling costs were considered as untaxed operating expense. This is in the same category of bureaucratic senselessness as the Interstate Commerce Commission's insistence on railroads charging more freight per pound for scrap steel than for iron ore, but on the other hand charging less for raw wood pulp than for waste paper.

Nothing pays off so fast in energy saving as insulation. If every house had 6 inches of Fiberglas or its equivalent in the attic, and 3 inches on the walls, Americans could save some 20 billion gallons of oil and over 1 trillion cubic feet of gas per year. And it is important to realize that one of the prime technical objects of insulation is to keep your walls, floors, ceilings, and windows warm on the inside, not so much to prevent heat from leaving or entering the house (although that is surely important) but to prevent your body and the bodies of your family from radiating heat to the surroundings. Heat loss by radiation depends on a monstrous law which says that the rate of loss depends on the fourth power of the temperature difference between the radiating object and the target of radiation.

If you are a regulation-size adult you give off about the same amount of heat as a 100-watt light bulb. But the rate at which the heat radiates from your body and hits a wall depends much more on how cold the wall is than on how cold the air in the room is. The difference between inadequate and proper insulation in a temperate climate can amount to 40 percent of your fuel bill. Storm windows (double glazing) cut in half the heat loss from the windows and also cut in half the difference between the air temperature in the room and the window temperature.

Much has been made of the unnecessary luxury of pilot lights for gas stoves or hot-water heaters. It is true that the pilot uses about one-third of all the gas you consume on the stove, but in the wintertime it is an efficient source of space heat which has to come from somewhere. In the summer an electric igniter is worthwhile.

Turn off the energy-wasting drying cycle on your dishwasher. Dishes dry perfectly well at room temperature. As mentioned earlier your water heater is the fiercest energy hound you control. Be sure to drain sediment from the bottom of it every month.

In any central home heating system, the tendency is to get out of balance and work overtime to keep one problem room warm while the others are too warm. Study the problem room a bit. Maybe it would save money to close it off or boost it with a separate space heater.

Evergreen trees planted to form a windbreak slow the rate at which winter winds suck heat from your house. In regard to other greenery, remember this: Your lawn is an incorrigible energy guzzler. It is worse than a monstrous 6,000 pound automobile, and it gives no awards except the questionable one of comparing it with your neighbor's when he has gone to Europe for the summer. If your lawn is going to be presentable, it must be fertilized. A 50 pound bag of nitrate fertilizer takes a vast number of Btus of hot natural gas to produce, while a 10,000 square foot lawn requires about 5 bags a season. When it has deigned to grow, it grows faster than your whiskers and takes half a million or more Btus worth of gasoline to mow—a harvest that is thrown away. If Americans had sense, they would use their lawn space to grow vegetables.

The central air conditioner is an energy swine of elephantine dimensions. Air-conditioning energy now costs so much that prudent people are thinking of returning to the attic fan, which in a well-insulated house can provide summer comfort. It takes about 300 kilowatt-hours a year to run an attic fan, whereas a central cooling system in a 1,500 square foot house may slurp about 4,000 kilowatt-hours. Put awnings on the south side of the house, so you can open the shaded window, when it's not too hot out there. Don't put a sunny patio next to the house, because you are going to get a blast of heat from the flagstones. On the other hand, the more plants or trees the better, since plants respire water and its evaporation gives a cooling effect along the house perimeter.

If you insist on buying an air conditioner, find out first the energy efficiency ratio (EER). That is a number, customarily guaranteed, simply obtained by dividing the number of Btus cooling capacity by the wattage (electric power required). A 10,000 Btu system that draws 1,000 watts would have an EER of 10, which is satisfactory. Anything lower than this should be viewed with suspicion. Don't get a unit that's too big, because it proceeds to cool the rooms so quickly that the compressor does not have time enough to work on its secondary chore—that of dehumidifying the air.

Then there's the heat pump.* It has been exuberantly claimed that if all dwellings in the United States were equipped with heat pumps, the net savings in the country would be 29 percent of the present heating-cooling bill. I wish I could believe this. In the experience of friends of mine that have been sold on the bouncy thermodynamic chatter that surrounds the heat pump, it simply doesn't work. It's fine on paper or on a blackboard, but the compressor always breaks down or some other factor in the equation fails to balance out right. I am still open to argument but I would rather regard the heat pump at present as economically if not physically an unproven gimmick.

Let us return briefly to offices. The General Service Administration (GSA), a pet agency more or less under the aegis of Congress, has small, 7-story demonstration buildings at Manchester, New Hampshire, and Saginaw, Michigan, where new ideas are being tried out. There are no windows at all on the north wall, whereas double-glazed window space on the other walls is limited to 15 percent of the wall area. Different lighting systems are being tried out on the various floors, including one that has the lights built into the furniture. One floor has large windows to experiment with natural light.

Perhaps the most crucial GSA experiment is designed to answer the question can janitors and cleaning women work in the daytime without the clerks and vice-presidents falling into water buckets and tripping over mops? This is not a frivolous issue, because in the metropolitan high-rise office buildings a large amount of energy goes into lighting up every story on the graveyard shift, when the custodial or clean-up work is normally performed. Although a city with towers ablaze at 3:00 A.M. gives a sense of tremendous work output, the old girls are not all that productive. They may not be entertaining themselves in the manner of Carol Burnett, but there is an awful lot of illumination going on for the amount of elbow grease expended.

As to metropolitan living space, the biggest landlord in New York City is Samuel J. Lefrak, who owns 60,000 apartments with 250,000 tenants. A few simple conservation rules have, he claims, made him rich. In the first place, all washing machines must use cold water (no exceptions whatever are allowed). In every apartment a piece of aluminum foil is placed between the radiator and the cold wall so that heat will be reflected back into the room. The radiators are painted with enamel, since he finds that the use of metallic or flat paint cuts down the radiation by about 25 percent.

---

*A heat pump is a device to use electrical power to heat or cool a house, essentially by compression or expansion of air. For heating it is theoretically much more economic than the standard electric space heater which, like an electric stove, works on the far more expensive principle of transforming the electrical resistance of a conducting metal into heat.

CONSERVATION IN INDUSTRY

It is always interesting to learn how people make a handsome living from the conservation of energy, since it is in the industries of America, where one would have expected close accounting of power leaks or fritterings that our most shocking wastages have occurred.

However, there is a more or less valid reason why American industry until quite recently has been nonchalant about its housekeeping on energy. Energy has been so cheap that out of every dollar the average manufacturer spent in costs, only a nickel went for energy. The value of energy saved was often less than the cost of trying to save it. The manufacturer would rather spend his money on psychological efficiency experts who knew how to get more work out of the hired help.*

The scene has changed. Dow Chemical went so far as to operate an infrared reconnaissance helicopter above some of its plants and discovered such things as a heated sidewalk that somebody had forgotten to turn off. Some of the wasteful practices, however, were so downright crude and stupid that one would have thought they would have been rectified without recourse to inspiration from the utility bill or the price of coal. For example, in one large manufacturing plant in the Southeast the first step in striking a blow for independence was to replace several hundred broken windows through which heated or refrigerated air had been leaking for years. No one could be found who even knew how many broken windows there were.

Basic industries such as steel—once the pride of this country—were the worst offenders. Industrial experts estimate that about 50 percent of the water-cooled skidrails in American heat-drawing furnaces are fully insulated compared with 90 percent in major steel plants abroad. Rolling mills 5 years ago were scandals of wasted heat. In a typical mill in Pennsylvania one day's survey by a pair of knowledgable eyes disclosed that the men would open a furnace door to warm themselves, ruining the work. The huge end of a heated warehouse would be opened to let out a little fork lift (one half expected a gigantic statue of Baal to emerge, pulled by a thousand slaves). Workers maintained the furnace flame as hot as possible, oblivious to the tenets of flame management, i.e., obtaining the maximum Btus per unit of fuel. The heat from the production facilities was vented outside, while separate and expensive equipment was used to heat the nearby office.

So much waste heat goes up the stacks! By inserting a simple recuperator for recapturing stack gas heat from a radiant fired tube and using it to preheat combustion air, it is easy to save 30 percent of the fuel used in many direct heating operations. The cost is about equivalent to installing a grate in a fireplace.

---

*I can recall a phase in the oil industry when every boss or prospective boss had to spend several hours a week learning how to get along with people and to persuade them (cunningly, not arrogantly!) to be productive.

THE WASTED MILES

In the first five years of the 1970s the energy consumed in this country by transportation amounted to about one-quarter of the energy consumed for all purposes. It seems to me important to bear this fact in mind, since too often we have the impression that simply by improving the fuel economy of our automobiles we would suddenly be out of the woods and free. Transportation extravagance is an easy descent to the hell of energy bankruptcy, but is not the only way to go to hell.

A few numbers on passenger-miles per gallon of fuel compiled by the Office of Emergency Preparedness are of interest, since they emphasize the extreme importance of sharing the ride. In the early 1970s, traveling expensively by the Boeing 747 Jumbo Jet (60 percent capacity) added up to 22 passenger-miles per gallon. For an average automobile (sedan) the corresponding figure was 32 passenger-miles to the gallon, reflecting the fact the average car ride took place with only 2 people in the car, while during commuting 56 percent of the automobiles were occupied only by the driver. The average commuter train gets 100 passenger miles to the gallon—figured as diesel fuel—the large bus 125 and the double-decker suburban train 200 passenger-miles to the gallon.

Why don't people use carpools any more? Although Senator Hubert Humphrey has incessantly called for and introduced bills to pay people to share rides, by tax exemptions, special parking privileges, and the like, I feel there is some stymie that has developed between the years of my youth when carpooling was taken as a matter of course and the present, when people will give up Sunday driving, will give up the second family car, will even give up a long-drive vacation, but they will not drive to work with 4 or 5 others. I had the idea it had something to do with the growing American obsession with time which has become acute, the notion that picking up passengers at different points of departure will result in the fatal expenditure of 27 minutes. On the other hand, I see Americans willing to queue as never before; to stand in line for an hour or even more to see a popular movie, even the seeing of which is in all probability another wasted couple of hours or so. When questionnaires are put out on the subject, the typical answers are "too much trouble" or "driving to and from work is the only time I have to think." The latter excuse strains credibility, since in 99 cases in 100 the thoughtful one is driving with the radio blaring at the top of its voice.

Is this possibly the answer? Since we have had car radios for about 50 years, people have got in the habit of hearing a certain program at a certain time, going to and from work. Is there a prickling fear that in a car full of people the program on the radio will not be the right one? Or, worse than this, in order to carry on conversation, the radio will be turned too low or (God save our souls!) turned off? I am holding to this theory because it fits in with the popular psychology of an age when we have become hypnotized by the subtle actions of electrons and electromagnetic waves. Radio and television are by far our most powerful addictions.

If we won't carpool and if we won't or can't use mass transportation, can we at least get more mileage from the gallon?

Yes, you can get 297.731 miles per gallon, the equivalent of going from New York to Los Angeles with about 10 gallons. But you have to work your butt off, something along the following line as prescribed by the economy champion Ben Visser of Shell Oil Company: First, tear your car apart. Throw away the frame, transmission, springs, shock absorbers, and rear axle. Construct a brand-new frame with the rear wheels side by side in the center where the trunk was located. Put the motor in where the back seat used to be and connect it to the rear wheels with a long bicycle chain. Pump up the tires to 8 times normal pressure and be sure the tires are worn treadless. Replace the carburetor with a motor-scooter version. Remove the fan, water pump, and generator. Wrap the engine in 6 layers of insulation to seal in the heat. Sit in the center so you rest on the single axle and 2 simple key bearings. Replace all grease with thin oil. (You should now be able to push your hideous skeleton of a once bonny automobile around with one hand.)

When you drive this apparition, you will have only high gear left. Accelerate to precisely 16 1/2 miles per hour. Shut off the engine and coast down to 7 miles per hour before starting over again. If you want, you can whistle "California, Here I Come!" remembering that you will get there in about 3 weeks.

But this is not the end point. Ben Visser is a big man with a large silhouette. If he hired a midget, who could ride the contraption bent over like a jockey, still more miles could be got out of a dribble of motor fuel, because of the decrease in air resistance and weight. Furthermore, note well that Visser's improvements have, except for the carburetor substitution, not even begun on the engine. He has got from about 13 to nearly 300 miles per gallon merely by reducing road friction, air resistance, and friction in the transmission of power from the engine to the wheels. At the speeds involved, one could probably get by on 2 cylinders. If special, very high octane fuel is used, the compression ratio could be upped to about 10 to 1, which should greatly raise the thermal efficiency. I would predict that Ben Visser with such further refinements could wind up at around 350 miles to the gallon.

We begin to see the trade-offs we have made in the modern automobile in getting speed and luxury in place of fuel economy.

In the 1975 model year most cars (except Fords) went up about 15 percent in mileage, averaging city and highway driving. As previously explained, the reason was that, whereas former methods of pollution control penalized fuel economy, the use of catalysts in the exhaust allowed more precise tuning of the engine. However, as we have seen in Chapter 16, the catalysts now may actually result in a more dangerous type of pollution and certainly cannot be regarded as more than a temporary answer to the older problems.

On looking at the tests in 1975 models, one is struck by the shocking discrepancy between imported and domestic cars, both of which naturally have to pass the same emission standards. Foreign subcompacts dominated the competition for economy. In fact, as mentioned before, the top-12 list for mileage per gallon in both city and highway driving did not include any American-made cars. The Datsun B210 was best in both kinds of driving, with 39 miles per gallon on the highway and an almost incredible 27 miles per gallon under simulated city-traffic conditions. (This is all the more astonishing since, except for the special California model, the Datsun does not use a catalyst, but meets EPA exhaust specifications by blowing extra air in the exhaust manifold and partially recycling exhaust vapors to reduce the formation of nitrogen oxides.)

Following fairly closely were 2 Volkswagen models, the Rabbit and the Sirocco, while other German and Japanese subcompacts trailed not too far behind. The best showing in city driving for an American car was that of the Chevrolet Vega subcompact at 22 miles per gallon (thirteenth), while on the highway the AMC Gremlin showed a fairly good 30 miles per gallon (seventeenth) and is notable for being the only 6-cylinder car among the front-runners, all the other subcompacts being powered by 4-cylinder engines. At the bottom of the list at 9 miles per gallon were the Mercury and Ford station wagons.*

There has not, to my knowledge at the time of writing, been an exhaustive and expert analysis of these results, which were obtained in cooperative work between EPA and the Society of Automotive Engineers, but one general explanation of the lower fuel economy of the 1975 American subcompacts vis-à-vis the Datsuns and Volkswagens and Toyotas suggests itself. It was with great reluctance that Detroit accepted the obvious fact in 1974 that the car-buying public had its eyes increasingly on smaller cars, because there is—comparatively speaking—no profit in subcompacts.† What Detroit did then turned out to be a disaster of greed and may indeed have helped trigger the recession of the 1970s: It fancied up the little cars, making normally optional equipment (gaudy trim, power seat and window adjustment) standard and upping the price so much that subcompacts turned out to cost as much as the intermediates of the year before. The result was not only lower fuel economy than the fat-free Japanese and German subcompacts but a historic gagging of the potential buyers at the sticker prices. People decided by the millions, as they did during World War II, to drive the old car for at least another year.

Although the American automotive industry promised President Gerald Ford that it could have a 40 percent over-all increase in fuel economy by 1980, if it were not inflicted with the tough 1977 EPA exhaust-emission standards, this does not mean very much in terms of national fuel conservation, because at 1974 and 1975 sales rates the guzzling cars are still going to be vastly in the majority through the present decade. Normally, over 8 million old cars a year disappear

---

*In the 1976 American models some over-all improvement in economy was gained in nearly all cars. Furthermore, Chevrolet brought out the Chevette, a subcompact with about the same performance as the Datsun. The Chevette, however, was entirely designed in West Germany (by engineers of G.M.'s subsidiary Adam Opel A.G.) and therefore can be described as a pseudo import.

†The reason for this is that, except for material (a much lower fraction of the total than labor), the manufacturing costs for all sizes of American cars are about the same; hence both the maker and the dealer have classically prospered by selling relatively big, expensive cars.

to the junkyards, but this is not an immutable number. During the depression years of the 1930s, as in present-day rural South America, hardly any junkyards existed. People took cars out of the junkyard.

There is a sort of sullen fatalism in the air which multiplies the energy drain. In going through Wichita, for example, one looks over the employee cars lined up beside private airplane factories—that city's specialty—and finds that an unbelievable proportion of the people have come to work in campers, getting all of 7 miles to the gallon, and driving, naturally, alone.

THE GREAT RECYCLE EXPERIMENT

Let us examine an entirely different aspect of conservation. Practical conservationists in this country have been interested in recycling garbage, sewage, and trash for several decades (the Chinese have done it for about 5,000 years). Early in the American campaign for cleaning up, in the 1950s, one of the discouraging discoveries was that it costs a lot of money just to collect trash and classify it. The state of Michigan discovered that picking up beer cans scattered beside highways costs 30 cents a can. Oregon found that the only answer is the law: Make nonreturnable cans and bottles illegal. Los Angeles halfheartedly experimented with compelling citizens to classify the garbage and trash before collection. Finally, with a great grunt and a heave, progress in the recovery of energy and recycling solids has definitely started in this country, notably in St. Louis and the state of Connecticut. And even sewage, which has so long in North America been figuratively swept under the rug, is now being looked upon as a source of methane, the main constituent of natural gas.

In the 1930s (to which we now return in many ways) sewage plants commonly used their own effluvia, so-called digester gas, to fuel engines for agitators, compressors, and the like. The plants switched to natural gas, when that became available, because the digester gas was slightly corrosive, containing in addition to methane, some hydrogen sulfide, carbon dioxide, and water vapor. The plants are switching back again, since even with the cost of extraction of the acid impurities, it is now cheaper than natural gas. Sanitation plants in Orange County in California have been burning digester gas since 1966. Methane is also formed in the course of time by bacterial decomposition of garbage in the landfills, and since the start of the smog furor the Los Angeles area has used landfills for garbage disposal. The Pacific Gas and Electric Company plans to tap such sites for methane, and in fact NRC Technology, Inc., has been draining gas from shallow wells at the Palos Verdes landfill for several years.

If you recover the equivalent of natural gas from human excrement, you can do it from animal excrement even more conveniently. Individual farmers and eventually big feed-lot operators have lately realized this. A single farmer in Indiana, for instance, pumps the manure from his 80 cattle into a closed tank, lets the anaerobic bacteria go to work, and recovers 40 cubic feet of gas a day, which is enough to heat his 10-room house all winter. At the other extreme, the

Montfort Company of Greeley, Colorado, the largest cattle feed-lot operator in the world, has completed a $4 million plant to gasify the manure at the rate of 4 million cubic feet per day.

Another recycling technique involves converting garbage into burnable fuel. Most garbages in this country are mixtures of material which is combustible as it is (paper), combustible when dried (food wastes), metal, and glass. The Connecticut system, initiated in Bridgeport, is quite typical in the first phase. Sixty trailer trucks bring the refuse from 5 transfer stations to the $30 million plant, dumping the waste into a sunken storage area. From storage it passes through automobile shredders. Heavy-duty magnets extract the iron or steel. Then it goes to classifier towers where blowers and vacuums separate the light from the heavy residue (mostly glass). The light fraction is put through dryers from which it emerges as a confettilike, low-sulfur fuel burned as a supplement to fuel oil in the boilers of a nearby electrical utility plant. Ten plants similar to the Bridgeport prototype are planned around the state. Connecticut is quite proud of this program, and it should be. They will have disposed of a nuisance, gained energy, while the steel scrap and glass are, so to speak, solid gravy.

The privately owned Union Electric Company in St. Louis is converting 2 of its coal-fired plants to allow them to burn 7,500 tons per day of organic garbage generated by the city and 6 surrounding counties. The coal-fuel mixture will consist of 80 percent coal and 20 percent dried garbage, and again there is a pollution bonus, for the garbage is low in sulfur. Because each ton of garbage contains 150 pounds of recoverable steel and 20 pounds of other metals, the utility will sell scrap metal. Finally, it will take over the dumping fees that the sanitation department had to pay for landfill or incineration. It is expected that by 1977 garbage will replace 6 percent of Union Electric's boiler coal.*

There is an alternative to simply burning the organic garbage, which in general gives trouble from ash in boilers other than those designed strictly for coal. It can be converted by cracking to liquid or gaseous fuel. This process looks like the old-fashioned beehive kilns used for making charcoal. The refuse is heated under pressure in the absence of air. There are various versions of converting garbage to liquid or to methane, controlled by Union Carbide, Monsanto, and Occidental Oil Company's Garrett Corporation (which is handling the Connecticut system).

The disposal of rubber tires presents a special problem. It now costs $15 a ton to ship old tires from Madison, Wisconsin, to Akron, Ohio, where they are worth $6 a ton. That is the reason why on my walks through the neighboring woods of the town where I live I have come across groves of half-standing, half-reclining old tires, hundreds of them, looking in the twilight like a convention of druids. One new process for handling old tires uses treatment with liquid

---

*The Dutch have been using garbage to produce steam heat and electricity for over 50 years. Copenhagen and Paris have been using similar systems almost as long. This year West Germany expects 25 percent of its total population to get electricity from garbage.

nitrogen followed by hammer-milling to reduce the tires to granular rubber. This powder can be used in the manufacture of artificial turf and in paving. The process is quite flexible in that it will handle all except polar plastics, such as nylon. It even works on dead rats, in which case the powder is fed as a "ratburger" to laboratory rats.

Aside from the energy yield, the fact of the matter is that we are running out of ways to dispose of solid waste. It is estimated that each person in America generates per year a ton of solid waste that would occupy a pile 9 feet square and 13 feet high. There is roughly a total of 4,000 billion pounds of garbage that now costs, depending on where you live, from $2 to $13 a ton, including a considerable proportion of energy, to get rid of. Chicago and Akron have run out of landfill space. Miami, Cleveland, Toledo, and Oklahoma City have a year or so to go.

Recycling plants are planned or under construction in New York, Chicago, Philadelphia, New Orleans, St. Louis, Baltimore, San Diego, Detroit, Boston, Washington, Cleveland, Buffalo, Memphis, Rochester, Albany, Knoxville, Akron, and Brockton, Massachusetts.

If the nation as a whole, including the small cities and towns where the greatest need for relief is, could go to recycling, we could conserve the equivalent of 290 million barrels of oil per year, recover up to $1 billion worth of metals, and completely forget about our desperate solid-waste dispersal problem.

THE NODDING OF HEADS

The Ford Foundation has come up with a fine monstrous book, the preparation of which was presided over by David Freeman who, under a Democratic administration, could doubtless expect to become "Mr. Energy." It is entitled *A Time to Choose: America's Energy Future.* The gist of the conclusions is that (1) mandatory and gradually increasing standards on automobile-fuel economy should be established (at 30 miles per gallon, it is emphasized that cars would be as efficient people-movers as present mass transit systems); (2) financial incentives should be set up for more efficient heating and cooling of buildings; (3) regulatory and tax policies should be revised to eliminate promotional rates and subsidies (e.g., electric rates should no longer include discounts for large users; in fact, higher rates should be charged on account of the higher costs of peaking power); (4) until conservation is well underway, we should forget about exotic sources of power; or rather we should argue about them rather than spend money on them.

This line of thought had little appeal to former secretary of the interior Rogers Morton who was said to have had John Sawhill fired for expressing almost precisely these opinions (plus Sawhill's tart language on Detroit, which especially offended President Ford). Rogers Morton thought that the conservation blueprints were "fancy footwork with computers." He also said, "Coal is the answer."

In spite of Morton's alleged temperamental distaste for mandatory conservation measures, the Federal Energy Administration's recent "Project Independence Blueprint" contains recommendations that are practically identical to those of the Ford Foundation. Conservation tricks of one kind or another, including those mentioned in this chapter, would hopefully reduce the yearly rate of increase in demand for energy to around 2 percent a year and by 1985 the consumption of energy in the United States would be less by 12 quadrillion Btus than if we continued at the usual rate of burning things.

In documents of this sort there is a new language in which the word *scenario* is always attached to charts. For example, the Ford Foundation considers the "Historical Growth Scenario," the "Technical Fix Scenario," and the "Zero Growth Scenario." The "Technical Fix" is the preferred one, the fixing consisting of degrees of conservation tailored to the 10 percent per year growth rate. The claim is made that this avoids capital expenditures which would otherwise amount to $300 billion between now and A.D. 2000.

One can see at once that the Ford Foundation people have been drinking beer instead of champagne. Compare this modest sum with the over $1 1/4 trillion that the Chase Manhattan Bank claims is necessary for the oil industry alone to spend to meet demands by 1985.

Numbers like this, whistling in the air of the Congress, have the sound of eagles and tend to make prudent men dizzy; such numbers also make men fearful of the power vouchsafed such a mysterious and imperial body as the Energy Resources Council, which sprang to cabinet level seemingly in a magic instant. One can sympathize with poor Congressman Robert Eckhardt's awed, historical characterization of the Standby Energy Emergency Authorities Act, "So far as I have been able to discover, no such broadly ranging authority has ever been bestowed by a parliamentary body in America, and the last precedent I find for it is the Statute of Proclamation passed by Parliament in 1539 at the behest of Henry VIII."

19 The Brain Power Shortage

It is from his fellow man that man's everyday danger comes.
—SENECA.

In the first chapter I tried to give the reader a feel of the inadequacy of the cheerful domino-playing corporate mind as I knew it—its clownish day-by-day open-field running in a world that had become physically and fiscally so tense and complex that attempts to predict or to act upon prediction were futile. In the petroleum business it was a plutocratic elite that did not conspire, because it was composed of Dickensian characters so eccentric and muddleheaded that conspiracy would be as easy to accomplish in a kennel of puppies. Yet the impending failure to accept and exploit all or even some of the massive technical challenges that I have reviewed in this book will not be the fault of stupid, greedy corporations but the fault of the United States government and in a larger, vaguer sense of the United States electorate—of you and me and of all the people who vote or who, more importantly, do not vote.

Somehow we all got on the wrong track about 1969—the very year of the greatest triumph of American technology—the year that should have inspired us but somehow depressed us incorrigibly—the year we got to the moon. Richard Nixon decided he did not need any scientific advisers. The apparatus that Dwight Eisenhower had leaned upon through the years of cold war and of Sputnik appeared to Nixon to be sorry and disobedient and supernumerary.

The bottom fell out of space science and space engineering and indeed practically all engineering in the early 1970s. After having performed an astronautic feat of unexampled brilliance and reverberation,* the government acted as if the poseurs and 19-year-old fairies of the antiscientific left and the old

*I trust the reader will have been impressed by the number of tentative and novel ideas that the space program proved out and gave substance to, which in the years to come should be woven into the future web of planetary energetics (for example, the fuel cell, the photovoltaic cell array, and the materials for an ideal, energy-storing flywheel).

know-nothing grumpsters of the equally antiscientific right, had to be immediately and desperately placated. The financial support of scientific and engineering graduates was discarded, as one throws off a cloak, and the space scientists and engineers in California found themselves in their thirties and forties, out of their jobs, and running taco stands. There was an almost total rejection of science and engineering on the part of the young (partly from a belief that science had become irrelevant if not immoral, and besides they saw their older brothers fired from scientific or engineering jobs). The colleges pullulated with students taking the snap courses of the humanities and the sugar-coated semidisciplines of sociology and political science, with the prelaw courses crammed, for every lad and lass who wanted either to make money or to do some undefinable good in the world wanted to become a lawyer. Now we have a country with an immense excess of young lawyers. Yet in 1973 only 200 mining engineers graduated in the entire United States and one coal company tried to hire 60 of them.

THE UNTOUCHABLES

Take the chemical industry; take it, because I've had it for too long. Six or seven years ago it was suddenly as static as the Salton Sea. Ph.D.s exchanged their little intricately glass-blown experimental setups for driving taxis or selling real estate. The real barometer of the storm, however, was the number of new chemical Ph.D.s who took postdoctoral research positions (also known as "holding patterns"), barely earning enough to eat one meal a day, unless they were so lucky as to have married a prudent girl who could be a provider.

Since the generation born after the baby boom of the early postwar period itself had matured and married, there was very little chance of getting a full-time teacher's job. Current instruction in the colleges had fallen way off because of the sudden unpopularity of science; hence the way to an assistant professorship was uncertain indeed. Current instruction of the next generation, in the grammar schools, had withered back because there was now far fewer young children. The babies of the baby boom had become as adults quite cautious and unfecund.

In the Great Depression, which happened before I got out of the University of California (Berkeley) I got to know these poor postdoctorate wretches. They breathed the chalk dust of extraordinary, brilliant young lecturers such as Linus Pauling, and they had come under the wing of G. N. Lewis, one of the most remarkable chemists of the century; but they had nothing to do but correct undergraduate papers, work unceasingly—sometimes all night—in their little laboratories which they had now occupied for half a dozen years, and go home to a boardinghouse where the landlady could afford only the 15 cents a pound it took to buy hamburgers. I learned to blow glass from one of these dogged, forlorn corporals of science, and later when I got to be a research boss I became prejudiced in favor of hiring Ph.D.s, not because they knew any more chemistry, but because at least they had learned by that time the art of glass blowing, for this is as important to a professional research chemist as knowing how to take a blood pressure is to a professional doctor or nurse.

The gross oversupply of chemists that began several years ago has receded to a point where there is going to be an acute shortage.* And as to chemical engineers, there is no one with such sex appeal to construction companies and government agencies. Bachelors in chemical engineering are getting median starting salaries of $13,000. Professor C. Judson King, head of the Chemical Engineering Department at the University of California (Berkeley), sees a profound shortage of chemical engineers continuing for at least 10 years.

And take the mining industry. In 1967 the University of Pittsburgh stopped enrolling students in its mining engineering program. The program's last graduating class in 1969 numbered only 2 students. In the fall of 1974 mining engineering was back in the curriculum with a rejuvenated program emphasizing the mining of coal. It takes at least 5 engineers to run a good-sized coal mine. Although there were once about 30 schools of mining in the United States, there are now only 16. Mining doesn't mean just coal. If the geothermal energy project is to amount to anything we will need in that field alone regiments of mining engineers or petroleum engineers plus brigades of chemical and electrical engineers to design the top-side power plants.

Before the still inflationary depression cast its deepening shadow, in the spring of 1974, the United States was about to start 4 low-Btu coal-gasification plants immediately and was planning as many as 30 synthetic natural gas plants, the number demanded by the Federal Power Commission for completion by 1985; there was speculation about 1 million barrels per day of shale oil from 10 to 20 plants; an increase in the number of nuclear-fission power plants from 40 to several hundred; the retrofitting of oil-and gas-fired power plants for coal; and at the same time the resumption of petroleum refinery construction again after a 4-year slumber. This does not include the important long-term research and engineering projects on wind, solar energy, geothermal energy, fuel cells, hydrogen, alcohols, and so on.

We can't hack it. The numbers are remorselessly against us. The number of physical scientists and engineers graduating each year is still decreasing. According to Betty M. Vetter of the Scientific Manpower Commission, these fields accounted for 20 percent of all bachelor degrees in 1950, 14 percent in 1960, 8 percent in 1971. The National Center for Educational Statistics projects a drop to less than 5 percent by 1982. These disciplines constituted 29.2 percent of all doctorates granted in 1965, but are expected to make up only 21.2 percent in 1975, and 17.7 percent in 1982.

The Engineers Joint Council estimates that by 1981, even without any big government splurge on the energy problem, the nation's top engineering and manufacturing companies will have 10,000 jobs they can't fill. This is because between 1969 and 1972 (according to the Engineering Manufacturers Council)

*All my statements, written in the winter and spring of 1975, are, of course, subject to the qualifications and caveats of an economic depression.

there were roughly 60,000 engineers out of work.* Freshmen enrollment in engineering schools fell 17 percent in 1970–71 and has since dropped another 11 percent, although the freshman enrollment in the fall of 1974 may happily be up by as much as 11 percent. Stanford University believes the long downward trend has ended and that engineer production is heading toward a higher plateau. But this won't do us much good until the graduates of the class of 1979 and the Ph.D.s of 1984 enter the job market.

In the meantime, corporations that depend on engineers have over 1,000 desperately gaping slots. According to engineering construction companies, it is now hard to get experienced men without pirating, but the young men will move for money since the old Victorian ethic of company loyalty is dead in the United States.

The oil shortage touched off a salary war for nuclear and fossil-fuel engineers and designers of coal-fired boilers. Engineers with nuclear training and background can command as much as $50,000 in today's market. But the energy crisis also will result in more layoffs of engineers in aerospace, automobile, and petrochemicals.

Nuclear power development is never going to meet any of the goals set without 37,000 more technical people in this industry, which chews up brain power at a greater pace than its rivals. In order to shorten the time for building nuclear plants from 10 to 6 years, as has been proposed, one would have to nearly double the number of nuclear-trained personnel. And it takes more time to develop a nuclear engineer who is earning his salary than it does to design and build a nuclear plant.

What is the transferability of skills? Can a chemical engineer in the petroleum or petrochemical business, for example, be trained in 2 or 3 years to be a nuclear engineer? Yes, he can. I know this to be true from firsthand observation. But transferability is a tricky question and may not be possible across the board. Thus if you ask, can one make a California aerospace engineer into an Illinois power-plant engineer, the answer seems to be no, because he'd rather run the proverbial taco stand in San Diego than work professionally in Chicago. Recently a large Midwestern gas company advertised for aerospace engineers on 4 consecutive Sundays in the Los Angeles *Times* and received only 30 applications, a tenth of what it had hoped for.

One factor that never influenced the competition for brain power very seriously before is the very aggressive role suddenly adopted by federal agencies. They now pay real money. The average annual salary of engineers in federal service in 1973 was $21,600; for scientists, $20,000.

Engineers with a fresh B.S. usually get in at civil service ratings of GS-7, $11,924; fresh Masters at $13,000 (GS-9); and newly minted Ph.D.s (GS-12) at

---

*The National Science Foundation supported survey data in the industry between 1950 and 1970. However, they ran into trouble with funding, data gathering, and arrangements with the states, so there is little hard data on the early 1970s.

$18,500. While government salaries in the last decade have risen rapidly, the amounts the government pays contractors for research and analytical work have not increased proportionately. As a result, the government has been able to hire scientists, engineers, mathematicians, and economists, who previously would have preferred to work for contractors, because of more chances upward. Now the good money and the better security of the government job usually tip the balance.

As we shall see a little later, there is a very realistic reason for anticipating that this trend will be immeasurably enhanced—indeed, to the point where governmental agencies do virtually all the designing, planning, and layout work for big construction projects of any sort.

The loss of loyalty to dear old Ichabod Ink, Inc., and the willingness to be seduced by governmental agencies, has understandably been stimulated by rather shabby company practices. Increasingly the companies have taken in young, recently graduated, relatively low-pay engineers through the front door and pushed older, higher salaried engineers out the back door. Also, they have committed the bad political error of trying to buy engineering talent at an hourly cost below that of unionized craftsmen. Where engineers, after an expensive education, are paid less than pipe fitters after an accelerated journeymanship, the engineers are going to fly away or become journeymen electricians. You have to lay it on the line these days, because the boys are no longer too proud to handle a wrench, if that pays more than running an electric calculator and balancing the design equations.

WOMEN ENGINEERS

The nonsensical underutilization of women both as scientists and engineers is part of the American and the whole Western World problem. When women go in for science, for no very logical reason except perhaps tradition and the comfort of other women's company, they usually go into biology or chemistry, 2 disciplines which (perhaps because of this very propensity) are anomalously crowded. In the academic year of 1972–73, 18 percent of the B.S. chemical graduating class was made up of women, precisely the same as in 1971–72. Of new Masters in chemistry, 22 percent were women, down from 23 percent the year before; while the percentage of female Ph.D. chemists had changed from 11 percent to 10 percent.

But if you go to the more needed discipline of chemical engineers, in 1973 only 3 percent of new B.S.s, 2 percent of Masters, and less than 1 percent of Ph.D.s were women. It would be convenient to say that this was simply the result of discrimination, but this is simply not the case. There is a bias in favor of women. Job offers for women with engineering B.S.s jumped 94 percent in 1973, compared to 83 percent for men, and the average salary offer was $936 per month for women compared with $929 for men.

Before the real surge began, for political or cosmetic reasons, there was also a bias for hiring black engineers, and the rarest of sought-after pearls was the black woman in engineering. Unfortunately, blacks have been unable to take advantage of the engineering opportunities mostly, it is reported, because they were inadequately prepared in math and basic science in high school. That remains a prickly question with which I do not propose to get my toes bloody; but the fact remains that today only 1 percent of all U.S. scientists and engineers are black.

While there are very few female chemical engineers, there are almost none, for some reason, in electrical engineering. One of the exceptions is Dr. Eleanor Baum at Pratt Institute in Brooklyn, who took her doctorate at Brooklyn Polytech a decade ago in a year when she was the only woman in the country to win a Ph.D. in "double e", as it is called. In an interview Dr. Baum is quoted as saying, "Before she thinks about engineering a woman must be interested in math—that's the single most important thing." She urges that women get out and meet professional women engineers in the Society of Women Engineers. The president of this society is Naomi McAfee, manager of quality and reliability engineering for Westinghouse, where she supervises 150 engineers, only 2 of them women. Ms. McAfee thinks that at the present, women seem reluctant to enter a field of work such as mining or civil engineering because of reservation about supervising hard hats.

As to Ph.D.s in particular, a recent study, *Women, Men and the Doctorate* by John A. Centra, compares 6 matched sets of Ph.D.s, not necessarily in the sciences or engineering, from the classes of 1950, 1960, and 1968. What is immediately apparent is the disparate sexual lives of men and women Ph.D.s. Nearly 40 percent of women from the 2 earlier classes and 30 percent from the 1968 class never married, compared to 5 and 8 percent of the men. Among those who did marry, one-quarter of the women and only one-tenth of the men are currently divorced or separated. There is a disgracefully wide discrepancy between the salaries of the contemporaneous men and women Ph.D.s, with the men averaging about $7,000 more per year.

There is something about women vis-à-vis science and engineering that I do not understand but am investigating. It is a notable superstition that women turn up their noses at mathematics or that they are incapable of understanding it, and if Dr. Baum is correct, this would explain why less than 1 percent of the engineers of the country are female. But the fact is that the superstition is totally wrong. While women represent such a lowly percentage of the engineers, they make up 29 percent of the professional mathematicians in the United States. Stanford University, which is carrying on a campaign to recruit women engineering students, calls attention to this whopping percentage in its special pamphlet.

A recent study of women in graduate schools prepared by the Carnegie Commission on Higher Education emphasizes that women graduate students in the hard sciences undergo a crisis of self-doubt and, even though they have better undergraduate grades than the men, they distrust their abilities to take on a piece of new research for their doctor's treatise. (Judging by the average quality of doctoral dissertations, the women are perhaps being simply more realistic rather than more timid than the men.)

HELP FROM IMMIGRATION?

During a temporary period of an almost desperate scarcity of qualified physicians, the United States was helped out of the emergency by immigrant doctors. Could we rely on a wave of immigrating scientists and engineers to help fill the immense hiatus of brain power that yawns before us? This does not seem very likely, because we are not the only industrial country with a brain-power shortage. A study by one large engineering firm projects a 3 million total engineer deficit in Germany, Great Britain, France, Belgium, Holland, Italy, Switzerland, Japan, and the United States by 1980. In 1973, 6,632 foreign scientists and engineers immigrated to the United States, down from 11,223 in 1970. The drop was primarily from the impact of the February 4, 1971, revisions of the Labor Department regulations for certifying scientists and engineers who apply for emigration to work in the United States. Under the new rules, technically trained immigrants cannot be certified to enter the U.S. without a specific job offer, or if this employment "will seriously affect the wages and working conditions of indigenous workers similarly employed in the area of intended employment." The Labor Department predicts an eventual plateau at about 2,000 immigrant scientists and engineers per year.

This may be optimistic and it is even possible that we could see a flow going the other way. Although we imagine we can outbargain all other countries, because of high pay, some nations, such as Saudi Arabia and Iran, can not only match our salaries but can promise lower taxes and probably a lower rate of inflation. Even in Europe, West Germany, because of markedly more restrained inflation, may soon be in a position to bid against us for young engineers.

THE BRAIN POWER WASTE

There is a rather spooky parallel between the way we waste energy and the way we waste brain power. The stunning lack of frugality in engineers is due to the fact that the United States is by far the most capitalistic or freely competitive of the industrialized countries. Although the impression has been established that our natural substance is being appropriated and inefficiently used because of monopolies (which is true in the case of transportation, as discussed in Chapter 17) the big wastes in brain power come precisely because of excessive competition.

In order to see how prodigally we spend brain power, it is convenient to examine the way big construction or engineering firms do business. There is no quicker route to this information than to listen to the very candid and forthright remarks of Clark P. Lattin, Jr., president of M. W. Kellogg, an engineering construction giant.

Spelling time out in engineering man-hours, a complete new oil refinery of 150,000 barrels per day capacity would require half a million hours to engineer. The same would be true of an energy-equivalent synthetic natural gas plant, when the fuel is liquid hydrocarbons. However, for the gasification of coal to produce the same amount of pipeline fuel, the engineering requirement is 4 times as great, because the men are working on an unstandardized process.

There are about 12,000 engineers in firms such as Kellogg, Lummus, Braun, Foster Wheeler, Ralph Parsons, Bechtel, and so forth. Working beside them are another 8,000 designers and draftsmen. As Lattin emphasizes, as much as 60 percent of the total engineering is "wasted" (the quote marks are Lattin's) *in competitive bidding.*

What Lettin is quite obviously concerned about is the problem of those 60 percent of engineering man-hours "wasted" on competitive bidding. I think he is hoping in a whisper that does not reach the written page that if we go in for superlarge, jointly owned plants, then we can tolerate joint, not competitive bidding, in which everybody gets a piece of every cake.

In my experience as a research boss, I can point to an even wilder waste of creative man-hours. The patent system gives a lot of jobs to attorneys and patent specialists. But the amount of duplicated research work can be utterly fantastic. In one field alone, with which I am especially familiar, that of the polymerization of olefins and diolefins to yield various plastics and synthetic rubbers, patent interference actions disclosed that in, for example, the catalytic polymerization of ethylene some particular experiments had been performed over and over again in at least 17 separate company laboratories. Until the "reductions to practice" were made public for the resolution of patent interferences, nobody of course knew what his competitor was doing.

I think the competitive free-enterprise system is a lot of fun, especially for Americans, who have such an instinct for competitiveness that if they cannot find it in a company versus company shoot-out, will invent it inside the company: our research division against your development division; our fifth-floor softball team against your third-floor team.

But can we afford the competitive system any more? Fun is fun, but if we don't have enough brain power to do the job on energy in an up front way, how can we possibly do it if we split the available brain power into groups that spend most of their time secretly duplicating each other's creative work?

20 The Stationary Economy

Everybody thinks of changing humanity and nobody thinks of changing himself.
—LEO TOLSTOY

IMITATORS OF OPEC

It was inevitable that the world model of OPEC (a cartel of small countries) should attract fascinated attention among other small countries which produced things the big ones needed. Revolutionizing international economies by showing how, even with a surplus of petroleum world-wide, the economic Indians could beat the economic cowboys by a policy of sheer stubborn togetherness, OPEC inspired other Indians in other places also to try to beat the cowboys. Thus there appeared almost immediately on the scene a Council of Copper Exporting Countries, consisting of Chile, Peru, Zambia, and Zaire.

Bauxite (aluminum ore) exporters, comprising Jamaica, the Dominican Republic, Surinam, Guyana, Guinea, Sierra Leone, Yugoslavia, and Australia formed the International Bauxite Associates. This body contained some wild Indians, especially Jamaica and Guyana, who proposed to get rich overnight. In June 1974, Jamaica raised the export taxes on its bauxite by almost the same multiple by which OPEC had increased the taxable base (posted price) of petroleum. The tax went up from $2.50 a ton of ore to $11.72 a ton. When the Reynolds Metal Company refused to pay an identical tax imposed by Guyana, the latter made fearful noises and threatened to sell the Reynolds property at public auction. There was an element of hysteria in this ferocity which was not very pleasing to cooler heads, such as those of Yugoslavia and Australia (the bigger you are, the cooler your head). Nevertheless Australia joined the associates in September 1974.

To extremely large users of aluminum, such as the United States, this threat of a bauxite squeeze was not particularly alarming, since we have a good deal of domestic bauxite and for years have been considering exploiting alternative sources of the metal, such as gray clay, which we possess in practically inexhausti-ble amounts. To switch to clay, however, would require more energy to recover the metal in an industry that is already a prodigious swallower of electric power. (As we review the coming shortages of practically everything, we shall be im-pressed by the fact that overcoming these shortages by recycling and by using low-grade ores always involves a power penalty. Until we have established an inexhaustible source of net energy, the dream of indefinite plenty in all metals by fiendishly clever methods of separation and retrieval is simply a science-fiction delusion.)

The United States not only consumes one-third of the energy used on the planet but one-third of the earth's resources of metals and other things. Looking back over a little more than a century ago, we realize how miserably fast mineral resources can fade away. In the nineteenth century Great Britain not only ruled the waves, but over these well-guarded waters the United Kingdom exported most of the things it now has to import. Once it was by far the foremost producer of lead, copper, tin, iron, and coal. In the years 1820 to 1840, 45 percent of the world's copper came from Britain. From 1850 to 1890, 50 percent of the world's iron and steel originated in this favored, sceptered isle. (Rural America in 1810 was so unimaginably rich in surface values that it could dig up iron ore in its backyard and smelt it with charcoal from a forest within an arrow's reach.)

Where now is England's tin, once the goal of daring Phoenician traders? Three small countries—Malaysia, Bolivia, and Thailand—now account for 70 percent of all tin that enters international trade channels. Cuba and New Cale-donia have well over one-half the world's known reserves of nickel. The main reserves of cobalt are in Zaire, Cuba, New Caledonia, and parts of Asia. And Mexico and Peru, along with Australia, account for 60 percent of the exportable supply of lead.

The available manganese is mostly located in Brazil, Gabon, South Africa, Zaire, and Ghana. Tungsten we get from Canada, Australia, Bolivia, Peru, Portu-gal, and South Korea; zinc from Canada, Peru, Mexico, and Australia; and titanium (a modern metal of growing importance) from Australia. Silver we probably have enough of, but platinum comes mainly from Russia and gold, for industrial uses, from South Africa.

Iron-ore exporters have been meeting together since 1968 and generally agree that world prices are lagging at least $15 per ton behind the cavalcade of international inflation. The countries represented number actually more than the numbers of OPEC, including Algeria, Australia, Bolivia, Brazil, Canada, Chile, India, Peru, the Philippines, Sweden, Tunisia, and Venezuela. Although the United States imports 30 percent of its iron ore, it could almost overnight cut back to 20 percent by boosting otherwise marginal domestic deposits, and eventually to 10 percent or less by going more heavily to taconite ores.

If Great Britain could come down from a net exporter of many things to a net importer of practically everything except coal in the course of a century, how long can we rely on the present various resources of nonferrous metals? Professor

E. J. Mishan of the London School of Economics, who is not even a member of the Club of Rome, about which we shall speak next, asserts firmly that at current rates of usage all known resources on the planet of silver, gold, copper, lead, platinum, tin, and zinc will have been used up within a couple of decades. In other words, some 5 years before the end of the century we shall for one thing be out of copper wire to transport the electric energy we hope to generate by then, and out of platinum to make our thousands upon thousands of domestic fuel cells.

THE CLUB OF ROME AND ITS DETRACTORS

In 1952 the Paley Commission forecast that the prices of new materials would keep rising indefinitely, a bad forecast as it turned out because actually most prices did not get back even to the 1951 level until about 1970. The community of professional and amateur economists has been greatly impressed by the fact that doomsayers have always been wrong, except in the prediction of wars. It was by no means surprising therefore that most economists and certainly all right-thinking editorialists poured their vitriol on the book sponsored by the Club of Rome, *The Limits to Growth.*

The Club of Rome is not a group devoted to the advocacy of zero economic growth. It is a loosely organized fraternity, informally although not titularly headed by Amelio Pecci, the Italian industrialist. Far from being a sort of extreme leftish society of long hairs, it is composed of thoughtful, solid intellectuals, mainly businessmen, who are preoccupied with futurology, only as it affects what they call the "world *problematique.*" It is what you would have hoped the United Nations would have included in its many mansions.

With the advent of computers that can handle a wide variety of inputs, the Club of Rome looked around for some computer group that could come up with a physical resultant to a number of separately calculated trends, including the rate of consumption of metal resources, food, population growth, and the like. They chose Professor Jay Forrester and his associates at MIT and persuaded the Volkswagen Foundation of Germany to provide the financial support. The book was written for not by the Club of Rome. When *The Limits of Growth,* authored by Dennis Meadows et alia came out in 1972 it sold some 3 million copies in about 27 languages, from Icelandic to Chinese. It caused almost that many tantrums and fits of apoplexy, for it predicted that economically the world as a going concern would fall to pieces in the twenty-first century if the present rates of increase in consumption of critical resources, mainly influenced by rate of population growth, continued.

Although the chief refutations of and attacks upon the book came from professional economists and roving reporters such as C. L. Sulzberger, it seems to have aroused the snarling, retaliatory beast in a wide variety of personalities, from the poor thin-panted editorial writers of a thousand American newspapers to the bristling socialistic adventurers of the third world. So deep-rooted in the heart of modern humanity is the idea of continued growth (an idea quite alien to ancient civilizations) that if you set out to prove it impossible, you threaten to cut the ground alike beneath gentle sociologists and cold-eyed corporation chairmen. You spark an incredibly white-hot counterfire.

The Limits to Growth is in fact rather naïve. If anything, it is basically overly optimistic, since it does not deal with the energy predicament. On the other hand, it assumes that the world, with its complex interdependence of resource exchange, would go to ruin as a mathematical whole. In an attempt to correct some of this monolithic image, a second report has been prepared by Professor Mohajlo Mesarovic of Case Western Reserve University and Edward Pestel of the Technological University of Hanover, in which the world is divided into 10 mutually interacting but basically independent regions. The mathematical input is hierarchical and, in taking energy into account, involves some behemoths of biased assumption, such as the rejection of nuclear reactors as even a partial solution of energy problems. In a bit of literary theatrics, the authors turn dramatically away from the Faustian bargain and assume a world economy based on solar energy. Everything comes out all right in the end. This is what everybody would like to see, but it is not sound futurology to assume that the world goes pleasantly.

There is also a poor man's "world *problematique*," the 'so-called Latin American model. In this the world is looked at, allegedly, from the standpoint of the third world. Scholars from 6 Latin American countries began work at the Institute Bariloche in Argentina with Amilear Hersera as leader, the work being financed, curiously enough, by the International Development Institute of Canada. As might be expected, this is a completely egalitarian model in which the untouchables of India, the peon, the gaucho, the *descamisado* eat as well and wear the same clothes as the debonair citizens of Beverly Hills or Westchester County. In this hopeful scenario Southcentral Asia remains the most vulnerable region, but even it (including the lowest of the low of Bangladesh) can expand food production and keep up with population growth for at least 80 years.

And what happens after 80 years? The Argentines themselves are fiercely propagandizing for an increase in the rate of population growth in their country, but what again happens to them after, let us say, 180 years? The critics of the original thesis of *The Limits to Growth* all exhibit what I take Nietzsche to have meant by his enigmatic phrase "the pathos of distance." The philosophy of growth must be embraced with almost ferocious loyalty until . . . until . . . until what? The answer is the heart of the pathos: until the genie of science and engineering finds a way to feed the countless billions and provide them with critical materials miraculously crafted from their own wastes or dredged from a land beneath the sea, a never-never land.

One never expected to look upon Keynesian economists so witty and chic as Kenneth Boulding and Herman Daly as images of pathos, but that is what their critiques of the idea of the no-growth society has made them. Without a steadily growing economy, the Keynesians are like dogs without noses. Forty years of vested interest and stylish dogma have hinged entirely on the notion of perpetual growth.

Strangely, it was not the same with the pre-Keynes classical economists. That nineteenth-century colossus, John Stuart Mill, in his *Principles of Political Economy* took the steady state society as a matter of course: "At the end of the progressive state lies the stationary state; all progress is but a postponement of this, and each step in advance is an approach to it." Furthermore, it was a state in which man could finally catch up with his destined quality of life.

Adam Smith did not go so far as to acknowledge the inevitability of the economic steady state. He frankly detested the idea of it because it seemed "too dull." He regarded the China of his time as a living embodiment of the stationary economy (and in a sense it remains so today).

But to fight continually and at the very boundary of man's wit and resoluteness to maintain a satisfactory steady state is far from a dull preoccupation. It is perhaps man's greatest challenge. Europe in the middle of the nineteenth century, with the maturing of the Industrial Revolution, had a chance to choose Utopia or the growth of populations. It chose the growth of populations, and that fork of the road led us to our present miserable predicaments.

THE FEARFUL MULTIPLIERS

Although family planning and zero population growth have been tentatively accepted in the industrialized countries and, perhaps unconsciously, put into practice,* the doctrine of continuous economic growth continues relatively unchallenged and the idea of a stationary but creative economy has not fully entered the public mind, except as a fragment of a bad dream. I believe that in the same way that unchecked population is an awesome multiplier for all our lacks and deficiencies, shortage of energy is a hidden multiplier of our frustration in trying to maintain our general store of physical amenities—gold from the sea, molybdenum from the ocean-bed nodules, steel and aluminum from scattered junk.

As to population explosions, demographers have generally agreed that no people voluntarily lower their birth rate until they have achieved a position of confidence for the security of their old age. Because this confidence exists in most highly industrialized nations, mainly because of savings plans and government or corporate pension systems, these nations all show an approach at least to zero population growth or in the case of some (e.g., West and East Germany, Luxembourg, Malta) to population decrease. Where there is no such confidence—when a man and his wife expect in old age to rely on the support of their children, then the more children, the more old-age insurance. This is especially pronounced in basically agricultural nations, where the children also function as unpaid farm hands.

That subcycles exist in this generalized cycle is shown by the population history of the United States. Until the Great Depression there was a steady if unspectacular decrease in the birth rate from the nineteenth-century highs of 7

*Much to the horror of eccentric poseurs and ersatz Renaissance men, such as Amital Etzione of Columbia University.

children per mother (with 4 surviving). During the Depression there was a very sharp birth-rate decrease, almost to the zero-population-growth level. Following World War II and especially in the early 1950s there was a veritable gusher of babies. This was explained most smoothly by Professor Richard Eastelin of the University of Pennsylvania in psychological terms: The man and woman who married and started families in the 1950s had been brought up as children in the midst of the Depression. To erase the memory of the deprivations they had experienced, they wanted some positive means of expressing their novel affluence, and how better to do this than by having 2 or 3 times as many babies as their parents? An extra baby was a status symbol, like an extra automobile or an extra TV set. Certainly they did not have the third world incentive of being helped in their old age by a squad of children.

On the other hand, the children of the babies of the baby boom—the grandchildren of the parents of the Great Depression came quickly back to the normal birth-rate curve approaching zero growth, and in the 1970s indeed broke all records for low birth rate in this country. Is this dependable? There are still a huge number of fertile women in the United States, and if some wave of fecundity, such as that of the 1950s, infected a majority of them, we would be in very serious trouble. Some illustrious demographers, such as Professor Judith Blake of the University of California (Berkeley), do not believe in the reliability of the present birth rate. It is greatly to be hoped she is wrong.

Population growth as a multiplier can do fearsome and unexpected things to the economic planning of a country and a planet. Moreover, without calling attention to itself, it can throw the blame on the character of a country: The inhabitants waste energy because they are born pigs—a common moral scolding the United States is used to receiving. As an example, the total energy requirements in the United States increased 1,100 percent (twelvefold) between 1880 and 1966, while the population grew 300 percent (fourfold). On a quick reading, one might infer from this statement that population growth was a minor factor. Yet actually the increase in energy consumption per capita was only 200 percent (threefold). The twelvefold increase in total use of energy is the product, not the sum of the fourfold increase in use per person and the threefold increase in population.

The recent vociferous objections of the third and fourth worlds to a planetary scheme that includes rigorous population control were based essentially on the idea that poor people cannot be expected to limit their fecundity. In effect these countries are saying, give us your wealth and we'll behave like you do.

Since I cannot imagine such a monstrous miracle of philanthropy as the voluntary sharing of total wealth between such rich countries as Sweden and such poor countries as Bangladesh,* one must hope that there is some instability in the monotonous theme of the poor being ever fecund.

---

*In fact there is no modern historical case of a really large transfer of wealth or of technology from one nation to another.

There do seem to be examples where intensive internal propaganda, tax incentives, or some inexplicable change of mood have very recently brought the birth rate down. R. I. Ravenholt of the Administration for International Development cites in fact 72 examples in which the birth rate has been reduced rapidly without waiting for a generation of social and economic progress. Among these examples are Taiwan, Mauritius, Costa Rica, Singapore, and Egypt.

There is some indication that the acquisition not of a guaranteed pension or of a Cadillac but simply of literacy may induce a people to reduce their fecundity. UNESCO has pointed out that it costs $8 to make an Asiatic or South American child literate. If the richer nations (which nowadays means especially the oil-producers, such as Saudi Arabia) contributed a few hundred million dollars apiece for an international education fund, theoretically one could have an essentially literate planet within a decade. That would seem to be one of the greatest bargains that the world could buy itself.

Yet with the seemingly helpless behemoth of India and the dubious behemoth of China, where the barracks discipline may or may not stifle the otherwise irresistible tendency of a billion people to become 2 billion, plus the devil-take-the-hindmost attitude of the ABC countries (Argentina, Brazil, Chile) of South America, it is evidently going to take several famines and possibly several nuclear wars to attain a world-wide no-growth population.

As to the ferocious advocates of a constantly expanding economy, regardless of how many human beings participate, there is something so irrational in the notion of constant and endless growth that one wonders whether these economists have actually studied arithmetic. Suppose, for instance, once we come out of our present retrograde condition, we settled upon a 4 percent annual rate of increase in Gross National Product of the United States as healthy and reasonable— forever. By the year 2126, we have a GNP of $3,000 trillion and 100 years later it would be over $150,000 trillion. Indeed the 4 percent annual increase in 2126 would be 120 times the present total GNP. These numbers are so astronomical as to be meaningless, because even supposing some gigantic breakthrough in the concentration of energy, we would have long since used up all the metallic and organic resources of the planet.

These mad projections are curiously consonant with the confessed personal attitude of certain political scientists. Professor Roland N. McKean of the University of Virginia confesses, "I don't honestly know whether I would voluntarily give up one-quarter of my disposable income even if this would, with 100 percent certainty, prevent the extinction of the human race 1,000 years hence." This is an *après-moi-le-déluge* attitude, and indeed the more saucy of the Keynesians recommend that one pay absolutely no attention to people who talk about things a hundred or more years from now.

Again the hidden implication is that the scientists and the engineers will find a way. I am a scientist and the way I see is a tunnel with no obvious light at the end, unless we abandon the progressive society and relax into the comforting arms of the steady state.

Perhaps the most brilliant exposition from the viewpoint of a pure scientist is Nicholas Georgescu-Roegen's *The Entropy Law and the Economic Process.* Here it is made plain, for those who are familiar with mathematical logic, that such facile solutions as the world of indefinite recycle of resources are thermodynamically unachievable, because at some point in the retrieval of small concentrations of valued materials (like small pieces of rusted steel scattered by the winds of a trackless desert) it takes more energy for retrieval and reconcentration than we could obtain from the sun.* And long before we reach such vast manipulations of power, we would have to make our peace with the climatologists.

DRIVE SLOW—MEN AT WORK

The eminent nuclear physicist and former director of the Energy Research and Development Office of the Federal Energy Administration, Alvin M. Weinberg, has pointed out that we know so little what the increased production of energy would do to the climate of the world that in as little as 30 or 40 years we may, so to speak, wake up dead. We aimlessly propose the questions but we do not know the answers. At what rate of energy production would the icecaps melt? Would carbon dioxide become thick enough to start us irreversibly on the way to being another Venus? What are the geographical distinctions, if any, in enormous transactions of power? Weinberg is confident that complete modeling of the type developed at the National Center for Atomic Research could be put to work on this specific *problematique.* He proposes that an institute (or institutes) of climatology be set up with long-term commitments to establishing the global effects of man's production of energy.

One should add to this most urgently: Man is fooling around with gigantic earth-moving and water-moving schemes to improve the agricultural yields in one part of the world with the possible ruination of another part.

Lester Brown of the Overseas Development Council has discussed the famous Soviet plan for changing the direction of flow of 4 major rivers in Western Siberia. When the virgin lands project of the late 1950s failed to live up to expectations, the Soviets fell back on trying to increase the grain yield in lands already under cultivation. This they could not do without a more reliable source of water, since seasonal droughts were becoming dangerously frequent. How about irrigation? The trouble was that all the big rivers in the wheat country flow north into the Arctic Sea; but the Soviets think very big, so they proposed to direct southward 4 of these giant rivers in one of the greatest engineering blueprints ever devised.

When these vast gaseous plans were made public, the international meterorological community was appalled, and in particular the climatologists of the United States and Canada would have been more comforted by the announce-

---

*Georgescu-Roegen did not include fusion energy in his studies since it is by no means certain that even if we could pull it off, it would actually represent net energy.

ment of a new generation of super-Soviet-H-bombs. The Soviets were urged to abandon these plans, the argument being that to interrupt the flow of warm water into the Arctic would change its nature entirely—indeed to an extent that it would trigger compensatory changes in the climate throughout the world. One careful study forecast that rainfall in Central North America, that is, the present most trustworthy granary of the planet, would be greatly reduced if the Soviets went ahead with their gargantuan plans.

It appears for the time being at least that these plans are on the shelf and the Russians are importing grain. This does not erase the possibility of eventual resumption of this calculated combination of triumph-cum-catastrophe nor does it avoid the problem posed by the prediction of the Food and Agriculture Organization of the United Nations that by the end of the century the world demand for fresh water will increase by 240 percent.*

A few years ago Clyde Cornen of Catholic University, Washington, suggested that a dam be constructed across the Bering Strait (56 miles wide). According to his calculations, the rebuilding of this ancient land bridge across which the proto-Indians were supposed to have migrated from Asia to the Americas, would turn the North Pacific into a warmer ocean and this change would have profound and beneficial climatologic repercussions in both North America and Siberia. It would turn the Pacific Southwest from a desert into a sort of semitropical rain forest. It would also alter the North Atlantic by drawing warm, mid-Atlantic currents into the Arctic Ocean.

Although the Soviets are in favor of a Bering dam and have talked about it for years, it seems obvious that without decades of experimental modeling, the construction of such a barrier would be foolhardy, because we do not know enough about climatology on a planetary scale to be sure what would happen. There is no doubt that the Bering Strait is the only place in the world where, as the Russians say, you can put your finger in the climate of the world, but if your finger gets stuck there, the great pitiless cycles of world weather might bring— who knows what? Perhaps a constant barrage of tornadoes, typhoons, hurricanes, gigantic floods. We have enough unpredictable weather troubles as it is, without uncorking Aladdin's lamp.

Another imprudent proposal was that we eliminate the Arctic Sea ice pack by spreading black soot or carbon black on the ice in the summer to induce melting. This has the same effect as the diversion of north-flowing rivers southward.

As previously noted, there is some indication of the coming of another ice age, similar to the little ice age of 1600 to 1900. The pack ice around Iceland is increasing annually while the crop failures across the USSR are growing in intensity. What this means in historical context is that it is a very good time to

---

*From this standpoint, energy sources that involve evaporating ocean water or underground brackish water will appear more and more attractive, especially if the planet goes through a dust-bowl cycle, as some predict.

pull in our oars, to put a stop to our insensately wild expanding economy, and to begin to nest up in the green, well-fenced grass of the steady state. The world-wide depression has been not only a warning but hopefully a signal for transition.

THE STEADY-STATE ECONOMY IS CREATIVE

The sharpest critics of the no-growth society, such as Kenneth Boulding, have emphasized that it leaves no incentive. With a constant amount of wealth, the poor can get richer only if the rich get poorer. The greatest fault of this criticism is its naked vulgarity, in that it equates richness to quantity. As John Stuart Mill was the first to realize, the steady-state society actually affords a breathing spell —a chance to celebrate life rather than simply to endure it. Throughout an economy in which the rate of through put of goods is greatly reduced, the challenge is the opposite of the vast mass markets of 1973. Instead of built-in obsolescence and tackiness, the trend would be toward built-in durability and loveliness. Figuratively speaking, every automobile (if such things persisted at all) would be a Rolls Royce.

It seems likely that in the attainment of the steady-state society, the concept of affluence would tend to disappear. But has affluence over and above the level of creature comfort and a delight in life ever helped anybody? It has turned Japan into a composite nervous wreck with the highest incidence of suicides in history. In the Western World, especially in the United States, affluence brought either know-nothing-ism or the banal problem of identity. When one is so affluent that one does not have enough work to occupy one's mind, one starts to wonder who one is.

And the technical and social challenges of the stationary economy are so enormous that there will be work enough for all. But let us not fool ourselves. In order to establish the no-growth society, a powerful centralized republic is necessary. A brutal wrenching of the backbone fiscally and monetarily is required to stop the floods of trash, of excess expenditure of energy, and of utter foolishness. Probably the first steps would be to place high taxes on all goods and transactions and to devote the proceeds first to energy projects too massive and daring for private capital and, second, to environmental repair. Whether this could be done by straightforward democratic means is problematical, since it might along the way involve such political events as the secession of Texas and Michigan and the wholesale removal of "eco-freaks" like myself.

What could make the setting up of the no-growth society a less dramatic and more probable process is the impending popular discovery that, in spite of all the shrugging and sneering of conventional economists and of the "good ole boys" the strict, complete, and complex control of wages and prices is the only way to run a modern world. By people who have never lived through the wartime controls of 1943–46, the myths have been accepted that these were days of black-market horrors and of a final collapse that sent everything sky-high in 1947.

I lived through that time at the busiest, most traveled period of my life—a period when my wife had to scrounge to find acceptable food, but she never experienced a black-market temptation—and in retrospect (with the last 2 years of ghastly inflation suffocating us) I can repeat again with full honesty that "I have seen the past and it worked."

As John Kenneth Galbraith and Arthur Schlesinger, Jr., remind us, the American economy was never in history under such unimaginable inflationary pressure as during World War II. In 5 years the national debt grew from $63 billion to $257 billion. In the war years cash deficits amounted to about 30 percent of the national product. Yet from June 1943, when the Office of Price Administration, with Chester Bowles, finally acquired enough clout to do its job, the retail price of food hardly budged at all. The increase in all wholesale prices in the last 3 years of the war were less than in the single month of August 1974. And the price explosion in late 1946 and 1947 took place precisely because the controls, at the roughhouse insistence of big-business lobbyists, were too hastily abolished.

Now the story is that the country is too big and too complicated to control any longer or that we could no longer afford the huge bureaucracy that would fatten itself on a nation under control. That is nonsense. The fact is that the percentage of federal employees to total employees is less now than in the 1950s.

However, the overshadowing fact is that the country can much better afford a bureaucratic multiplication than it can tolerate the indefinite continuance of stagflation. I predict that the appetite for wage-price controls and even rollbacks will become so ravenous that, whatever the results of the 1976 presidential campaign, we will by 1980 be a country under strict federal fiscal guidance, and from that point on, the transition to a steady-state economy might be a natural, not a revolutionary process.

In addition to the energy problems, under a no-growth system, we will, as mentioned, need to concentrate on the betterment of life quality in general. Although the rat race is an accepted shorthand description of a man or a woman earning a living in modern America, there need be no relevance for such a phrase. The enormous waves and surges, to and from an urban place of business, are mostly by file clerks, typists, sales people, and accountants. But their jobs can be handled either at remote control or can be abolished. Managers, all the way from the board chairman to the group leader, have no business commuting to work at all. An easily reachable ramification of our electronic communications system (which, in spite of all its glorification, has remained through the last 2 decades virtually stationary in development) could put all managers and all clerks, accountants, all computerists and their computers in intimate and constant communications via advanced videotelephony without the need to leave the places where they live.

There is no necessity for all the paper shuffling and letter filing that goes on in business. Computers and their memory banks can do these classificatory jobs much better than young women. Let the young women learn to boss the computers from a distance. Within a few decades we might abolish the tremendous tidal energy drains of going to and from work in a skyscraper—either by advances in communication or by advances in architecture—by living in the same skyscraper we work in. Both solutions need to be tried.

OR TRY FOR THE INSIDE STRAIGHT FLUSH

There is a good deal of wishful thinking in the above paragraphs. Because I believe so firmly in the idea of the steady-state economy, I have imagined it coming to pass in a planet of 4 billion people, some few million of whom have even been exposed to the idea. Furthermore, of those intellectuals who have understood it, few can stand it. There is an incorrigible, almost instinctual affection for the growth economy, even if one could be persuaded by mathematical and thermodynamic proof that it is ruinous. People would rather take their chances in the fateful scrimmage.

So I propose the courageous alternative that at least would keep us occupied and in a state of monolithic tension for several decades. I propose quite earnestly that we devote ourselves to the monstrous gamble referred to in Chapter 12; that is, that we include in the NASA Space Shuttle program a quite definite goal of establishing solar-power relay satellites along the lines suggested by Peter Glaser. This would be a wildly expensive gamble, both in terms of money and of net energy, since before the relay stations were constructed and active, the energy investment would be colossal. But, if successful, the net energy returns would be ultimately beyond the limitations of terrestrial solar collection devices, both because of the wider cross-section of sunlight interception and the much higher energy of the solar radiation collected. Georgescu-Roegen's entropy limits for an advanced economy would no longer apply. And we could begin to salvage the metallic resources of the moon and of the asteroid belt.

Even if this fails, and the experiment of Western civilization comes to an end, our diminished descendants, fighting the squirrels for acorns, may have the racial recollection that mankind went down fighting and clawing for his place in the sun, and that once there was to be a Camelot, if he found that place.

. . . We won't go down, let's pretend. We fill the inside straight flush and it's a royal one. With at least a constant or decreasing world population, the complete recycling of metals—supplemented by acquisitions from the moon and from other planets—and successful solar-energy relays plus perhaps fusion energy, Camelot rocks along for a million years or so. By that time, however, we might have colonized inhospitable planets, such as Mars, Venus, and Mercury. Some of our projects might involve more energy than even the sun gives us. We might send for an angelic consultant.

The angel, an agile, old, bearded man, something like an athletic Charles Darwin, would (in the manner of angels) instantly understand our telepathic language and our problems.

"Have you thought," he would ask in his kindly way, "of building a shell around the sun? You have enough material in your big outer planets to cocoon yourselves in—to avoid the radiation losses of your sun to outer space. Many of my clients have taken this route. That is the reason for the apparent mass deficit in the universe as observed by your telescopes. A good many billion suns have had shells built around them."

Some musing and table rapping with angelic knuckles.

"Your sun and the fusion processes of your own, as you know, are rather distressingly inefficient affairs." He sighs. "It seems to me you are ready to attack some more—er—let us say, robust methods. Reactions between matter and antimatter are very efficient, I assure you. Look at the quasars. If that does not appeal to you, why not try to exploit your black holes? I noticed several on my trip here. Or along with that, the interuniverse energy transfer—the white holes. Surely you are aware of the multiworld engineering extension of your own quantum theory? Or if you would prefer, you can always borrow energy from the future. You are aware that this is possible? Your sun is going to be a nova in 3.73 thousand million years. You can easily borrow anything you need from this unfortunate future explosion."

The angel gazes amiably at the beings around him.

"Or are you ready for psychic energy? The unlimited energy of the fully developed mind?"

He shakes his head, courteously. "I fear you are not ready for that. If you will forgive me, it takes a very advanced society. Very, very advanced," he repeats, disappearing gently.

APPENDIX A

The attached example shows how large companies will have an easy time buying independent oil property if the percentage depletion allowance is eliminated.

In the attached example Poverty Petroleum drills a well which costs $100,000 to drill and complete and $2,000 leasehold costs. The well produces 100,000 barrels in 5 years and goes dry. As you can see from the summary, the present-worth value of the profit after taxes to Poverty Pete would be $349,741, when discounted at 10 percent per year if percentage depletion allowance is retained. If percentage depletion allowance is eliminated Poverty Pete would only realize $272,486 present-worth profit if he produced the well until abandonment.

If instead of producing the well to abandonment they sold the property (prior to any production) for $500,000, they would realize $296,497 present-worth profit (after taxes) and they would not have to mess with producing it. The purchaser, Big Giant Oil and Gas, would also realize $75,067 present-worth profit after taxes. As you can see, the total after-tax profit (present worth) of both companies is more than that of Poverty Pete under percentage depletion allowance—however, there is no advantage to an independent to sell with depletion allowance because he would realize $53,244 more present-worth profit.

Poverty Petroleum Drills Oil Well Discovery in Osage County, Oklahoma, 1974

Well discovers reserves of 100,000 barrels
Leasehold cost, $2,000
Intangible drilling costs, $60,000
Tangible drilling costs, $40,000
    Oil price, $10 per barrel
    Taxes on production, 5%
    Operators' net revenue, 85%
    Lease operation expense, $5,000
    Well drilled December, 1974
    First production, January 1975
    Well produced as follows: 1st year (1975) 30,000 bbls.
                           2nd year (1976) 25,000 bbls.
                           3rd year (1977) 20,000 bbls.
                           4th year (1978) 15,000 bbls.
                           5th year (1979) 10,000 bbls.
                           6th year (1980) well plugged and abandoned

Poverty in 50% tax bracket

I.

With % Depletion Allowance	1974	1975	1976	1977	1978	1979
Gross Income	(102,000)	$255,000	$212,500	$170,000	$127,500	$85,000
Production Taxes		(12,750)	(10,625)	(8,500)	(6,375)	(4,250)
Lease Operating Expenses		(5,000)	(5,000)	(5,000)	(5,000)	(5,000)
(A) Cash Flow B/T*	(102,000)	237,250	196,815	156,500	116,125	75,750
Intangible Drilling Operations	(60,000	-0-	-0-	-0-	-0-	-0-
(B) Depletion		(56,100)	(46,750)	(37,400)	(28,050)	(18,700)
Investment Credit	(2,800)	-0-	-0-	-0-	-0-	-0-
Depreciation (5 years)	(	(8,000)	(8,000)	(8,000)	(8,000)	(8,000)
(C) Net Taxable Income	(62,800)	173,150	142,125	111,100	80,075	49,050
(D) Tax	(31,400)	86,575	71,062	55,550	(40,031)	(24,525)
(E) Tax Flow after Income Tax	(70,600)	150,675	125,813	101,000	76,088	51,225
(F) Actual Cash Flow						
after Income Tax		80,075	205,888	306,888	382,976	434,207
DCFAT*@ 19%		143,953	109,055	79,588	54,730	33,375
						349,741

II.

Without % Depletion Allowance						
(A) Cash Flow B/T	(102,000)	$237,250	$196,875	$156,500	$116,125	$75,750
(B) Depletion		(600)	(500)	(400)	(300)	(200)
(C) Net Taxable Income	(62,800)	228,650	188,375	148,000	107,825	67,550
(D) Tax	(31,400)	114,325	94,187	74,050	53,912	33,775
(E) Cash Flow after Income Tax	(70,600)	122,925	102,688	82,450	62,213	41,975
(F) Actual Cash Flow						
after Income Tax		52,325	155,040	237,490	299,703	341,678
DCFAT† 10%		117,209	89,009	64,970	44,563	27,339
						272,485

*Before Taxes.

†Discounted Tax Flow after Taxes.

Big Giant Oil and Gas buys Poverty Petroleum's interest in 1975—after repeal of percentage Depletion—for $500,000.

Poverty Sells to Big Giant

III.

	Poverty Pete		Big Giant Oil & Gas				
	1974	1975	1975 sale: (500,000)	1976	1977	1978	1979
Cash Flow B/T	(102,000	$500,000	$237,250	$196,875	$156,500	$116,125	$75,750
Intangible Drilling Expenses	(60,000)		—				
Depletion	—		(150,000	(125,000)	(100,000)	(75,000)	(50,000)
Depreciation	—		(8,000)	(8,000)	(8,000)	8,000)	(8,000)
Investment Credit	(2,800)		(2,800)	—	—	—	—
Capital Gain Credit		(230,000)	—	—	—	—	—
Net Taxable Income	(62,800)	(230,000)	76,450	63,875	48,500	33,125	17,750
Tax, Federal @ 50%	(31,400)	(115,000)	38,225	31,937	24,250	16,566	8,875
CFAT*	(70,600)	385,000	(300,975)	164,938	132,250	99,563	66,875
Actual CFAT	(70,600)	314,400	(300,975)	(136,037)	(3,787)	95,776	162,651
DCFAT	(70,600)	367,097	(286,980)	142,968	104,213	71,317	43,549
Actual CFAT		296,497					75,067

Summary

	Poverty Pete	Big Giant Oil & Gas	Total
I Poverty Retains Property with			
Percentage Depletion Allowance			
Actual CFAT	$434,201	-0-	$434,201
Actual CFAT @ 10%	349,741	-0-	349,741
II. Poverty Pete Retains Property without			
Percentage Depletion Allowance			
Actual CFAT	341,678	-0-	341,678
Actual DCFAT @ 10%	272,486	-0-	272,486
III. Poverty Sells to Big Giant without			
Percentage Depletion Allowance			
Actual CFAT	314,400	$162,651	477,051
Actual DCFAT @ 10%	296,497	$75,067	371,569

*Cash Flow after Tax.

SELECTED BIBLIOGRAPHY

Most of the facts and background material in this book have come either from personal contacts and recollections, technical documents, or technical periodicals. Because of the bulk and tediousness of arranging such references in any useful form, I have decided that for a book for which I do not claim extreme scholarly precision, I could do without the fussy annotations that I applied to *Death of the Sweet Waters*. Besides, I'm 10 years older.

I have kept complete notes, however, and if any earnest reader wants some back-up for any statement, I shall be glad to furnish it if he or she will write me through the publisher.

The list of books that follows is by no means complete but is in the nature of recommended reading.

Acheson, Dean. *Present at the Creation.* New York: Norton, 1969.

Adelman, M. A. *The World Petroleum Market.* Baltimore: Johns Hopkins University Press, 1972.

Baldwin, Malcolm F. *Public Policy on Oil: An Ecological Perspective.* Washington, D.C.: Conservation Foundation, 1971.

Ball, Gordon R. *Electric Energy Consumption and the Nuclear Opportunity.* Toronto, Canada: Canavest, 1972.

Bell, Daniel. *The Coming of the Post-Industrial Society.* New York: Basic Books, 1973.

Berkowitz, David A., and Squires, Arthur M. *Power Generation and Environmental Change.* Cambridge, Mass.: MIT Press, 1971.

Brodeur, Paul. *Expendable Americans.* New York: Viking, 1974.

Brown, Keith C. *Regulations of the Natural Gas Producing Industry.* Baltimore: Johns Hopkins University Press, 1972.

Brown, Lester R., with Eckholm, Erik T. *By Bread Alone.* New York: Praeger, 1974.

Brown, Theodore L. *Energy and the Environment.* Columbus, Ohio: Charles E. Merrill, 1971.

Bryerton, Gene. *Nuclear Dilemma.* New York: Ballantine, 1970.

Caro, Robert A. *The Power Broker.* New York: Knopf, 1974.

Carr, Donald E. *The Breath of Life.* New York: Norton, 1965.

———. *Death of the Sweet Waters.* New York: Norton, 1966.

Centra, John A. *Women, Men and the Doctorate.* Princeton, N.J.: Educational Testing Service, 1974.

Cornelius, W., and Agnew, W. G. *Emissions from Continuous Combustion Systems.* New York: Plenum, 1972.

Daly, Herman. *Towards a Steady State Economy.* San Francisco: Freeman, 1973.

Daniels, Farrington. *Direct Use of the Sun's Energy.* New Haven: Yale University Press, 1964.

Eaton, Robert. *Black Tide: The Santa Barbara Oil Spill and its Consequences.* New York: Delacorte, 1972.

Finer, Herman. *The TVA: Lessons for Industrial Application.* New York: Da Caro, 1972.

Fisher, John C. *Energy Crises in Perspective.* New York: Wiley, 1972.

Ford Foundation. *A Time to Choose: America's Energy Future.* Cambridge, Mass.: Ballinger, 1974.

Frankel, Paul H. *Mattei: Oil and Power Politics.* New York: Praeger, 1971.

Freeman, S. David. *Energy: The New Era.* New York: Walker, 1974.

———. *A Time to Choose: America's Future.* Cambridge, Mass.: Ballinger, 1974.

Garfield, Paul J., and Lovejoy, William F. *Public Utility Economics.* Englewood Cliffs, N.J.: Prentice-Hall, 1964.

Georgescu-Roegen, Nicholas. *The Entropy Law and the Economic Process.* Cambridge, Mass.: Harvard University Press, 1971.

Goldman, Marshall I., ed. *Controlling Pollution: The Economics of a Cleaner America.* Englewood Cliffs, N.J.: Prentice-Hall, 1967.

Goodwin, Richard C. *The American Condition.* Garden City, N.Y.: Doubleday, 1974.

Gordon, Richard L. *The Evolution of Energy Policy in Western Europe: The Reluctant Retreat from Coal.* New York: Praeger, 1970.

Hammond, Allen L.; Metz, William D.; Maugh, Thomas H. *Energy, and the Future.* Washington, D.C.: American Association for Advancement of Science, 1973.

Heilbroner, Robert A. *An Inquiry into the Human Prospect.* New York: Norton, 1974.

Hellman, Richard. *Government Competition in the Electric Utility Industry.* New York: Praeger, 1972.

Hesketh, H. E. *Understanding and Controlling Air Pollution.* Ann Arbor, Mich.: Ann Arbor Science Publications, 1972.

Hickel, W. J., et al. *Geothermal Energy.* Fairbanks: University of Alaska Press, 1972.

Higgins, C. M. *A New Concept for In-Situ Coal Gasification.* Berkeley, Calif.: Lawrence Livermore Laboratories, 1972.

Hottel, Hoyt J., and Howard, J. B. *An Agenda for Energy.* Cambridge, Mass.: MIT Press, 1974.

Jacobs, Jane. *The Death and Life of Great American Cities.* New York: Modern Library, 1969.

Lappe, Frances Moore. *Diet for a Small Planet.* New York: Ballantine, 1974.

Lowey, H. H., ed. *Chemistry of Coal Utilization.* New York: Wiley, 1963.

Lundsberg, Hans H., and Shurr, Sam M. *Energy in the United States: Sources, Uses and Policy Issues.* New York: Random House, 1960.

MacAvoy, P. W. *Economy Strategy for Developing Nuclear Breeder Reactors.* Cambridge, Mass.: MIT Press, 1969.

McLennan, H. J. *Elements of Physical Oceanography.* Elmsford, N.Y.: Pergamon, 1965.

McPhee, John. *The Curve of Binding Energy.* New York: Farrar, Straus and Giroux, 1974.

Meadows, Dennis L.; Meadows, Donella H.; Randers, Jorgen; and Behrens, W. W. *The Limits of Growth: A Report for the Club of Rome.* New York: Universal Books, 1972.

Mesarovic, Mihajlo, and Pastel, Edward, *Mankind at the Turning Point.* New York: Dutton, 1974.

Mill, John Stuart. *The Principles of a Political Economy.* Clifton, N.J.: Kelley, 1909.

Mishan, Ezra. *The Costs of Economic Growth.* New York: Praeger, 1974.

Nef, John V. *The Rise of the British Coal Industry.* London: Cass, 1966.

Nelkin, Dorothy. *Nuclear Power and Its Critics: The Cayuga Lake Controversy.* Ithaca, N.Y.: Cornell University Press, 1971.

Novick, Sheldon. *The Careless Atom.* New York: Dell, 1969.

O'Connell, W. H. *Ride Free, Drive Free.* London: John Day, 1973.

Odum, Howard. *Environment, Power and Society.* New York: Wiley, 1973.

Oliver, John W. *The History of American Technology.* New York: Ronald Press, 1950.

Potter, D. M. *People of Plenty: Economic Abundance and the American Character.* Chicago: University of Chicago Press, 1954.

Rand, Christopher. *Los Angeles, the Ultimate City.* London: Oxford University Press, 1967.

Ridker, Ronald G. *Economic Costs of Air Pollution.* New York: Praeger, 1967.

Rothschild, Emma. *Paradise Lost: The Decline of the Auto-Industrial Age.* New York: Random House, 1973.

Schurr, Sam M., et al. *Energy in the American Economy, 1850–1975, Resources for the Future.* Baltimore: Johns Hopkins University Press, 1960.

Shepherd, William G. *Economic Performance under Public Ownership: British Fuel and Power.* New Haven and London: Yale University Press, 1965.

Stacks, John F. *Stripping: The Surface Mining of America.* San Francisco: Sierra Club, 1971.

Sutherland, Thomas C., Jr., and McCleery, William. *The Way to Go.* New York: Simon and Schuster, 1973.

Szczelkun, Stefan A. *Survival Scrapbook 3: Energy.* New York: Schocken, 1973.

Tarbell, Ida. *The History of the Standard Oil Company.* New York: Norton, 1969.

Taylor, Theodore. *Nuclear Theft: Risks and Safeguards,* New York: Ballinger, 1974.

Theler, G. F. M., and Bonk, S. P. *Advances in Standard Composites.* New York: Society of Aerospace Material and Process Engineers, 1967.

Tugendhat, Christopher. *Oil: The Biggest Business.* New York: Putnam, 1968.

Veesey, George. *One Sunset a Week. The Story of a Coal Miner.* New York: Dutton, 1974.

Vicker, Ray. *The Kingdom of Oil.* New York: Scribners, 1974.

Votaw, Don. *The Six Legged Dog: Mattei and ENI—A Study in Power.* Berkeley and Los Angeles: University of California Press, 1964.

Watt, Kenneth E. *The Titanic Effect.* New York: Dutton, 1974.

Weaver, John. *El Pueblo Grande.* Pasadena, Calif.: Ritchie, 1973.

Willrich, Wilson. *Global Politics of Nuclear Energy.* New York: Praeger, 1971.

————, ed. *Civil Nuclear Power and International Security.* New York: Praeger, 1971.

Wagner, Richard H. *Environment and Man.* New York: Norton, 1974.

Young, Louise B. *Power over People.* London: Oxford University Press, 1973.

INDEX

DATE DUE

DEC 1 4 '79			